ARGOPREP

STUDY SMARTER, NOT HARDER

+20%

OFF TO OUR FULL ONLINE SHSAT COURSE

# NEW SHSAT

SPECIALIZED HIGH SCHOOL ADMISSIONS TEST

## 5 | FULL-LENGTH PRACTICE TESTS

BOOK 4

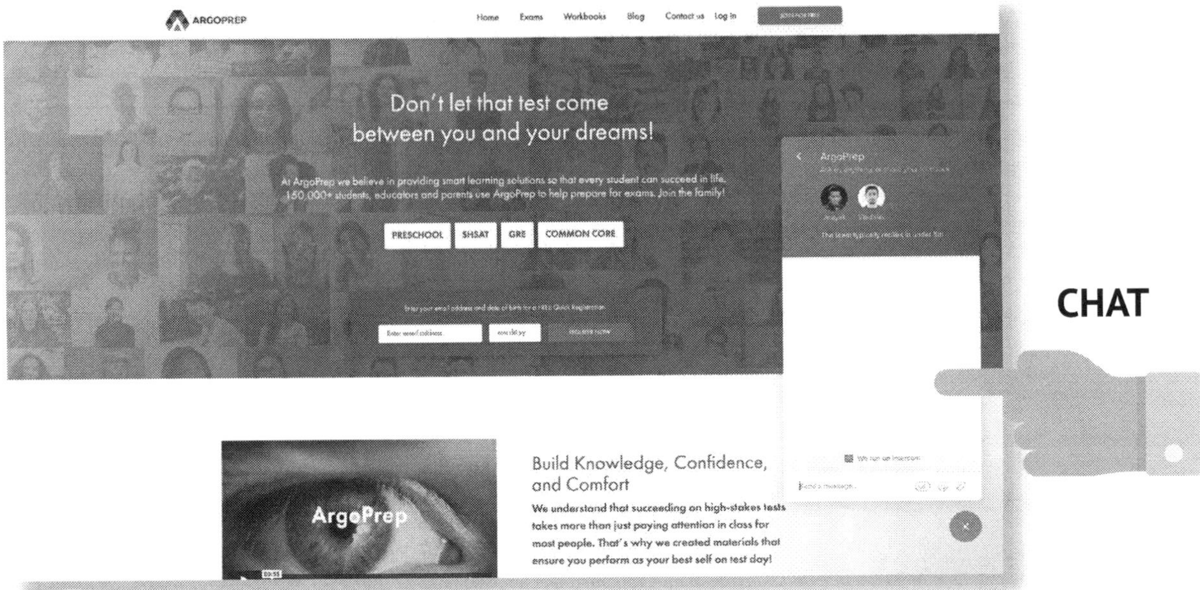

# Want FREE printable worksheets for additional practice?

Simply chat with us on our website at:
**www.argoprep.com**



ISBN-13: 9781946755582

Published by Argo Brothers Inc.

# TABLE OF CONTENTS

# INSTRUCTIONS FOR STUDENTS

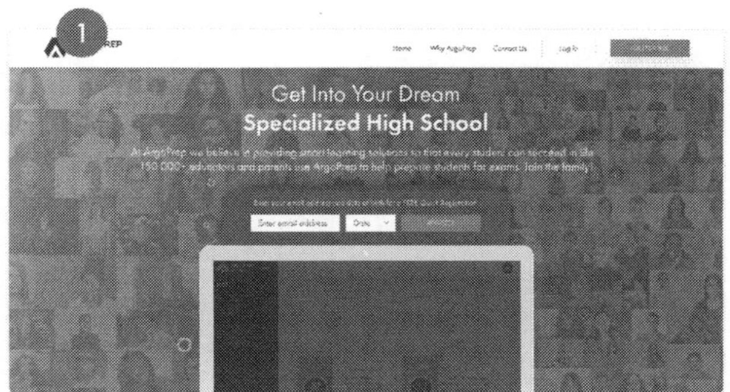


Visit our website at argoprep.com/ shsat

Click on the JOIN FOR FREE button.

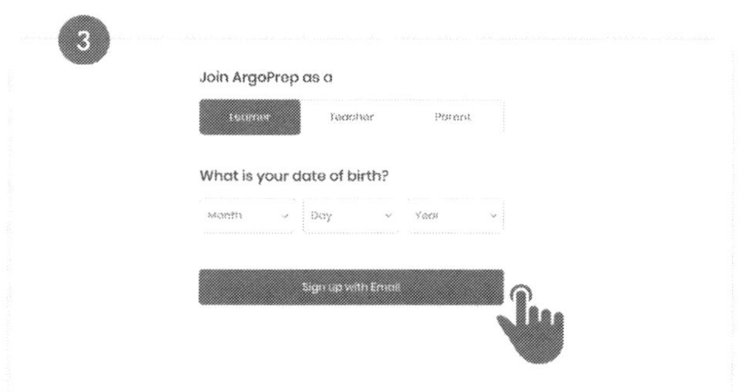


Enter date of birth and e-mail address.

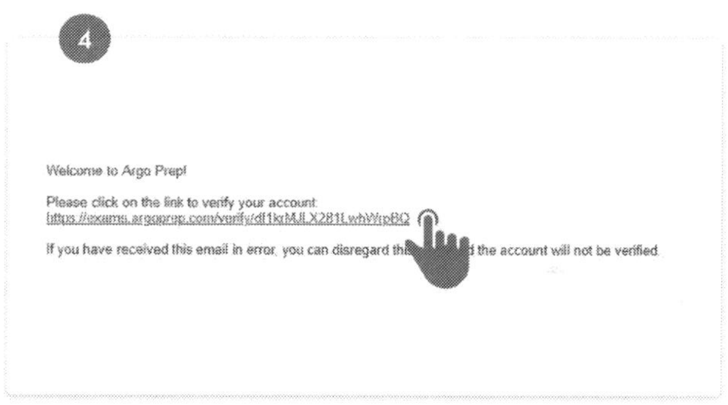


Verify your email address by clicking on the verification link in your inbox.

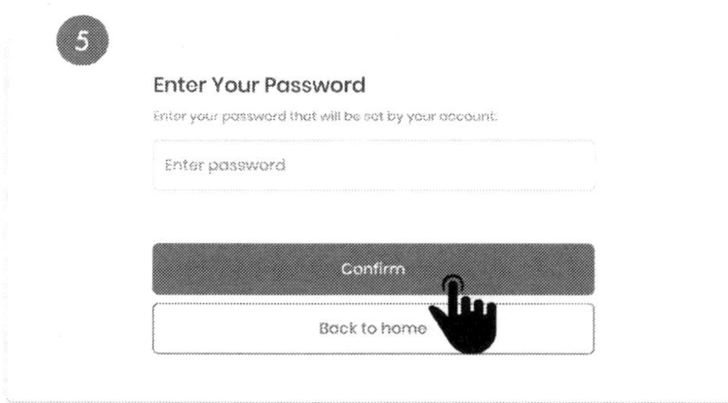


Create a password.

Click on Book Video Explanations.

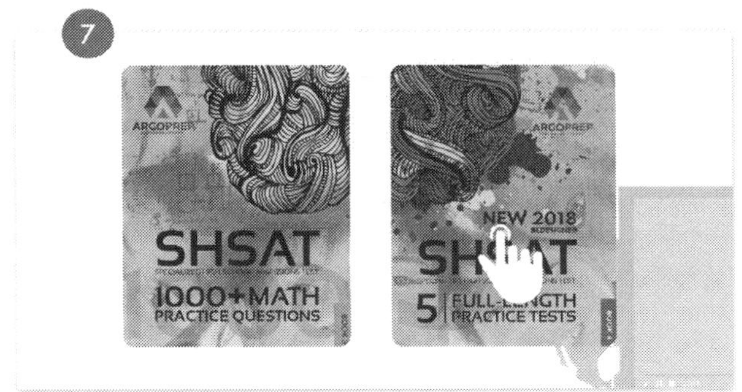


Select the workbook you are using.

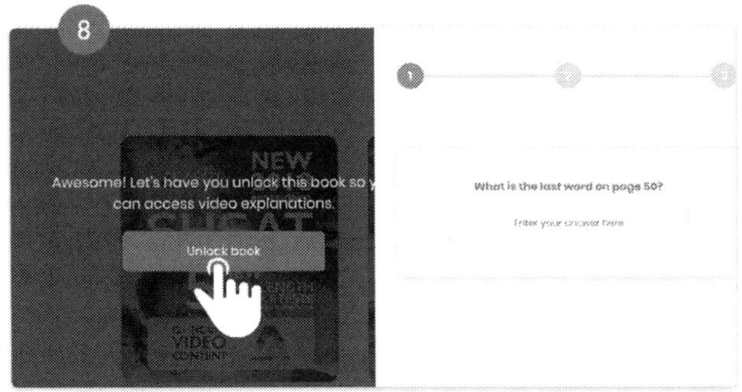


Unlock this section by answering security questions.

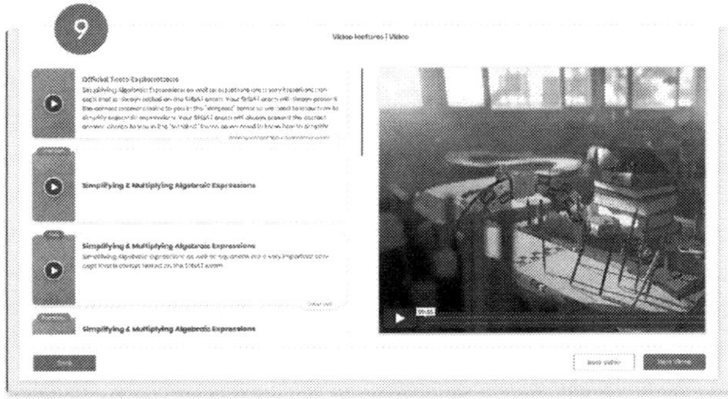


Congratulations! You can now access video explanations to all the questions in the workbook.

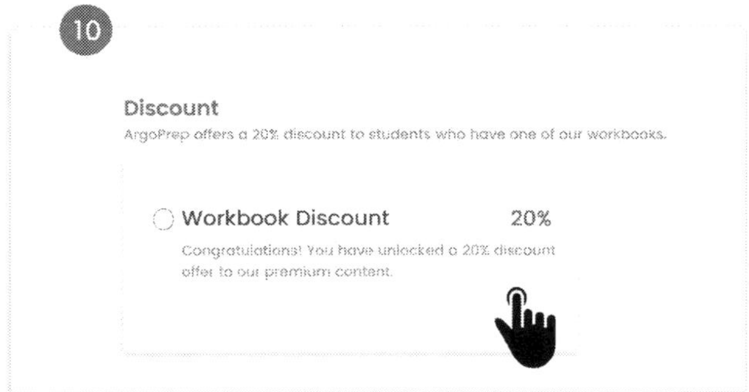


**Awesome news! A 20% discount has been automatically applied for access to our full online SHSAT test prep course.**

## INSTRUCTIONS FOR PARENTS

(Students under the age of 13 will need parental consent. As a parent, you can create an account for them by following the steps below!)

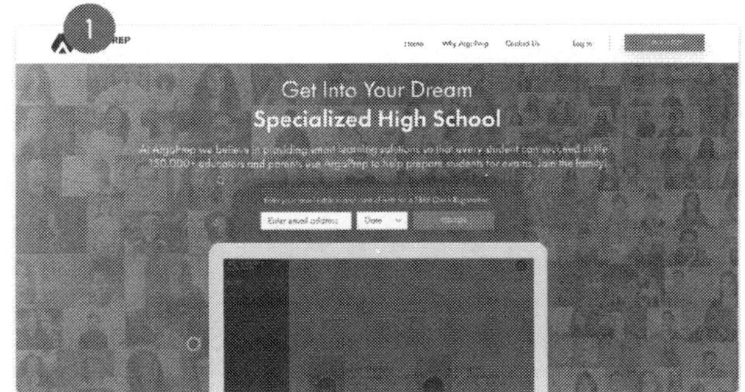


Visit our website at argoprep.com/ shsat

Click on the JOIN FOR FREE button.

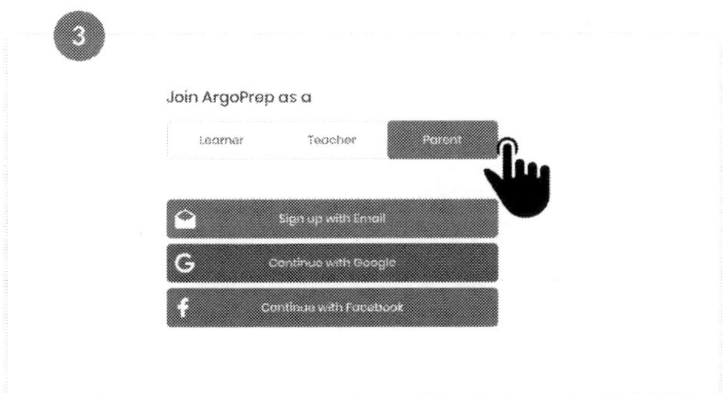


Choose Parent.

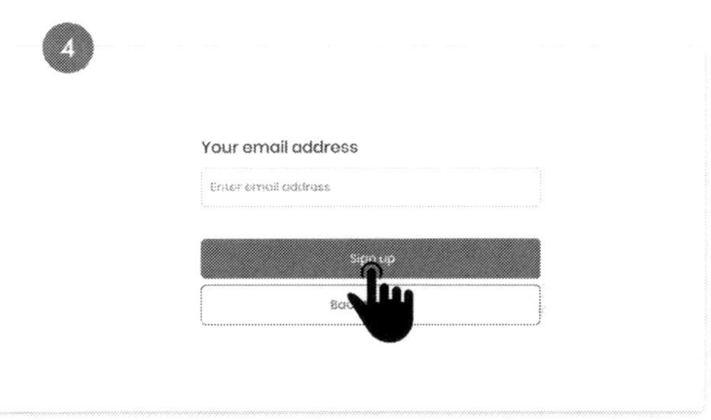


Enter your email address.

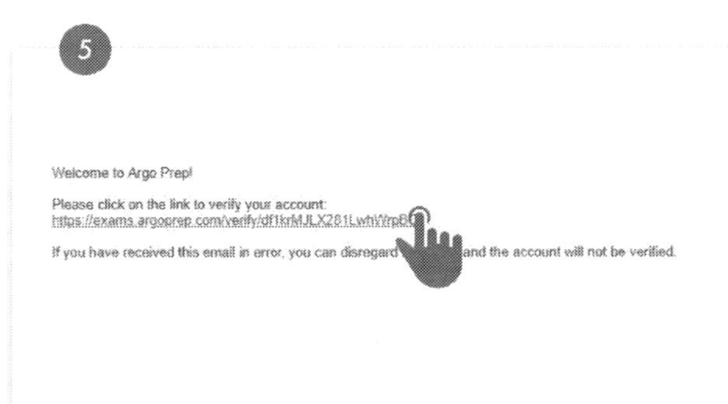


Verify your email address by clicking on the verification link in your inbox.

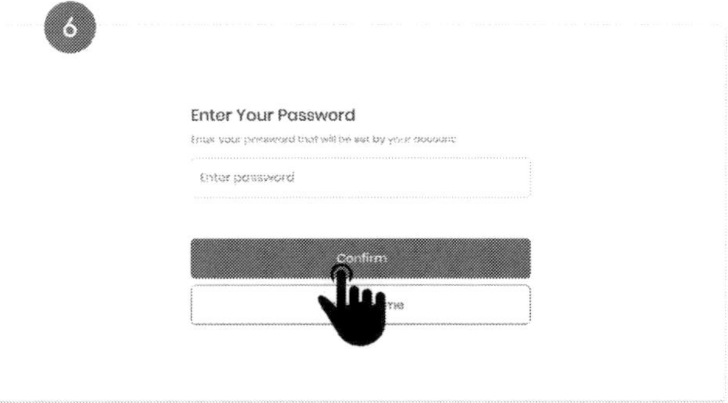


Create a password.

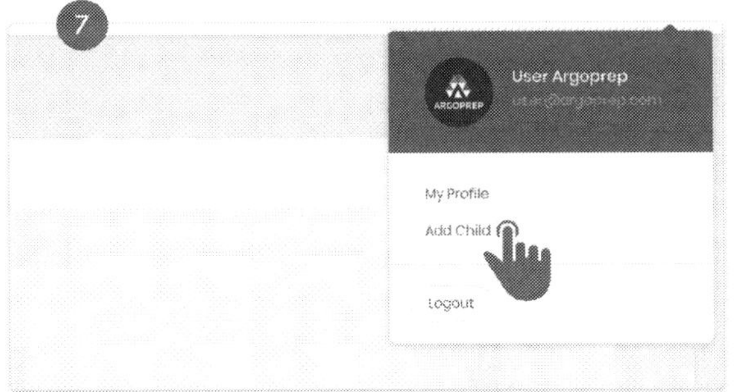


Add your child by clicking ADD CHILD in your profile menu.

8
Children
Add your child

Click Add Child.

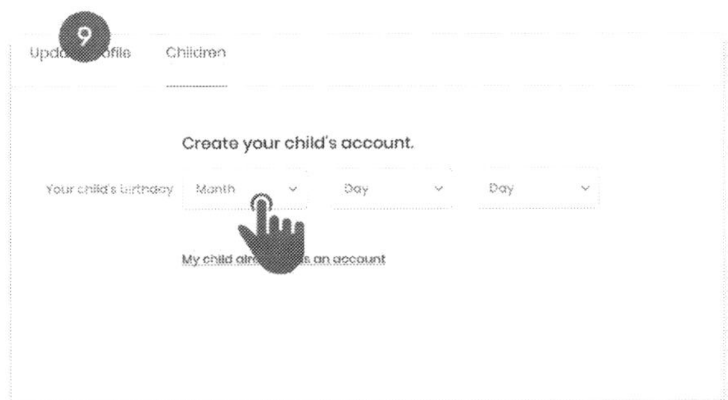


Put child's date of birth.

10
Create a username and password for your child
Child's Username
Enter username
Child's Password
Enter password

Create Nickname and password for your child account.

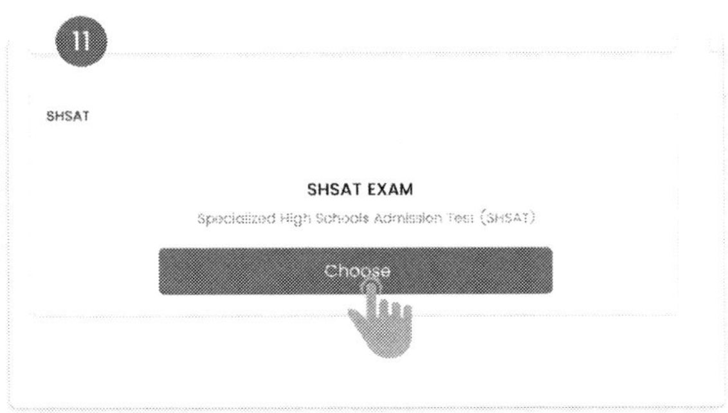


Choose SHSAT Exam.

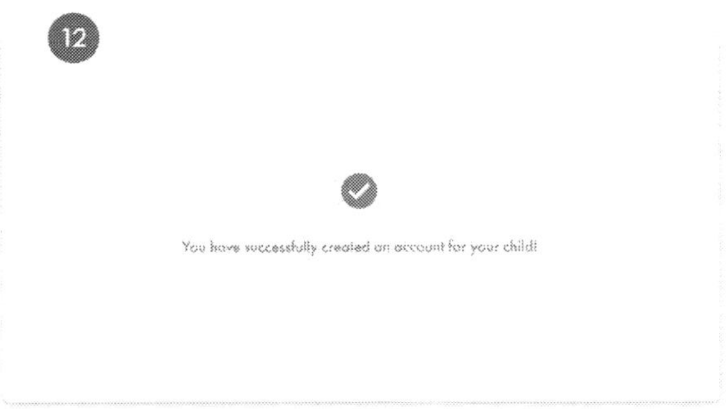


Your child account has been successfully created.

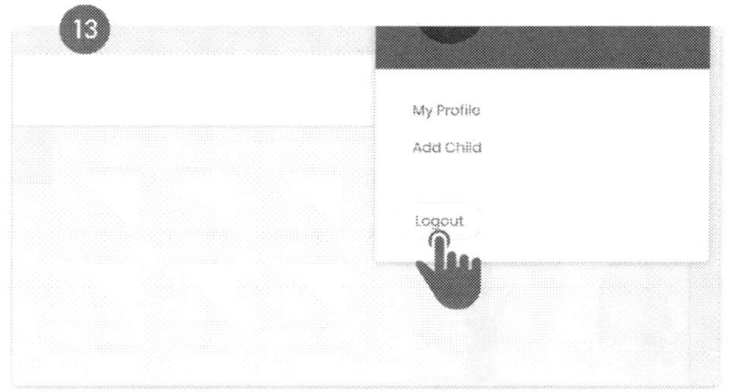


Log out and log in to child's account.

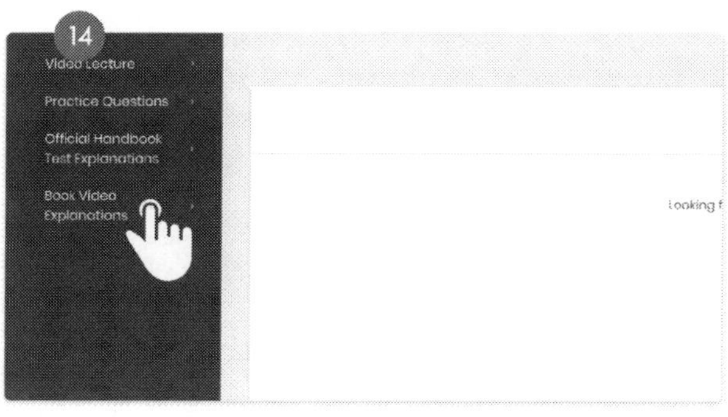


Click on Book Video Explanations.

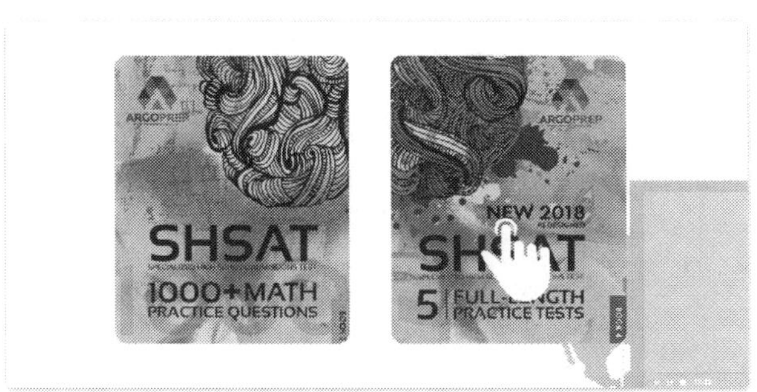


Select the workbook you are using.

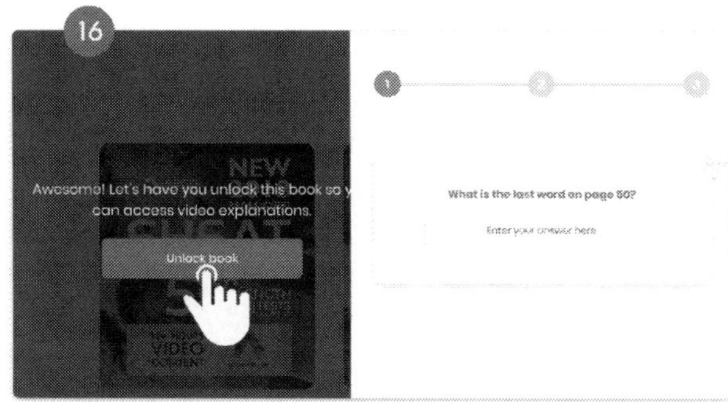


Unlock this section by answering security questions.

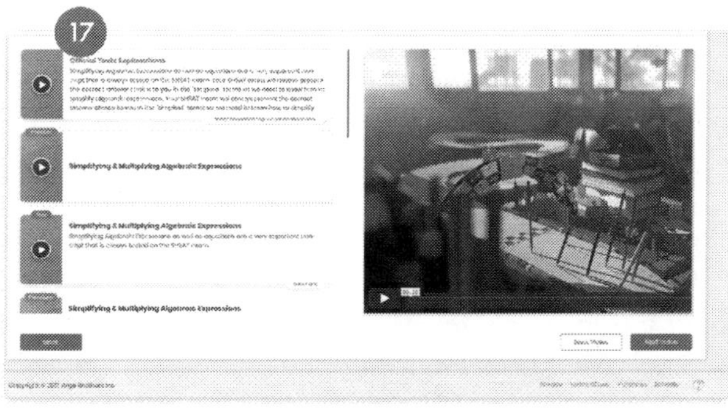


Congratulations! You can now access video explanations of all the questions in the workbook.

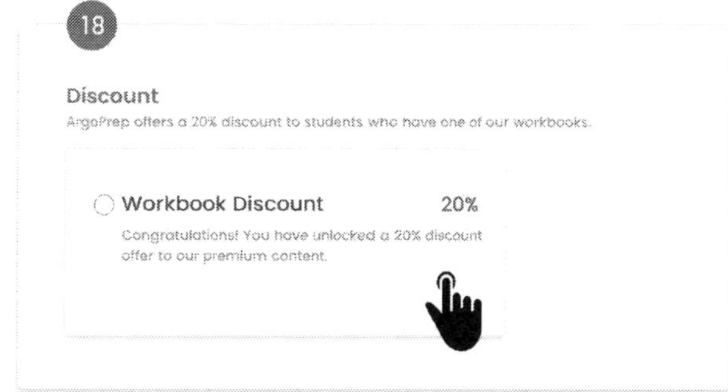


**Awesome news! A 20% discount has been automatically applied for access to our full online SHSAT test prep course.**

## SHSAT COMPREHENSIVE STUDY

ArgoPrep offers comprehensive resources for students studying for the Specialized High Schools Admissions Test (SHSAT). Check out our three other workbooks along with our online learning platform!

# OTHER BOOKS BY ARGOPREP

Here are some other test prep workbooks by ArgoPrep you may be interested in. All of our workbooks come equipped with detailed video explanations to make your learning experience a breeze!

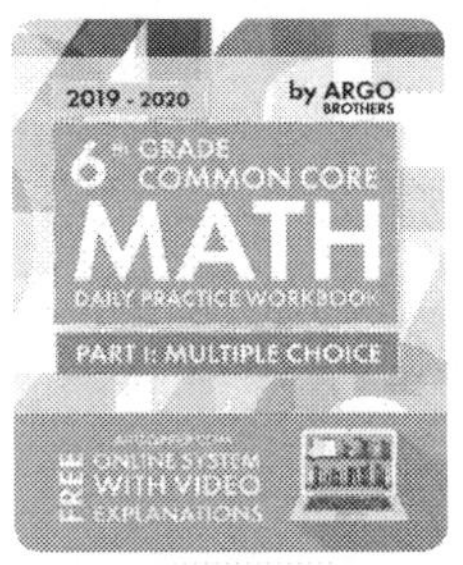

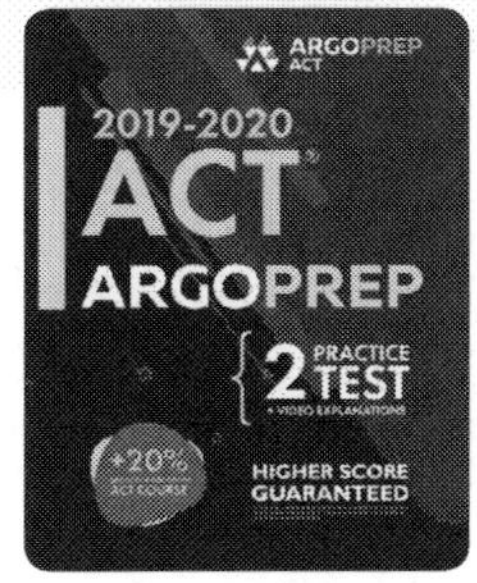

# INTRODUCTION

The Specialized High Schools Admissions Test (SHSAT) is an exam that students take in order to gain admission into one of the New York Specialized High Schools. Out of the nine Specialized High Schools, eight of the schools admit students solely on the SHSAT score. Fiorello H. LaGuardia High School of Music & Art and Performing Arts (LaGuardia), is the only specialized high school which admits based on an audition and academic review.

Here is a list if the Specialized High Schools along with their contact information.

**The Bronx High School of Science**
75 West 205th Street, Bronx, New York 10468
Contact Number: (718) 817-7700
www.bxscience.edu

**Brooklyn Technical High School**
29 Fort Greene Place, Brooklyn, New York 11217
Contact Number: (718) 804-6400
www.bths.edu

**The Brooklyn Latin School**
223 Graham Avenue, Brooklyn, New York 11206
Contact Number: (718) 366-0154
www.brooklynlatin.org

**High School for Mathematics, Science & Engineering at the City College of New York**
240 Convent Avenue, New York, New York 10031
Contact Number: (212) 281-6490
www.hsmse.org

**High School for American Studies at Lehman College**
2925 Goulden Avenue, Bronx, New York 10468
Contact Number: (718) 329-2144
www.hsas-lehman.org

**Queens High School for the Sciences at York College**
94-50 159th Street,Jamaica, New York 11433
Contact Number: (718) 657-3181
www.qhss.org

**Staten Island Technical High School**
485 Clawson Street, Staten Island, New York 10306
Contact Number: (718) 667-3222
www.siths.org

**Stuyvesant High School**
345 Chambers Street, New York, New York 10282-1099
Contact Number: (212) 312-4800
stuy.enschool.org

**Fiorello H. LaGuardia High School of Music & Art and Performing Arts**
100 Amsterdam Avenue, New York, New York 10023
Contact Number: (212) 496-0700
www.laguardiahs.org

---

## Ready for the NEW redesigned Specialized High Schools Admissions Test?

**The NEW SHSAT is a 3 hour timed multiple choice test with two sections, ELA and Math.**

| Number of Questions | Content |
|---|---|
| 9 to 11 | Revising/Editing |
| 46 to 48 | Six reading comprehension passages with 6 to 10 questions each. One of the six passages will be a poem. |
| 52 | Math multiple choice problems |
| 5 | Grid-in math questions |

## SHSAT 2018 CHANGES

The SHSAT is changing! If you are taking the Fall 2018 SHSAT Exam, you should be aware of the following changes so you can properly prepare for the exam. The old SHSAT test comprised of two sections: verbal and math. The verbal section included five scrambled paragraphs, followed by ten logical reasoning questions followed by 5 reading comprehension passages. The math section included 50 multiple choice questions. The time limit for the exam was 150 minutes.

**So... what are the new changes you should be aware of?**

- The new time limit for the SHSAT exam is now 180 minutes. (30 minutes more than the old SHSAT exam)
- NO MORE SCRAMBLED PARAGRAPHS.
- NO MORE LOGICAL REASONING QUESTIONS.
- Verbal section is renamed to the English Language Arts (ELA) section.
- There is 57 questions per section (57 questions for ELA and 57 questions for Math). 47 out of 57 questions in each section will be scored. 10 questions are field test items which will not count toward the students score. Students will not know which 10 questions are classified as field test items.
- The ELA section will include 9 to 11 revising and editing questions along with 6 reading passages.
- The math section will include 5 grid-in questions
- All multiple choice questions will have 4 answer choices instead of 5.

---

If you did not watch our video yet which outlines **EVERYTHING** you need to know regarding the new changes for the SHSAT exam, please watch our video here:

**www.argoprep.com/shsat**

---

## The Importance of Ranking Schools

When you take the SHSAT test, you will be required to rank the Specialized High Schools you want to attend. It is extremely important that you know ahead of time which schools you would like to attend. You will only be admitted into one school if your score meets the level. Acceptance is based on the score you get on the SHSAT exam followed by your choices of schools.

When making the decision to rank the schools, some important things to think about are:

- How far away is the school from you?
- Does the school have a program you are interested in?
- Is there a certain sport or activity you would like to do in high school?
- Is the school a good fit for you? Each school differs in class size and specialty.

## What do I need on test day?

You will need to bring your signed Admission Ticket which will have your school choices. There are **no calculators** permitted on the exam. Have more than one number 2 pencil, an eraser and a watch to keep track of time. Water and snacks are allowed, however you must wait until your proctor gives you permission to eat the snacks. Most importantly, bring your confidence! If the exam seems difficult, do not stress. Give it your best shot and have fun!

## How can I study for this exam?

The first thing you need to understand is to do well on this exam, you must put in the time and effort to study. This is a challenging exam, so here is a list of a few important tips.

- **Practice and PRACTICE!**
  Take as many practice exams as you can find. Taking simulated exams will give you a very good idea on the type of questions that will be asked during the exam and will make you more confident.
- **Read Books**
  The best way to raise your score in the English Language Arts section of the exam is to read books, articles and newspapers. You will develop a better vocabulary list and find it easier to read the passages provided in the exam.
- **Learn from your mistakes**
  When you go over your practice exams, make sure you understand **why** you got the question wrong. Did you read the corrections correctly? Was it a simple calculation error? Try to understand why you got the answer wrong.

## Test Day Strategies

There is no penalty for wrong answers, so **do not** leave anything blank. If you do not know the answer to a question, then circle the question and move on. When you are done with all solvable questions, return to the circled questions. If you still do not know the answer, make an educated guess.

If you still have time after finishing all questions, then check your answers. While you practice, find roughly fifteen questions from throughout your practice that you believe to exemplify the test. You should know how to answer these questions perfectly. On test day, use these fifteen questions as a warmup. Make sure that you go through all steps when going through the question. You should be able to explain why each wrong answer is wrong.

You do not need to take the exam in the order that it is presented. Take the test in the order that you believe will maximize your time on those questions which you are most likely to get correct. It is better to spend time on questions you know you can get right than spending an excessive amount of time on questions that you find more difficult.

# SHSAT ELA REVIEW

## ENGLISH LANGUAGE ARTS

The new SHSAT now includes 9 to 11 revising/editing questions. Below is a basic overview about grammar rules that you should be familiar with. This review serves as a basic guide and should not be your only guide to fully prepare you for the SHSAT exam.

## GRAMMAR

***What is a sentence?***

A proper sentence has, at the very least, a *subject* and a *verb*.

The *subject* is the person, place or thing that is causing an action to occur.
The *verb* is the action that is taking place by the subject.

For example, let's say we have the very simple sentence:

*The boy kicks.*

The subject in this sentence would be "the boy", and the verb would be "kicks". Simple enough, right?

There is one more part that, while it is <u>not</u> necessary, is usually found in a sentence: the *object*.
The *object* of a sentence is the person, place or thing that the subject performs the action on.

Let's look at the previous sentence with an object added:

<u>The boy kicks the ball.</u>

In this sentence, the subject is again "the boy," the verb is "kicks," and finally, the object is "the ball."

The sentence can also be broken down more roughly to just the *subject* and *predicate*. The *predicate* can be made up of just the verb, or both a verb and an object.

In the above sentence, "kicks the ball" would be the predicate.

Here are a few more examples of proper sentences:
- Henry loved to eat apples.
- Jenna and Margaret will get ready for the party.
- Moe needs a haircut.

***Subject-Verb Agreement***

As mentioned before, every subject must be connected to a verb. However, the conjugation (form of the verb) must also agree with the subject given.

*The three friends play video games every Saturday and Sunday. (CORRECT)*
*The three friends plays video games every Saturday and Sunday. (INCORRECT)*

*The book on animals provides a good understanding on habitats. (CORRECT)*
*The book on animals provide a good understanding on habitats. (INCORRECT)*

Depending on the sentence, this may or may not prove to be difficult. For all sentences, the subject of the sentence, whether it is a person, place or thing, can be changed to its appropriate *pronoun*.

A *pronoun* is a word that is used in place of a person, place or thing (noun).

**Pronouns:**

| | **Singular (ONE)** | **Plural (TWO OR GREATER)** |
|---|---|---|
| **1st Person** | I | we |
| **2ns Person** | you | you |
| **3rd Person** | he, she, it | they |

**Example of Conjugated Verbs:**

| *to eat* | **Singular (ONE)** | **Plural (TWO OR GREATER)** |
|---|---|---|
| **1st Person** | I eat | we eat |
| **2ns Person** | you eat | you eat |
| **3rd Person** | he, she, it eats | they eat |

The core idea is to be able to identify the subject of the sentence and then determine whether the verb agrees with the pronoun.

Looking back at the two previous examples for sentences, the subjects can be changed as such:

*The three friends play video games every Saturday and Sunday.*
*They play video games every Saturday and Sunday.*

*The book on animals provides a good understanding on habitats.*
*It provides a good understanding on habitats.*

Understanding how to change a subject to its appropriate noun is crucial in being able to grasp subject-verb agreement. The focus is mainly on *3rd-Person Singular (he, she, it)* and *3rd-Person Plural (they)*

Here are some examples of each:

- He: the boy, the man, the male cat, Tom
- She: the girl, the woman, the female cat, Ashley
- They: the boys, the girls, the men, the women, the cats, Tom and Ashley

## Collective Nouns:

_Collective nouns_ are subjects that refer to *groups* of things. A collective noun can be a class of students, a team, or a committee. It can even be a collection of *ideas*.

*Collective nouns can be both singular and plural.*

**It**: singular collective nouns
**They**: plural collective nouns

Examples of singular collective nouns include:
- team
- squad
- audience
- analysis of reports
- interaction between two students

*Note: For the last two examples, the grouping itself is the subject. The rest of the subject is a description of the group.*

Example of plural collective nouns include:

- teams
- squads
- audiences
- analyses of reports
- interactions between two students

## Individuals Among Groups

The opposite can be said for subjects that are considered to be individuals among collective nouns.

Such nouns are associated with the pronoun, *it*.

Examples of individual subjects include:

- each of the boys
- every teacher
- one of the women
- a member of the group

### Indefinite Pronouns (Singular or Plural)

Indefinite pronouns can be define as words that replace nouns without specifying the noun being replaced. There are a few words that can be used as *either* singular or plural.

Singular or Plural Pronouns:

- all
- any
- some
- more
- most
- none

## Pronoun-Antecedent Agreement

In some examples, the pronoun in the sentence will be used later to refer to the subject that has already been introduced. These questions are easily answered using the principles of Subject-Verb agreement to identify the associated pronoun.

Some examples include:

*Students must provide his or her homework at the beginning of class. (INCORRECT)*
*Students must provide their homework at the beginning of class. (CORRECT)*

In the example above, the subject of the sentence is "Students" and as such, the pronoun associated to it would be "they" or "their," not the singular pronouns "his or her."

*The person can pick up their bag on the way out. (INCORRECT)*
*The person can pick up his or her bag on the way out. (CORRECT)*

The opposite idea is provided in this example. The "person" is the subject of the sentence, and the associated pronoun would be the 3rd - Person singular "his or her" and not 3rd - Person plural "their."

## Subject vs. Object Pronouns

Since you can now identify and differentiate between subjects and objects, it is crucial to understand that there are significant differences in the pronouns used for both instances.

**Subject Pronouns:**

| | **Singular (ONE)** | **Plural (TWO OR GREATER)** |
|---|---|---|
| **1st Person** | I | we |
| **2ns Person** | you | you |
| **3rd Person** | he, she, it | they |

**Object Pronouns:**

| | **Singular (ONE)** | **Plural (TWO OR GREATER)** |
|---|---|---|
| **1st Person** | mine, me, myself | mine, me, myself |
| **2ns Person** | your, yourself | your, yourself |
| **3rd Person** | his, her(s), its | his, her(s), its |

I vs. me

One of the biggest mistakes that many test takers make is misusing "I" and "me." The first is used in the context of the subject of the sentence, and the second for the object of a sentence.

**SUBJECT**: I
**OBJECT**: me

The following two examples provide context to the misuse of the subject pronoun.

*John and me are both extremely hungry. (INCORRECT)*
*John and I are both extremely hungry. (CORRECT)*

The next two sentences provide examples of the misuse of the object pronoun.

*Ms. Evergreen gave John and I failing grades this marking period. (INCORRECT)*
*Ms. Evergreen gave John and me failing grades this marking period. (CORRECT)*

### Who vs. whom

The same context can be provided for who and whom:

**SUBJECT**: who
**OBJECT**: whom

*Whom is going to open that door for me? (INCORRECT)*
*Who is going to open that door for me? (CORRECT)*

*Who are you going to the movies with? (INCORRECT)*
*Whom are you going to the movies with? (CORRECT)*

Note that in the second pair of examples given, the subject of the sentence is "you." Thus, the object MUST be "whom." Another example of such has been provided below:

*To whom is she writing that letter? (CORRECT)*
*Whom did he hire for the new position? (CORRECT)*

## Reflexive Pronouns

Reflexive pronouns are object pronouns that end in either "-self" or "-selves" and refer back to the subject of the sentence.

**Object Pronouns:**

| | Singular (ONE) | Plural (TWO OR GREATER) |
|---|---|---|
| **1st Person** | myself | ourselves |
| **2ns Person** | yourself | yourself |
| **3rd Person** | himself, herself, itself | themselves |

Here are a number of examples of reflexive pronouns in use:

- *I gave me a note to read in the near future. (INCORRECT)*
- *I gave myself a note to read in the near future. (CORRECT)*

- *You must give yourself some time to rest from the injury. (CORRECT)*

- *He cannot help himself out of bed. You should go aid him. (CORRECT)*

## Ambiguous Pronouns

The word ambiguous itself means unclear, and an ambiguous pronoun is found in situations when it is unclear which noun the pronoun refers to.

*Between Ms. Jameson and Ms. Richard, she gives the harder exams. (INCORRECT)*
*Among Ms. Jameson and Ms. Richard, Ms. Richard gives the harder exams. (CORRECT)*

In the first sentence, who is "she" referring to in this sentence? Both the subjects are female, making it hard to differentiate between who the pronoun is referring to.

*Christie loves their artwork. (INCORRECT)*
*Christie loves the Metropolitan Art Students' artwork. (CORRECT)*

In the first example, who is "their" referring to? There is no indication of who the artists are.

## *SENTENCE STRUCTURE*

While a basic sentence can be broken down to just a subject and predicate, most sentences are much more complex and are made up of two components: clauses and phrases.

**Clause vs. Phrase**

A *clause* is a part of a sentence that **contains both a subject and predicate**. There are two types of clauses:

1. **Independent clause**: a clause that can stand on its own as a sentence
   Example: Alicia eats two pies.

2. **Dependent clause**: a clause that cannot stand on its own as a sentence
   Example: When John jumps very high...

*The most basic sentence consists of just a clause:*

- *Cats meow.*
- *Girl runs.*
- *Jack cooks.*

A phrase is a part of a sentence **that lacks either a subject, predicate or both**.

Example: By the way...
Example: Without Jimmy...

Sentences can be comprised of all three of these concepts:

*By the way, when John jumps very high, Alicia eats two pies.*

A. Phrase  B. Dependent clause  C. Independent clause

## *PUNCTUATION*

### Commas

Notice how in a previous example, commas were used to separate the clauses and phrase in the previous example:

By the way, when John jumps very high, Alicia eats two pies.

A *comma* **separates segments of a sentence**.

The use of a comma includes:

1. Separate two **independent clauses** when they are separated by the following words:
   a. and, but, or, nor, so, yet, for

*Amy is very hungry today*, ***but*** *she does not have any food at home.*

2. Separate **dependent clauses**, **phrases**, and **words** that come before the **main independent clause**.

*However, before his mother could answer the phone,* ***John was out of the house***.

3. Separate three or more clauses, phrases or words that are written in a series.

*Jumping rope, climbing fences, and running on the track are all exercises.*

*John likes to read comics written by Marvel, DC, and Image Comics.*

**Misuse of Commas**
Unless in extreme cases, **commas are not needed for dependent clauses or phrases**.

*I went to eat some apples, after swimming ten laps. (INCORRECT)*
*Tim does not want to see her, while he is eating. (INCORRECT)*

## Semicolons

A *semicolon* **separates major sentence elements or independent clauses**.

In other words, a semicolon is used to separate two stand-alone sentences that are not already joined by a period or conjunction.

*Hint*: Consider semicolons to be almost identical to periods. If a period cannot fit in the sentence provided, neither can a semicolon.

Look at the following few examples, and just replace the periods with semicolons.

*John loves snowballs. He eats them whenever there is a blizzard. (CORRECT)*
*Without any money. Tara cannot go to Florida to search for her missing pants. (INCORRECT)*

↓

*John loves snowballs; he eats them whenever there is a blizzard. (CORRECT)*
*Without any money; Tara cannot go to Florida to search for her missing pants. (INCORRECT)*

*In the first example, both "John loves snowballs" and "He eats them whenever there is a blizzard" are considered to be independent clauses: they can be read as complete sentences. Therefore, either a period or semicolon can separate the clauses.*

*In the second example, "Without any money" is a **phrase**, and "Tara cannot go to Florida to search for her missing pants" is an independent clause. As such, the two parts should be separated by a **comma**, as was discussed in the previous section.*

*Without any money, Tara cannot go to Florida to search for her missing pants. (CORRECT)*

## Colons

A *colon* **introduces quotations, examples or lists.**

A few examples of each are as follows:

Quotations:

- *I will recite the first sentence on the note: "Always remember to brush and floss."*
- *Never forget his final choice of words: "Live, laugh and love."*

Examples:

- *We all know who will win this fight: the dog.*
- *There are only two options right now: stand up or back down.*

Lists:

- *I want to visit a number of places while in Europe: London, Rome and Athens.*
- *Here is the full list of items needed from the store: eggs, milk, orange juice and double-stuffed chocolate cookies.*

## Quotation Marks

*Quotation marks* are **used to indicate either dialogue or direct quotes**. While that is simple enough to understand, punctuation is a bit trickier to grasp.

The rules of punctuation in quotation marks are as follows:

1. If the quotation is at the start of the sentence and is followed by a clause, the first word is capitalized and ends in a comma inside the quotation marks. If the quote is a question, use a question mark in place of the comma.

   - *"The door is open," said John.*
   - *"One of these days, I will win," replied Ralph.*
   - *"Where is the bathroom?" asked Brienne of Tarth.*

2. If a clause precedes a quotation, the ending punctuation is placed within the quotation marks. The first word of the quote is capitalized.

    - Albert asked, "Are you hungry?"
    - She replied, "I will always love basketball."
    - Did he really ask, "Is that a tree?"

3. In some instances, the quotation may be separated with a clause in between. Separate such quotes with commas as such.

    - "When you were walking," Ralph asked, "did you see a black dog?"
    - "You can walk," Beth said uneasily, "if you are ready to walk."
    - "One day," Mufasa told Simba, "this entire valley will be yours."

## Question Marks and Periods

A *question mark* is **used at the end of a direct question**. A *period* is **used at the end of a direct statement**. Understanding the difference between a statement and question is the key to avoiding mistakes between the two.

Here are a few examples of differentiating between statements and questions.

- *Will Timothy run ten laps today. (INCORRECT)*
- *Renee will never be a great martial artist? (INCORRECT)*
- *I must write a hundred page paper tomorrow? (INCORRECT)*
- *Did the chicken come before the egg. (INCORRECT)*

- *Will Timothy run ten laps today? (CORRECT)*
- *Renee will never be a great martial artist. (CORRECT)*
- *I must write a hundred page paper tomorrow. (CORRECT)*
- *Did the chicken come before the egg? (CORRECT)*

## Apostrophes

An *apostrophe* has two specific functions: **to indicate contractions and to show possessive form**.

Examples of contractions include:
- will not: won't
- cannot: can't
- I am: I'm
- he is: he's

Examples of possessive form include:
- Lisa's jacket
- Jeff's basketball
- The Yankees' field
- Ross' hat

**Common Mistake: It's vs. Its**
It is crucial to understand the difference between "it's" and "its"

*Contraction: It's (it is)*
- *It's getting hot in here.*
- *It's almost time for bed.*

*Possessive: Its*
- *Its tail is now blue!*
- *Can you please give its hair back?*

## *SENTENCE STRUCTURE ERRORS*

### Run-on Sentences

A run-on sentence is a combination of two or more independent clauses that are joined inappropriately.

Remember, there are four different ways to join or separate independent clauses. The following will be a review of the list, used to appropriately fix the given run-on sentences.

1. Combination of commas with the conjunctions: and, but, or, nor, so, yet, for

*John loves to go skiing he cannot due to Pasadena's warm weather. (INCORRECT)*
*John loves to go skiing,* ***but*** *he cannot due to Pasadena's warm weather. (CORRECT)*

2. Semicolons

*John loves to go skiing he cannot due to Pasadena's warm weather. (INCORRECT)*
*John loves to go skiing; he cannot due to Pasadena's warm weather. (CORRECT)*

3. Subordinate conjunctions and commas (although, if, since, while, after)

*John loves to go skiing he cannot due to Pasadena's warm weather. (INCORRECT)*
***Although** John loves to go skiing, he cannot due to Pasadena's warm weather. (CORRECT)*

4. Periods

*John loves to go skiing he cannot due to Pasadena's warm weather. (INCORRECT)*
*John loves to go skiing. He cannot due to Pasadena's warm weather. (CORRECT)*

## Sentence Fragments

Sentence fragments are otherwise known an incomplete sentence. An incomplete sentence **lacks either a subject, predicate, both, or is not a complete thought**.

Remember, just because a sentence is long and connected with a number of phrases and clauses does not mean that it is a complete sentence.

Examples of sentence fragments include:

<u>Incomplete Thoughts:</u>
- *Because his mother told him to **(...what did he do?)***
- *After the snowstorm ends. **(...what after?)***
- *If you are willing to buy a ticket from Expedia for a one-way trip to Alaska. **(...what will happen?)***

## *VERB TENSES*

*Grammatical tenses are forms taken to show the time of action.*

**Simple Tense:**

| | |
|---|---|
| **Present** | I eat |
| **Past** | I ate |
| **Future** | I will eat |

**Perfect Tense**

The perfect tense shows that the action has already been completed.

| | |
|---|---|
| **Perfect Present** | I have eaten |
| **Perfect Past** | I had eaten |
| **Perfect Future** | I will have eaten |

Example: *I had eaten by the time the news about Antonio reached me.*

Example: *Thank you, but I have eaten my share of food today.*

**Progressive Tense**

The progressive tense shows an action that is still continuing.

| | |
|---|---|
| **Present Progressive** | I am eating |
| **Past Progressive** | I was eating |
| **Future Progressive** | I will be eating |

Example: *I am eating right now.*

Example: *I was eating while they burned down my house.*

**Perfect Progressive Tense**

The progressive tense shows an action that is still continuing.

| | |
|---|---|
| **Perfect Present Progressive** | I have been walking |
| **Perfect Past Progressive** | I had been eating |
| **Perfect Future Progressive** | I will have been eating |

## ADJECTIVES VS. ADVERBS

Adjectives and adverbs are both used to describe words. It is essential to know the different uses of the two.

- Adjectives describe or modify pronouns and nouns.
  EXAMPLE: red ball, angry Jim, funny clown

- Adverbs describe or modify verbs, adjectives or other adverbs.
  EXAMPLE: hardly running, recklessly paint, drastically different

HINT: Most adverbs ends in "-ly".

Here are a few examples of the incorrect use of adverbs.

*Driving <u>reckless</u> in the snow and ice is a very dangerous decision. (INCORRECT)*
*Driving <u>recklessly</u> in the snow and ice is a very dangerous decision. (CORRECT)*

*Amber finished her homework <u>quick</u>. (INCORRECT)*
*Amber finished her homework <u>quickly</u>. (CORRECT)*

## *COMPARATIVES AND SUPERLATIVES*

Comparatives and superlatives are adjectives used to compare different objects.

- Comparatives compare two objects.
  "-er" is added to the end of the adjective.
  If adding "-er" is inappropriate, the word "more" is added.

- Superlatives compare more than objects.
  "-est" is added to the end of the adjective
  If adding "-er" is inappropriate, the word "more" is added.

HINT: "More" and "most" is added to adjectives with three or more syllables (beautiful, important).

| COMPARATIVES AND SUPERLATIVES | | |
|---|---|---|
| **Adjective** | **Comparative** | **Superlative** |
| fast | faster | fastest |
| big | bigger | biggest |
| rich | richer | richest |
| ridiculous | more ridiculous | most ridiculous |

In some instances, the entire structure of the adjective changes to suit the comparative and superlative.

| IRREGULAR COMPARATIVES AND SUPERLATIVES | | |
|---|---|---|
| **Adjective** | **Comparative** | **Superlative** |
| good | better | best |
| bad | worse | worst |
| much | more | most |
| little | less | least |
| far | farther | farthest |

Remember that comparatives are used when comparing two nouns or pronouns, and superlatives are used for three or more nouns or pronouns.

*Between Jacob and Edward, Jacob is the <u>strongest</u>. (INCORRECT)*
*Between Jacob and Edward, Jacob is the <u>stronger</u>. (CORRECT)*

*Among Harry, Ron and Hermione, Hermione is the <u>smarter</u>. (INCORRECT)*
*Among Harry, Ron and Hermione, Hermione is the <u>smartest</u>. (CORRECT)*

## Illogical Comparisons

When comparing two or more objects, the nouns or pronouns must be of the same entity. For instance, one cannot compare a painter to a painting, or an author to a book. Painters are compared with other painters, and books are compare with other books.

*Satoshi's <u>test scores</u> are higher than <u>John</u>. (INCORRECT)*
*Satoshi's <u>test scores</u> are higher than <u>John's</u>. (CORRECT)*

*The coffee from Starbucks is much better than Dunkin Donuts. (INCORRECT)*
*The coffee from Starbucks is much better than Dunkin Donuts coffee. (CORRECT)*

### *OTHER GRAMMATICAL TRAITS*

### Double Negatives

The use of two negative words can turn the sentence into a positive one, which may not be the intent of the writer. Double negatives are usually discouraged.

*Don't say nothing. (INCORRECT)*
*Don't say anything. (CORRECT)*

### Redundancy

Unnecessary repetition makes writing more difficult to read and makes the sentence seem longer than it actually is. The objective is to remove any repeated information.

*The meeting on Tuesday has been postponed until later. (INCORRECT)*
*The meeting on Tuesday has been postponed. (CORRECT)*

The definition of "postpone" is to take place at a later time; "until later" is not needed.

*The attack was an unintentional mistake. (INCORRECT)*
*The attack was a mistake. (CORRECT)*

A "mistake" is something that is misguided and unintentional.

ARGOPREP
ARGOPREP.COM/SHSAT

## LIST OF MOST COMMONLY MISUSED WORDS

| | |
|---|---|
| **A, an** | The article *a* is used before a consonant sound, and *an* is used before a vowel sound.<br>*a car, an apple* |
| **Accept, except** | *Accept* is a verb meaning to receive, and *except* means to leave out.<br>*I accepted the gift.*<br>*Everyone went to the party except me.* |
| **Affect, effect** | *Affect* is a verb meaning to influence, and *effect* is a noun that means result.<br>*The disaster affected everyone in town.*<br>*The effect of the disaster was saddening.* |
| **Already, all ready** | *Already* means by a certain time, and *all already* means completely ready.<br>*I have already completed my homework.*<br>*My homework is all ready to be submitted.* |
| **Altogether, all together** | *Altogether* means entirely, and *all together* means as an entire group.<br>*He is altogether a very capable individual.*<br>*All together, there is a total of twenty members.* |
| **Among, between** | *Among* is used in groups of three or more, whereas *between* is used for two individuals.<br>*Among the three friends, Henry is the coolest.*<br>*Between the two friends, Henry is the uglier.* |
| **Amount, number** | *Amount* is a numberless bulk, and *number* refers to a specific count.<br>*The amount of homework I have is ridiculous.*<br>*The number of homework packets I have is ridiculous.* |
| **As, like** | *As* is a conjunction that is followed by a verb, while *like* is a preposition and is not followed by a verb.<br>*Please cook the recipe as I instructed.*<br>*This food looks like dung.* |
| **Beside, besides** | *Beside* means next to, and *besides* means apart from.<br>*The bird flew beside his fellow friends.*<br>*Besides watching birds fly, I enjoy eating pie.* |
| **Farther, further** | *Farther* is used to compare distances that are measurable, and *further* is used to describe the advancement of an idea or object.<br>*The boat is twenty miles farther than from here.*<br>*We must explore this experiment further* |

**Fewer, less** — *Fewer* applies to objects that can be counted, and *less* is used for degrees that cannot be measured.
*There are five fewer cupcakes than there was yesterday.*
*I am less happy today.*

**Its, it's** — *Its* is possessive, and *it's* is a contraction for it is.
*Its horns are enormous.*
*It's quite enormous.*

**Principal, principle** — *Principal* refers to the head of something, and *principle* refers to a fundamental truth.
*The principal of the school laid down the rules.*
*The principle behind survival is to lay low at all times.*

**Than, then** — *Than* is used to compare things, whereas *then* is used in reference to time.
*I am smarter than you.*
*I will study for the test and then get a higher score than you.*

**Their, there, they're** — *Their* is the possessive form of they, *there* is an indication of place, and *they're* is the contraction of they are.
*I can't wait to go to their party.*
*Over there, you will find a list of party foods.*
*They're 30 minnutes away from the party.*

## CAPITALIZATION

Here is a list of nouns, otherwise known as "proper nouns" that must be capitalized in any sentence.

- Proper first and last names, names of organizations
  - Amanda Greenberg, Yankees, Wall Street
- Titles that precede names
  - Doctor Johnson, Mister Freddy, Aunt Jemima
- Days of the week and months in a year
  - Monday, January, Thursday
- Holidays
  - Fourth of July, Thanksgiving, Halloween, Memorial Day

The first word of a sentence or quotation must also be capitalized.

*My name is Diane Johnson.*
*John replied, "The dog is blue."*

## READING PASSAGES ARE NOTHING TO BE WARY OF.

Reading questions can be intimidating and even overwhelming at times. Nonetheless, they are a large part of the SHSAT exam and cannot afford to be ignored.

---

### Common Reading Comprehension Mistakes

Remember, the Reading section is not quizzing you on how well you read and understand the passage; rather, it tests you on how easily and swiftly you recognize the author's intended answer. Increasing your score by earning points is only achieved by arriving to the correct answer choice. The main focus should always be placed on spending as much time as possible on the reading questions provided. The best way to do so is by avoiding a few common reading mistakes:

- Studying all of the questions before the passage
- Reading the passage too closely
- Nitpicking sentences you have difficulty understanding

Notice how all of the main difficulties listed above center around one element: time management. The last two mistakes go hand in hand. Recall that the primary purpose is to gain only a general understanding of the passage to tackle the questions. You will be required to reread certain parts of the passage when attempting to answer the questions anyway, so why waste additional time fussing over specific details?

### Tackling Reading Comprehension Questions

### Phase I: Read the Passage

### Phase II: Identifying the Question Types

Now that you've gained a good understanding of how to approach the passage itself, you can finally start to look at the most important part of the section: the questions themselves. Determining the type of question being asked is the first step; doing so will allow you to effectively read parts of the passage to answer appropriately.

#### A. Main Idea Questions

The main idea question focuses on summarizing the most important idea of the passage. It is helpful to understand that the main idea ties all of the paragraphs together and is the overall central theme.

Common Traps in Main Idea Questions. The main idea should be neither too narrow nor too broad. Too narrow of an answer choice tends to cover some details in the passage, but not all that were discussed. Adversely, an answer choice may cover all of the ideas in the passage, but may include others that were not mentioned directly in the reading. Any answer covering unsupported or new information will be incorrect.

Examples of main idea questions can include:

- What is the main idea of this passage?
- What is the passage mainly about?
- A good title for this passage would be...?
- Which of the following most accurately describes the passage?
- What is the author's primary purpose in this passage?

**B. Detail Questions**

Detail questions are the most common form of questions found in the Reading Comprehension section. Thankfully, they are very easy to master and answer correctly; just consider them to be a part of an open book test. Whatever the question is asking, the passage must provide the details. Depending on what you are asked, you just have to locate that information in the passage.

It is always important to read information outside of the reference provided in the question. The questions most likely require some amount of context clues to fully answer, so reading the sentence before and after the following sentence can help. Identifying detail questions is simple enough. In some instances, a phrase in the question may refer to back to the passage: "According to the passage...".

Examples of detail questions can include:

- According to the passage, which of the following is true?
- John was best known for his ability to do what?
- During its final trip to the Atlantic Ocean, what did the ship come across?

**C. Inference Questions**

Inference questions mainly ask you to draw conclusions based on information provided directly in the passage. Note that the inference is never directly stated in the passage.

For example, a passage can discuss the travels of a character. It may describe in great detail surroundings of the area that the character is set in, but may not explicitly state the location. Take a look at the passage below.

"Hundreds of cars honked on the road as Jim walked down the littered streets. The view of the sky was completely blocked by the dozens of skyscrapers. The air was thick with smoke and smog. Jim felt sickened and disgusted; this was not what he had imagined at all."

From this excerpt, a number of details can be inferred. While it is not directly stated, it can be concluded that Jim is most likely visiting a city. It is most likely his first time stepping into the city as well, according to his

negative reaction to his experience. All of this can easily be interpreted without having any direct details on Jim's whereabouts or past travels.

**Common Traps in Inference Questions.** Remember, the answer to inference questions are never directly stated in the passage – answers that discuss the exact details are to be avoided.
Examples of inference questions can include:
- The character in this passage is most likely...
- This passage can most likely be found in a...

### D. Vocabulary Questions

Vocabulary questions ask you to find synonyms of specific words that are to be found in the reading passage. The word provided may or not be a word that you recognize, but the key to answering such questions correctly lies in using context clues.

Answering vocabulary questions is very simple. Read the sentence that the word is located in, as well as the sentences that come both before and after for better reference. Once you have a general understanding of what the word is, replace the vocabulary word with each of the answer choices and select the word that best fits the definition of the word.

Examples of vocabulary questions can include:
- The word ____ most nearly means...
- According to the passage, which word most closely represents ____?

This concludes a basic review of the ELA section for the NEW SHSAT Exam. In this book you will find five full-length exams to practice and get a better understanding of the NEW SHSAT Exam.

## Important information:

Please note that video explanations on our online platform all contain the answer choices ABCD. This workbook and the real exam alternates between answer choices ABCD and EFGH.

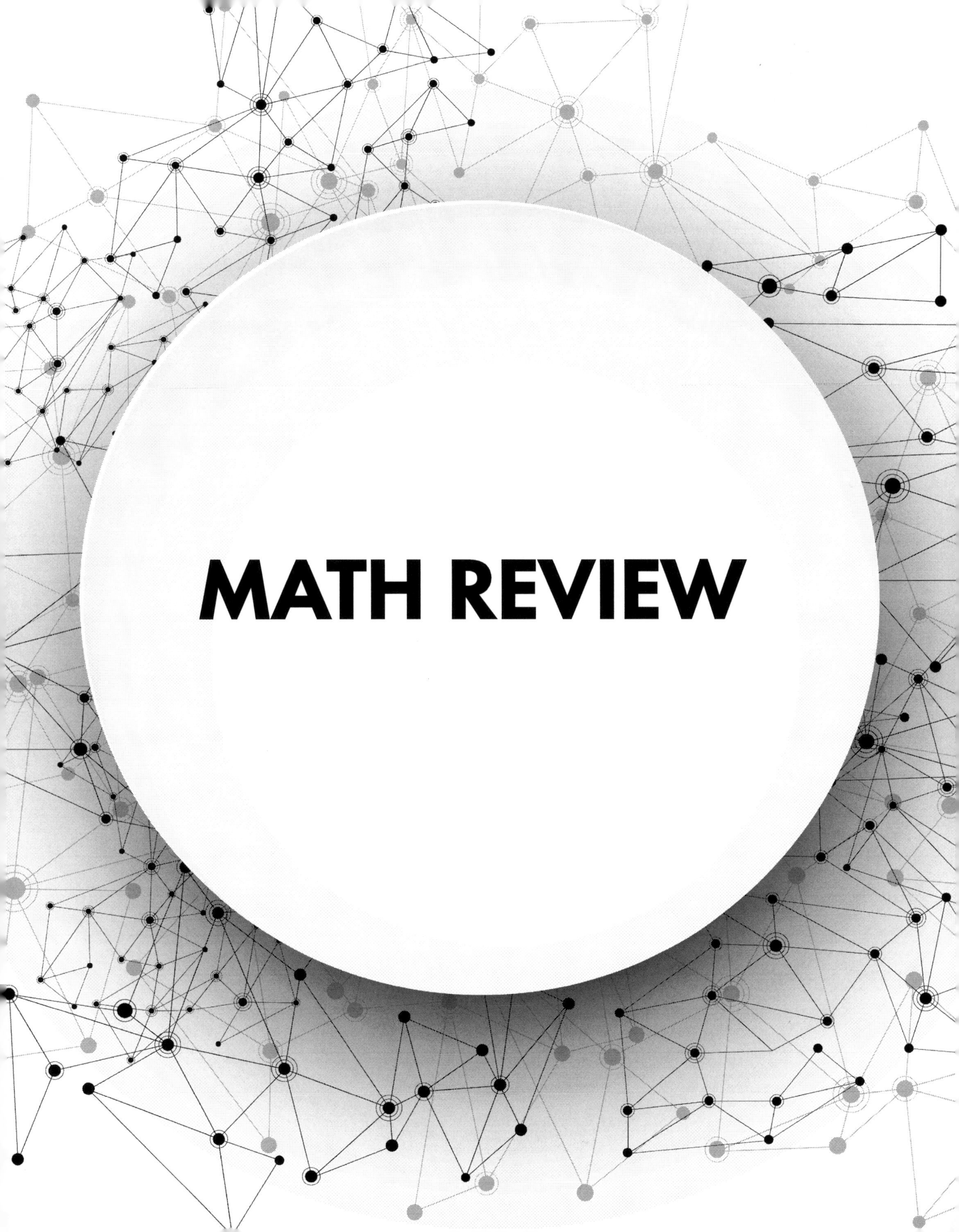

# MATH REVIEW

## Math on the SHSAT

Let us explore the major concepts tested in each of the subject areas. Again, this is not a comprehensive list.

**Arithmetic**

- Real numbers including integers, prime numbers, rational numbers and irrational numbers
- Number sequences
- Factors and multiples
- Fractions and decimals
- Arithmetic operations
- Percentages, ratios, and rates
- Absolute value

**Algebra**

- Algebraic expressions
- Coordinate planes, slopes, and intercepts
- Functions and relations
- Linear equations
- Quadratic equations
- Inequalities
- Rules of exponents and Roots

**Geometry**

- Right, isosceles, and other special triangles
- Pythagorean theorem
- Properties and measurements of circles
- Polygons
- Perimeter, area, and volume
- Properties and measurements of three-dimensional figures

**Data Interpretation**

- Descriptive statistics
- Understanding data from charts and graphs
- Frequency distributions
- Probability
- Permutations
- Means and averages

## Mathematical Conventions on the SHSAT

While math can be straightforward at times, there are many nuances that need to be considered when working with problems to determine how you interpret information. Here are some of the key conventions:

- All numbers on the exam are real numbers. There will be no questions relating to imaginary numbers.
- Geometric figures are **not** drawn to scale unless otherwise indicated.
- While you should not assume lengths based on how geometric figures look, you should assume that all lines in a figure are straight lines and that the figure lies on a plane unless otherwise indicated.
- Contrary to geometric figures, coordinate planes and numbers lines **are** drawn to scale.
- Graphs on the exam, including histograms, pie charts, and line graphs are drawn to scale and you can make assumptions based on the visual presentation of the data.
- $\pi$ is assumed to represent the value 3.14.
- For geometry questions, the sum of the measure of the interior angles of a triangle equals 180°.

# Arithmetic: The Basics

Arithmetic encompasses the fundamental building blocks of math. It includes basic concepts like the mathematical operations of addition, subtraction, multiplication and division. Almost all the questions you encounter on the exam will require you to apply principles of arithmetic in some capacity. You will need to understand the order of operations, real numbers, ratios, and fractions. The concepts discussed in this section will help you refresh your understanding of basic arithmetic and prepare you to navigate the more difficult exam concepts such as algebraic expressions and geometry.

## Math Building Blocks

Before we dive into the specifics of arithmetic and the other concepts tested on the math section of the exam, let us review the fundamental building blocks of math, especially common symbols and types of numbers. These concepts will appear in some form on the exam and a clear understanding of these fundamentals is key to your success.

***What's That Sign?***

| Math Symbol | Common Name | Description |
|---|---|---|
| $<$ | Less than | Used to signify that the quantity to the left of the symbol is less than the quantity to the right. |
| $>$ | Greater than | Used to signify that the quantity to the left of the symbol is greater than the quantity to the right. |
| $\leq$ | Less than or equal to | Used to signify that the quantity to the left of the symbol is less than or equal to the quantity to the right. |
| $\geq$ | Greater than or equal to | Used to signify that the quantity to the left of the symbol is greater than or equal to the quantity to the right. |

| Math Symbol | Common Name | Description |
|---|---|---|
| $\sqrt{\ }$ | Square root | An irrational number that produces a specified quantity when multiplied by itself. |
| $\lvert x \rvert$ | Absolute value | Reflects the positive distance of the expressed number from zero. |
| ! | Factorial | The product of the whole numbers from 1 to a given number. |
| $\parallel$ | Parallel Lines | Signifies that two lines are parallel to each other and do not intersect at any point. |
| $\perp$ | Perpendicular Lines | Signifies that two lines separated by this symbol intersect to form a right angle. |
| $\pi$ | Pi | The geometric ratio of a circle's circumference to its diameter; the value used on the SHSAT is 3.14. |

## *Real Numbers*

You will encounter only real numbers on the SHSAT, so you need not concern yourself with studying concepts related to imaginary numbers. Real numbers are numbers found on the number line and are, with the exception of zero, either positive or negative. Several classes of numbers are included in the real numbers category and will appear on the exam. Let's look at the various types of real numbers you can expect to see.

### *Whole Numbers*

Whole numbers are positive counting numbers including zero that contain no decimal or fraction parts.

0, 1, 2, 3, 4, 5...

### *Integers*

Integers are all positive and negative numbers, including zero. Integers that occur in a sequence like the ones below are called consecutive integers.

-2, -1, 0, 1, 2, 3...

### *Rational Numbers*

Rational numbers are any numbers, positive or negative, that can be expressed as a ratio of two numbers. All integers and fractions are considered rational numbers.

$\frac{1}{2} \quad \frac{3}{4} \quad \frac{1}{4}$

### *Irrational Numbers*

Irrational numbers are all numbers, positive or negative, that are not rational and cannot be expressed as a ratio.

$\pi, \sqrt{5}$

### *Prime Numbers*

A prime number is a number that has only two positive divisors, 1 and itself. For example, 5 is a prime number because it is only divisible by 1 and itself. Prime numbers are tested often on the exam.

It is best to familiarize yourself with the most common prime numbers, which are those that occur below 100:
2, 3, 5, 7, 11, 13, 17, 19, 23, 29, 31, 37, 41, 43, 47, 53, 59, 61, 67, 71, 73, 79, 83, 89, & 97

There are some other properties of prime numbers you should know:

- Neither 0 nor 1 is a prime number
- Only positive numbers can be prime numbers
- 2 is the only even prime number

### *Factors*

A factor is an integer that divides into another integer evenly and has no remainder.

Take the number 24 as an example:

- 1, 2, 3, 4, 6, 8, 12, and 24 are all factors of 24 since they all divide evenly into the number and have no remainder. On the other hand, the number 5 is **not** a factor since when you divide 5 into 24, there **is** a remainder.

*Greatest Common Factor*

The greatest common factor of two numbers is the largest factor shared by both numbers.

Suppose you wanted to find the greater common factor of 48 and 60. You would first start by identifying the factors for each number:

- Factors of 48: 1, 2, 3, 4, 6, 8, **12**, 16, 24, 48
- Factors of 60: 1, 2, 3, 4, 5, 6, 10, **12**, 15, 20, 30, 60

The greatest common factor of 48 and 60 is 12. The least common factor—in this case, 1—is not likely to be tested on the exam.

### *Multiples*

A multiple is essentially the opposite of a factor. Instead of division, multiples are determined by multiplication. A multiple of a number is the product of the number and any other whole number. Zero is a multiple of every number.

0, 8, 16, 24, 32, 40, 64, and 800 are all multiples of 8 because they are the product of multiplying 8 by another number. When any whole number is multiplied by 8, the product is a multiple.

*Least Common Multiple*

The least common multiple of two or more whole numbers greater than zero is the smallest whole number divisible by each of the numbers.

If you wanted to find the least common multiple of 5 and 6, for example, you would start by identifying the multiples of each.

- Multiples of 5: 10, 15, 20, 25, 30, 35, 40...
- Multiples of 6: 12, 18, 24, 30, 36, 42...

Since you are looking for the least common multiple, you want to select the smallest number that occurs in both lists. In the case, the least common multiple is 30. The greatest common multiple is not likely to be tested on the exam.

## Numeric Operations

The SHSAT Math section includes problems that will require you to add, subtract, multiply, and divide real numbers, including fractions, decimals, roots, and algebraic expressions with non-numeric variables. There are key operations you should keep in mind when dealing with numbers in order to work more efficiently and minimize mistakes.

### *Laws of Operations*

*Commutative Property:* Addition and multiplication are commutative operations; the order in which they are performed does not impact the answer.

$$a \cdot b = b \cdot a$$
$$a + b = b + a$$

*Associative Property:* Addition and multiplication are also associative; when written as an expression, they can be regrouped without impacting the final answer.

$$a + (b + c) = (a + b) + c$$
$$(a \cdot b) \cdot c = a \cdot (b \cdot c)$$

*Distributive Property:* The distributive property outlines how values in an expression should be distributed to the terms being added or subtracted. The distributive property can also be used in division.

$$a(b + c) = ab + ac$$
$$\frac{a + b}{2} = \frac{a}{2} + \frac{b}{2}$$

## *Order of Operations*

The commutative, associative, and distributive properties outline some standard approaches to dealing with addition and multiplication. When other operations are involved, it is important to understand the proper order in which to solve each component of the problem.

The acronym **PEMDAS** outlines the correct order for mathematical operations. Performing operations out of order, specifically those dealing with more than addition and multiplication, will often lead you to the incorrect answer.

*Parentheses:* Complete anything in **parentheses** first.

*Exponents:* Next, calculate any **exponents.**

*Multiplication/Division:* Then attack **multiplication** and **division** elements from left to right.

*Addition/Subtraction:* Finally, attack **addition** and **subtraction** elements from left to right.

Not all equations will contain all these elements. However, be sure to still follow the order when attacking the elements that are present.

Let us look at an example:

| | |
|---|---|
| $100 - 4(7 - 4)^3$ | First, solve for the values in the parentheses |
| $100 - 4(3)^3$ | Solve (7 − 4) and replace the value in parentheses with 3 |
| $100 - 4(3)^3 = 100 - 4(27)$ | Solve the exponent |
| $100 - 4(27) = 100 - 108$ | Multiply and divide |
| $100 - 108 = -8$ | Solve addition and subtraction elements |

The final answer is −8. Remember to work equations in the proper order and that multiplication, division, addition, and subtraction should be solved from left to right.

### *Absolute Value*

Absolute value is the distance of a number from zero. The value is always expressed as a positive number. Absolute value is symbolized by a number being enclosed in two vertical bars.

$$|12|$$

The absolute value of a positive number is always just the number itself.

$$|12| = 12$$

The absolute value of a negative number is derived by dropping the negative sign in front of the number.

$$|-14| = 14$$

You may see absolute value appear in a number of ways on the exam, including as expressions where you must solve for a value. Here's an example:

$4 - 2 + |5 - 7| =$

| | |
|---|---|
| $|5 - 7| = |-2| = 2$ | Solve what is in the brackets |
| $4 - 2 + 2 = 4$ | Plug in the value to the rest of the expression and solve |

## Fractions

Now, let us look at a subset of rational numbers, namely fractions and ratios.

There is no shortage of fractions on the SHSAT. You will see them appear in word problems, as part of algebraic expressions, and in pure problem solving questions. The two main components of a fraction are the numerator and the denominator.

$$\frac{a \longrightarrow \text{numerator}}{b \longrightarrow \text{denominator}}$$

You will need to know how to perform various operations with fractions, including addition, subtraction, multiplication, division, simplifying, and converting them to mixed numbers. Let us look at some of the key facts about fractions and operations related to them.

### *Reciprocals*

The reciprocal of a fraction is found simply by reversing the numerator and the denominator. For example, the reciprocal of $\frac{2}{3}$ is $\frac{3}{2}$. The product of any fraction and its reciprocal is always 1. All whole numbers except zero have a reciprocal where the reciprocal of $a$ is $\frac{1}{a}$.

### *Equivalent Fractions*

Since fractions represent the part of a given whole, increasing the whole and the part by the same amount does not change the relationship. Consider the fraction $\frac{1}{2}$. If you multiplied the numerator and denominator by 3, for example, you would end up with the equivalent fraction $\frac{3}{6}$.

### *Reducing Fractions*

There are a number of instances in which you will need to reduce fractions on the exam; in fact, whenever you are able to do so, you should. When you reduce a fraction, you simply express the fraction in its lowest terms.

Let us suppose you have the fraction $\frac{40}{80}$. To reduce the fraction, identify the greatest common factor shared by the numerator and denominator. In this case, 40 and 80 share several factors:

Factors of 40: 1, 2, 4, 5, 8, 10, 20, **40**
Factors of 80: 1, 2, 4, 5, 8, 10, 20, **40**

The greatest common factor of the numerator and the denominator is **40**. To reduce the fraction, determine how many times the greatest common factor divides into both the numerator and the denominator.

Numerator: $\frac{40}{40} = 1$ Denominator: $\frac{80}{40} = 2$ Reduced fraction: $\frac{40}{80} = \frac{1}{2}$

### *Mixed Numbers*

A mixed number is a fraction that is preceded by an integer. For example: $2\frac{3}{7}$.

It is often not possible to work with mixed numbers and perform operations like addition and subtraction. You must instead convert a mixed fraction into a standard fraction having just a numerator and a denominator. Converting a fraction is rather straightforward. First, you multiply the denominator and the integer, then add the product to the numerator. The denominator from the mixed fraction will remain the same.

$$2\frac{3}{7} = \frac{7 \cdot 2 + 3}{7} = \frac{17}{7}$$

### *Adding and Subtracting Fractions*

Adding and subtracting fractions is a straightforward operation when the fractions have the same denominator. In these cases, you simply add or subtract the numerators; the denominator remains the same.

*Examples*: $\frac{2}{4} - \frac{1}{4} = \frac{1}{4}$ $\frac{8}{13} + \frac{23}{13} = \frac{31}{13}$

Adding and subtracting fractions that do not have the same denominator involves a bit more calculation. The most efficient way to approach adding and subtracting fractions is cross-multiplying. Let us take $\frac{11}{21} + \frac{4}{11}$ as an example.

First, multiply the denominator of the second fraction by the numerator of the first fraction:

$\frac{11}{21} \nwarrow \frac{4}{11}$ $\quad 11 \cdot 11 = 121$

Then, multiply the denominator of the first fraction by the numerator of the second fraction:

$\frac{11}{12} \nearrow \frac{4}{11}$ $\quad 12 \cdot 4 = 48$

The sum of these two operations is your new **numerator:** 48 + 121 = **169**. You are not done yet, however: to find your new denominator, multiply both denominators:

$\frac{11}{12} + \frac{4}{11} = \frac{11(11) + 4(12)}{12(11)} = \frac{169}{132}$ The sum of the fractions

The process is the same for subtracting fractions, except that instead of adding the products of the cross-multiplication to get the new numerator, you will subtract.

### *Multiplying Fractions*

When multiplying fractions, the process is the same regardless of whether or not the denominators are the same.

$$\frac{8}{11} \cdot \frac{7}{13} = \frac{8 \cdot 7}{11 \cdot 13} = \frac{56}{143}$$

### *Dividing Fractions*

Dividing fractions is similar to the process of multiplying fractions since multiplication and division are inverse operations. To divide fractions, multiply the first fraction by the reciprocal or inverse of the second fraction.

$$\frac{1}{5} \div \frac{3}{7} = \frac{1}{5} \cdot \frac{7}{3} = \frac{7}{15}$$

### *Ratios*

Ratios are often written as fractions and compare two quantities. Ratios, like fractions, deal with parts of the whole, but also express the relationship between two quantities that may not be part of the same whole.

Ratios can be written as fractions or using the common notation $x : y$. For example, if a word problem tells you that the ratio of girls to boys in the class is four boys for every three girls, you can write that as: $\frac{4}{3}$ or 4 : 3.

If a question asks you what the ratio of girls to boys is, whatever follows the term ***of*** is the numerator and whatever follows ***to*** is the denominator.

Ratios often appear on the exam in word problems. Be careful and make sure you understand what ratio the question is asking you to examine. Let us look at a few examples:

> Nathan has 7 sodas and 4 bottles of water in his cooler. What is the ratio of sodas to bottles of water in the cooler?

Since you are looking for the ratio of sodas to bottles of water, your ratio would look like this:

$\frac{soda}{bottles\ of\ water}$ **or** sodas : bottles of water

$\frac{7}{4}$ or 7 : 4 — Once we know what our ratio looks like, we plug in the numbers.

7 : 4 : 2 — Ratios are not always expressed with just two variables. Suppose Nathan has 7 sodas, 4 bottles of water, and 2 juice boxes. To express the ratio of the drinks in the cooler, add the juice boxes to the original ratio.

This is a fixed ratio, meaning that each portion of the ratio directly corresponds to a particular item in the cooler. So, if you reordered the ratio so that it read 4 : 7 : 2, you no longer have the ratio of sodas to bottled waters to juice boxes. Instead, you had the ratio of bottled waters to sodas to juice boxes.

> Tori's soccer team loses 10 games out of every 30 games that it plays. What is the ratio of Tori's soccer team's wins to losses?

$\frac{wins}{losses}$ or wins : losses — You are looking for the ratio of wins to losses.

Be careful not to assume the ratio of wins to losses is 10 : 30. While that is the order the parts are listed in the problem, the order does not correspond to the question. Further, the question does not explicitly tell you the number of wins. 30 is the number of games played, so we need to calculate the number of wins before we can determine the ratio.

$30 - 10 = 20$ — Subtract the number of losses from the total number of games

$\frac{wins}{losses} = \frac{20}{10} = \frac{2}{1} = 2:1$ — Insert the number of wins into your ratio formula

### *Proportions*

Proportions are an extension of ratios. Proportions are equations that set two ratios equal to one another and are helpful to determine ratios when quantities in a specific ratio relationship increase or decrease.

> If Nathan has 7 sodas and 4 bottles of water, proportions tell us that if Nathan has 14 sodas, he would have 8 bottles of water. This proportion can be expressed as:
>
> $$\frac{14}{8} = \frac{7}{4}$$

## Decimals

A decimal, like a fraction, expresses a part of a whole. Decimals are tested often on the SHSAT and it is important to understand the fundamentals of a decimal, including how the specific digits of the decimal are described. Take the decimal 123.456, for example. Each digit has its own mathematical label:

1 2 3 . 4 5 6

| | | |
|---|---|---|
| 1: Hundreds | 3: Ones | 5: Hundredths |
| 2: Tens | 4: Tenths | 6: Thousandths |

## *Fractions to Decimals*

You may occasionally need to change either the expressions in the problem or your answer from fractions to decimals or decimals to factions.

> To change a fraction to a decimal, simply divide the denominator into the numerator.
>
> $\frac{7}{20} = 7 \div 20 = 0.35$

## *Decimals to Fractions*

Suppose you have the decimal 54.67. To convert a decimal to a fraction, first remove the decimal point and make the resulting whole number your numerator and, for right now, make 1 your denominator:

$54.67 = \frac{5467}{1}$

Then, count the number of digits after the decimal point. In this case, .67 follows the decimal point. So, two digits follow the decimal point. Place a 0 after the 1 in the denominator for each digit that occurs after the decimal point in order to determine the fractional equivalent to your decimal.

$54.67 = \frac{5467}{100}$

In order to verify that you have the correct fraction, simply divide the denominator into the numerator--you will end up right back at 54.67.

## *Percentages*

Percentages, like fractions and decimals, represent a portion of the whole and are heavily tested on the exam in a number of ways. Percentages are based on the whole of 100. 20% of something is essentially 20 parts of 100. Percentages can be written a number of different ways. For example, we can write 20% as follows:

20% or $\frac{20}{100}$ or .20

On the exam, you may be asked to calculate what percentage an integer is of another integer. For example, a problem solving question may ask you: *5 is what percentage of 20?*

| | |
|---|---|
| $5 = ?\%(20)$ | Write the problem as an equation |
| $5 = \frac{x}{100}(20)$ | Since percentages are always based on 100, you can add more information to the equation to help you solve and substitute an unknown variable for the value we are missing. |
| $5 = \frac{20x}{100} = \frac{2x}{10} = \frac{x}{5}$ | Reduce the fraction |
| $5 = \frac{x}{5}$ | Cross-multiply |
| $25 = x$ | 5 is **25**% of 20 |

You solved the problem and got the correct answer, but it took a lot of steps, which translates to a lot of time. There are some common formulas you can use on the exam to help approach percentage problems of various types. Let us look at these in more detail.

### *Part of the Whole Formula*

Problems involving percentages on the exam will normally, like the previous problem, give you two of the values and ask you to calculate the third. In the previous example, you had 5, the part, and 20, the whole. You were looking for the percentage. You can solve the problem with fewer steps by using a formula:

**Formula:** $percent = \frac{part}{whole}$

$$percent = \frac{5}{20} = .25 \text{ or } 25\%$$

Let us look at a few more examples:

**Example 1:**
*What is 20% of 42?*

| | |
|---|---|
| $percent \cdot whole = part$ | Percentage Formula |
| $.20 \cdot 42 = 8.4\%$ | Solve |

**Example 2:**
*12 is 40% of what number?*

| | |
|---|---|
| $\frac{part}{percent} = whole$ | Percentage Formula |
| $\frac{12}{.40} = 30$ | Solve |

### *Percent Increase and Decrease*

The SHSAT commonly tests the percent of increase and decrease. While word problems are most common, questions are presented in a number of different ways and may ask you to determine, for example, a new price based on a price increase of a certain percentage, or the decreased percentage of revenue for one fiscal year compared to a previous year. Like the previous problems, you will be given some pieces of information and asked to find the missing element. Let us look at some common formulas to help you calculate percentage increase and decrease.

**Example:**
*The staff at Salsa Kitchen was reduced from 40 to 29 employees. What is the percent decrease in staff?*

To calculate the percentage decrease, use the following formula:

$$\textbf{percentage decrease} = \frac{\text{amount of decrease}}{\text{original whole}} \cdot 100$$

In order to calculate the *amount of decrease*, you must find the difference of the number of current employees and the number of original employees. In this case, Salsa Kitchen started with 40 employees and now has 29, for a difference of 11.

$$percentage\ decrease = \frac{11}{40} \cdot 100$$

$$percentage\ decrease = .275 \cdot 100 = \mathbf{27.5}\%.$$

**Example:**
*Ansley works in a bookstore for $12.00 per hour. If her pay is increased to $14.00, then what is her percent increase in pay?*

To calculate percentage increase, use this formula:

$$\textit{percentage increase} = \frac{\textit{amount of increase}}{\textit{original whole}}$$

In order to calculate the *amount of increase*, you must find the difference of Ansley's current hourly pay and her previous hourly pay. In this case, Ansley started off earning $12.00 an hour before her pay increased to $14.00 an hour. The amount of increase is $2.00.

$$\text{percentage increase} = \frac{2}{12} \cdot 100$$

$$\text{percentage increase} = \frac{1}{6} \cdot 100 = \mathbf{16.66\%}$$

### *Combined Percentages*

Sometimes questions on the exam will ask you to calculate more than one percentage. You may also be asked to find the percentage of a percentage. It is important to understand that you cannot compare percentages that are not part of the same whole. This is a common trap on the exam and you can count on an answer choice that matches the outcome of this mistake.

**Example:**
*During the semi-annual sale, dresses were reduced by 20%. Then, the price was further reduced by 10%. If a dress was originally $200, what is the final price of the dress?*

The dress was first reduced by 20% then by 10%. While it may be tempting to calculate the new final price by reducing the original price of $200 by 30%, that is not correct.

| | |
|---|---|
| .20 · $200 = $40.00 | First, calculate the first price reduction of 20% |
| $200.00 − $40.00 = $160.00 | Subtract $40.00 from the original price |

If the price of dress was reduced by 20%, there would be a $40.00 price difference from the original price. So, after the first reduction, the price of the dress would be $160.00.

| | |
|---|---|
| .10 · $160 = $16.00 | Calculate the second price reduction |
| $160.00 − $16.00 = $144.00 | Reduce the dress by the new discount |

If you had erroneously decreased the original price of $200 by 30%, you would have arrived at $140, which is incorrect.

## Algebra: The Basics

Algebra involves many of the same concepts as arithmetic like absolute value, fractions, and numerical operations. Algebra often uses variables, which are letters used to represent an unknown quantity. Variables are incorporated into expressions and you will often be asked to solve equations to find their value. The concepts discussed in this chapter present themselves in various mathematical capacities on the exam. You will need to understand concepts like factoring, polynomials, algebraic expressions, exponents, roots, and inequalities. Let us start by reviewing some important vocabulary associated with algebra.

## Essential Algebra Vocabulary

*Coefficient:* A multiplier in front of a variable that indicates how many of the variable there are. For example, for the term 5x, 5 is the coefficient. Whenever a term occurs without a coefficient in front of it, like $x$, the coefficient is 1.

*Constant:* A numerical quantity that does not change.

*Equation:* Equations are the building blocks of algebra. An equation is two expressions linked together with an equal sign where values of each expression can be solved or simplified. $2x + 1 = x - 10$ is an example of an equation.

*Expression:* An expression is made up of a single or multiple algebraic term(s), linked together by operations. $5x - 6$, $6xy$, and $x - 1$ are all expressions.

*Term:* A component of an algebraic equation that either represents the product or quotient of a constant and variable, or a specific value separated by arithmetic operations. In the expression $4x + 3b - 2$, $4x$, $3b$, and 2 are all terms.

*Variable:* A letter used to represent an unknown value. Any letter may be used for variables and you many not always need to or be able to find the specific value associated with the variable. In many cases on the exam, however, you will solve to find the value of variables.

## Simplifying Algebraic Expressions

Before you dive into solving more complicated equations, you need to understand a few simplification tools that allow you to change algebraic expressions into simpler but equivalent forms.

### *Algebraic Laws of Operations*

Like with arithmetic, algebra also has three basic properties for dealing with equations: commutative, additive, and distributive.

*Commutative Property:* Addition and multiplication are commutative operations; the order in which they are performed does not impact the answer. The commutative property does not hold for subtraction.

$$2a \cdot 3b = 3b \cdot 2a$$
$$2a + 3b = 3b + 2a$$

*Associative Property:* Addition and multiplication are also associative; when written as an expression, they can be regrouped, and like terms can be combined without impacting the final answer.

Addition:

$$= 2a - 3a + 5b + 2b$$
$$= (2a - 3a) + (5b + 2b)$$
$$= -a + 7b$$

Multiplication:

$$= (6a \cdot 5b) \cdot 4b$$
$$= 6a(5b \cdot 4b)$$
$$= 6a(20b^2)$$
$$= 120ab^2$$

*Distributive Property:* The distributive property outlines how values in an expression should be distributed when performing more than one operation (addition, subtraction, multiplication).

$$3a(4b - 6c) = (3a \cdot 4b) - (3a \cdot 6c)$$
$$= 12ab - 18ac$$

The associative, commutative, and distributive properties apply to many of the problems you will see on the exam. In some expressions and equations, you may need to combine the operations of the properties to arrive at your answer.

## Combining Like Terms

Combining like terms is an effective approach to simplifying and solving algebraic expressions. As you work through the expression, using the appropriate law(s) of operation, look for terms that have the same characteristics and combine them into a single term. Any term that shares the same variable in the same form can be combined.

| | |
|---|---|
| $x^3 + x^2 + 2x + 3x - 4$ | In this case, $2x$ and $3x$ are like terms and can be combined. |
| $x^3 + x^2 + 5x - 4$ | Notice that $x^3$ and $x^2$ cannot be combined. While they share the same base, the exponent $x$ is different. |

## Substitution

Substitution is also another effective way to solve algebraic expressions or to express them in terms of other variables. Let us look at a sample question:

Evaluate $4x^2 - 8x$ when $x = 3$.

Here, you would substitute the value 3 for every $x$ in the expression. Remember the order of operations; solve the parentheses and exponents first:

$$4(3)^2 - 8(3) =$$
$$4(9) - 24 = 36 - 24$$
$$= 12$$

Substitution may sometimes require you to replace non-mathematical symbols with values or operations. For example, you may see a question that uses a non-mathematical symbol instead of an operation sign. In this case, the question will always outline what the symbol represents.

Suppose $x\blacksquare \frac{8 - x}{x^2}$ where $x > 0$. Evaluate $3\blacksquare$.

While it may appear confusing at first, this is simply a substitution question.

| | |
|---|---|
| $\frac{8 - x}{x^2}$ | $x$ times $\blacksquare$ is equal to this expression |
| $3\blacksquare = \frac{8 - 3}{3^2} = \mathbf{\frac{5}{9}}$ | $3\blacksquare$ tells you that 3 is the value of $x$. You will need to substitute the value 3 wherever you see an $x$, then solve. |

## Factoring and Polynomials

Factoring is another approach to simplifying algebraic expressions and is essentially the opposite of distribution, though they are commonly used together. Factoring allows you to evaluate complex expressions by breaking it into simpler expressions, taking into consideration monomials, polynomials, binomials, and trinomials.

*Monomials:* A single term expression. For example, $3x$ or $4y$.

*Polynomials:* An expression with more than one term. For example, $3x^2 + 2y + 3$.

*Binomials:* A polynomial expression with exactly two terms. For example, $4x + 6$.

*Trinomials:* A polynomial expression with exactly three terms. For example, $4y^2 + 3x - 2$.

When there is a monomial factor common to all the terms in the polynomial expression, it can be factored out to create simpler expressions. Suppose you have the following expression:

$4x + 8xy$

$4x(1 + 2y)$ — $4x$ is the common factor and can be used to simplify the expression

### *Common Polynomial Equations*

There are common polynomials that you may encounter on the exam. Knowing how to recognize and factor these can save you time on exam day.

The difference of squares can be factored out into the product of two simpler expressions.

$$a^2 - b^2 = (a - b)(a + b)$$

Some polynomials can be factored into two matching binomials.

$$a^2 - 2ab + b^2 = (a - b)(a - b)$$

Some polynomials are trinomials that are perfect squares.

$$a^2 + 2b^2 + b^2 = (a + b)^2$$

Since factoring is the opposite of distribution, these equations are all commutative.

## Roots and Exponents

### *Exponents*

You may have noticed that polynomials often involve exponents. While this is not always the case, exponents are an important component of algebra and have their own set of rules you should be familiar with going into the exam.

An exponent tells you how many times to multiply a number by itself to find a particular value. If we have the exponent $3^2$, the number 3 is called the base while the number 2 is referred to as the exponent or power.

To solve an exponent, multiply the base by itself the number of times expressed by the exponent. Take $5^3$, for example. If you were to rewrite the expression without exponents and solve, it would look like this:

$$5 \cdot 5 \cdot 5 = 125$$

Any base with an exponent of 2 is commonly referred to as *squared* and any base with an exponent of 3 is referred to as *cubed*. It is helpful to be familiar with some of the common exponents you may see on the exam. The following chart outlines common squares and cubes that commonly appear in arithmetic and algebra problems.

| Common Squares | Common Cubes |
|---|---|
| $1^2 = 1$ | $1^3 = 1$ |
| $2^2 = 4$ | $2^3 = 8$ |
| $3^2 = 9$ | $3^3 = 27$ |
| $4^2 = 16$ | $4^3 = 64$ |
| $5^2 = 25$ | $5^3 = 125$ |
| $6^2 = 36$ | $6^3 = 216$ |
| $7^2 = 49$ | $7^3 = 343$ |
| $8^2 = 64$ | $8^3 = 512$ |
| $9^2 = 81$ | $9^3 = 729$ |
| $10^2 = 100$ | $10^3 = 1000$ |

### *Rules of Exponents*

Working with exponents is pretty straightforward when you only have a base and a positive exponent like $3^2$. But you will see exponents on the exam that include negative numbers and involve mathematical operations like multiplication and division. The following chart is a helpful tool to familiarize yourself with the rules of exponents and how to deal with various presentations of exponents on the exam.

| Exponent Rule | Example |
|---|---|
| $x^0 = 1$ | Any nonzero number to the zero power is equal to 1. Note that $0^0$ has no defined value.<br>*Example:* $5^0 = 1$ |
| $x^1 = x$ | Any nonzero number raised to the power of 1 is equal to the number itself.<br>*Example:* $6^1 = 6$ |

| Exponent Rule | Example |
| --- | --- |
| $(x^a)(x^b) = x^{a+b}$ | When you multiply exponents with the same base, add the exponents to calculate the value of the expression.<br>*Example:* $(4^2)(4^3) = 4^{2+3} = 4^5 = 1024$ |
| $\frac{x^a}{x^b} = x^{a-b}$ | When you divide exponents with the same base, subtract the exponents to calculate the value of the expression.<br>*Example:* $\frac{4^3}{4^2} = 4^{3-2} = 4^1 = 4$ |
| $(xy)^a = (x^a)(y^a)$ | The product of two bases raised to a power can be simplified and solved by raising each number in the expressions to the same power.<br>*Example:* $(4^2)(2^2) = 8^2 = 64$ |
| $(x/y)^a = \frac{x^a}{y^a}$ | The quotient of two bases raised to a power can be simplified and solved raising each number in the expressions to the same power.<br>*Example:* $(3/4)3 = \frac{3^3}{4^3} = \frac{9}{64}$ |
| $x^{-a} = \frac{1}{x^a}$ | Any nonzero number raised to a negative power is equivalent to its reciprocal raised to a positive power.<br>*Example:* $3^{-2} = \frac{1}{3^2} = \frac{1}{9}$ |
| $(x^a)^b = x^{ab}$ | When a power is raised to another power, multiply the exponents.<br>*Example:* $(3^2)^3 = 3^{2\cdot3} = 3^6 = 729$ |

### *Exponents in Expressions and Equations*

The exponent rules cover the basics of dealing with exponents that primarily involve multiplication. It is important to note that it is not possible to add and subtract exponents in an expression if they do not have the same base and the same exponent. Consider the following expression:

$2^9 + 2^7$

This expression is in its simplest form. You cannot add the terms to get a new expression of $2^{16}$. Each part of the expression should be solved separately to arrive at your answer: $2^9 = 512$ and $2^7 = 128$. When you add the two together, you get 640. When you calculate $2^{16}$ you get 65,536. That's a vast difference in answers!

Exponents in these cases **must** be computed separately. The same goes for subtraction. However, when working with terms that share the same base and have the same exponents, you can add and subtract to simply the expression. Suppose you have the algebraic expression $3x^4 + 6x^4$. Here your base and exponent, $x$ and 4, respectively, are the same. You can add the two terms together, keeping the base and exponents intact. Your new expression will be $9x^4$.

You may or may not have the information needed to fully solve the expression, but you can put it in its simplest terms.

### *Negative Numbers and Exponents*

There is another possible situation involving exponents to keep in mind when a negative number is raised to a positive power.

When you raise a negative number to a positive power, the same rules apply for multiplying negative and positive numbers together. The product of a negative and positive number is a negative number, while the product of two negative numbers is a positive number. How does that relate to exponents? Since an exponent represents the number of times you multiply a number by itself, when you have a negative number raised to an exponent, whether it is an odd or even exponent will impact whether your final answer is positive or negative.

$$-4^2 = (-4)(-4)$$

In this case, the value of the expression $(-4)(-4)$ is 16. However, the value of $-4^3$ is calculated $(-4)(-4)(-4)$, which is $-64$.

When you raise a negative number to an even exponent, the result will be a positive number. When you raise a negative number to an odd exponent, the result will be a negative number.

## *Roots*

Exponents are closely linked to roots, another mathematical concept that deals with the number of times a number goes into another number. Like exponents, roots appear on the exam in various forms, and an understanding of the basic principles of roots will help you simplify expressions and solve equations.

Roots are the inverse function of exponents. The roots you will encounter on the exam are generally confined to square roots and cube roots. You will need to either solve or simplify them. A root is symbolized by a figure that looks like a check mark with a trailing bar which extends over the number whose root is being taken: $\sqrt{4}$.

The above example is the standard notation for a square root. In this case, the expression is translated as "the square root of 4." To solve, you are looking for a number that, when squared equals 4. If you look back at the common exponents table you will find that $2^2 = 4$. So the square root of 4 is 2.

You may sometimes see the root symbol with an exponent in front of it: $\sqrt[3]{27}$.

In this case, you must take the *cubed* root of 27. You need to identify the number that when cubed, equals 27. Again, if you refer back to the chart of common squares and cubes, you will see that $3^3 = 27$. So the cubed root of 27 is 3.

The SHSAT will only ask you to find the square root of positive numbers. However, the square root may be negative or positive, because any real number squared will always yield a positive number. If you are comparing quantities, for example, and have the equation: $\sqrt{100} = x$, it is easy to assume $x = 10$. Yet $x$ could also be $-10$, and must be considered.

### *Simplifying Roots*

You cannot add or subtract roots that appear in equations or expressions. You can, however, multiply or divide them in order to solve or simplify. In some cases, you may be able to solve for the value regardless of the operation being performed. For example:

$\sqrt{4} + \sqrt{16}$

Here, you can take the root of each of the terms separately, so 2 and 4, then find the sum, 6. You are not adding the roots; instead, you are adding values of the solved roots. Solving for $\sqrt{20}$ would be incorrect.

You can multiply the same roots in a given expression. You cannot, however, multiply a square root by a cubed root. Consider this example:

$\sqrt{2} \cdot \sqrt{8} \cdot \sqrt[3]{27}$

$\sqrt{16} \cdot \sqrt[3]{27}$ Simplify

$\sqrt{16} = \pm 4 \quad \sqrt[3]{27} = 3$ Solve for roots

$4 \cdot 3 = 12$ **OR** $-4 \cdot 3 = -12$

You can also divide roots of the same type. Here, you can complete the division as you would without the roots to simplify the expression. Then, solve the new simplified root to determine your answer.

$$\frac{\sqrt{16}}{\sqrt{4}} = \sqrt{\frac{16}{4}} = \sqrt{4} = \pm 2$$

Using these general principles, you can also reduce numbers under the root sign to create smaller but equivalent expressions. You can simplify the original root and create a new expression that includes simpler terms and solve:

$$\sqrt{81} = \sqrt{9} \cdot \sqrt{9} = \pm 3 \cdot \pm 3 = \pm 9$$

### *Fractional Exponents*

You may have a number raised to a fractional exponent. To simplify and solve, convert the exponent to a root.

$$4^{\frac{1}{2}} = \sqrt{4^1} = \pm 2$$

In these instances, the denominator tells you the type of root, while the numerator tells you what power to raise the base number or variable.

## Solving Algebraic Equations

Equations are algebraic functions that set two expressions equal to each other. Equations consist of numbers, operations, variables, or non-mathematical symbols. Your goal is usually to isolate the variables and solve or simplify as much as possible.

Since equations set two expressions equal to each other, when you manipulate the equation, you must ensure that you perform all operations to **both** sides of the equation. This is the most fundamental principle of working with algebraic equations.

Equations can have any number of variables. On the exam, you will see equations with one variable, on up to four or five unique variables. Equations that do not contain any exponents are the most common on the exam and are referred to as **linear equations**.

$x + 20 = 45$ The equation is telling you that the sum of $x$ and 20 is equal to 45.

$x + 20 - 20 = 45 - 20$ You want to isolate $x$ in order to solve for its value. Subtract 20 from each side of the equation. This keeps $x$ positive and isolates it at the same time.

$x = 25$

Equations with one variable on one side tend to be easier to solve than those with multiple variables or variables on both sides of the equation. Naturally, the latter requires more manipulation and computation. In a time crunch, seeking out one-variable equations may help you get to more questions in the time you have remaining.

Let us look at an equation with the same variable on both sides:

| | |
|---|---|
| $5x - 7 = 3x + 10$ | To solve for $x$, you still need to isolate the variable. Solve to get all the terms with the variable on one side of the equation. First, subtract $3x$ from both sides. |
| $5x - 3x - 7 = 10$ | Next, finish isolating the variables by adding 7 to both sides. When you add 7 to the left side of the equation, it cancels out the −7 already there. |
| $5x - 3x = 17$ | Calculate |
| $2x = 17$ | Divide by 2 |
| $x = 8.5$ | |

To make sure you have the right answer, you can plug the value you have for $x$ into the original equation.

$$5(8.5) - 7 = 3(8.5) + 10$$

$$42.5 - 7 = 25.5 + 10$$

$$35.5 = 35.5$$

### ***Absolute Value Equations***

Solving equations with absolute value expressions involves a little more work than equations that do not. Remember that the absolute value of a number is the positive distance from zero to that number on a number line. When you take absolute value of algebraic equations, you will have two answers: one where the expression between the absolute value brackets is positive and one where the expression in the absolute value brackets is negative. Here's an example:

If $|x + 3| = 10$, then $x = ?$

Just like you would in any other equation, you want to isolate the variable. You can worry about the implications of the absolute value later. In fact, write the equation out, without the absolute value notation:

$$x + 3 = 10$$

$$x = 10 - 3 = 7$$

You have solved for $x$, but you are not done yet. Since the expression on the left side asks you to take the absolute value of the expression, and absolute value is always expressed as a positive number, you need to consider that instead of 10, the expression can also yield an answer of −10. To do so, adjust the right side of the equation to −10 and solve.

$$x + 3 = -10$$

$$x = -10 - 3 = -13$$

You can plug your answers back in to the original equations to see if they are correct. Both these values are correct. It is important to consider both possibilities when dealing with absolute value although the question may not specifically prompt you to so.

### *Variables in the Denominator*

When variables are in the denominator, they warrant special attention. You still want to isolate the variable and solve or simplify. Consider this example:

$9 = \frac{1}{x+3} + 5$

$4 = \frac{1}{x+3}$ Subtract 5 from both sides to try to isolate the variable

$4(x+3) = (x+3) \cdot \frac{1}{(x+3)}$ Multiply each side by the expression in the denominator

$4(x+3) = 1$ The expression $x + 3$ on the right side cancels out

$x + 3 = \frac{1}{4}$ You could distribute the 4, but you are trying to isolate the variable. Divide each side by 4 to further isolate the variable.

$x = \frac{1}{4} - 3 = \frac{1}{4} - \frac{12}{4}$ Subtract 3 from both sides to solve for $x$ by turning the integer into a fraction with the same denominator

$= -\frac{11}{4} = -2.75 = -2\frac{3}{4}$

### *Equations with More than One Variable*

Of course, the test creators won't let you slide with solving for just one variable. Sometimes you will see equations with two variables. As with one variable expressions, your goal is to either solve or simplify. You can do so using many of the methods previously discussed. Equations with more than one variable, as you might imagine, can be more challenging than their one variable counterparts, and often require more steps to arrive at the answer. Usually, you are also given two separate equations to help you arrive at the answer.

**Example:**
Solve for $x$ and $y$ if $2x + 5y = 7$ and $x + 4y = 2$

$x + 4y = 2$ Solve for one of the variables in terms of the other variable

$x = 2 - 4y$

$2(2 - 4y) + 5y = 7$ Now plug in the expression for $x$ into the first equation and solve for $y$

$4 - 8y + 5y = 7$

$4 - 3y = 7$

$-3y = 3$

$y = -1$

$x = 2 - 4(-1)$ Now that you have the value for $y$, plug it in and solve for $x$

$x = 2 + 4 = 6$

Remember, plug in the values you calculated to check your answers. To determine which variable to try to solve for first, look for the equation where one variable is easier to isolate and start there.

## *Quadratic Equations*

The quadratic equation is a special equation where specific polynomials are set to equal zero.

$$ax^2 + bx + c = 0$$

For the quadratic equation, $a \neq 0$, and $a$, $b$, and $c$ are constants representing the coefficients that precede the variable $x$.

Earlier in this section, we reviewed factoring and binomials, which are key components to finding values in a quadratic equation. Consider the example:

| | |
|---|---|
| $x^2 - 5x + 6 = 0$ | |
| $(x - 2)(x - 3) = 0$ | To solve for $x$, first factor out the binomial terms: |

**Math Prep Tip:** If you are unsure if you have factored properly and identified the correct binomials, check your work using distribution. As you multiply in order, write out the products; if you have factored correctly, your distribution should yield the original equation.

| | |
|---|---|
| $(x - 2)x - (x - 2)3$ | Distribute the first term in the first binomial into both terms in the second binomial |
| $((x)(x) - 2x) - (3x - 6)$ | Next, do the same with the second term in the first binomial |
| $x^2 - 2x - 3x + 6 = x^2 - 5x + 6$ | Now, combine the products to see if it matches your original equation |

Everything looks good! Let us get back to solving the problem.

| | | |
|---|---|---|
| $x - 2 = 0$ | $x - 3 = 0$ | Quadratic equations **always** have two solutions. The two solutions may be the same number. To solve for the values of $x$, set each of the binomial factors to 0. |
| $x = 2$ | $x = 3$ | Both 2 and 3 are solutions to the equation. Plug in your answers to check if the values are correct. |
| $(2)^2 - 5(2) + 6 = 0$ | $(3)^2 - 5(3) + 6 = 0$ | |
| $4 - 10 + 6 = -6 + 6 = 0$ | $9 - 15 + 6 = -6 + 6 = 0$ | Solve |

The values check out when plugged in. The solution for the quadratic equation is $x = 2$ **OR** $x = 3$.

**Math Prep Tip:** The quadratic equation may be rewritten to generate the quadratic formula:

$$x = \frac{-b \pm \sqrt{b} - 4ac}{2a}$$

The quadratic formula is not tested on the exam.

## Inequalities

Inequalities are similar to equations. Instead of setting two expressions equal, however, inequalities describe their relative value. Inequalities express four quantity comparisons:

$x$ greater than $y$: $x > y$
$x$ less than $y$: $x < y$
$x$ greater than or equal to $y$: $x \geq y$
$x$ less than or equal to $y$: $x \leq y$

### *Solving Inequalities*

Inequalities are approached using the same techniques as the equations in this section. Your goal is still to isolate the variables and solve for their value, if possible. As with equations, whatever function you perform on one side, you must perform on the other. Inequalities have one difference that can impact your answer choice if you are not careful. Whenever you divide or multiply both sides by a negative number, you must flip the inequality sign to ensure the inequality remains valid. Let's look at an inequality example:

$$3 - \frac{x}{4} \geq 2$$

$-\frac{x}{4} \geq 2 - 3 = -\frac{x}{4} \geq -1$ First, isolate the variable

$$(-4)\left(-\frac{x}{4}\right) \leq (-4)(-1)$$

$x \leq 4$ Since we multiplied both sides by a negative number we changed the direction of the inequality sign. The negative signs cancel out.

The expression reads $x$ is less than or equal to 4. While you have solved for $x$, this is not your answer. The complete answer is all the values equal to or less than 4. Inequalities are sometimes represented on a number line. The above example on a number line would look like:

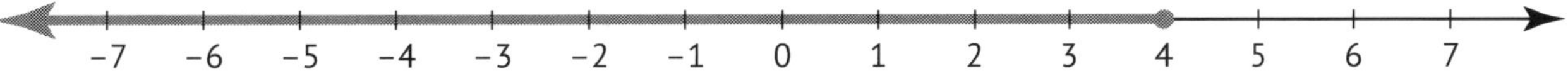


The filled-in point over the 4 indicates that 4 is included in the possible list of values. If the final answer was $x < 4$, the circle would **not** be filled in. The number line in that case would look like:

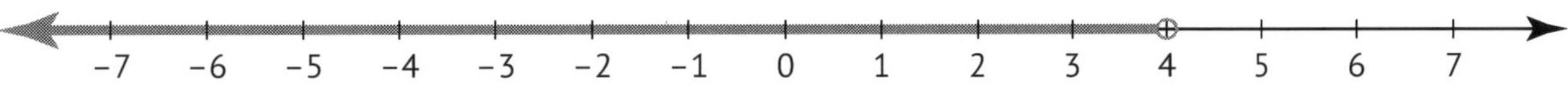


## Coordinate Geometry

Coordinate geometry is the transition point from algebra to geometry and involves the use of algebraic expressions to create graphical displays on a coordinate plane. The coordinate plane is composed of a vertical and horizontal axis that run perpendicular to each other. All points on a coordinate plane can be plotted in reference to these axes, which intersect at zero. This meeting point is referred to as the **point of origin**.

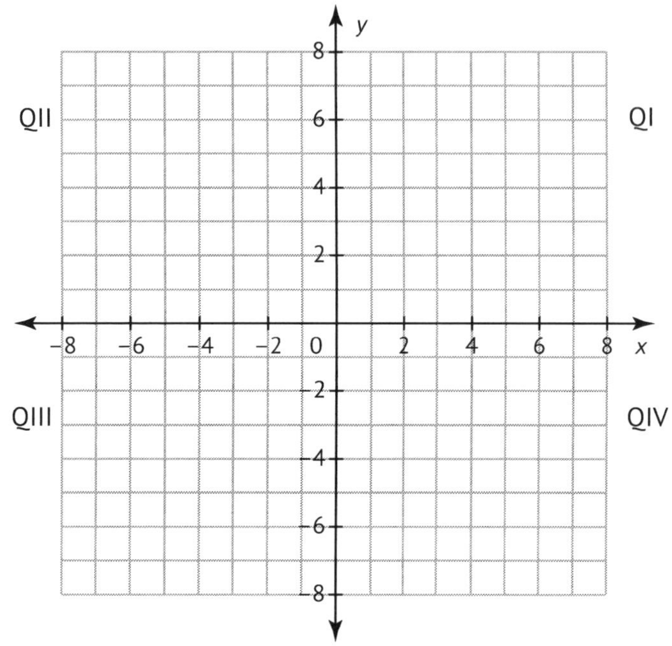


| Quadrant | *x*-coordinate | *y*-coordinate |
|---|---|---|
| I | positive | positive |
| II | negative | positive |
| III | negative | negative |
| IV | positive | negative |

The coordinate plane has four distinct quadrants when the origin is placed at the center. Quadrant I is in the upper right corner, quadrant II is in the upper left corner, quadrant III is in the lower left corner, and quadrant IV is in the lower right corner.

Points are plotted on a coordinate plane. Every point has two coordinates, one on the $x$-axis and one on the $y$-axis. The origin sits at the intersection of the two axes and has coordinates (0,0). The coordinates of points not at the center are determined by their positive or negative difference from the origin. Coordinates are always written with the $x$ coordinate first: $(x,y)$. You can determine whether the $x$ and $y$ coordinates are positive or negative based on the quadrant they fall in.

On the exam, it is helpful to know these quadrant locations for coordinates to save time and prevent you from having to plot the points on the coordinate plane each time.

## *Graphing Coordinates*

Sometimes you need to either graph coordinates or determine the value of coordinates already on the graph. When given a set of coordinates, simply start at zero and plot the distance across (left or right) for the value of $x$, then up or down for the value of $y$.

Let us look at a set of coordinates and how to graph them on the coordinate plane. Suppose you are asked to identify a graph that has a point with the coordinates (3,2). Your graph would look like this:

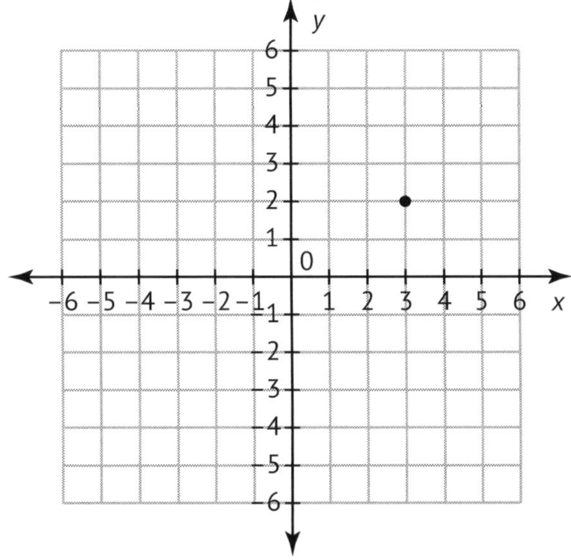


You can see the coordinates start at the point of origin, shift 3 spaces to the right, then shift 2 spaces up. If you refer back to the quadrant chart, you can see that it predicted our coordinates, which are both positive, would be in quadrant I.

## *Calculating Distance on the Coordinate Plane*

You may be asked to calculate the distance between two points on a coordinate plane. If the points are in the same vertical or horizontal plane, you can simply count the spaces between the points. Distance is always positive.

You can also use the distance formula to plug in coordinates and calculate the distance between two points.

**Distance Formula:**

$$distance = \sqrt{(x_2 - x_1)^2 + (y_2 - y_1)^2}$$

To find the distance between two coordinates—let us say (5,−2) and (−4,9)—plug in the values in the equation and solve.

$$distance = \sqrt{(-4 - 5)^2 + (9 - (-2)^2}$$

$$distance = \sqrt{(-9)^2 + 11^2}$$

$$distance = \sqrt{202}$$

# MATH

## *Midpoint*

The midpoint is also a measure of distance between points on a coordinate plane. Instead of the distance from one point to another, the coordinates of the midpoint are the average of the endpoints. To find the midpoint of two points, take the average of your endpoints using the midpoint formula:

**Midpoint Formula:**

$$midpoint = \frac{x_1 + x_2}{2}, \frac{y_1 + y_2}{2}$$

Suppose you have the points (−1,2) and (3,−6). Plug in the coordinates to find the midpoint:

$$midpoint = \frac{-1 + 3}{2}, \frac{2 - 6}{2}$$

$$midpoint = (1,-2)$$

## *Slope*

Points on a coordinate plane connect to form lines. The slope is the measure of how steep a line is in relation to the $x$-axis and $y$-axis. The equation of a line can be written as: $\mathbf{y = mx + b}$, where $m$ is the slope, $b$ is the $y$-intercept, and $x$ and $y$ represent possible coordinate values. This equation is commonly referred to as **slope-intercept form**.

**Slope-Intercept Form:**

$$y = mx + b$$

The $y$-intercept is just another way of describing the point that falls directly on the $y$-axis. Likewise, the $x$-intercept describes the point that falls directly on the $x$-axis. All lines will have no more than one $x$ and one $y$ intercept.

The slope is the measure of *the rise over the run* of a line, or the change in the $y$-coordinate values (rise) and the change in $x$-coordinate values (run). You need two points to find the slope of a line.

Consider the coordinates (4,3) and (−2,−1). Calculate the change in $x$ and $y$ to find the slope, $m$.

$$m = \frac{\text{change in } y}{\text{change in } x} = \frac{3 - (-1)}{4 - (-2)} = \frac{4}{6} = \frac{2}{3}$$

You may sometimes be asked to find the slope of a line from an equation instead of coordinates. Suppose you have the equation $2x + y = 5$. To find the slope, put the equation in slope-intercept form, $y = mx + b$:

$$2x + y = 5$$

$y = 5 - 2x$ OR in slope-intercept form: $y = -2x + 5$

The slope of this line is −2.

### *Properties of Slopes*

Knowing some of the common properties of slopes and what they look like graphically can help save you time and calculation on the exam.

- The slope of a line can be either positive or negative.
- Slopes do not have to be whole integers, they can be fractions as well.

- Parallel lines on the same coordinate plane will always have the same slope. For example, if the slope of line *a* is 3, **all** lines parallel to that line will also have a slope of 3.
- The slope of a line on the same coordinate plane that is perpendicular to another line is the **negative reciprocal**. If a line has a slope of 2, **all** lines perpendicular to that line will have a slope of $-\frac{1}{2}$.

A **positive** slope rises from left to right.

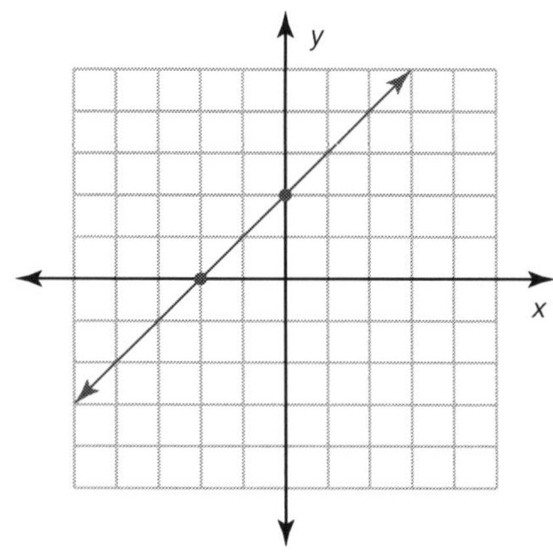


A **negative** slope falls from left to right.

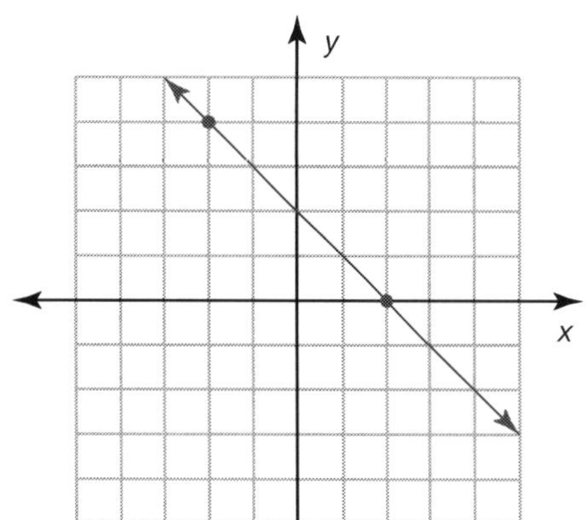


Any **horizontal** line has a slope of 0 since there is no change to the *y* value.

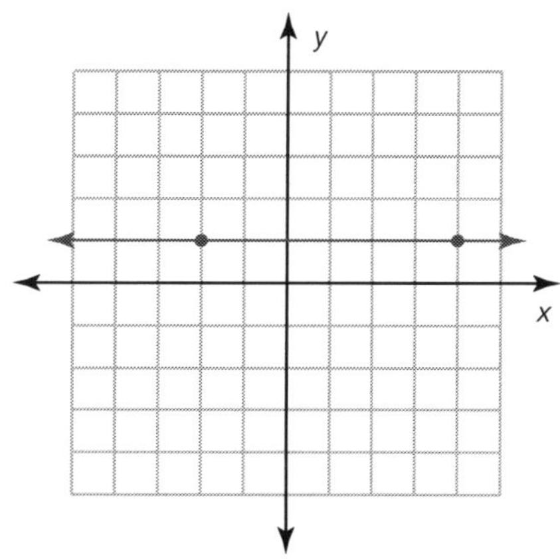


The slope of any **vertical** line cannot be defined because all of its points have the same *x*-coordinate.

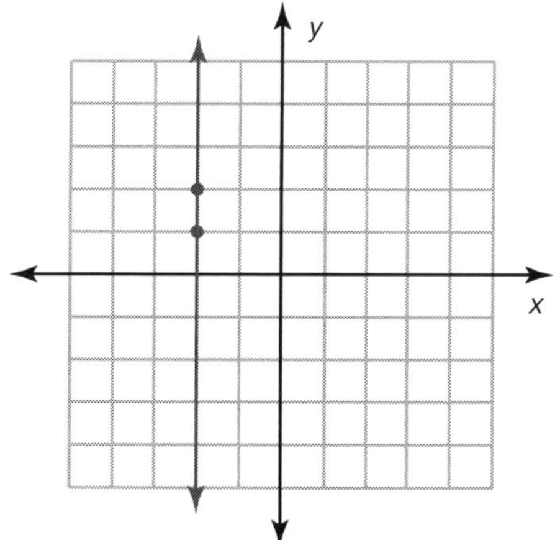


## Functions

Let's briefly review functions. Functions are tested on the 9th grade SHSAT exam. Functions can be expressed as a graph or as an equation and describe a relationship between corresponding inputs and outputs. Functions are typically represented by the notation $f(x)$ and indicates calculations to be performed.

For example, you may see something similar to the following:

$f(x) = 2x + 4$

For the function above, $f$ is the name of the function. Any letter can be used in place of $f$ to name a function.

A question may present you with the above equation and ask you to solve $f(3)$. To solve, replace each $x$ in the equation with the input of 3. For $f(3)$:

$f(3) = 2(3) + 4$

$f(3) = 10$

Functions can also be graphed on a coordinate plane. Depending on the equation, the graph may not always be a straight line. Instead, functions can be parabolas.

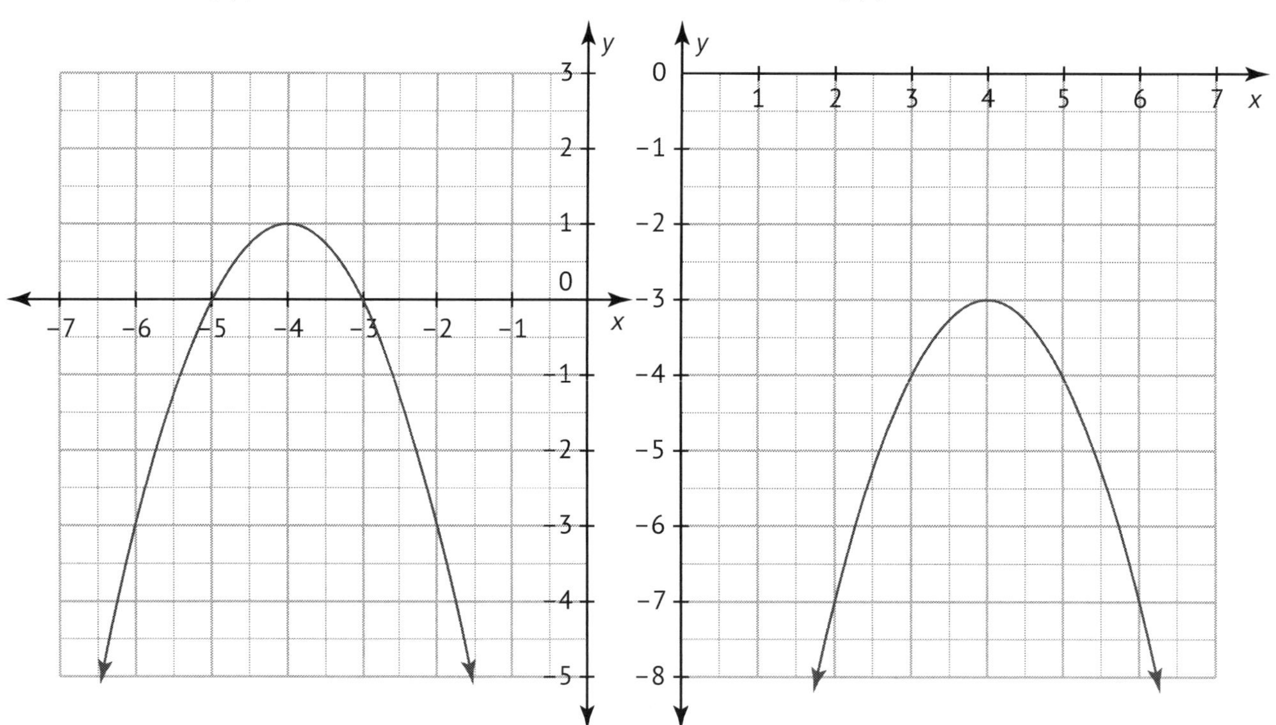


## Geometry: The Basics

Geometry focuses primarily on the measurements of shapes, lines, angles, and planes. Several key areas of geometry are tested on the SHSAT. You will see problems that involve triangles, circles, and two-dimensional shapes of various sizes with different numbers of sides. This section will refresh your memory of the related formulas and concepts, outline key geometric concepts that occur frequently on the exam, and equip you with problem solving strategies to improve your accuracy.

## Diagrams and Formulas

Most of the geometry questions on the exam will be accompanied by a diagram. In most cases, this works to your advantage. Often the diagrams contain useful information to help you answer the question. For example, if you have a diagram of a circle and the diameter is noted as 4 cm, you can calculate the radius of the circle, which is half the diameter.

It is important to note that geometry diagrams on the exam are typically **not** drawn to scale. You should not make assumptions based on how diagrams "look." Instead, you should use the information presented in the questions and any given measurements to calculate the information you are looking for to find a corresponding answer choice.

We will review key geometric formulas in this section. While the formulas are helpful to know, they are useless if you are unsure of how to use them. Questions on the exam, particularly those dealing with triangles, will require you to think beyond simply plugging numbers into a formula. Instead, you will have to critically analyze the given components to arrive at the correct answer.

## Lines, Angles, Planes, and Shapes (L.A.P.S)

The building blocks of geometry are lines, angles, planes, and shapes. You will encounter one or more of these components in all the geometry questions on the exam. While geometry is a dense subject matter that includes some very complex principles, remember that the SHSAT is a test of your understanding of high-school level math and is primarily concerned with your basic math skills. As such, complex topics like differential geometry, model theory, and geometric proofs will not appear on the exam.

The exam will focus specifically on coordinate and plane geometry. Planes are two-dimensional flat surface areas that extend infinitely in all directions. The surfaces of geometric shapes like polygons, triangles, and hexagons all lie on planes; lines and points are also essential components of geometric planes. Using points, angles, and units of measurement, you can calculate critical information about a shape, plot coordinates on a plane, and draw conclusions about angle measurements. This section will cover the **L.A.P.S** fundamentals, including key definitions, formulas, and approaches to various problems.

### *Lines*

A line is a one-dimensional figure on a plane. Lines are always straight and drawn with arrows at each end to indicate their infinite nature. Lines extend in both directions infinitely.

Lines are uniquely determined by two points. Points are found on all geometric shapes. They are not measurable units, although the distance between two points is a common calculation which you will be asked to perform. In the diagram below, **A** and **B** are points on the line. These points are unique and only one line runs through them. Remember that the line extends infinitely in both directions.

Instead of figures, you may see the common notation $\overleftrightarrow{AB}$ used. The notation indicates that you have a line, with no defined end, that crosses through points **A** and **B**.

#### *Rays*

A ray can be defined by two points where it begins at one of the points and passes through a second point while extending infinitely in one direction. The length of a ray cannot be determined and thus, neither can you find its mid-point.

In the diagram below, the ray begins at point **A**, passes through point **B**, and continues infinitely in one direction. As with a line, you can use a shorthand notation for this figure. The notation $\overrightarrow{AB}$ shows the points on the ray and that it continues infinitely in one direction.

### *Segments*

A segment is a part of a line. However, segments have a measurable length. Unlike a line, segments do not continue infinitely. The annotation for a segment is written as $\overline{AB}$.

The key characteristics of a segment are its two end points and its midpoint. The end points mark finite ends of a segment while the midpoint is positioned at the center of a segment. Only segments have midpoints.

In the diagram below, **A** and **B** are the end points of the segment. **M** represents the midpoint or center of the segment.

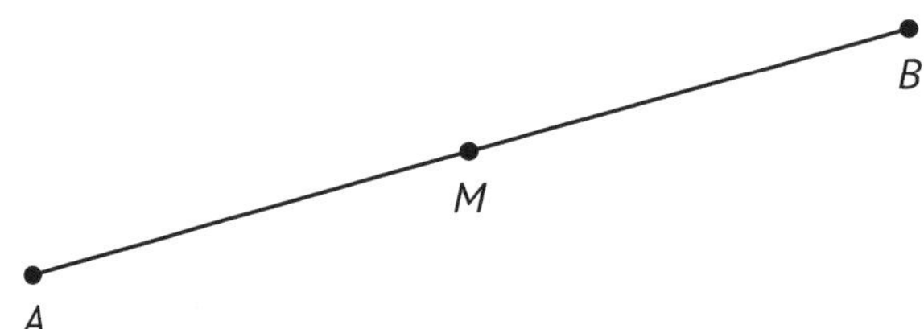


**A** and **B** are the same distance from the midpoint: $\overline{AM} = \overline{MB}$. If you have an exam question that tells you **M** is the midpoint of segment $\overline{AB}$ and that $\overline{MB} = 3$, you can deduce that $\overline{AM}$ is also 3.

### *Parallel Lines*

Parallel lines are two lines which exist on the same plane but do not intersect each other. You should not assume that because two lines are not touching in a diagram that they are parallel lines, since it is possible they may intersect at some point. For exam questions addressing parallel lines, the question will explicitly state the lines are parallel or will use the common notation for parallel lines.

$\overleftrightarrow{AB}$ and $\overleftrightarrow{CD}$ are parallel lines. Their relationship can be annotated as $\overleftrightarrow{AB} \parallel \overleftrightarrow{CD}$.

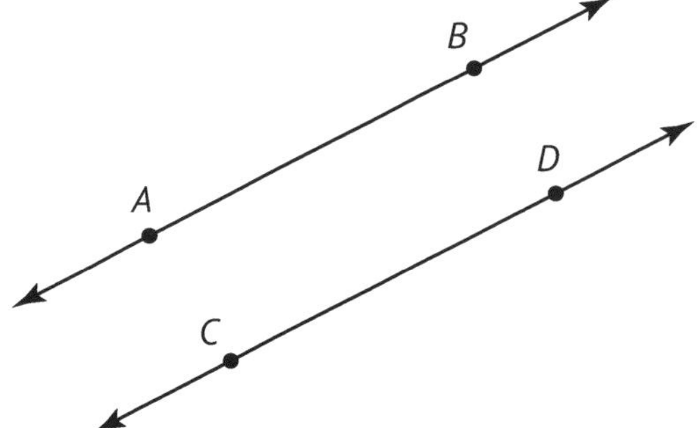


### *Perpendicular Lines*

Perpendicular lines are two lines that intersect each other forming a 90° angle. We will discuss angles in more detail below. Just like with parallel lines, never assume you are dealing with perpendicular lines

unless the instructions specifically tell you so or you can identify the 90° angle. The standard notation for two lines that are perpendicular is $\overleftrightarrow{AB} \perp \overleftrightarrow{CD}$.

### *Intersection*

An intersection, as its name implies, refers to the point where two lines, segments, or rays intersects. Perpendicular lines have an intersection point, but not all lines that intersect are perpendicular since they do not all form 90° angles.

## *Angles*

Angles are formed when two lines intersect. The point of intersection is referred to as the **vertex** of the angle. Angles are measured in degrees and can be either acute, obtuse, right or straight. The measure of the angle determines its classification.

| Type of Angle | Degree Measurement | Visual Representation |
|---|---|---|
| Acute | Acute angles are angles that measure less than 90° | |
| Right | Right angles measure **exactly** 90° | |
| Obtuse | Obtuse angles are angles that measure between 91° and 180° | |
| Straight | Straight angles are angles that measures **exactly** 180° and are equivalent to a straight line | |

The typical naming convention for angles is to use the labels for the three points on the intersecting lines, segments, or rays, making sure to place the vertex in the middle. The common symbol to represent an angle is ∠.

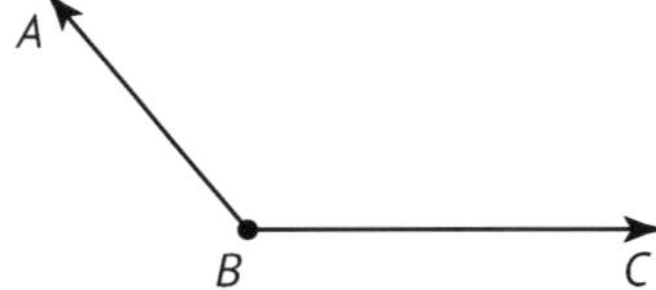


This angle can be written as ∠*ABC* or ∠*CBA*. This angle can also be simply named ∠*B*. However, only use this notation when there are no other angles that share *B* as the vertex.

### *Other Types of Angles*

Any time a line intersects another line, at least one angle is formed. Questions will ask to you identify the

measures of angles. Knowing a few fundamentals about different type of angles occurring on the same line and how they relate to each other will help you save a lot of time. Let us look at the key angle relationships.

*Supplementary and Complementary Angles*

Two angles with a sum of 180° are called **supplementary angles**.

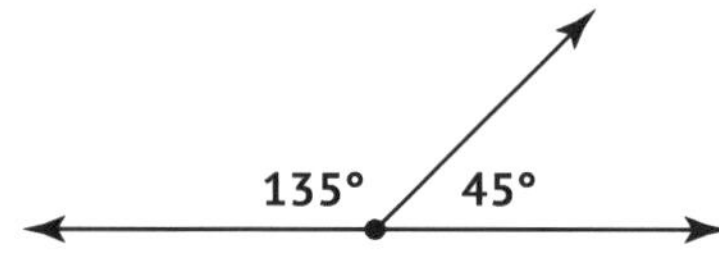


Two angles with a sum of 90° are called **complementary angles**.

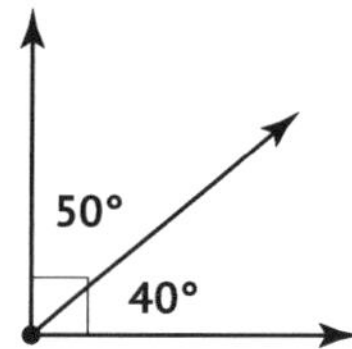


*Vertical Angles*

Two lines or line segments that intersect form **vertical angles**. Vertical angles, or opposite angles, are congruent and have the same angle measurement.

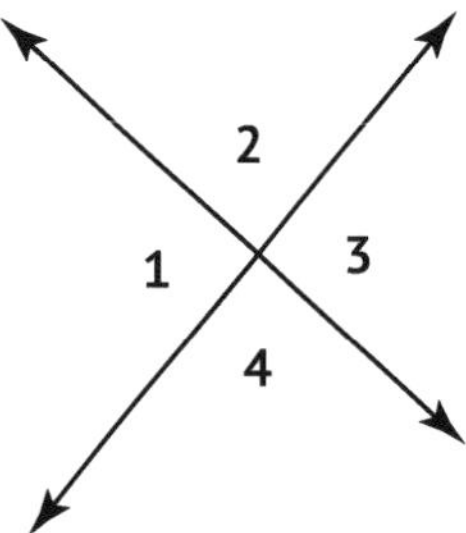


In the figure above, $\angle 2$ and $\angle 4$ are vertical angles. $\angle 1$ and $\angle 3$ are also vertical angles. If $\angle 4 = 50°$, then $\angle 2 = 50°$ since they are vertical angles. Moreover, if $\angle 4 = 50°$, then $\angle 1 = 130°$ because $\angle 4$ and $\angle 1$ are supplementary.

*Adjacent Angles*

Angles that share a common vertex and common side are called **adjacent angles**. Take a look at the following example.

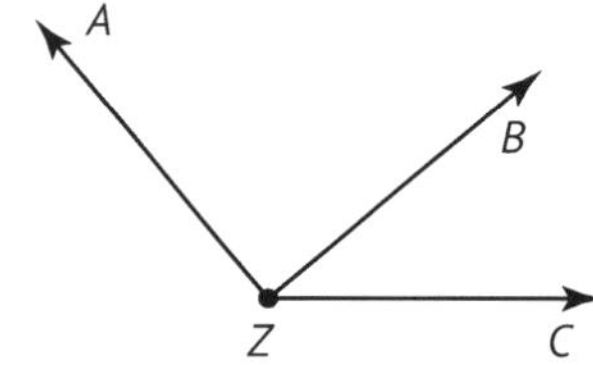

$\angle AZB$ and $\angle BZC$ are adjacent angles because they share a common vertex, $Z$, and a common side, $\overrightarrow{ZB}$.

*Transversals*

A transversal is a line that intersects two or more lines at two or more points.

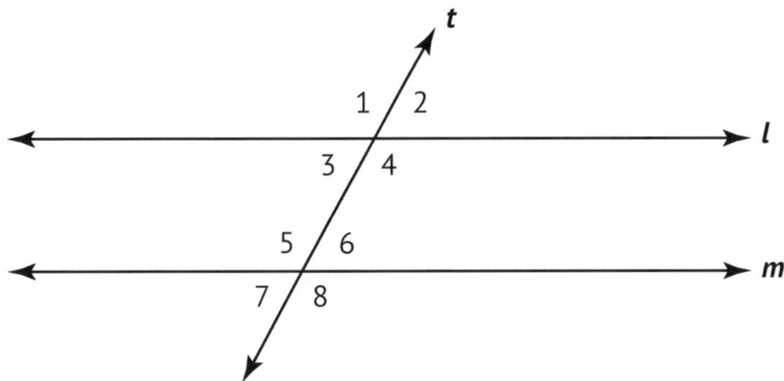


When a transversal intersects a pair of parallel lines, as in the above example, the resulting angles are related in some way:

- Angles 1, 4, 5, and 8 are equal.
- Angles 2, 3, 6, and 7 are equal.
- The sum of any two adjacent angles, such as 1 and 2 or 7 and 8, equals 180° since they form a straight angle on a line.
- The sum of any large angle + any small angle = 180° since the large and small angles in this figure combine into straight lines, all the large angles are equal, and all the small angles are equal.

You will see these concepts of angles appear again in the next sections where we will explore properties and measurements of polygons.

## *Shapes: Polygons*

You will encounter a number of different types of polygons on the exam. A polygon is a two-dimensional enclosed figure with three or more straight sides. Polygons are named based on the number of sides they have.

| Polygon Name | Number of Sides |
|---|---|
| Triangle | 3 |
| Quadrilateral | 4 |
| Pentagon | 5 |
| Hexagon | 6 |
| Heptagon | 7 |
| Octagon | 8 |

| Nonagon | 9 |
| --- | --- |
| Decagon | 10 |
| Dodecagon | 12 |

Polygons can be either regular or irregular. Regular polygons have all sides of equal length and equal angles. Irregular polygons do not. It is important to understand the difference so that you do not make erroneous assumptions about the size of a figure that could lead you to an incorrect answer. The test questions will tell you if you are dealing with a regular or irregular polygon.

While all polygons are different in the number of sides they have, they do share some fundamental characteristics.

- The area of a polygon is the measure of the area of the region inside the polygon.
- A polygon with equal sides and equal interior angles is a regular polygon.
- The sum of the exterior angles of any polygon is 360°.
- The perimeter of a polygon is the sum of the lengths of its sides.

Geometry questions will focus primarily on finding various measurements, like volume, area, and circumference, of the polygons. A majority of the polygons on the exams will be triangle and four-sided polygons, also known as quadrilaterals.

This section will look at the basic properties of polygons, and the formulas used to calculate the measurement of the sides and angles. It will also discuss circles and how to approach figures that include more than one polygon or circle. Triangles have many properties, rules, and calculations and merit a deeper review given their complexity and popularity on the exam. First, let us look at some general principles of quadrilaterals.

### *Quadrilaterals*

Quadrilaterals are four-sided polygons. Quadrilaterals can be regular or irregular and the sum of their interior angles is 360°. The most common quadrilaterals tested on the exam are squares and rectangles, but there are also several others.

*Rectangles*

A rectangle is a quadrilateral where the opposite sides are parallel and the interior angles are all right angles. The opposite sides of a rectangle are of equal length. The diagonals of a rectangle are also of equal length.

**Formula for the Area of a Rectangle**

$area = length \cdot width$

Diagonals of a Rectangle

The two diagonals of a rectangle are always equal to each other. Both diagonals divide the rectangle into two equal right triangles. Since the diagonals of the rectangle form right triangles that include the diagonal and two sides of the rectangle, if you know two of the values, you can calculate the third with the Pythagorean equation (discussed below).

*Square*

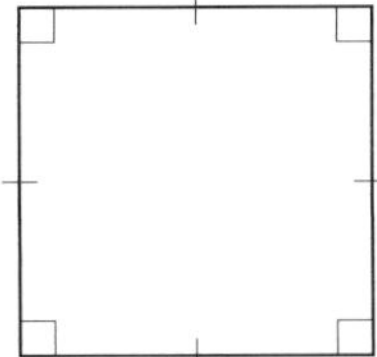

A square is a rectangle with four equal sides. All squares are rectangles but not all rectangles are squares.

**Formula for the Area of a Square**

$area = s^2$

In the formula, $s$ is the length of a side.

Diagonals of a Square

The diagonals of a square bisect each other at right angles and have equal lengths. The diagonals also cut the square into two 45-45-90 triangles. If you know the length of one side of the square, you can calculate the length of the diagonal.

*Parallelogram*

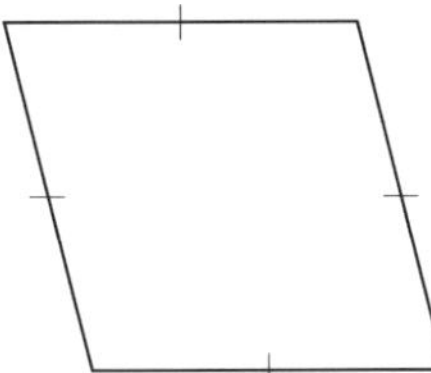

A parallelogram is a quadrilateral with two sets of parallel and equal sides. The length and width do not need to be the same in a parallelogram but the opposing sides will always be equal and the adjacent angles will be supplementary.

**Formula for the Area of a Parallelogram**

$area = base \cdot height$

Diagonals of a Parallelogram

The diagonals of a parallelogram divide the figure into two congruent triangles.

### *Polygon Angles*

The sum of the interior angles inside of a polygon is determined by the number of sides in the figure; this is true for both regular and irregular polygons. The figures you will see most often on the exam, triangles and quadrilaterals, both have set measures for their interior angles. Triangles will always total 180 degrees and quadrilaterals will total 360 degrees.

You can always figure out the total measurement of the internal angles of a polygon by using the formula:

$$(n - 2) \cdot 180$$

In the formula, $n$ equals the number of sides.

Triangles

Triangles are three-sided polygons. The sum of the interior angles is 180°. The height of the triangle is the perpendicular distance from the vertex to opposite leg and can be found inside or outside of the triangle.

**Formula for the Area of a Triangle**

$$area = \frac{1}{2}\ base \cdot height$$

Equilateral Triangles

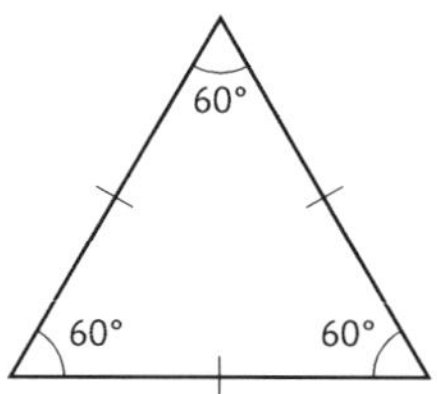


An equilateral triangle has three equal sides and three equal angles.

Once you know that you have two 60° angles, you can assume you are dealing with an equilateral triangle.

Isosceles Triangles

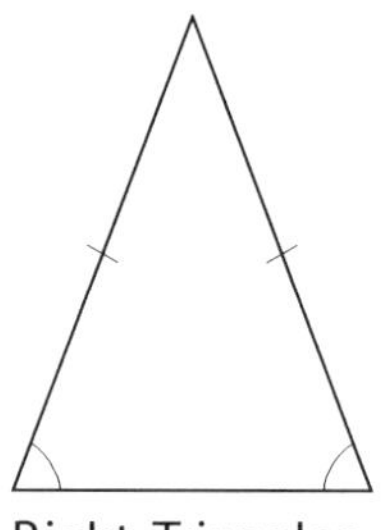

An isosceles triangle has two equal sides and two equal angles.

The two equal angles are opposite the two equal sides. The sides opposite equal angles are always equal, and the angles opposite equal sides are always equal.

Right Triangles

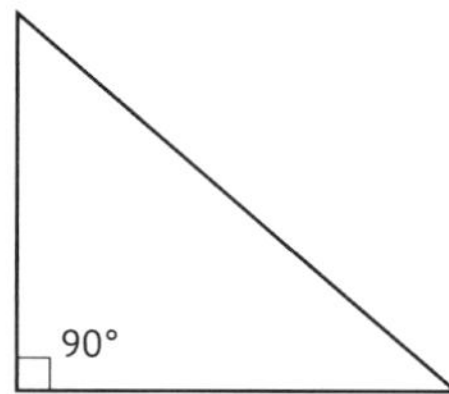


Right triangles are tested more than any other type of triangle on the exam. A right triangle is any triangle that contains a right angle. The side opposite the right angle is the hypotenuse. The other two sides are called legs. The remaining two angles add up to 90 degrees.

Right Triangles and the Pythagorean Theorem

The Pythagorean Theorem is one of the most tested theories on the exam, which makes sense as it applies to right triangles and right triangles are tested frequently. The theory establishes the relationship of a right triangle's legs to its hypotenuse.

**Pythagorean Theorem**

$$a^2 + b^2 = c^2$$

In this equation, **a** and **b** are the legs and **c** is the hypotenuse.

Since right triangles adhere to the Pythagorean Theorem, they rarely yield integers for the lengths of the legs. But a few integer triplets perfectly conform to the Theorem. These are referred to as **Pythagorean triples**. The ones you will see on the exam include:

- 3, 4, 5
- 5, 12, 13
- 7, 24, 25
- 8, 15, 17

Also note that any multiples of these triples conform. For example, 6, 8, 10 are multiples of the triples 3, 4, 5. Memorizing these will help you identify measurements and answer questions more quickly.

# MATH

## *Shapes: Circles*

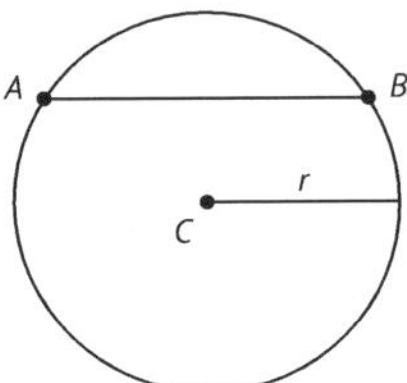


Circles are not polygons because they do not have straight sides. Circles are tested on the exam and you will mainly be asked to find some part of its measurements. Here are some quick facts about circles:

- All circles contain 360°
- The distance from the center to any point on the circle is called the radius. The radius of a circle is a critical piece: if you know a circle's radius, you can figure out all its other measurements.
- The diameter of a circle stretches between endpoints on the circle and passes through the center.
- A chord also extends from endpoint to endpoint on the circle, but it does not necessarily pass through the center.
- In the figure above, point C is the center of the circle, $r$ is the radius, and $\overline{AB}$ is a chord.

**Formula for the Circumference of a Circle**

The circumference is the distance around the circle.

$$circumference = 2\pi r$$

The standard value for *pi* on the exam is 3.14.

**Formula for the Area of a Circle**

$$area = \pi r^2$$

In this formula, $r$ is the radius. When you need to find the area of a circle, your real goal is to figure out the radius. For an added challenge, sometimes a question may give you the diameter or the circumference and you will need to calculate the radius (half the diameter) to solve for the area.

## *Shapes: Solids*

### *Rectangular Solids*

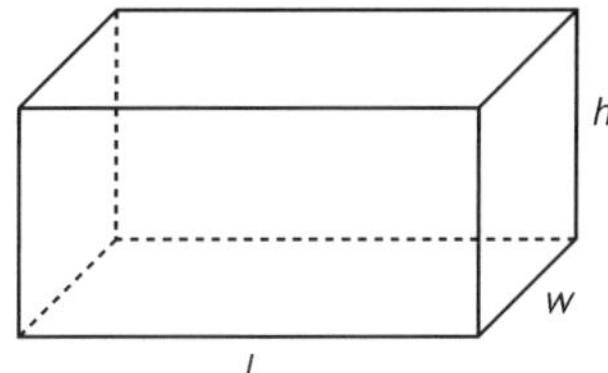


A rectangular solid is a prism with a rectangular base and edges that are perpendicular to its base.

A rectangular solid has three key dimensions: length, width, and height. If you know these three measurements, you can find the solid's volume and surface area.

**Formula for the Surface Area**

$A = 2 \cdot w \cdot l + 2 \cdot l \cdot h + 2 \cdot h \cdot w$

**Formula for the Volume**

volume = $l \cdot w \cdot h$

### *Cubes*

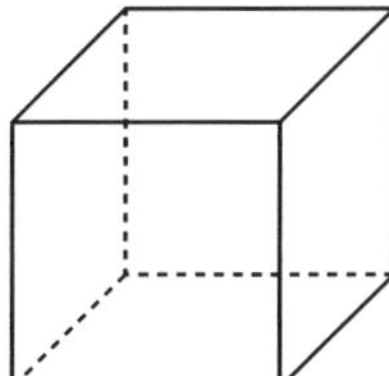

A cube is a rectangular solid with sides ($s$) that are all equal. Cubes have six faces, each of which is a square, meaning the length, width, and height of each are equal.

**Formula for the Surface Area**

*volume* = $6s^2$

**Formula for the Volume**

*volume* = $s^3$

### *Right Circular Cylinders*

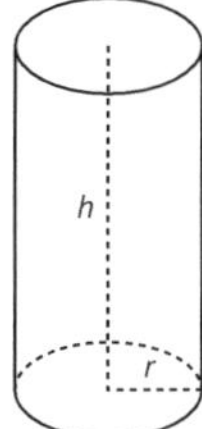


A right circular cylinder is a geometric solid that has two circular bases. A right circular cylinder has a lateral measurement, and its height forms a rectangle.

**Formula for the Volume**

The only measurement you will be asked to calculate for right cylinders is the volume.

*volume* = $\pi r^2 h$

## Data Interpretation: The Basics

Data interpretation questions test your ability to derive information from graphs, charts, and other visual displays. Data interpretation questions are more of an extension of problem solving questions than a unique question type or concept. For these questions, you will interpret data from charts, graphs, and other images and use this information to solve for the correct answer(s).

This section will provide a brief overview of central tendency, probability, and frequency distributions.

### Measures of Central Tendency

Measures of central tendency identify the distribution of certain values in an attempt to make data more understandable and allow for accurate interpretation. The three measures of central tendency are the mean, median, and mode.

#### *Mean*

The **mean** is commonly referred to as the average, and is the sum of all terms divided by the number of terms. To express the mean as an equation, set the mean equal to its relationship with the terms in the data set:

$$mean = \frac{sum\ of\ terms}{number\ of\ terms}$$

Suppose on your last four statistics exams, you received the following scores: 84, 92, 93, 87. If you wanted to find the mean of your scores, calculate using the equation for the mean:

$$mean = \frac{84 + 92 + 93 + 87}{4} = \frac{356}{4} = 89$$

Sometimes, instead of all the terms, a test question might provide you with the mean and ask you to identify the other values. You can rearrange, simplify, and substitute to arrive at your answer.

#### *Median*

The **median** of a set of data is the middle term when the numbers are written in ascending order. For example, to calculate the median of the group 7, 12, 14, 6, 4, 3, and 17, you would first list the numbers in order.

3, 4, 6, 7, 12, 14, 17

Then find the middle number, which is in this case is 7. If, however, the number 21 was added to this set, you would have **two** numbers in the middle: 7 and 12. In this case, you average the two numbers (7 + 12, divided by 2) to reach a median of 9.5.

#### *Mode*

The **mode** is simply the number that occurs the most. In the group 1, 2, 3, 3, 3, 3, 4, and 7, the mode is 3 since it appears the most frequently in the group.

### Range

The **range** of a data set is the difference between the largest term and the smallest term. For example, the range of 12, −24, 13, 2, and 4 is 13 − (−24) = 37.

### Probability

**Probability** is the measure of the number of specific outcomes compared to the number of possible outcomes:

$$p = \frac{\#\ of\ specific\ outcomes}{\#\ of\ possible\ outcomes}$$

If you have 10 cookies in a bag—3 chocolate chip, 2 oatmeal, 4 lemon, and 1 peanut butter—the probability of your reaching into the bag and selecting a lemon cookie is $\frac{4}{10}$ or $\frac{2}{5}$. Probability can be written as a fraction or a decimal.

You may be asked to determine multiple-event probability, such as the probability of reaching into the bag of cookies a second time and grabbing a lemon cookie. In these instances, you must find the probability for each event and then multiply them.

## Frequency Distribution

A **frequency distribution** is a table used to describe a data set. It also lists intervals or ranges of data values—called **data classes**—together with the number of data values or **frequency** from the set that are in each class.

Suppose that the exam scores of 20 psychology students are as follows:

97, 92, 88, 75, 83, 67, 89, 55, 72, 78, 81, 91, 57, 63, 67, 74, 87, 84, 98, 46

You can construct a frequency table with classes 90–99, 80–89, 70–79 etc., by counting the number of grades in each grade range.

| Class | Frequency ( $f$ ) |
|---|---|
| 90–99 | 4 |
| 80–89 | 6 |
| 70–79 | 4 |
| 60–69 | 3 |
| 50–59 | 2 |
| 40–49 | 1 |

Note that the sum of the frequency column is equal to 20, the total number of test scores that you were given.

**This concludes your review for the math section. In the following pages you will find 5 full-length exams to practice with. Good luck!**

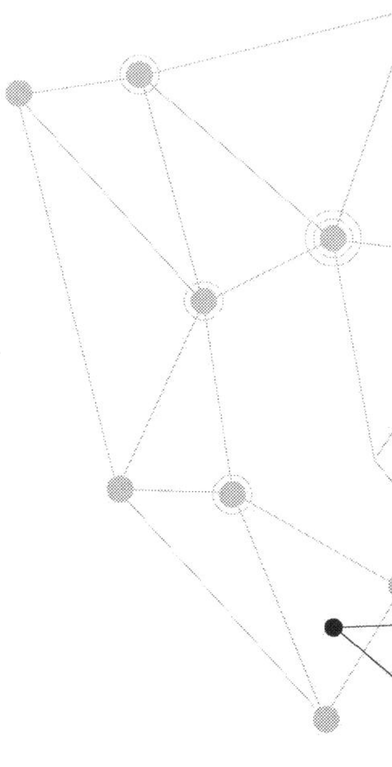

ARGOPREP
ARGOPREP.COM/SHSAT

# SHSAT
# PRACTICE TESTS

ARGOPREP
ARGOPREP.COM/SHSAT

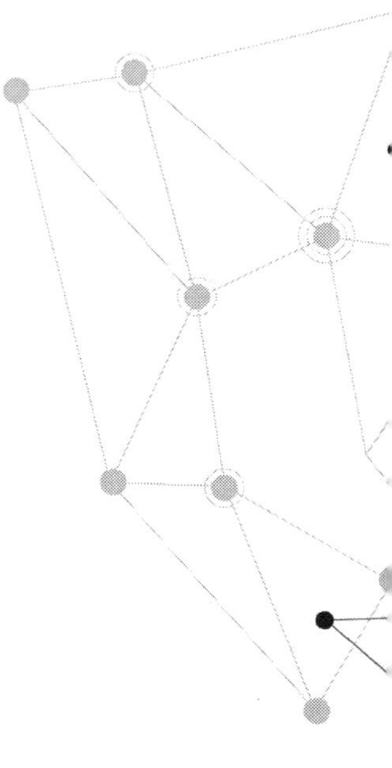

# Practice Test 1
# SHSAT

- This exam is 3 hours long. Try to take this full exam in one sitting to simulate real test conditions.
- While taking this exam, refrain from hearing music or watching T.V.
- Please note, calculators are not permitted! You are permitted to answer questions in any order you see fit.
- Allocate your test time accordingly.
- Concentrate and GOOD LUCK!

!

## Important information:

Please note that video explanations on our online platform all contain the answer choices ABCD. This workbook and the real exam alternates between answer choices ABCD and EFGH.

**You can find detailed video explanations to each problem in the book by visiting: ArgoPrep.com**

**DIRECTIONS:** For questions 1 to 5, you will be asked to recognize and correct errors in sentences or short paragraphs.

**1.** Read this sentence.

> The Space Race which began in 1955, was a memorable part of the Cold War between the United States and the Soviet Union.

Which edit should be made to correct this sentence?

**A.** Insert a **comma** after **Race**
**B.** Insert a **comma** after **part**
**C.** Insert a **comma** after **War**
**D.** Insert a **comma** after **States**

---

**2.** Read this sentence.

> From 1952 to 1988, the United States and Soviet Union engaged in a legendary Olympic rivalry, during which the Soviets capture over a thousand medals, while the Americans won 774.

Which edit should be made to correct the sentence?

**E.** Change **engaged** to **engage**
**F.** Change **which** to **that**
**G.** Change **capture** to **captured**
**H.** Change **won** to **win**

**3.** Read this paragraph.

> (1) It's easy to see that the magnificent pets in a dog show are cute, but it's much harder to understand how they are actually judged. (2) Each animal in a dog show is rated based on its adherence to breed standards, which are established guidelines for how dogs of a particular type are supposed to look and behave. (3) First, judges determine which dog at the show is the finest example of each breed. (4) Then, those dogs compete in groupings of similar dogs, including working dogs, sporting dogs, toy dogs, and terriers. (5) Again, the goal is to be the dog that best represents its breed's ideals. (6) Finally, the winners of the group stages compete to see which of them is the best example of its breed in the show.

Which sentence is the least related to the main ideas of the paragraph and could be removed?

**A.** Sentence 1
**B.** Sentence 2
**C.** Sentence 3
**D.** Sentence 4

CONTINUE ON TO THE NEXT PAGE ➡

**4.** Read this paragraph.

(1) Walt Disney's name is synonymous with outstanding cartoons, but few people appreciate how many iconic characters Disney created himself. (2) His most iconic creation, Mickey Mouse, was born in 1928, alongside his love interest Minnie Mouse. (3) Disney created Pluto and Goofy in 1930 and 1932, respectively. (4) Appearing in over 150 cartoons between 1934 and 1959, Mickey's grouchy pal Donald Duck was introduced in 1934. (5) In addition to this core of favorites, Disney created a robust supporting cast that made his cartoons feel as though they occurred in a rich, fully inhabited world.

Which sentence needs to be revised to correct a dangling participle?

**E.** Sentence 2
**F.** Sentence 3
**G.** Sentence 4
**H.** Sentence 5

**5.** Read this sentence.

After the assassination of Abraham Lincoln, the civil war continued for almost two months before the last Confederate forces surrendered in Oklahoma, ending the war.

Which edit should be made to correct the sentence?

**A.** Change **civil war** to **Civil War**
**B.** Change **Confederate** to **confederate**
**C.** Change **forces** to **Forces**
**D.** Change **ending the war** to **ending the War**

CONTINUE ON TO THE NEXT PAGE ➞

**DIRECTIONS:** Read the passage below to answer questions 6 to 11. The questions will focus on improving the writing quality of the passage to follow the conventions of standard written English.

---

**Salmonella**

(1) Salmonella is a rod-shaped bacterium that can cause the illness commonly known as "food poisoning" in humans. (2) According to the Centers for Disease Control and Prevention (CDC), Salmonella sickens more than a million Americans every year and causes as many as 380 deaths. (3) People infected with Salmonella typically experience abdominal pain, fever, and diarrhea. (4) Most healthy adults can fight off the infection in less than a week, but Salmonella can be deadly for infants, senior citizens, and people with compromised immune systems.

(5) Salmonella infections usually come from consuming food infected with the bacteria. (6) Meat (especially poultry) and eggs are the most common sources of Salmonella infections in the United States. (7) It can be difficult for chicken farmers to ensure their products are completely free of Salmonella because the bacteria does not make chickens sick. (8) When infected hens lay eggs, they pass along one or two bacteria into the yolk, where they can reproduce quickly under the right conditions.

(9) The CDC provides a variety of strategies for preventing Salmonella infection. (10) Refrigerating foods that may contain Salmonella prevents the bacteria from reproducing, lowering the chance that a sickening load of the bacteria will form. (11) All meat, poultry, and eggs should be cooked fully to an internal temperature of at least 160° F. (12) This guarantees that any existing bacteria will be killed before the food is eaten. (13) Finally, anybody handling or processing food should wash their hands and any surfaces touched by food frequently to prevent cross-contamination.

---

**6.** In sentence 2, why is the parenthetical note "(CDC)" necessary?

- **E.** When discussing a government agency, it is required to give both its formal name and initials.
- **F.** It explains the meaning of an acronym that is used later in the passage.
- **G.** It establishes a formal tone for the passage.
- **H.** It's not necessary. It can be removed.

CONTINUE ON TO THE NEXT PAGE ➡

7. What information could be added to sentence 4 to best improve clarity?
   - **A.** What percentage of adults comprises "Most healthy adults..."
   - **B.** An explanation of how the immune system fights Salmonella
   - **C.** Age limits defining the terms "infant" and "senior citizen"
   - **D.** An example of a situation in which somebody might have a compromised immune system

---

8. How could sentence 6 be rewritten to eliminate the use of parentheses?
   - **E.** Meat, especially poultry, and eggs are the most common sources...
   - **F.** Meat especially poultry and eggs are the most common sources...
   - **G.** Meat – especially poultry – and eggs are the most common sources...
   - **H.** E or G

---

9. What kind of major error can be found in sentence 7?
   - **A.** Subject-verb agreement
   - **B.** Spelling
   - **C.** Capitalization
   - **D.** Punctuation

10. Which change would best clarify the repeated use of the pronoun "they" in sentence 8?
    - **E.** When infected hens lay eggs, those hens pass along one or two bacteria into the yolk, where they can reproduce quickly under the right conditions.
    - **F.** When infected hens lay eggs, they pass along one or two bacteria into the yolk, where the eggs can reproduce quickly under the right conditions.
    - **G.** When infected hens lay eggs, they pass along one or two bacteria into the yolk, where Salmonella can reproduce quickly under the right conditions.
    - **H.** When infected hens lay eggs, Salmonella passes along one or two bacteria into the yolk, where they can reproduce quickly under the right conditions.

---

11. Which transition word would make the most sense at the beginning of sentence 11?
    - **A.** However
    - **B.** Additionally
    - **C.** Subsequently
    - **D.** Unfortunately

---

**CONTINUE ON TO THE NEXT PAGE ➡**

# READING COMPREHENSION
## Practice Test 1

**DIRECTIONS:** Analyze the passages below, and answer the commensurate questions. Only use information provided within the passage for your answers. There is only one answer for each question.

---

Despite being a notorious luddite and curmudgeon about technology in general (Gabriel Marcel refused for years to even use a typewriter, though before his death, he finally acquiesced to allowing one in his apartment for his transcriber), Marcel's warnings seem prescient even decades after he died. He writes, "Technical progress seems to many to be the necessary and infallible way to obtain human wellbeing and happiness, and the latter is identified with pleasure and satisfaction on a material level." But human well-being can never result from material satisfaction. Instead, a hyper-focus on technology leads to what Marcel calls a "broken world", a "world divided" and "at war with itself".

By 'broken', 'divided' and 'at war with itself', Marcel mean that, existentially, we treat others (and are treated by others) as mere objects, functions, and problems to be solved. But, he also means that our brokenness leads to literal schisms and war. Marcel's generation lived through the rise and ultimate deployment of nuclear weapons, and like his, our generation constantly faces the threat of their use. The possibility of world war, Marcel believed, throws us into a situation in which humanity could actually eradicate itself, "The fruits of our amazing technological progress are weapons of mass destruction possessed by many states whose relationships with each other are primarily in terms of power, often blatantly manifest in the desire of conquest."

For a philosopher like Gabriel Marcel, truth can survive even in today's threats. But, this modern age differs from Marcel's, because technologically-enhanced weapons (chemical, nuclear, and digital) are proliferated among state and non-state actors. Ours uses atrocities and the threat of atrocities to subject others into submission. And this age uses the fear of acute suffering to commodify whatever is being sold to the mass public. Philosophers today have the benefit of recent history and a knowledge of power structures, however, as tools with which to stand in the gap, between those who would perpetuate atrocity and those who would suffer from it. On a smaller scale, philosophers are able to name the inevitable despair that comes to those who put their faith in material things, since there is no material thing which is capable of helping the powerless contend with the fundamental loss of meaning in the world.

But philosophers are those who respond to a *call,* the vocation of naming evil, fostering meaning, and providing hope to the world. Herein lies the prophetic nature of philosophy's gate-keeping. In *Creative Fidelity,* Marcel writes, "Hope consists in asserting that there is at the heart of being, beyond all data, beyond all inventories and all calculations, a mysterious principle which is in connivance with me....I assert that a given order shall be reestablished, that reality is on my side in willing it to be so. I do not wish: I assert; such is the prophetic tone of true hope."

**CONTINUE ON TO THE NEXT PAGE →**

**12.** Which of the following best tells us what the passage is about?

- **E.** the relationship between philosophy and science
- **F.** the science of how technology leads to nuclear war
- **G.** the brokenness of humanity
- **H.** the difficulty of producing material things without technology

**13.** What is the principal role the philosopher is supposed to play as described in the 2nd paragraph?

- **A.** to predict a hopeful future for the world
- **B.** to develop principles of fear that can be used against non-state actors
- **C.** to produce power in those who suffer
- **D.** to protect those who suffer from those in power

**14.** Which of the following can be concluded from Marcel's view that we are at war with ourselves?

- **E.** human brokenness cannot be fixed through technological advances
- **F.** philosophers are modern day prophets
- **G.** science and philosophy will always be at odds with each other
- **H.** we must reduce access to chemical weapons by non-state actors

**15.** Why does the author mention philosophy's call in the 4th paragraph?

- **A.** to suggest that despair is inevitable in a technologically-advanced world
- **B.** to explain the prophetic nature of philosophy today
- **C.** to demonstrate that faith in material things leads to problems
- **D.** to give an example of philosophy done well

**16.** The author describes the role that hope plays for being (lines 54-60) in order

- **E.** to emphasize that the mystery of being is discovered beyond data
- **F.** to highlight that humans, by their nature, are calculating beings
- **G.** to emphasize that creativity can lead to hope
- **H.** to highlight the difficulty in finding out what is real

**17.** The author includes details about using fear over suffering (lines 36-38) in order:

- **A.** to show that fear is easy to create through technology
- **B.** to demonstrate that fear is better than suffering that comes through atrocity
- **C.** to highlight that fear is found in a variety of commodities
- **D.** to suggest that groups benefit financially by using fear of atrocities

**CONTINUE ON TO THE NEXT PAGE ➞**

**Edward's Castles in Wales**

Although we now think of England, Scotland, and Wales as connected pieces of Great Britain or the United Kingdom, England was highly antagonistic toward both its nearest neighbors throughout much of the middle ages. King Edward I of England, who ruled for 1272 to 1307, is mostly remembered for his campaigns of aggression to subdue the Scottish and Welsh. Although his actions were considered tyrannical and unjust by the people whose borders he invaded, Edward I was undeniably successful at bringing the Welsh under English rule. He achieved that feat by establishing a system of castles throughout Wales that stands as one of the great architectural achievements of his era.

Edward's castle-building strategy is known as the "Iron Ring" because he created a circle of four castles one day's march apart from each other around the area he controlled in Wales. As Edward's influence and military success spread, more castles were added to reflect the expansion of territory. As he gained new land, Edward also refurbished older Welsh castles to incorporate into his system, and Welsh nobles who wanted to find favor with the increasingly powerful English king would even build small castles or fortifications for his troops to use.

The castles of the Iron Ring shared several general characteristics. For one, they all featured thick, high stone walls. In fact, many of the castles had multiple sets of concentric walls to discourage Welsh warriors from attempting to climb their way into the strongholds. The castles also featured a huge number of arrow loops cut into their stone walls. Arrow loops were thin slits in the dense walls that allowed archers inside the castle to shoot outward and downward at potential invaders without exposing themselves to the shots of enemy archers outside the castle. As this design feature illustrates, the strategy of the "Iron Ring" wasn't necessarily to bring the fight to the Welsh but rather to communicate that the King of England was in the area to stay, and no resistance, siege, or assault was going to send his nobles back across the border.

While Edward's iron ring of castles was a successful military strategy to frustrate Welsh resistance, it ultimately won the Welsh over for economic purposes. The areas around Edward's castles grew into thriving farm towns and merchant communities, in which laws were well-enforced (which was not the case in the wild woods and back roads of medieval Britain) and local artisans and merchants could get a fair price for their work. While the Welsh did not want to sacrifice their heritage or identity, the prosperity that grew around the castles of the Iron Ring showed them that embracing English rule could be mutually beneficial. In this way, the castles helped create a true middle class in Wales.

Today, four of the original castles of the Iron Ring make up a World Heritage Site. Caernarfon, Conwy, Harlech, and Beaumaris castles still stand as reminders of Edward I's incredible military and economic vision in Wales. Although the original living quarters of the castles have not stood the test of time, the breathtaking walls designed to keep the English in Wales and the Welsh out of English castles still stand as a testament to the long and complex history between the two neighbors.

CONTINUE ON TO THE NEXT PAGE →

| "Iron Ring Castles" Included in the modern World Heritage Site | | | | |
|---|---|---|---|---|
| | Caernarfon | Conwy | Beaumaris | Harlech |
| Year Construction Began | 1283 | 1283 | 1295 | 1282 |
| Year Construction Concluded | 1330 (Abandoned) | 1289 (Completed) | 1330 (Abandoned) | 1289 (Completed) |
| Uses Arrow Loops? | Yes | Yes | Yes | Yes |
| Located on a Water Feature? | Yes (Bay) | Yes (Coastline) | Yes (Moat) | Yes (Coastline; not observable today) |
| Uses Concentric Walls? | Yes | No | Yes | Yes |

**18.** How does the incorporation of water features align with ideas from the passage about the philosophy of the "Iron Ring?"

- **E.** It shows that the English were mostly concerned with creating safe economic zones where laws were enforced and people had access to clean water
- **F.** It shows that the English had no fear of the Welsh attacking them using ships
- **G.** It shows that the English were concerned with the Welsh attempting to burn down their castles
- **H.** It shows that the English were mostly concerned with defending their castles rather than using them as bases for attack

---

**19.** What is the main purpose of Paragraph 1 within the passage?

- **A.** To provide a general introduction to the content of the passage
- **B.** To provide historical context for the castles discussed in the body of the passage
- **C.** To provide the reader with additional topics they might be interested in if they enjoy the content of the passage
- **D.** To provide an explanation of the historic relationship between England, Scotland, and Wales

**20.** Which of these words is a synonym for "campaigns of aggression" as it is used in Paragraph 1?

- **E.** Castles
- **F.** Arguments
- **G.** Sabotages
- **H.** Wars

---

**21.** Based on context, what is the most likely reason that only four of the Iron Ring castles are part of the current World Heritage Site?

- **A.** The other castles of the Iron Ring are not well enough preserved to appreciate
- **B.** The World Heritage Site only includes the original castles of the Iron Ring, not the ones added later
- **C.** The four castles that make up the World Heritage site were the most important to the English campaign in Wales
- **D.** The World Heritage Organization rules stipulate that no more than four individual locations can be associated with any single "site"

**CONTINUE ON TO THE NEXT PAGE →**

**22.** How does the information in the table "'Iron Ring Castles' Included in the Modern World Heritage Site" correspond to the content of the passage?

**E.** The table primarily reinforces information from the passage
**F.** The table primarily provides specific details that were excluded from the large-concept focus of the passage
**G.** The table primarily provides large-concept context for the specific details that were included in the passage
**H.** The table primarily provides dates to communicate when the conflict between the English and Welsh began, peaked, and ended

---

**23.** Based on the passage and table, what can we infer about the year 1330?

**A.** King Edward I must have died in 1330
**B.** Castle building must have been obsolete by 1330
**C.** Relations between the English and Welsh must have improved by 1330
**D.** Concentric walls were more popular in 1330 than they were in 1280

CONTINUE ON TO THE NEXT PAGE →

**Excerpt from Chapter VIII of *Great Expectation* by Charles Dickens**

She was dressed in rich materials,—satins, and lace, and silks,—all of white. Her shoes were white. And she had a long white veil dependent from her hair, and she had bridal flowers in her hair, but her hair was white. Some bright jewels sparkled on her neck and on her hands, and some other jewels lay sparkling on the table. Dresses, less splendid than the dress she wore, and half-packed trunks, were scattered about. She had not quite finished dressing, for she had but one shoe on,—the other was on the table near her hand,—her veil was but half arranged, her watch and chain were not put on, and some lace for her bosom lay with those trinkets, and with her handkerchief, and gloves, and some flowers, and a Prayer-Book all confusedly heaped about the looking-glass.

It was not in the first few moments that I saw all these things, though I saw more of them in the first moments than might be supposed. But I saw that everything within my view which ought to be white, had been white long ago, and had lost its lustre and was faded and yellow. I saw that the bride within the bridal dress had withered like the dress, and like the flowers, and had no brightness left but the brightness of her sunken eyes. I saw that the dress had been put upon the rounded figure of a young woman, and that the figure upon which it now hung loose had shrunk to skin and bone. Once, I had been taken to see some ghastly waxwork at the Fair, representing I know not what impossible personage lying in state. Once, I had been taken to one of our old marsh churches to see a skeleton in the ashes of a rich dress that had been dug out of a vault under the church pavement. Now, waxwork and skeleton seemed to have dark eyes that moved and looked at me. I should have cried out, if I could.

"Who is it?" said the lady at the table.

"Pip, ma'am."

"Pip?"

"Mr. Pumblechook's boy, ma'am. Come—to play."

"Come nearer; let me look at you. Come close."

It was when I stood before her, avoiding her eyes, that I took note of the surrounding objects in detail, and saw that her watch had stopped at twenty minutes to nine, and that a clock in the room had stopped at twenty minutes to nine.

"Look at me," said Miss Havisham. "You are not afraid of a woman who has never seen the sun since you were born?"

I regret to state that I was not afraid of telling the enormous lie comprehended in the answer "No."

"Do you know what I touch here?" she said, laying her hands, one upon the other, on her left side.

"Yes, ma'am." (It made me think of the young man.)

"What do I touch?"

"Your heart."

"Broken!"

She uttered the word with an eager look, and with strong emphasis, and with a weird smile that had a kind of boast in it. Afterwards she kept her hands there for a little while, and slowly took them away as if they were heavy.

"I am tired," said Miss Havisham. "I want diversion, and I have done with men and women. Play."

I think it will be conceded by my most disputatious reader, that she could hardly have directed an unfortunate boy to do anything in the wide world more difficult to be done under the circumstances.

CONTINUE ON TO THE NEXT PAGE ➡

**24.** Which of these best describes the attitude of the narrator, Pip, throughout the passage?

- **E.** Adventurous and excited
- **F.** Nervous and excited
- **G.** Apprehensive but enthusiastic
- **H.** Apprehensive and uncomfortable

---

**25.** Which is the best definition for "dependent" as it is used in Paragraph 1?

- **A.** Hanging
- **B.** Reliant upon
- **C.** Trustworthy
- **D.** A child or other family member for whom someone is financially responsible

---

**26.** Which of these words best describes Miss Havisham's room?

- **E.** Regal
- **F.** Messy
- **G.** Festive
- **H.** Ruined

---

**27.** How is Miss Havisham's appearance ironic or paradoxical?

- **A.** Typically, brides only wear their dress for one day and experience happy times in it; she has been wearing her dress for years and is seemingly miserable.
- **B.** She looks like she could be dead, but she is somehow alive.
- **C.** Miss Havisham has expensive jewelry, but her wedding dress is surprisingly ugly.
- **D.** Typically, brides take excellent care of their wedding dress after their ceremony, but Miss Havisham has allowed hers to become yellowed over time.

**28.** Why does Pip mention his trip to the fair in Paragraph 2?

- **E.** To describe another time he was very scared like he was meeting Miss Havisham
- **F.** To use a pleasant memory to try to block out the horror of meeting Miss Havisham
- **G.** To provide a reference point from his own experience to describe Miss Havisham better
- **H.** To contrast the joy of the fair with the depressing atmosphere at Miss Havisham's house

---

**29.** Based on the text, what can the reader infer happened to Miss Havisham?

- **A.** She lost her money and is in financial ruin
- **B.** She was emotionally devastated by the loss of her children
- **C.** She was left at the alter by a man she was supposed to marry
- **D.** She was disfigured by a horrible curse

---

**30.** What major physical change has Miss Havisham gone through since her wedding dress was made?

- **E.** She has gained a considerable amount of weight
- **F.** She has lost a considerable amount of weight
- **G.** She has begun to dye her hair
- **H.** She has died

CONTINUE ON TO THE NEXT PAGE ➡

**31.** Which of these sets of words provides the closest synonyms to "disputatious," as it is used in the final paragraph of the passage?

**A.** Incredulous or skeptical
**B.** Frightened or horrified
**C.** Disgusted or sickened
**D.** Argumentative or disagreeable

---

**32.** Why is Pip especially uncomfortable at the end of the passage?

**E.** Miss Havisham's ugliness makes her difficult for him to look at
**F.** He empathizes a great deal with Miss Havisham's broken heart
**G.** Miss Havisham insists on watching him play, which feels unnatural given the context
**H.** Miss Havisham kicks him out of her house for being rude

**CONTINUE ON TO THE NEXT PAGE ➞**

**Ghost House**
**By Robert Frost**

I dwell in a lonely house I know
That vanished many a summer ago,
And left no trace but the cellar walls,
And a cellar in which the daylight falls
And the purple-stemmed wild raspberries grow.

O'er ruined fences the grape-vines shield
The woods come back to the mowing field;
The orchard tree has grown one copse
Of new wood and old where the woodpecker chops;
The footpath down to the well is healed.

I dwell with a strangely aching heart
In that vanished abode there far apart
On that disused and forgotten road
That has no dust-bath now for the toad.
Night comes; the black bats tumble and dart;

The whippoorwill is coming to shout
And hush and cluck and flutter about:
I hear him begin far enough away
Full many a time to say his say
Before he arrives to say it out.

It is under the small, dim, summer star.
I know not who these mute folk are
Who share the unlit place with me—
Those stones out under the low-limbed tree
Doubtless bear names that the mosses mar.

They are tireless folk, but slow and sad—
Though two, close-keeping, are lass and lad,—
With none among them that ever sings,
And yet, in view of how many things,
As sweet companions as might be had.

O'er = over
Copse = a group of trees

**33.** Which of these best describes the speaker's attitude throughout the poem?

- **A.** He or she is happy to reminisce about his or her childhood home
- **B.** He or she is trying to fight back negative memories about the place where he or she grew up
- **C.** He or she is frustrated with how difficult it is to control nature
- **D.** He or she finds both sadness and beauty in what has happened to his or her childhood home

---

**34.** Which parts of the speaker's former house does he or she specifically mention still exists?

- **E.** The doorway
- **F.** The roof
- **G.** The cellar
- **H.** His or her bedroom

---

**35.** What does the speaker mean when he or she describes that "The woods come back to the mowing field" (Line 7)?

- **A.** Trees have grown back in what used to be a cleared field
- **B.** There are woods at the back of the field behind the house
- **C.** The trees have come to life and are mowing the grass
- **D.** The field used to be wild, but it has recently been mowed

**CONTINUE ON TO THE NEXT PAGE ➡**

**36.** Which of these is the best definition for "healed" as it is used in Line 10?

- **E.** Cured from disease or injury
- **F.** To repair the worn-down part of a shoe
- **G.** Regrown or recovered
- **H.** Relieved from distress or anguish

---

**37.** How is the setting of the second half of the poem markedly different from the setting of the first half of the poem?

- **A.** The first half of the poem takes place at night; the second half of the poem takes place during the daytime
- **B.** The first half of the poem takes place during the daytime; the second half of the poem takes place at night
- **C.** The first half of the poem takes place in the past; the second half of the poem takes place in the present
- **D.** The first half of the poem takes place in the present; the second half of the poem takes place in the past

---

**38.** Based on the poem, which of these is the best definition for "whippoorwill" as it is used in Line 16?

- **E.** A farmhand or laborer
- **F.** A kind of bird
- **G.** A kind of tree
- **H.** An unfortunate child

**39.** When the speaker explains how "Those stones out under the low-limbed tree / Doubtless bear names that the mosses mar" (Lines 24-25), what kind of place is he or she most likely describing?

- **A.** A cemetery
- **B.** A field with a stone boundary wall around it
- **C.** A quarry
- **D.** A place in the woods where the speaker used to play as a child

---

**40.** Which of these is an example of how the absence of people from the farm has negatively impacted nature or wildlife?

- **E.** The road no longer provides toads with dust to bathe in
- **F.** The whippoorwill does not have anybody to sing to
- **G.** The raspberry and grape vines have grown out of control
- **H.** The trees in the orchard have stopped producing fruit

---

**41.** Based on the text, which of these is a reasonable inference about the speaker of the poem?

- **A.** He or she grew up poor but is now very rich
- **B.** He or she wants to rebuild the house that used to be on the property
- **C.** He or she is regretful about abandoning rural life for the city
- **D.** He or she may be dead or dying

**CONTINUE ON TO THE NEXT PAGE →**

The phrase "it's a witch hunt" is used in many pop culture domains. But, the reality of the history of the phrase is startling, at a minimum, and terrifying, at a maximum. In an American society that celebrates witches, goblins, demons, and ghouls every year on Halloween, it might seem antiquated to think about a time in which most people believed that real witches walked among us, casting dark spells on their neighbors and enemies. Not too long ago, in this very country that now adores *Harry Potter*-style myths, large-scale witch hunts took place in which hundreds of men and women were accused, hunted, and either burned or hanged for the crimes of witchcraft and sorcery.

We need to go back further in history to learn about the origin of witch hunts. The Celts, living in what is now the Fenlands of Great Britain, believed that on the night of Halloween, those who had died could cross over from the land of the dead. For one night, the souls of those who were evil could haunt and cause physical harm to people and animals, and to wreak havoc on crops. Witches were especially frightening on Halloween, because they were able to make a pact with the Devil—in exchange for their souls, they would be given the ability to fly, and they could cast spells by channeling Satanic power, which they used to harm others. Halloween was association with real fear, danger, and physical pain.

It's not completely clear when the witch hunting phenomenon caught on this side of the Atlantic. In the 1620s, farms in the colonies were undergoing extreme hardship. Whenever natural or other disasters occurred that made life unsustainable, colonists usually looked for a supernatural cause that acted on individuals within the community. (After a severe frost in May 1626, for example, women were taken to court, where they confessed to conspiring to freeze and destroy the crops.) Famines were attributed to evil doing, and insect infestations were caused by some spiritual flaw in the families associated with the ruined harvests. By the 1620s, accusing people of witchcraft in early America was a regular occurrence.

Men were not excluded from the allegations. (Under torture, farmers would admit to casting spells that would cause horrendous weather disasters and fires.) Whether male or female, those who accused were already thought to be guilty. People who were thought guilty were in a Catch-22 predicament: if any proof emerged that cast doubt on their guilt, it was rejected as dishonest; and if the evidence seemed credible, it was dismissed as being the product of someone who worked with the Devil to connive against righteous people. Even more, if someone brought evidence to support someone accused of witchcraft, they were charged with being co-conspirators. All participants were seen as a poison to the community, and the only way to rid a community of poison is to completely eradicate it. So, the accused were tortured (to elicit confessions from them), then publicly hanged or burned at the stake to serve as a reminder to the community that justice for witchcraft required a blood payment.

**42.** Which of the following best tells what this passage is about?

**E.** the origin and nature of witch hunting in America
**F.** the Celtic roots of American witch hunting
**G.** the relationship between crop destruction and witch hunting
**H.** the irony of American passion for sorcery

**CONTINUE ON TO THE NEXT PAGE ➞**

**43.** What is the principal goal of bringing up *Harry Potter* in paragraph one?

- **A.** to predict that witch hunting will continue in America in the future
- **B.** to develop an argument that we owe families reparation for witch hunts
- **C.** to produce an interesting comparison between American culture then and now
- **D.** to improve the claim that males accused of sorcery were also hunted

---

**44.** Which of the following can be concluded from the fact that torture led people to confess to witchcraft?

- **E.** that the accused did, in fact, participate in witchcraft
- **F.** that torture is ineffective to get people to tell the truth
- **G.** that the spells cast by the accused effectively destroyed the crops
- **H.** that the women were disproportionately tortured compared to the men.

---

**45.** Why does the author mention insect infestations in the third paragraph?

- **A.** to suggest that God was displeased with the early colonists
- **B.** to explain that the early Americans had made pacts with the Devil to harm those who were enemies
- **C.** to demonstrate how precarious the survival of the early colonists really was
- **D.** to give an example of a natural disaster that was explained through the spiritual

**46.** Based on the text, what does the author mean by "Catch-22" (line 50)?

- **E.** the accused faced a situation that will produce a negative outcome for them regardless of what actions are performed
- **F.** the accused were going to catch the consequences of their actions
- **G.** the judges faced an unwinnable situation in which they could make no one happy
- **H.** the evidence presented on one hand, exonerated the accused and, on the other, showed they were guilty

---

**47.** What most directly enabled witch hunts to occur in America?

- **A.** famine and poverty were unexplainable except for supernatural causes
- **B.** in the New World, families were walking away from their religious beliefs
- **C.** all evidence was turned against the accused
- **D.** public execution was already a socially acceptable punishment used by the courts

**CONTINUE ON TO THE NEXT PAGE ➞**

**The Evolving Classroom**

Between 1945 and 2000, educators across the U.S. employed a fairly uniform approach. The teacher was the sun in the classroom, and all lessons and activities revolved around him or her. Educators stressed discipline and obedience within the classroom, and students were expected to follow very rigid standards for behavior and academic performance or suffer the consequences. The stated goal of this model was to ensure fairness by applying the same expectations across the board; however, the result was often a classroom in which a few students succeeded while many others were left by the wayside.

The main issues with this approach were that it failed to account for the very real differences between individuals and often stressed respecting the authority of the teacher over learning. For students who liked to listen and take notes and study, school was relatively easy because all they had to do was follow directions in order to succeed. On the other hand, though, students for whom following rules and focusing on a single task for a long time was challenging were often singled out as behavioral problems or branded "problem students." In short, the model worked well for some students but had minimal positive impacts for others.

When computer and internet technology entered the classroom a few decades ago, progressive educators immediately saw the opportunity to change the way school looked for students across America. Instead of needing to focus on the teacher for the vast majority of the day, students could use computers, web sites, and even games to learn new material, practice their skills and knowledge, and even take tests or quizzes in a livelier environment. Not all educators embraced this shift, however, as some believed it took power and responsibility away from the teacher and cheapened the educational experience for learners.

Over the last decade or so, two distinct camps of educators have emerged: one that believes we should harness technology to significantly change what school looks like in classrooms around America and one that believes we should preserve the classroom model that worked in the 20th century. Tech advocates stress that computers and internet technology allow students to learn at their own pace in an environment that makes them feel comfortable, whereas the traditional classroom set a pace that many learners couldn't keep up with and often made students feel uncomfortable. Traditionalists, on the other hand, believe that over-reliance on tech inhibits students' ability to build their own knowledge and skills and does little to prepare them for the realities of being an adult in the real world.

Regrettably, the inability of these two parties to find a consensus has stunted the growth of our education system in the 21st century. We cannot truly move forward as a system or a country until we officially define how we are going to approach school. We must learn from what worked in the past while integrating the best of our new technologies to create an education system that reflects our modern world and the needs of our communities. If we can't get all our teachers on the same page, then we're at risk of failing future generations of American students.

**48.** What is the best definition for "uniform" as it is used in Paragraph 1?

**E.** An official outfit of clothing
**F.** Formal and stuffy
**G.** Dated and unengaging
**H.** Consistently similar

**49.** Which of these behaviors would be most encouraged under the education model described in Paragraphs 1 and 2?

- **A.** Not doing a homework assignment if you don't understand the material
- **B.** Raising your hand every time you have a question
- **C.** Obeying the teacher's instructions, even if you feel they're wrong or unfair
- **D.** Using computer and internet technology to fill gaps in your understanding

---

**50.** Which of these best describes the teachers the author refers to as "traditionalists?"

- **E.** Traditionalist teachers believe we should stick to the teacher-centric model that was used throughout most of the 20th century.
- **F.** Traditionalist teachers believe we should overhaul learning to create a more student-centered approach.
- **G.** Traditionalist teachers believe we need to find a balance between the best aspects of old style education and the best aspects of tech-enabled learning.
- **H.** Traditionalist teachers believe the needs of individual students should drive the education process.

**51.** Based on the passage, which of these is an argument that a traditionalist might make about integrating tech in the classroom?

- **A.** If we integrate computer technology into the classroom, students will have greater access to the curriculum.
- **B.** If we integrate computer technology into the classroom, students will just use the computers to do all their thinking for them.
- **C.** If we integrate computer technology into the classroom, we can ensure each student receives a high-quality, individualized experience.
- **D.** If we integrate computer technology into the classroom, we'll be preparing students for adulthood in the 21st century world.

---

**52.** Based on the passage, which of these is an argument that a tech advocate might make about integrating tech into the classroom?

- **E.** If we integrate technology into the classroom, it could cheapen the bond between teachers and students.
- **F.** If we integrate technology into the classroom, it will create a low-accountability environment.
- **G.** If we integrate technology into the classroom, education will be more accessible and engaging for students.
- **H.** If we integrate technology into the classroom, students can learn the same material it currently takes them 12 years to learn in just 10 years.

**CONTINUE ON TO THE NEXT PAGE →**

**53.** Based on the passage, which of these best describes how teachers around the country approach education today?

- **A.** Teachers throughout the country still embrace the 20th century teacher-centric model.
- **B.** Teachers throughout the country have embraced teach-enabled learning.
- **C.** Teachers throughout the country currently use a variety of approaches, some of which involve tech and some of which do not.
- **D.** Teachers throughout the country are broken into two camps.

---

**54.** Which of these best describes the author's point of view throughout the passage?

- **E.** The author approaches education from a traditional, teacher-centric point of view.
- **F.** The author approaches education from a progressive, tech-enabled point of view.
- **G.** The author approaches education objectively, from an impartial outsider's point of view
- **H.** The author has no clear vision or point of view about education but feels it's an important topic to discuss.

---

**55.** Which of these is the best definition of "cheapened" as it is used in Paragraph 3?

- **A.** Reduced the price of
- **B.** Provided an unfair advantage
- **C.** Reduced the quality of
- **D.** Reduced the importance of

**56.** Why does the author begin the final paragraph with the transition "Regrettably?"

- **E.** To signal the transition from the main body of the essay to the conclusion
- **F.** To clarify his or her point of view on the content of the preceding paragraph
- **G.** To express that he or she believes the education system is broken
- **H.** To appeal to the emotions of the reader

---

**57.** Which of these terms is used in the text as an antonym for "progressive educators" (Line 29)?

- **A.** Not all educators (Line 37)
- **B.** Two distinct camps (Line 41)
- **C.** Tech advocates (Line 47)
- **D.** Traditionalists (Line 53)

CONTINUE ON TO THE NEXT PAGE ➡

ARGOPREP
ARGOPREP.COM/SHSAT

# MATHEMATICS INSTRUCTIONS

## 90 MINUTES • 57 QUESTIONS

Select the best answer from the choices given by carefully solving each problem. Bubble the letter of your answer on the answer sheet. Please refrain from making any stray marks on the answer sheet. If you need to erase an answer, please erase thoroughly.

**Important Notes:**

1. There are no formulas or definitions in the math section that will be provided.
2. Diagrams may or may not be drawn to scale. Do not make assumptions based on the diagram unless it is specifically stated in the diagram or question.
3. Diagrams are not in more than one plane, unless stated otherwise.
4. Graphs are drawn to scale, therefore, you can assume relationships according to the graph. If lines appear parallel, then you can assume the lines to be parallel. This is also true for right angles and so forth.
5. Simplify fractions completely.

# Practice Test 1

**GRID IN PROBLEMS (Questions 58-62)**

*Directions: The following five questions are grid-in problems. On the answer sheet, please be sure to write your answer in the boxes at the top of the grid. Start on the left side of each grid.*

**58.** After a 20% discount at the book store, a recipe book sells for $10. What was the original price of the book?

| | | | | |
|---|---|---|---|---|
| ⊖ | | | | |
| | ⊙ | ⊙ | ⊙ | ⊙ |
| | ⓪ | ⓪ | ⓪ | ⓪ |
| | ① | ① | ① | ① |
| | ② | ② | ② | ② |
| | ③ | ③ | ③ | ③ |
| | ④ | ④ | ④ | ④ |
| | ⑤ | ⑤ | ⑤ | ⑤ |
| | ⑥ | ⑥ | ⑥ | ⑥ |
| | ⑦ | ⑦ | ⑦ | ⑦ |
| | ⑧ | ⑧ | ⑧ | ⑧ |
| | ⑨ | ⑨ | ⑨ | ⑨ |

**59.** If the measure of angle $P$ of triangle $PQR$ is $3x$, the measure of angle $Q$ is $5x$, and the measure of angle $R$ is $4x$, what is the value of $x$?

| | | | | |
|---|---|---|---|---|
| ⊖ | | | | |
| | ⊙ | ⊙ | ⊙ | ⊙ |
| | ⓪ | ⓪ | ⓪ | ⓪ |
| | ① | ① | ① | ① |
| | ② | ② | ② | ② |
| | ③ | ③ | ③ | ③ |
| | ④ | ④ | ④ | ④ |
| | ⑤ | ⑤ | ⑤ | ⑤ |
| | ⑥ | ⑥ | ⑥ | ⑥ |
| | ⑦ | ⑦ | ⑦ | ⑦ |
| | ⑧ | ⑧ | ⑧ | ⑧ |
| | ⑨ | ⑨ | ⑨ | ⑨ |

**CONTINUE ON TO THE NEXT PAGE ➡**

**60.** If Katie scored an 80, 83, and an 88 on her first three tests, what must she score on her fourth test if she wants an average of 85? Enter your answer in the text box below.

**61.** Suppose $2(a - 3) + 9 = 4a - 7$. What is the value of $a$?

**62.** Solve the equation: $\frac{n + 4}{10} = \frac{n - 8}{2}$

CONTINUE ON TO THE NEXT PAGE ➡

## MULTIPLE CHOICE PROBLEMS (Questions 63-114)

**63.** Convert $\frac{7}{20}$ to decimal form.

**E.** 0.0035
**F.** 0.035
**G.** 0.35
**H.** 3.50

---

**64.** The value of 500,000 + 400 + 5 is

**A.** 500,450
**B.** 540,005
**C.** 540,500
**D.** 500,405

---

**65.** If $x = 4$ and $y = 3$, what is $(x + y)^2$ ?

**E.** 25
**F.** 32
**G.** 7
**H.** 49

---

**66.** $(\sqrt{144})(\sqrt{16}) =$

**A.** 16
**B.** 48
**C.** 12
**D.** 32

---

**67.** 1 Knot = 3 Vines
2 Shings = 4 Knots

How many Shings are in 9 Vines?

**E.** $\frac{4}{5}$
**F.** $\frac{2}{3}$
**G.** $\frac{5}{4}$
**H.** $\frac{3}{2}$

---

**68.** What number is halfway between $2 \bullet (\frac{3}{6})$ and 4 ?

**A.** 2
**B.** 2.5
**C.** 3
**D.** 1.5

---

**69.**

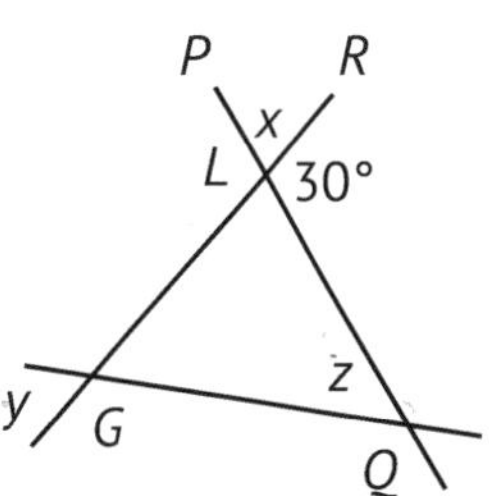


In the figure shown above LGQ is a triangle. What is $z$ in terms of $y$?

**E.** $30 - y$
**F.** $y + 150$
**G.** $2y + 30$
**H.** $2y - 30$

CONTINUE ON TO THE NEXT PAGE ➞

**70.** $-2 + 5(-18 \div 3 + 9) - 13 =$

**A.** 3
**B.** –4
**C.** 13
**D.** 0

---

**71.** The area of a square is equal to the area of a circle, whose diameter is 10. What is the length of a side of the square?

**E.** $\pi r\sqrt{5}$
**F.** $25\pi r$
**G.** $5\sqrt{\pi}$
**H.** $25\sqrt{\pi r}$

---

**72.** $4a(3b - 6)$

**A.** $7ab - 2a$
**B.** $12ab - 6$
**C.** $12b - 24$
**D.** $12ab - 24a$

---

**73.** $\frac{(-39)^2}{13^3} =$

**E.** –3
**F.** $\frac{-1}{13}$
**G.** $\frac{9}{13}$
**H.** 3

---

**74.** In a scaled diagram, 1 inch represents 20 feet. How many square inches on the diagram represent 1 square foot?

**A.** 0.0025
**B.** 0.04
**C.** .4
**D.** 400

---

**75.** What is the greatest common factor of 2,240 and 3,360?

**E.** 105
**F.** 280
**G.** 1,120
**H.** 2,240

---

**76.** If 50% of $2y$ is 12, what is $y^2$ ?

**A.** 36
**B.** 6
**C.** 16
**D.** 144

**CONTINUE ON TO THE NEXT PAGE ➞**

**77.**

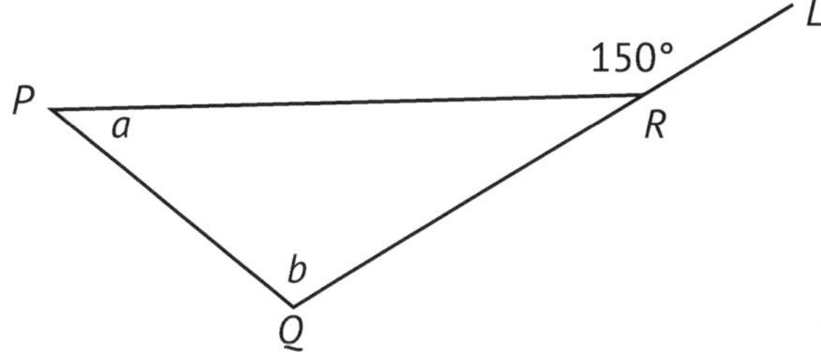


In the figure above ∡ $PRL$ is 150°. What is $\frac{a^2 - b^2}{(a - b)}$ ?

**E.** 30°
**F.** 120°
**G.** 150°
**H.** 160°

---

**78.** If $y = \frac{3}{4}$ and $xy^2 = \frac{9}{16}$, what is $(x - 4)$?

**A.** −3

**B.** $\frac{-13}{4}$

**C.** $\frac{-9}{16}$

**D.** −4

**79.** If $P$ is an odd integer, which of the following must be an even number?

**E.** $\frac{P^2 - (\frac{P}{4})}{(a - b)}$

**F.** $\frac{P - 2P^2}{2P + 5}$

**G.** $P^2$

**H.** $\frac{2P^2 - 2P^3}{2P}$

---

**80.** If the diameter of a circle is $P$, and $\frac{P^2}{4} = 2$ what is the area of the circle?

**A.** $4\pi$
**B.** $8\pi$
**C.** $2\pi\sqrt{2}$
**D.** $2\pi$

---

**81.** If a regular polygon has $(N - 10)$ sides, where, $N = (\frac{40}{10})^2$, what is the measure of one of its angles?

**E.** 120°
**F.** 160°
**G.** 240°
**H.** 720°

**CONTINUE ON TO THE NEXT PAGE ➡**

**82.**

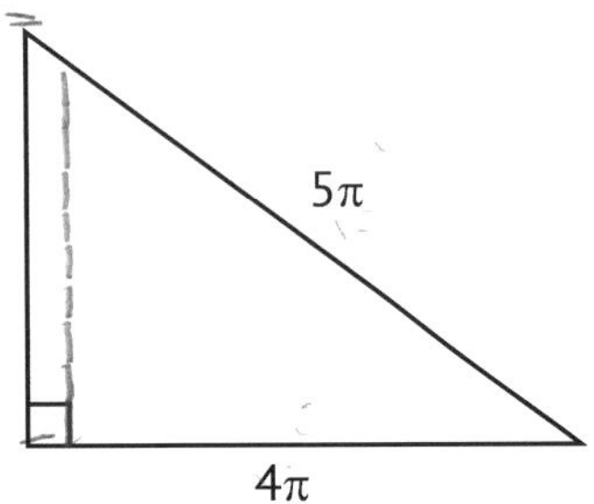


If the perimeter of the triangle shown above is the circumference of a circle, then what is the radius of the circle?

**A.** $9\pi$
**B.** 4
**C.** 6
**D.** $6\pi$

---

**83.** If $\dddot{x} = \frac{7}{x}$, what is the value of $\dddot{14}\ (\dddot{14})$

**E.** 0.25
**F.** 0.50
**G.** 7
**H.** 14

---

**84.** What is the least common multiple of 4, 16, 25 and 30?

**A.** 160
**B.** 240
**C.** 480
**D.** 1200

**85.** How many positive integers are between $\frac{-7}{3}$ and $\frac{5}{2}$?

**E.** 0
**F.** 1
**G.** 2
**H.** 3

---

**86.** The perimeter of a rectangle is 80 inches. If the width is 18 inches, what is the area of the rectangle?

**A.** 22 sq. in
**B.** 324 sq. in
**C.** 396 sq. in
**D.** 6,400 sq. in

---

**87.** $7|-x-3| = b$. If $x = -3$, what is $b$?

**E.** 24
**F.** 40
**G.** 42
**H.** 0

---

**88.** $1 + 2 + 3 + 4 + 5 + \ldots + 100 =$

**A.** 1010
**B.** 5050
**C.** 5000
**D.** 1000

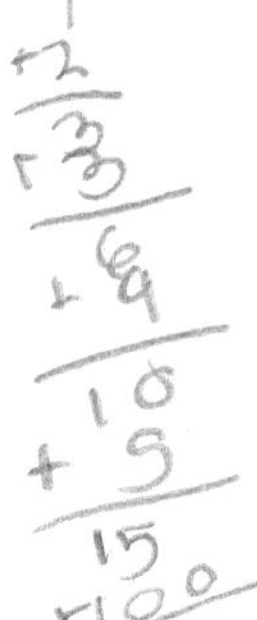

**CONTINUE ON TO THE NEXT PAGE ➡**

**89.** After a 10% increase, a population was 55. What was the population before the increase?

**E.** 44
**F.** 50
**G.** 40
**H.** 45

---

**90.** The length of a rectangular solid is 10. The width, $w$ and the height, $h$ follow the relationship, $w^3h^3 = 27$. What is the volume of the rectangular solid?

**A.** 270
**B.** 30
**C.** 90
**D.** 60

---

**91.**

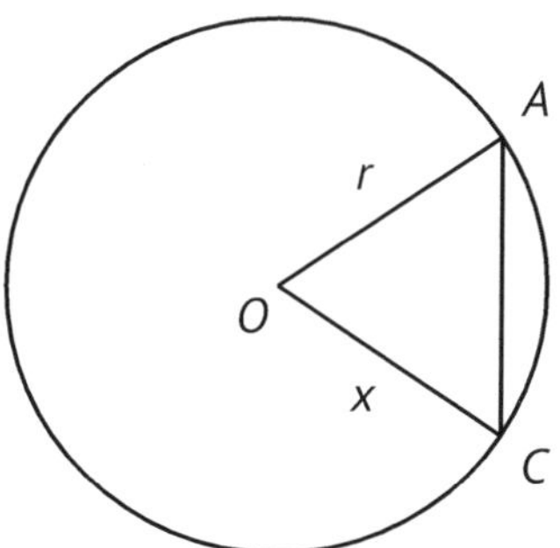


Figure not drawn to scale.

$\overline{AC}$ has a length of 10 and $r$, the radius, is 7. What is $x$?

**E.** 5
**F.** 7
**G.** $7\sqrt{2}$
**H.** 10

**92.**

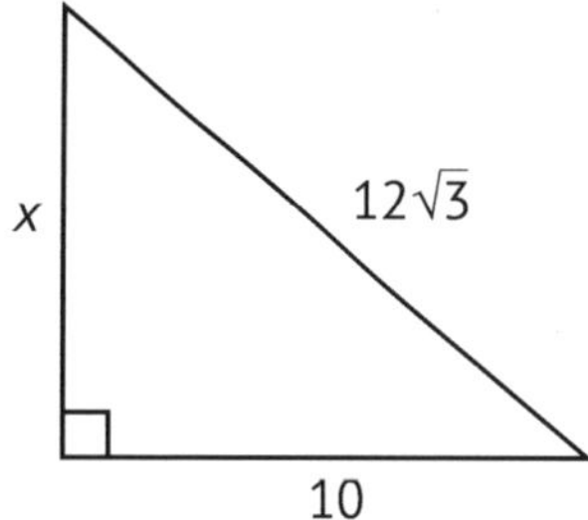


Figure not drawn to scale.

Find the length of $x$?

**A.** $\sqrt{83}$
**B.** $2\sqrt{83}$
**C.** $2\sqrt{332}$
**D.** 332

---

**93.** If $A = 3r^2h^2$, and $(rh)$ increases by 100%, then the new $A$ is how many times greater than the old $A$?

**E.** 2
**F.** 3
**G.** 4
**H.** 12

---

**94.** If $x^a = \sqrt[q]{x^p}$, what is $\frac{p^2}{q^2}$ ?

**A.** $\sqrt{a}$
**B.** $a^{1/3}$
**C.** $a^2$
**D.** $a$

CONTINUE ON TO THE NEXT PAGE →

**95.** Set $A = \{1, 2, 3, a\}$
Set $B = \{2, 4, 5, a^2, b\}$
What is $A \cap B$?

**E.** $\{2, a^2, b\}$
**F.** $\{2, \frac{b}{a}\}$
**G.** $\{2\}$
**H.** $\{2, \frac{a}{b}\}$

---

**96.** $2\sqrt{75} - (\sqrt{25})(\sqrt{3})$

**A.** $5\sqrt{3}$
**B.** $10\sqrt{3}$
**C.** $2\sqrt{3}$
**D.** 5

---

**97.** Express $\frac{0.0345}{10}$ in scientific notation.

**E.** $3.45 \times 10^{-2}$
**F.** $.0345 \times 10^{-2}$
**G.** $3.45 \times 10^{-3}$
**H.** $0.345 \times 10^{-3}$

---

**98.** ☆ × ☆ = $3x$, if $x$ is even and negative **OR**
☆ × ☆ = $4x$, if $x$ is odd.
Following the rule above, what is the value of ☆ – 23 ☆ ?

**A.** 92
**B.** −92
**C.** 529
**D.** −529

---

**99.** $y = x^3$
The only possible values of $x$ are those in the set $\{\frac{-1}{3}, \frac{1}{2}, \frac{1}{3}\}$. What is the maximum value of $y$?

**E.** $\frac{-1}{27}$
**F.** $\frac{1}{4}$
**G.** $\frac{1}{8}$
**H.** $\frac{1}{6}$

---

**100.** What is $\frac{x^3y^2z^4}{z^3y^3}$ equal to

**A.** $\frac{x^3}{3}$
**B.** $x^3yz^2$
**C.** $\frac{x^3z}{y}$
**D.** $\frac{x^3y}{z}$

---

**101.**

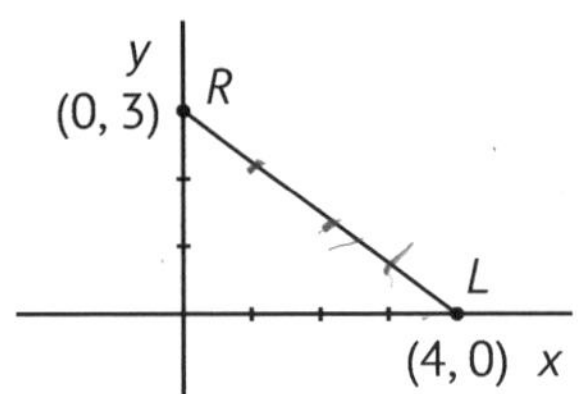


What is the length of $\overline{RL}$?

**E.** 6
**F.** 5
**G.** 4
**H.** 7

CONTINUE ON TO THE NEXT PAGE ➡

**102.** In a triangle, the sum of two angles equals the third. Find the measure of the third angle.

**A.** 45°
**B.** 60°
**C.** 90°
**D.** 30°

---

**103.** If Anthony and Bridget take turns watching T.V. every 4 hours and Anthony's third watch was at 10:00 P.M. and Bridget was the first to watch T.V., then when did Bridget begin her second watch?

**E.** 6:00 P.M.
**F.** 10:00 A.M.
**G.** 10:00 P.M.
**H.** 6:00 A.M.

---

**104.** There are a total of 9 bicycles and unicycles in a path. There are 13 wheels in total. If $x$ is the number of bicycles, what is $x^2$?

**A.** 16
**B.** 12
**C.** 23
**D.** 13

**105.** A boy moves 4 miles south. Then he turns 90° to the left. He moves forward 6 miles. He turns 90° to the left. He moves forward 4 miles. How far is he now than from his starting point?

**E.** 4 miles
**F.** 3 miles
**G.** 6 miles
**H.** 5 miles

---

**106.**

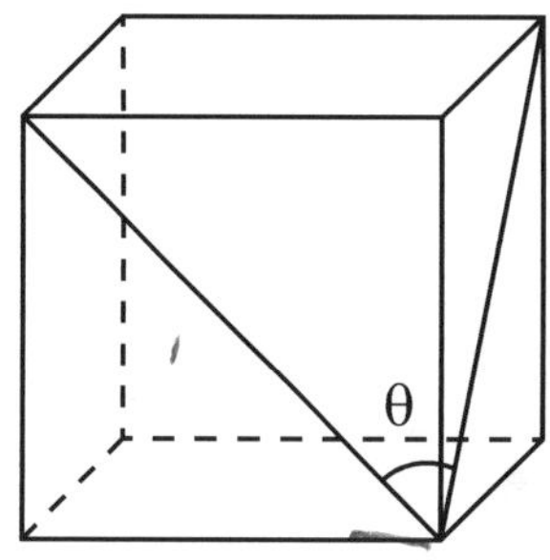


Note: The angle is between the two diagonal lines of the cube.

In the figure above, what is the angle, $\theta$?

**A.** 45°
**B.** 56°
**C.** 60°
**D.** 30°

**CONTINUE ON TO THE NEXT PAGE ➞**

**107.**

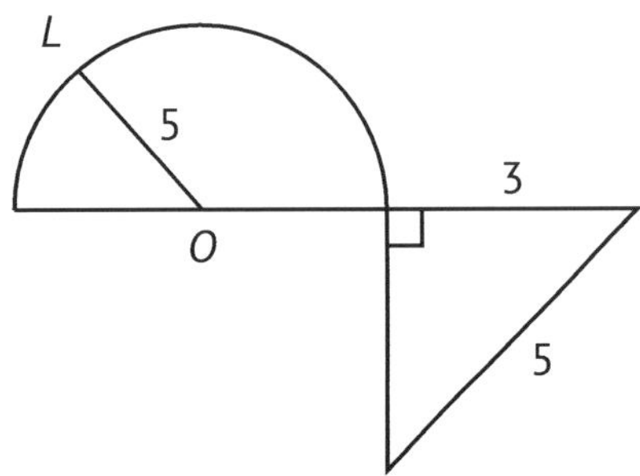


Figure not drawn to scale.

$\overline{OL}$ is the radius. What is the perimeter of the figure above?

**E.** $12 + 25\pi$
**F.** $12 + 5\pi$
**G.** $22 + 5\pi$
**H.** $22 + 25\pi$

---

**108.** What is $0.\overline{53} - 0.\overline{36}$?

**A.** $\frac{7}{50}$

**B.** $\frac{7}{99}$

**C.** $\frac{17}{99}$

**D.** $\frac{7}{9}$

**109.** The sum of two positive numbers is 6 times their difference. What is the reciprocal of the ratio of the larger number to the smaller?

**E.** $\frac{5}{7}$

**F.** $\frac{7}{5}$

**G.** $\frac{5}{2}$

**H.** $\frac{2}{5}$

---

**110.** The mean weekly salary of 9 teachers in a school is $1,000. If there are 9 teachers and 11 assistant principals and the mean weekly salary for assistant principals and teachers is $1,275, what is the mean salary of the assistant principals?

**A.** $1,100
**B.** $1,500
**C.** $1,137.50
**D.** $1,300

CONTINUE ON TO THE NEXT PAGE ➞

**111.** Given $x_n = x_{n-1} + x_{n-2}$, what is $\frac{x_6}{x_5}$, knowing that $x_4 = 3$ and $x_3 = 2$?

**E.** $\frac{3}{2}$
**F.** $\frac{5}{8}$
**G.** $\frac{8}{5}$
**H.** $\frac{2}{3}$

---

**112.** $f(x) = \frac{1-x}{1-x}$, which of the following set is not a possible domain for the given function?

**A.** $\{2, 3, 5\}$
**B.** $\{1, 0, 6\}$
**C.** $\{\pi, 2.17, 10\}$
**D.** $\{2\pi, \pi^2, 0.65\}$

**113.** The new video game console was priced at $400 when it was released last year. This year, the price decreased by 15% during the holiday sale period. The game manufacturer recently announced that the same console will be re-released with new updates and expanded functionality. The retail price will be 25% greater than the previous sale price. When the game console is re-released, what will be the retail price?

**E.** $360
**F.** $425
**G.** $380
**H.** $415

---

**114.** Jimmy stands at the window of an apartment which is 40 feet above the ground. He releases a glider which flies a straight path to his friend, who catches the glider 10 feet above the ground in the neighboring building. If the buildings are 40 feet apart, what is the distance traveled by the glider?

**A.** $10\sqrt{17}$ feet
**B.** $10\sqrt{41}$ feet
**C.** $40\sqrt{2}$ feet
**D.** 50 feet

**THIS IS THE END OF THE TEST. IF THERE IS TIME REMAINING,YOU MAY CHECK YOUR ANSWERS TO PART 1 OR PART 2**

# SHSAT PRACTICE TEST 1
## ANSWER KEY

### PART 1 (ENGLISH LANGUAGE ARTS)

**Revising/Editing**

1. **A**
2. **G**
3. **A**
4. **G**
5. **A**
6. **F**
7. **D**
8. **H**
9. **A**
10. **G**
11. **B**

**Reading Comprehension**

12. **E**
13. **D**
14. **E**
15. **B**
16. **E**
17. **D**
18. **H**
19. **B**
20. **H**
21. **A**
22. **F**
23. **C**
24. **H**
25. **A**
26. **F**
27. **A**
28. **G**
29. **C**
30. **F**
31. **D**
32. **G**
33. **D**
34. **G**
35. **A**
36. **G**
37. **B**
38. **F**
39. **A**
40. **E**
41. **D**
42. **E**
43. **C**
44. **F**
45. **D**
46. **E**
47. **A**
48. **H**
49. **C**
50. **E**
51. **B**
52. **G**
53. **C**
54. **F**
55. **C**
56. **F**
57. **D**

### PART 2 (MATHEMATICS)

**Math**

58. **$12.50**
59. **15°**
60. **89**
61. **5**
62. **11**
63. **G**
64. **D**
65. **H**
66. **B**
67. **H**
68. **B**
69. **E**
70. **D**
71. **G**
72. **D**
73. **G**
74. **A**
75. **G**
76. **D**
77. **G**
78. **A**
79. **H**
80. **D**
81. **E**
82. **C**
83. **E**
84. **D**
85. **G**
86. **C**
87. **H**
88. **B**
89. **F**
90. **B**
91. **F**
92. **B**
93. **G**
94. **C**
95. **G**
96. **A**
97. **G**
98. **B**
99. **G**
100. **C**
101. **F**
102. **C**
103. **F**
104. **A**
105. **G**
106. **C**
107. **G**
108. **C**
109. **E**
110. **B**
111. **G**
112. **B**
113. **F**
114. **D**

You can find detailed video explanations to each problem in the book by visiting:
**ArgoPrep.com/SHSAT**

# Practice Test 1 (Answers and Explanations)

**1. A** The phrase "which began in 1955" is a nonessential phrase whose main job is to provide extra information about "The Space Race." Nonessential phrases appearing in the middle of sentences should be separated with a comma on each side. Therefore, the sentence should read "The Space Race, which began in 1955, was a memorable part of the Cold War between the United States and the Soviet Union," making Answer A correct. Answers B, C, and D are all incorrect because each answer would create a sentence that was improperly spliced by commas.

**2. G** This sentence is consistently written using past tense verbs, which makes Answer G correct. Using a past tense verb is additionally important in this sentence because it clearly establishes that the events in question are matters of history and occurred in the definite past. For this reason, answers E and H are both incorrect because they would bring inconsistent present tense verbs into the sentence, creating confusion for the reader. Answer F is also incorrect because "that" and "which" are not interchangeable in this context, an error that could be quickly discovered by reading (or imagining reading) the sentence out loud.

**3. A** Even though it appears first, Sentence 1 is actually minimally related to the other sentences in the paragraph. Sentences 2 through 5 explain the process of dog show judging, describing it in a systematic way that immediately negates Sentence 1's assertion that the topic is hard to understand. A topic sentence like Sentence 1 undermines the reader's confidence that they'll explain an upcoming topic and should therefore be removed. Sentences 2, 3, and 4 all clearly connect to the same overarching topic (explaining how dog show judging works), and do so in a systematic, logical way so that removing any of them would weaken the paragraph overall.

**4. G** A dangling participle occurs when a modifying phrase at the beginning of a sentence has an unclear subject, creating reader confusion. The phrase "Appearing in over 150 cartoons between 1934 and 1959" in Sentence 4 is a dangling participle because it could be unclear to the reader that the phrase is describing Donald Duck, its intended subject who is not mentioned until later in the sentence. As written, the phrase could be interpreted by the reader to be describing any of the four characters previously mentioned (Mickey, Minnie, Pluto, and Goofy). Answer G is correct because Sentence 4 contains the dangling participle.

**5. A** Answer A is correct because, when speaking of the American Civil War in Standard American English, "Civil War" is considered a proper noun and therefore needs to be capitalized. Answer B is incorrect because "Confederate" is a proper adjective (meaning an adjective created from a proper noun, in this case "Confederacy" or "Confederate States of America"), and therefore must be capitalized. Answer C is incorrect because the term "forces" is a common noun referring to military troops generally, not any particular units, battalions, or agencies. Answer D is incorrect because "war" is a common noun when no particular war is specified. If the sentence read "... ending the Civil War," then that would be citing a specific, named war, creating a situation in which a proper noun is used. Since the sentence simply says "the war" in a nonspecific way, the common, non-capitalized form is used.

**6.** **F** "CDC" is used in sentence 9. Without the note at the beginning of the passage, readers unfamiliar with public health might not understand the meaning of the acronym.

**7.** **D** Of all the ideas in sentence 4, the concept of a "compromised immune system" is the most advanced and most likely for a reader to have questions about. Additionally, the writer would only have to add a few words to the existing sentence to provide an example. Answer A would provide the reader with interesting information, but it's not the best way to clarify the main ideas of the sentence. Answer B is incorrect because an explanation of immune function would require its own sentence (or paragraph). Answer C is incorrect because "infant" and "senior" are both commonly used terms that most readers would understand at least generally.

**8.** **H** Answer E is correct because two commas can be used to separate out a nonessential clause ("bonus information" that the sentence would be correct without). Answer G is also correct because dashes can be used to separate parenthetical information.

**9.** **A** "Bacteria" is a plural noun (the singular "bacterium" appears in sentence 1), so it takes the plural verb "do."

**10.** **G** The first use of "they" clearly refers to the word "hens," which immediately precedes it, making answers A and D incorrect. Answer G is the best choice because it clarifies that it is the Salmonella bacteria that are reproducing.

**11.** **B** "Additionally" is the best choice because the author is providing the reader with additional information about CDC guidance. "However" is incorrect because it implies the main idea in sentence 11 is contrary to that of sentence 10. "Subsequently" is incorrect because it implies a causal connection between sentences 10 and 11. "Unfortunately" is incorrect because there is nothing negative or bad about the temperature to which meat should be cooked.

## READING COMPREHENSION

### Passage 1 ("Despite being a notorious luddite and curmudgeon..."):

**12.** **E** Answer E is the best choice because all the content of the passage is connected to either the concept of scientific advances, philosophy's role in the world, and the intersection of those two disciplines. Therefore, it's accurate to say this passage explores the relationship between science and philosophy. Answer F is incorrect because, while nuclear war is mentioned as an access point, the topic is used to introduce the tricky relationship between science and philosophy, making Answer E a better choice. Answer G is incorrect because, while human fears and brokenness are a feature of the text, they speak to the importance of philosophy, making Answer E a better choice. Finally, Answer H is incorrect as well because the importance of technology is merely a background detail in this passage, which primarily seeks to connect the topics of philosophy and science, making Answer E the best overall choice.

**13. D** We can eliminate choices that don't make any sense compared to the text—both (B) and (C), since this text suggests philosophy has a positive impact for the world (and power isn't necessarily positive in this text). That leaves us with (A) and (D); certainly the author wants a hopeful future, but the question asks the *principle role* for the philosopher, so only (D) fully answers the question.

**14. E** (E) seems obviously to be true, but we'll work the rest of the answers to be sure. Philosophers have a prophetic role (F), but that is *not* a conclusion that we come to in the passage *because* we are at war with ourselves. It isn't true from the passage that (G) science and philosophy will always be at odds, and even though it is factually true that the text thinks the role of non-state actors in war-like violence is atrocious, that doesn't come from the fact that Marcel thinks we are at war with ourselves. So, only E can be true.

**15. B** The difficulty with this question is that each of the answer choices *is true*, according to the passage. Remember here that we have to figure out the answer choice that not only is true, but which addresses the question most fully. So, we have to turn to philosophy's call in the 4th paragraph, specifically. In the 4th paragraph, the author moves away from despair (A) and materialism (C), and does provide an example of good philosophy (D), but the best answer is (B), since the passage includes the prophetic nature of philosophy as philosophy's call.

**16. E** We have to isolate lines 32-36 to answer this question directly. The subject of those lines is the direct Marcel quote, which includes, "Hope consists in asserting that there is at the heart of being, beyond all data...." Immediately, you should be honing in on answer (E), since the quote indicates that the heart of being is tied up with hope, and can't be quantified through data. You can eliminate (H) since this idea isn't in the passage at all, as well as (F) because it contradicts the quote. Certainly, (G) is an important component of the passage, but is not the meaning of the Marcel quote.

**17. D** To properly solve this question, we need to isolate the lines indicated. The main idea of lines 23-25 hinges on the sentence preceding it, that the key difference between our modern age and those of previous times is that now, many people have access to weapons that can devastate the world. This isn't to show (A) that fear is easy to create, or (B), since fear is not better than suffering. (C) is a possibility, since fear is bound up with a commodification of ideas in the passage. But, the best answer is (D), because what is being commodified is fear. Commodification is the process of buying and selling, and this text suggests that many make money off of the fear others have of suffering.

**Passage 2 ("Edward's Castles in Wales"):**

**18. H** Answer H is the best choice because it conceptually connects the advantage of being surrounded on one or more sides by water to the advantages of arrow loops and high, thick walls described in Paragraph 3. The passage consistently reinforces that the goal of the Iron Ring was to create an easily-defended system of castles. Having water on at least one side of the castle limits access, making the castle still easier to defend. This idea connects to the strategic thinking outlined in the passage. Answer E is incorrect because the table clearly describes that several of these castles were located on coastlines, which would have saltwater. Saltwater is undrinkable, so it would not be correct to assume the use of water features had any connection to water cleanliness or access. Answer F is incorrect, although it is a somewhat reasonable inference, because it is not tied to any ideas in the passage (no mention of a navy or boats is ever mentioned). Answer H, on the other hand, is directly connected to the line of thinking described in Paragraph 3, making it a better choice that's tied directly to the text. Answer G is incorrect because the castles are clearly described in Paragraph 3 as being made from "thick, high stone walls." Since stone is unlikely to burn, the reader can infer that firefighting considerations had little to do with the location of Iron Ring castles.

**19. B** Answer B is the best choice because the content of Paragraph 1 describes when the castles discussed throughout the passage were created and explains the circumstances which led to their creation. This is valuable context for the reader that helps them feel oriented as they move into the main content of the passage. Answer A is incorrect because a "general introduction" would provide more specific previews of the content to follow in the body paragraphs of the passage. Answer B is a much better choice because it speaks to *how* the Paragraph introduces the passage rather than simply saying that it does. Answer C is incorrect because, while readers might find topics for further research in Paragraph 1, that is not the true purpose of the paragraph. The paragraph's role in providing context is far more important to the function and readability of the passage, making Answer B a better choice. Answer D is incorrect as well because Paragraph 1 focuses on a very specific time in history (1272 – 1307) and narrows to a clear focus (the castles built in Wales during that time). "An explanation fo the historic relationship between England, Scotland, and Wales" would be much more detailed and cover a much wider timeframe.

**20. H** Answer H is the best choice because the content Paragraph 1 strongly indicates that Edward I fought a series of wars against the Scottish and Welsh. The term "campaign" has a clear military context, and the phrase "...the people whose borders he invaded..." strongly suggests crossing boarders in an antagonistic manner, which indicates warfare. Answer E is incorrect because the castles were just a key aspect of the "campaign," not the entire campaign. Answer F is incorrect because it fails to appreciate the scope and scale of the conflict. Given the information in Paragraph 1 about crossing borders, tense histories, and tyranny, the reader should be able to infer that something much more complex and violent than an argument is taking place. Answer G is incorrect because, while the English were trying to "sabotage" the Scottish and Welsh in some sense, Answer H is still a better answer because "sabotage" would've just been part of the larger strategy of warfare and aggression.

**21. A** Answer A is the best choice because it is the only available answer that connects to specific details from the text. Paragraph 5 states that "...the original living quarters of the castles have not stood the test of time..." suggesting that even the four castles that make up the World Heritage Site are in somewhat rough shape. Additionally, the dates provided for Edward I's rule in Paragraph 1 (1272 to 1307) communicate that the castles in question are over 700 years old, making them high susceptible to decline. Based on these details, the reader can reasonably infer that many of the other castles in the Iron Ring are no longer in good enough condition to become key historical sites. Answer B is incorrect because there's nothing in the passage or table that communicates whether the four castles that make up the World Heritage Site were the first four. Answer C is incorrect because there's nothing in the passage or table to suggest definitively that those castles were the four most important. Answer D is incorrect because the passage gives no information whatsoever about the WHO or how they create sites. The only answer actually supported by the text is Answer A, making it the best choice.

**22. F** Answer F is the best choice because the table supplements the passage by providing specific details excluded from the passage, such as years in which the castles were built, and presenting information that further reinforces the similarity of the castles (such as the adjacency to water features). Answer E is incorrect because the table contains a great deal of information that's never mentioned in the passage (particularly the incorporation of water features and the emphasis on specific dates). It is not a simple reflection of the passage since it introduces additional interesting/important information. Answer G is incorrect because it has the relationship between the table and the passage completely backwards. The passage lays out the high-concept ideas and the table reinforces the passage by providing data that enhances the reader's understanding of the Iron Ring, making Answer F a better choice. Answer H is incorrect because, while the dates on the table certainly tell a narrative about when the "Iron Ring" strategy was being employed, the table focuses squarely on the qualities of the castles described in the passage rather than the chronology of the root conflict, making Answer F a better choice.

**23. C** Answer C is the best choice because the passage clearly states repeatedly that the English "Iron Ring" castles were built as part of Edward I's plan to conquer Wales. Given the fact that the table states that the building of two castles was "abandoned" (which is not to say "completed") in 1330, the reader can infer that these castles were no longer serving their intended purpose by the 1330s. That suggests that the military/economic conflict between England and Wales must have improved. Answer A is incorrect because Paragraph 1 of the passage states that Edward I only ruled until 1307, strongly suggesting he died more than 20 years before 1330. Answer B is incorrect because there is nothing in the text or the table about how technological advances affected castle design, meaning that Answer B has no textual basis. Answer D is incorrect because there are not enough data points in the table to make a sound conclusion about when concentric walls were most popular. All the data table tells us for sure is that, for one reason or another, Conwy castle did not use concentric walls.

**Passage 3 (Excerpt from Chapter VIII of Great Expectation by Charles Dickens...)**

**24. H** Answer H is the best choice, as it represents both the best understanding of the tone of the passage and the best interpretation of the narrator's descriptions. Pip describes Miss Havisham's room as being unnerving and her appearance as corpse-like, and his response to her request for him to play at the end of the passage demonstrates that he is in a very uncomfortable position that he's not sure how to handle. Answer E is incorrect because Pip is not feeling adventurous, outgoing, or excited at all, but is rather uncomfortable, concerned, and more than a little freaked out. Answer F is incorrect because it's only half-right. Pip is certainly nervous, but the passage does not make him seem excited at all; on the contrary, he seems excited to remove himself from the situation. Answer G is incorrect because it is only half-right as well. Pip is apprehensive in the passage, but he is not enthusiastic.

**25. A** Answer A is the best choice, as it displays the most complete understanding of the passage's opening lines. When Miss Havisham's clothing is being described, it says, "And she had a long white veil dependent from her hair, and she had bridal flowers in her hair, but her hair was white." If the reader visualizes the positioning of a bridal veil, it is clear that the veil was attached to or hanging from her hair. Answer B is incorrect because it provides the wrong definition for the word in this context. Answer C is incorrect because it conflates the word "dependent" with "dependable." Answer D is incorrect as well because it also fails to choose the correct, context-specific definition, but rather relying on the way the term is used within the tax code.

**26. F** Answer F is the best choice because Paragraph 1 clearly describes "Dresses, less splendid than the dress she wore, and half-packed trunks, were scattered about." The visual of dresses lying open on the floor communicates the idea that, while the room is filled with expensive objects, many of them are flung around the room carelessly. In fact, Miss Havisham's appearance – with only one shoe one – reinforces this idea that the room is a messy space. Answer E is incorrect because, although there are many expensive objects in the room, they are presented as being in a state of disarray, so they cannot be seen as regal. Answer G is incorrect because, while the room may have once been festive, it is now dark and creepy, as evidenced by Pip's descriptions. Answer H is incorrect as well because, while the room is in disarray, the house still stands and everything is structurally fine, it's just messy and neglected, making Answer F a better choice.

**27. A** Answer A is the best choice because it reflects both high-level comprehension of the details of the passage and an ability to think beyond the text. Miss Havisham wears a bridal dress, and yet, she lives as though she is in mourning. That is inherently ironic or paradoxical. Answer B is incorrect because, while Pip's description of her is grim, there's nothing ironic or paradoxical about her condition as an elderly woman. Answer C is incorrect because her wedding dress is described as "splendid," or at least something that used to be splendid. Answer D is incorrect because it sticks to the surface level detail (the faded color of the dress) without attaching any deeper meaning to it (the symbolism of her sadness), making Answer A a better, more complete choice.

**28. G** Answer G is the best choice because the final sentences of Paragraph 2 show Pip using previous experiences from his life to provide context for the scariness of Miss Havisham. He only mentions the fair to discuss the "ghastly waxwork" that reminds him of Miss Havisham. Answer E is incorrect because it is not as specific a choice as Answer G. It's fair to say Pip is horrified, but it's more accurate to say he's telling the story as a reference point for horribleness. Answers F and H are both incorrect because they fail to indentify that Pip mentions the fair to introduce a scary story, not a happy one. Both Answer F and Answer H mistakenly assume Pip had fun at the fair, but a closer examination of the text reveals he primarily remembers the scary wax statue, making Answer G a better choice.

**29. C** Answer C is the best choice because it draws on the many context clues in the passage to draw an educated inference. The faded wedding dress, her half-applied jewelry and footwear, and the phrase "(It made me think of the young man)" all suggest that Miss Havisham was traumatized by being left at the alter. Answer A is incorrect because the passage communicates that Miss Havisham is still rich (as she is covered in jewels and surrounded by dresses), she is just miserable. Answer B is incorrect because there's nothing at all in the passage about Miss Havisham having children or a family. Answer D is incorrect because there is nothing in the passage to suggest the existence of magic or curses in the world of the story.

**30. F** Answer F is the best choice because it correctly interprets the details of Paragraph 2. The text says, "I saw that the dress had been put upon the rounded figure of a young woman, and that the figure upon which it now hung loose had shrunk to skin and bone." Here, the narrator describes that the dress was fitted for Miss Havisham when she was young and curvaceous, but now she almost skeletally thin in her old age. Answer E is incorrect because it completely inverts the meaning of the passage to suggest she has gained weight rather than loosing it. Answer G is incorrect because Paragraph 1 definitively says, "her hair was white." Answer H is incorrect because, although Miss Havisham is described as somewhat corpselike by Pip, she is clearly still alive, as the passage includes some dialogue between her and Pip.

**31. D** Answer D is the best choice as it uses the context clues within the key sentence to correctly define "disputatious" as "argumentative." The sentence reads: "I think it will be conceded by my most disputatious reader, that she could hardly have directed an unfortunate boy to do anything in the wide world more difficult to be done under the circumstances" In the sentence, the narrator effectively says, "Even someone who disagrees with everything I say and do will agree it's creepy for someone to want to watch you play." In addition to the clues contained within the sentence, "disputatious" also contains the root word "dispute," which should be a hint to the reader. Answer A is incorrect because the sentence isn't just saying "Even the most skeptical person would agree..."; it's saying "Nobody could ever possibly argue this," which is a completely different idea. Answer D remains a better, more specific answer, given the context. Answer B is incorrect because, while Pip is probably frightened and horrified, he's accusing the reader of being prone to disagreeing or arguing with his course of action. Similarly, Answer C is incorrect because, while Pip might be sickened by what he sees at Miss Havisham's, in the sentence in question, he's directly accusing the reader of being argumentative or contrarian, making Answer D the best possible choice.

**32. G** Answer G is correct because it reflects the best understanding of the closing paragraphs of the passage. Miss Havisham commands Pip, "Play," and he says, "I think it will be conceded by my most disputatious reader, that she could hardly have directed an unfortunate boy to do anything in the wide world more difficult to be done under the circumstances." Here, he plainly states that he is massively uncomfortable with the idea of playing in front of Miss Havisham. Answers E is incorrect because the question clearly asks why Pip is uncomfortable at the *end* of the passage. The topic of discussion in the final paragraphs is his lack of comfort playing, whereas the descriptions of Miss Havisham as ugly come in the beginning and middle of the passage. Answer H is incorrect and represents a misunderstanding of the text, as Miss Havisham never kicks Pip out, but rather, commands him to stay and play.

**Passage 4 ("Ghost House...")**

**33. D** Answer D is the best choice because the poem contains a mixture of both uplifting and sad imagery throughout the text. There is a great deal of language that supports both emotions, as words like "lonely," "ruined," "aching heart," etc. speak to sadness while other words like "new," "healed," and the phrase "as sweet companions as might be had" all speak to positive, uplifting feelings. Given the balance of both emotions throughout the poem, Answer D is the best choice. Answer A is incorrect because it would be wrong to say the speaker is uniformly happy throughout the poem. Similarly, Answer B is incorrect because it would also be wrong to say the speaker is uniformly unhappy throughout the poem. Answer C is incorrect because, while the difficulty of controlling nature is certainly a theme in the poem, it is something the speaker actually seems to be impressed by rather than dismayed (which is most evident in Stanzas 2 and 3).

**34. G** Answer G is the best choice because Lines 3 and 4 of the poem clearly state, "...And left no trace but cellar walls, / And a cellar in which the daylight falls." This indicates that nothing of the above-ground structure of the house exists any longer, and only the cellar remains. Answers E, F, and H are all incorrect because they fail to identify the importance of the phrase "left no trace but cellar walls" in Line 3. No doors, roofs, or bedrooms are described at any point in the poem, so only Answer G reflects a proper understanding of the text.

**35. A** Answer A is the best choice because the content of Stanza 2 clearly focuses on how nature has reclaimed areas that had previously been cleared or managed by people. Several examples are provided, such as a new cluster of trees growing in the orchard, untrimmed apple trees with extensive amounts of dead branches, and the "healing" of the footpath to the well. All these images point at Answer A, as does the phrasing "come back to" in Line 7, which suggests something returning. Answer B is most likely a correct statement based on the content of the poem, but it is not as detailed and specific an answer to the question as Answer A, which explains specifically what the author is saying rather than simply providing a loose description of the situation, like Answer B does. Answer C is incorrect because there is nothing in the poem about the trees coming to life and performing the jobs of people. Answer D is incorrect and represents a major misunderstanding of the poem, as the speaker emphasizes repeatedly that things used to be more organized and controlled but are currently in a state of wildness and reclamation.

**36. G** Answer G is the best choice because it reflects the best overall understanding of Stanza 2, which emphasizes how wild growth is overtaking what was once a maintained farm or homestead. When the speaker says the footpath has been "healed," he or she means that the trail is no longer maintained and wild growth has reappeared, as though nature was "healing" the path (like the body heals a cut over time). Answers E and H are both incorrect because they take the word "healed" at its literal meanings rather than understanding it as a poetic metaphor for the growth of plants. Answer F is incorrect and conflates "heal" with "heel," a homophone with a completely different meaning.

**37.** **B** Answer B is the best choice because it correctly identifies the shift from night to day that takes place at the end of Stanza 3. Stanza 1 clearly establishes that the early part of the poem is describing "daylight" events (Line 4). However, when the speaker states, "Night comes; the black bats tumble and dart" (Line 15), it should be an indicator to the reader that the poem has shifted from day to night. In Line 21, the speaker also mentions the presence of a star in the sky, further cementing that it is night. Answer A is incorrect because it reverses the order of the events, incorrectly putting night first. Answers C and D are both incorrect because they suggest a time or era change in the poem, which never occurs. While it is true that the events of the present and past seem to bleed together at times in the poem, there is no official "time travel" moment in which the speaker shifts from describing the past to describing the future or vise versa.

**38.** **F** Answer F is the best choice because the words "cluck" and "flutter" in Line 17 clearly describe the actions of a bird. The description of bats in Line 15 also indicates to the reader that the speaker is discussing different animals that are flying around, which is suggestive of birds as well. Answers E and H are both incorrect because the speaker does not describe any people at all in the poem, but rather animals, plants, stones, and other non-human objects. Answer G is incorrect because the speaker clearly describes the sights and sounds of a bird in Lines 16-17, which suggests that the whippoorwill is a bird flying around in the trees, not the trees themselves.

**39.** **A** Answer A is the best choice because there are a number of hints in Stanzas 5 and 6 that suggest they take place in a cemetery. The description of "stones" that "doubtless bear names" that are now obscured by moss suggests that the speaker is describing old tombstones. The speaker also describes others in this place as "mute folk" who are "tireless... but slow and sad," which is suggestive of ghosts or zombies. Cumulatively, these details suggest a cemetery. Answer B is incorrect because the field is described in Stanza 2, not the portion of the poem the question focuses on. Answer C is incorrect because there is no mention of a quarry anywhere in the poem, and the only detail supporting a quarry is the existence of rocks. Answer D is incorrect because, while the lines do mention a tree, the description of the area is far from playful and actually evokes darker imagery, making a cemetery much more likely than a child's playground.

**40.** **E** Answer E is the best choice because it is the only answer that gives voice to a specific example from the poem in which the absence of humans from the homestead or farm has negatively impacted nature or wildlife. The dust-baths that toads no longer receive (Line 14) are the only

aspect of human inhabitants that the speaker identifies as missing. Answer F is incorrect because the passage makes it clear that the whippoorwills still "shout / And hush and cluck and flutter about" (Lines 16-17), so the lack of an audience does not seem to prevent the birds from singing. Answer G is incorrect because the "out of control" growth of the vines would be a problem for humans, not for nature. From nature's perspective, the massive growth of the vines is good and healthy. Answer H is incorrect as well because the speaker clearly states the orchard is still thriving by saying, "The orchard tree has grown one copse of new wood and old," suggesting the trees are still growing a producing fruit, even though people are no longer maintaining and harvesting them.

**41. D** Answer D is the best choice because there are many hints throughout the poem that the speaker is either dead or reflecting back on his or her life as he or she is dying. The nostalgic/melancholy descriptions of the former home which now lays in ruins (Stanzas 1-2), the transition from light to darkness (between Stanza 3 and Stanza 4), and the description of the graveyard filled with "mute folk... who share the unlit place with me" (Stanza 5) all point to the idea that the speaker of the poem is either dead or transitioning toward death. Answers A and C are incorrect because, although its strongly suggested the speaker grew up living a rural lifestyle, there are no specific discussions of economics or where the speaker lived after the house mentioned in the poem. Answer B is incorrect because there is no mention anywhere of rebuilding the house; on the contrary, it seems like a foregone conclusion that the property's decline/reclamation will continue.

**Passage 5 ("The phrase "it's a witch hunt"...")**

**42. E** Focus in here on the *main idea* of this passage. Although answers (F) and (H) are correct, according to the text –(G) is too vague to be correct–neither are the main point. Instead, they support the main idea, which is (E).

**43. C** To answer correctly, you need to identify context clues in the first paragraph where the author invokes *Harry Potter*. At that moment in the passage, the author compares our love for the fictional wizard with the witch hunting done hundreds of years ago. That means (D) has to be eliminated as irrelevant. (A) is outside of the scope of our fascination with *Harry Potter*, and (B) is not supported by any of this passage at all. That leaves (C) as the best response, especially as a comparison point between two cultural moments in American history.

**44. F** Here, we have to make inferences based on the facts presented in the passage. We do not know from the passage whether accused individuals did participate in witchcraft (although we are led to doubt that they did), so we can eliminate both (E) and (G). The text actually argues against (H) by explicitly including the torture of men in its evaluation of the subject. (F) is the best inference, because the passage suggests that the accused did not actually tell the truth when, under torture, they said they were witches and wizards.

**45. D** The key to the 3rd paragraph instance of "insect manifestations" is the idea that a *spiritual flaw* in the accused was the source of the plague. This fact allows us to eliminate (C). But, (A), (B), and (D) all relate to the spiritual, so we have to look further to see the relationship between the loss of crops and the spiritual. (A) is not the best choice, because if it was true that God was displeased, the early Americans would be upset with *God* over the loss of the crops, and not their neighbors. (B) is true, given the other information in the passage, but that relationship is drawn in paragraph two, and not paragraph three. Rather, the 3rd paragraph suggests that the insect manifestations are one example of a physical event—insects wiping out crops—occurring because of a spiritual flaw. That means (D) is the best answer.

**46. E** Even if you don't know what a "Catch-22" is, you can use context clues to figure out the meaning in line 24. The phrase cannot simply mean that the accused would experience a consequence (F), because the Catch-22 is about evidence and not consequences. (G) would be a Catch-22 for the judges, but line 24's Catch-22 is not about the judges, but about the results for the accused. Unfortunately for the accused, (H) is not correct, because none of the evidence presented was allowed to exonerate them, *because of the Catch-22*, provided in (E), that regardless of the evidence presented, they were going to be cast as witches and put to death.

**47. A** Answer A is the best choice because Paragraph 3 of the passage states, "Whenever natural or other disasters occurred that made life unsustainable, colonists usually looked for a supernatural cause." That means that the colonists' lack of scientific knowledge or ability to understand their hardship was the root cause of the witch hunts. Answer B is incorrect because there's nothing in the passage about people abandoning religion in the New World. If anything, the existence of superstitious witch hunts suggests that colonists were very steadfast in their religious beliefs. Answer C is incorrect, although it is a true statement based on the passage, because the wording of the question asks, "What most directly enabled witch hunts to occur?" The fact that all evidence was turned against the accused demonstrates why witch hunt trials almost always ended in a guilty verdict, but Answer C does little to explain what phenomena led to the occurrence of witch hunts. Finally, Answer D is similarly incorrect, although based in the passage, because the use of public execution has nothing to do with the witch hunts happening in the first place. Only Answer D makes sense because it represents text-based root causes that led to the witch hunts occurring.

### Passage 6: ("The Evolving Classroom")

**48. H** Answer H is the best choice because, in this context, uniform means "the same." The way the paragraph goes on to describe a single, unified approach to education should be a major hint to the reader. Answer E is incorrect because it misinterprets "uniform" to mean a specific outfit or set of clothing, which is not the case here. Answer F is incorrect because it fails to recognize the sameness described in Paragraphs 1 and 2. Answer G is incorrect because, while the approach described is arguably dated an unengaging, that is not the concept being accessed by the word "uniform." Since "uniform" is used to emphasize consistent sameness, only Answer H makes sense.

**49. C** Answer C is the best choice because the content of Paragraphs 1 and 2 repeatedly stresses that teacher needs are placed first under the traditional model, while students are expected to obey and follow directions. Answer A is incorrect because Paragraph 1 states traditional teachers were "applying the same expectations across the board," which means that everybody would be expected to at least attempt a homework assignment, regardless of their comfort level with the material. Answer B is incorrect because, in a traditional classroom, the teacher would pace lessons based on the needs of the overall group. If one individual student had a large number of questions, the teacher might not be interested in answering every single one of them because they might feel they don't apply to the group as a hole. Individual student needs are not a value of traditional education, as is laid out in the passage. Answer D is incorrect as well and shows a major misunderstanding of the passage, as the traditional model does not embrace technology.

**50. E** Answer E is the best choice because Paragraphs 3 and 4 both describe how traditionalists do not embrace technology in the classroom. The line, "Traditionalists, on the other hand, believe that over-reliance on tech inhibits students' ability to build their own knowledge and skills and does little to prepare them for the realities of being an adult in the real world" from Paragraph 4 should be a major hint to the reader. Answers F, G, and H are all incorrect because they assume traditionalists would embrace or like tech-enabled learning, which is contrary to the content of Paragraphs 1-4.

**51. B** Answer B is the best choice because the closing sentence of Paragraph 4 clearly states: "Traditionalists, on the other hand, believe that over-reliance on tech inhibits students' ability to build their own knowledge and skills and does little to prepare them for the realities of being an adult in the real world." This sentence directly connects the concept of a "traditionalist" to the belief that computers actually damage students' educational experience. Answer A is incorrect because it represents the viewpoint of a "tech advocate," as described in Paragraph 4 rather than that of a traditionalist. Answer C is incorrect because it fails to identify the main idea that "traditionalists" are typically against a high level of tech infusion in the classroom. Similarly, Answer D is also incorrect because it fundamentally fails to recognize that Paragraph 4 establishes "traditionalists" as being against classroom tech integration.

**52. G** Answer G is the best choice because Paragraphs 3 and 4 describe how tech advocates believe integrating technology can revolutionize education. The line, "Tech advocates stress that computers and internet technology allow students to learn at their own pace in an environment that makes them feel comfortable" from Paragraph 4 should have been a major hint to the reader. Answers E and F are both incorrect because they assume tech advocates are against integrating technology, which shows a flawed understanding of the passage as a whole and the word "advocate" in particular. Answer H is also incorrect with no basis in the text because there is nothing in the passage about shortening the number of years students spend in school.

**53. C** Answer C is the best choice because Paragraphs 4 and 5 both detail how there is no unified approach to classroom teaching today, with educations using a variety of approaches. Answer A is incorrect because it's clear in Paragraphs 3-5 that some teachers embrace technology. Answer B is incorrect because Paragraphs 1-5 make it clear that some traditionalists have not yet accepted tech in the classroom. Answer D is incorrect because it does not provide enough detail about the nature of the two camps and how they relate to educational approaches. Without further explanation, Answer C is still the much better choice.

**54. F** Answer F is the best choice because the tone of Paragraphs 1-2 as well as Paragraph 5 clearly establishes that the author is in favor of adopting technology into the classroom over the traditional model. In Paragraphs 1 and 2, the author concludes with a sentence about the problems of the traditional system. In Paragraph 1, he or she writes, "... the result was often a classroom in which a few students succeeded while many others were left by the wayside." In Paragraph 2, he or she continues, "...the model worked well for some students but had minimal positive impacts for others." These two quotes both show that Answer E is incorrect, as the author clearly is not on the side of traditional educators. Answer G is incorrect because Paragraph 5 clearly states, "We must learn from what worked in the past while integrating the best of our new technologies to create an education system that reflects our modern world and the needs of our communities." This shows the author is, in fact, in support of adopting technology. Answer H is incorrect because a close reading of the passage clearly reveals that the author is dissatisfied with the traditional model and believes in tech adoption.

**55. C** Answer C is the best choice because when the text says, "...some believe it took power and responsibility away from the teacher and cheapened the educational experience for teachers," it's generally saying that some teachers argued that technology made education worse. Answer A is incorrect because it misinterprets "cheap" to mean inexpensive, which is a legitimate definition, but not the proper choice in the is context. Answer B is incorrect and misinterprets "cheap" to mean "unfair," as it is sometimes used in popular culture, which is not the proper choice in this context. Answer D is incorrect as well because there is no question at any point in the passage that education is extremely important; rather, the word "cheapened" is used to mean "made worse," so Answer C remains the better overall choice.

**56. F** Answer F is the best choice because the word "Regrettably" signals to the reader that the author endorses neither point of view expressed in Paragraph 4 and rather sees the conflict between them as part of the larger problem. This clarifies for the reader that the author is exploring what he or she feels is an important problem or issue from an outside perspective rather than simply endorsing one of the presented viewpoints wholesale. Answer E is incorrect because "Regrettably" does little to signpost the transition into a conclusion, making Answer F a much better answer. Answer G is incorrect because, while the author clearly believes the system needs to be improved, there is no sense of total despair that everything is ruined or unsalvageable at any point in the passage. What's regrettable is that all teachers can't get on the same page; the author is not saying the system has regrettably fallen apart. Answer H is incorrect because the author is not trying to sway the readers emotionally, but rather expressing his or her own frustration with the conflict described in the previous paragraph, making Answer F a better choice.

**57.** **D** Answer D is the best choice because "traditionalists" and "progressive educators" are the two opposing groups of teachers discussed in Paragraphs 3 and 4. To answer the question, the reader first must determine that "antonym" means "opposite" and then dive back through the text beginning at the cited line to find like and unlike terms. Answer A is incorrect because, while it's true that not all teachers are progressives, it's inaccurate to say "not all teachers" is an antonym for "progressive educators." Answer B is incorrect as well because it simply identifies that there are two "camps" or schools of thought on this issue rather than identifying the one of them that is not "progressive." Answer C is incorrect because "progressive educators" and "tech advocates" are used as synonyms in the passage; the two terms are used to discuss the same group.

**58.** **$12.5**

This problem tests your understanding of how to work with percentages. A 20% discount is calculated as 100% – 20% = 80%. You are therefore being told that the sale price of $10.00 is **80%** of the original price (*n*). 80% is represented as .80 in decimal form. You can set up the calculation as:

| | |
|---|---|
| $\$10.00 = .80 \times n$ | given |
| $\frac{\$10.00}{.80} = n = \$12.50$ | divide both sides by .80 and calculate |

**59.** **15°**

If you draw a diagram you can see that the interior angles of triangle *PQR* is 3*x*, 5*x* and 4*x* respectively. We know that the sum of the interior angles in a triangle is 180 so we can set up an equation:

| | |
|---|---|
| $3x + 5x + 4x = 180.$ | simplify like terms |
| $12x = 180.$ | solve for *x* |
| $x = 15°$ | |

**60.** **89**

This problem tests your ability to set up an average calculation. In order to find the average of the test scores, use the formula:

$$\frac{\text{sum of test scores}}{\text{number of tests}} = \text{test score average}$$

The number of tests is 4 and the desired average is 85. You have 3 of the test scores, and are asked to find the fourth to achieve this average. So let *x* be the fourth test score.

Now write your equation:

| | |
|---|---|
| $\frac{x + 80 + 83 + 88}{4} = 85$ | given |
| $x + 80 + 83 + 88 = 85(4)$ | multiply both sides by 4 |
| $x + 251 = 340$ | calculate |
| $x = 340 - 251 = 89$ | solve for *x* |

The answer is 89.

**61.** **5**

This problem tests your skills at algebraic manipulation.

| | |
|---|---|
| $2(x - 3) + 9 = 4x - 7$ | given |
| $2x - 6 + 9 = 4x - 7$ | distributive |
| $-6 + 9 + 7 = 4x - 2x$ | isolate your *x* terms by adding 7 – 2*x* to both sides |
| $10 = 2x$ | simplify |
| $5 = x$ | divide both sides by 5 |

The correct answer choice is **5**. NOTE: Be sure to substitute 5 as the value of *x* back into the original equation in order to verify your work.

**62.** **11**

This problem asks you to solve the given equation for the value of $n$.

| | |
|---|---|
| $\frac{n+4}{10} = \frac{n-8}{2}$ | given |
| $n + 4 = 5(n - 8)$ | multiply both sides by 10 |
| $n + 4 = 5n - 40$ | distribute |
| $44 = 4n$ | simplify by adding $40 - n$ to both sides |

**63.** **G** $(\frac{7}{20}) \bullet (\frac{5}{5}) = (\frac{35}{100}) = 0.35$

**64.** **D** $500{,}000 + 400 + 5 = 500{,}405$

**65.** **H** Substitute and perform the respective operations.
$x = 4$
$y = 3$
$(4 + 3)^2 = (7)^2 = 49$

**66.** **B** $(\sqrt{144})(\sqrt{16}) = (12)(4) = 48$

**67.** **H** One approach to this type of problem is to look at the two equations and see what is common. Both equations have the word **Knot** in common.

Manipulate the equation so that both equations have the same number of Knots. You can do this by dividing the second equation by 4, to get
$\frac{1}{2}$ Shings = 1 Knot.

Therefore, 3 Vines = $\frac{1}{2}$ Shings.

Since you are trying to find out how many Shings are in 9 Vines, simply multiply the equation by 3 to get 9 Vines = $\frac{3}{2}$ Shings.

**68.** **B** Simplifying the first number gives us 1. So, the question is asking for what number is between 1 and 4. As a general rule for these types of problems, we must divide the difference of the numbers by 2 and add that value to the original number. This gives us:
$(\frac{4-1}{2}) + 1 = (\frac{1.5}{2}) + 1 = 2.5$

**69.** **E** $\measuredangle GLQ = 150°$ since angles on a straight line add up to 180°.

$\measuredangle LGQ = y$ since vertical angles are always equal. Using this and the fact that the interior angles of a triangle add up to 180°, find $z$ in terms of $y$.

$y + 150° + z = 180°$ and by solving for $z$, you get
$z = 30 - y$, which is answer choice E.

**70.** **D** Use PEMDAS (Parenthesis, Exponents, Multiplication, Division, Addition, Subtraction).

**71. G** You must remember the formula for the area of a circle and square. Given that the side of the square is, "*s*" and the radius and diameter of the circle are "*r*" and "*O*" respectively, we have:

A square = $s^2$

A circle= $(\pi)(r^2) = (\pi)(\frac{D^2}{4})$, since the radius is half the diameter (substitute the radius for $(\frac{D}{2})$.

We are given that the diameter is 10, and the areas are equal, so after setting both areas equal to each other, we have:

$s^2 = (\pi)(\frac{10^2}{4}) = 25\pi$, and solving for *s*, we get:

$s = 5\sqrt{\pi}$, which is answer choice G.

**72. D** Use distributive property
$4a(3b - 6) = 12ab - 24a$

**73. G** The trick here is to realize that 39 is the product of 13 and 3. Using that, we have:

$(\frac{(-3 \cdot 13)^2}{13^3}) = (\frac{(-3)^2 \cdot (13)^2}{13^3}) =$

$9 \cdot (\frac{13^2}{13^3}) = \frac{9}{13}$, which is answer choice G.

**74. A** If 1 inch represents 20 ft, you can square both sides to get 1 square inch equals 400 ft squared. We want to find how many square inches are in one square foot. Using this information, we can write a proportion:

$(\frac{1in^2}{400ft^2}) = (\frac{xin^2}{1ft^2})$

and solving for *x*, we get:

$x = \frac{1}{400} = 0.0025$, which is answer choice A.

**75. G** List the prime factors for each number

2240 : $2^6 \cdot 5 \cdot 7$

3360: $2^5 \cdot 3 \cdot 5 \cdot 7$

Multiply the factors that are common in both sets.

$2^5 \cdot 5 \cdot 7 = 1{,}120$, which is answer choice G.

**76. D** 50% of 2*y* is half of 2*y*, which is just *y*. So we have: *y* = 12, so then the square of y is 144. The answer choice is D.

**77. G** We know that:

$(a + b) = 150°$ because of the rule that an exterior angle of a triangle is equal to the two opposite interior angles *(a* and *b)*. And, simplifying:

$(\frac{a^2 - b^2}{a - b}) = (\frac{(a - b)(a + b)}{a - b}) = (a + b) =$ 150°, which is answer choice, G.

**78. A** If $y = (\frac{3}{4})$ then $y^2 = (\frac{9}{16})$ which means x must equal 1 for $xy^2$ to equal $(\frac{9}{16})$.

Now we have to solve for $(x - 4)$. Since we know the value of $x$ is 1, we can substitute the value of $x$ in to get (1-4) which is equals to -3.

The answer choice is A.

**79. H** One way to solve this problem would be to use hypothetical values and test which answer choice always results in an even number. Another way to solve the problem is by realizing if an integer is divided or multiplied by 2, it will always result in an even number. If you look carefully at answer choice H, the variable P is being multiplied by 2 and in this case also being divided by 2. Try to plug in any value for P, and using the expression in answer choice H will always result in an even integer.

**80. D** If the diameter is P, then we know that the radius is $(\frac{P}{2})$ and using the given information, we can substitute and find that the area is just:

$A = \pi(\frac{P}{2})^2 = \pi(\frac{P^2}{4}) = 2\pi$,

which is answer choice D.

**81. E** We must find what $N$ is first.

Simplifying, we find that $N = 16$ and so the polygon has (16 – 10) sides or 6 sides. Now we need to find the total number of degrees in this hexagon, and then divide by 6. We can use the formula:

Total number of Degrees = $(N - 2)180°$, and so when $N = 6$, this simplifies to 720°. Dividing this by 6, gives us:

120° for each interior angle. The answer is E.

**82. C** It is important to note that this is a variation of a 3, 4, 5 right triangle. The fact that there is $\pi$ multiplied with 4 and 5 does not change this relationship. Knowing this, the perimeter is $12\pi$. This perimeter equals to the circumference of a circle, which gives way to this equation:

$12\pi = 2(\pi)r$, where $r$ is the radius. Solving for the radius gives: $r = 6$, so the answer choice is C.

**83. E** In this problem, we just need to plug into the formula. We get:

$(\frac{7}{14}) \cdot (\frac{7}{14})$,

which simplifies to a quarter, which is 0.25, or answer choice E.

**84. D** Since 25 can only go into 1200, K is the answer choice.

**85. G** We can simplify each fraction to a mixed number. Then, we are just looking for the positive integers that are bigger than $-2\frac{1}{3}$ and less than $2\frac{1}{2}$. If we wrote all the integers between those two numbers, we would get −2, −1, 0, 1, 2. Eliminating the negative ones gives us: 1 and 2, which is 2 integers giving us answer choice G.

**86. C** The formula of the perimeter of a rectangle is $2l + 2w$, where $l$ and $w$ are the length and width respectively. They give us the width as 18 inches and the perimeter at 80 inches. Which means when we solve for the length, we get 22 inches.

To get the area, we just need to multiply the length and width together, so we get 18in × 22in, which is 396 sq. inches or answer choice C.

**87. H** All we need to do is plug in $x = -3$ in the first expression. We then get $b = 7 \bullet |0|$, which is just 0.

The answer is H.

**88. B** Here, we need to find the sum: 1 + 2 + 3 + 4 + ... + 100.

Well, if we take the first and last number and add them, we get 101. If we take the 2nd and 99th number and add them, we get 101. If we continue this pattern, we will always get 101. So, we have 50 pairs of numbers that add up to 101 and we are adding them all up. So the answer is:

$50 \bullet 101 = 5050$, or answer choice B.

**89. F** Let's say that the original population was $Y$. Then we have that $1.1Y = 55$ because we increase $Y$ by 10%.

Solving for $Y$ gives us 50, or answer choice F.

**90. B** The volume of a rectangular solid is the product of the length, the width and the height.

$V = lwh$. We are given $l = 10$, so all we need is, $wh$. We can find this by taking the cube root of both sides of the equation below which is given to us:

$w^3h^3 = 27$ becomes $wh = 3$, so then:

$lwh = 30$, which is answer choice B.

**91. F** The key here is to realize that there are two radii of the circle drawn, $OA$ and OC. All radii are equal, so $x = 7$. The answer is F.

**92. B** Using the Pythagorean Theorem, we get,

$x + 100 = 432$

$x = 332$

$x = \sqrt{332} = 2\sqrt{83}$, which is answer choice B.

**93. G** Another way of writing $A$ is $A = 3(rh)^2$, and if we increase $(rh)$ by 100%, we are actually doubling it. We can label the new A as A'. Since we doubled (rh) we can represent A' now as $A' = 3(2rh)^2 = 3 \bullet 4(rh)^2 = 12(rh)^2$ which is 4 times as large as the original A. The answer is G.

**94. C** We have,

$x^a = x^{\frac{p}{q}}$, which means $a = \frac{p}{q}$ so then,

$\frac{p^2}{q^2} = (\frac{p}{q})^2 = a^2$

The answer is C.

**95. G** The only common value(s) in both sets is 2. So the answer is {2} which is answer choice G.

**96. A** This can be simplified to

$2\sqrt{75} - \sqrt{25}\sqrt{3} = 10\sqrt{3} - 5\sqrt{3} = 5\sqrt{3}$

The answer is A.

**97. G** This can be reduced to 0.00345, which in scientific notation is $3.45 \times 10^{-3}$.

The answer is G.

**98. B** Since −23 is odd, we must use the second rule. The answer is 4(−23) = −92.

The answer is B.

**99. G** The maximum value for $y$ occurs when

$x$ is positive and large. This value of $x$ is $(\frac{1}{2})$ giving us $y = (\frac{1}{8})$.

The answer is G.

**100. C** By simplifying, we get, $\frac{x^3z}{y}$ or answer C.

**101. F** This is a special 3, 4, 5 right triangle. The length of $RL$ must be 5. The answer is F.

**102. C** If the sum of 2 angles equals the third, then the only value of the third angle that is possible is 90°.

One way of thinking of this is to realize that the sum of the third angle and the sum of the other two angles must be 180°.

The answer is C.

**103. F** Bridget and Anthony take turns watching T.V. with 4 hour intervals. We progress in the order of Bridget (B), Anthony (A), Bridget (B), Anthony (A), etc. We can write a list where we know that Anthony's 3rd turn is at 10PM.

B-
A-
B-
A-
B-
A-10PM

Now, we can work backwards to find Bridget's time for her second turn. That turns out to be at 10 AM.

The answer is F.

**104. A** We can write a system of two linear equations. The first represents the number of bikes and unicycles as $x$ and $y$ respectively as a sum. The second represents the number of wheels for each bike and unicycle as a sum.

$x + y = 9$
$2x + y = 13$

Solving these equations by either substitution or addition, we get that $x = 4$. So, $x^2 = 16$

The answer is A.

**105. G** The direction of his path is shown below.

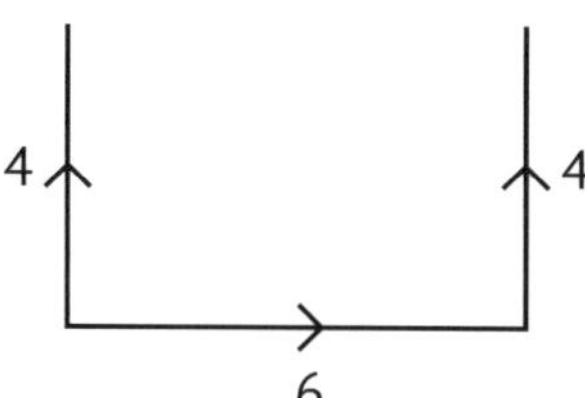


He is 6 miles from his starting point, which is answer choice G.

**106. C** Since all the diagonals of a cube are equal,the angle is part of an equilateral triangle. So the angle measure is 60°.

The answer is C.

**107. G** We must know the equation for the circumference of a semi-circle, which is simply half the circumference of a circle. We must also realize that the triangle is a special 3, 4, 5 right triangle. Adding the circumference of the semicircle, with the diameter of the semicircle and the perimeter of the triangle, we get the perimeter as $22 + 5\pi$.

The answer is G.

**108. C** You must know that these repeating decimals can be simplified to, $\frac{53}{99}$, $\frac{36}{99}$ respectively. Subtracting these two repeating decimals, we get, $\frac{17}{99}$, which is answer choice C.

**109. E** We can set up equation as follows, $(x + y) = 6(x - y)$ and solving for the ratio gives us: $\frac{x}{y} = \frac{7}{5}$
The question asks for the reciprocal of the ratio of the larger number to the smaller number. Therefore, the reciprocal of $\frac{7}{5}$ is $\frac{5}{7}$. The answer is E.

**110. B** We are given the mean weekly salary for the 9 teachers as $1,000. If $x$ is the total for the salary of the teachers, then we have:

$$\frac{x}{9} = 1000$$

Now let's let $y$ equal the total salary of the 11 assistant principals.

Then we have:

$$\frac{x + y}{9 + 11} = \frac{x + y}{20} = \frac{9000 + y}{20} = 1275$$

and solving for $y$, we get, $y = 16{,}500$. The mean weekly salary of the 11 assistant principals is just y divided by 11, giving $1,500 or answer choice B.

**111. G** The recursion formula just requires us to take the two previous terms to get the next. So the 5th term is the sum of the 4th and 3rd terms, or 5. The 6th term is the sum of the 5th and 4th terms or 8.

The 6th term divided by the 5th term is $(\frac{8}{5})$ or answer G.

**112. B** We cannot divide by 0, so the set that is not a possible domain is any set with the value 1 in it , or answer B.

**113. F** This problem tests your understanding of increasing and decreasing percentages. You are given an initial value of $400, followed by a decrease of 15%, which is then followed by an increase of 25%. You need to provide the final value. To calculate a change by percentage, use the formula: *initial value* • (1 - *percentage change*) Your two changes are −15% and −25%, respectively, so you can write out the entire expression as:

$$\$400 \times (1 - 15\%) \times (1 - 25\%) =$$
$$\$400(.85)(1.25) = \$425.$$

The answer choice is F.

**114. D** This problem tests your ability to set up a geometric word problem. The given data lays out the dimensions of a right triangle. The clue you are given is that the start of the glider is 40 feet above the ground (distance to the ground is **always** measured along a line perpendicular to the ground). The glider starts its journey 40 feet above the ground and ends 10 feet above ground. Therefore, the height of the triangle is 30 feet. You are given the distance between the two buildings as 40 feet. You thus have the two legs of the triangle at 30 and 40. You should recognize this as a multiple of the Pythagorean Theorem proportions of 3:4:5 and so arrive at 50 for the last side. The calculation is:

$a^2 + b^2 = c^2$ Pythagorean Theorem
$30^2 + 40^2 = c^2$ substitution
$900 + 1600 = c^2$ calculate
$2500 = c^2$ simplify
$\sqrt{2500} = c = 50$ calculate

The correct answer is D. REMEMBER: The negative result of the square root can be ignored in this instance because we are looking for a distance, which will always be a positive number.

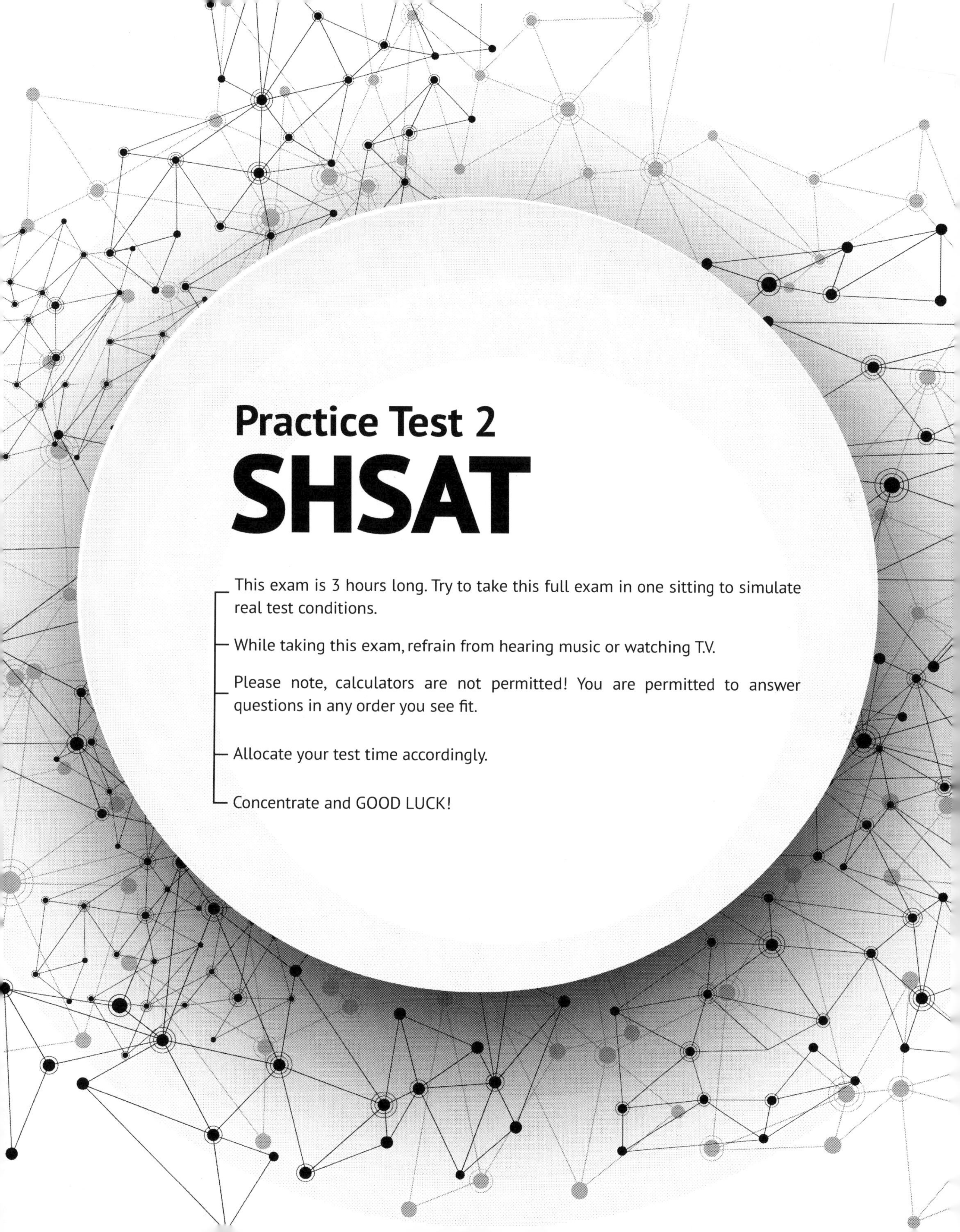

# Practice Test 2

# SHSAT

- This exam is 3 hours long. Try to take this full exam in one sitting to simulate real test conditions.
- While taking this exam, refrain from hearing music or watching T.V.
- Please note, calculators are not permitted! You are permitted to answer questions in any order you see fit.
- Allocate your test time accordingly.
- Concentrate and GOOD LUCK!

**You can find detailed video explanations to each problem in the book by visiting: ArgoPrep.com**

# SHSAT PRACTICE TEST 2
## ANSWER SHEET

### ENGLISH LANGUAGE ARTS

| | | | | |
|---|---|---|---|---|
| 1. | A | B | C | D |
| 2. | E | F | G | H |
| 3. | A | B | C | D |
| 4. | E | F | G | H |
| 5. | A | B | C | D |
| 6. | E | F | G | H |
| 7. | A | B | C | D |
| 8. | E | F | G | H |
| 9. | A | B | C | D |
| 10. | E | F | G | H |
| 11. | A | B | C | D |
| 12. | E | F | G | H |
| 13. | A | B | C | D |
| 14. | E | F | G | H |
| 15. | A | B | C | D |
| 16. | E | F | G | H |
| 17. | A | B | C | D |
| 18. | E | F | G | H |
| 19. | A | B | C | D |
| 20. | E | F | G | H |
| 21. | A | B | C | D |
| 22. | E | F | G | H |
| 23. | A | B | C | D |
| 24. | E | F | G | H |
| 25. | A | B | C | D |
| 26. | E | F | G | H |
| 27. | A | B | C | D |
| 28. | E | F | G | H |
| 29. | A | B | C | D |
| 30. | E | F | G | H |
| 31. | A | B | C | D |
| 32. | E | F | G | H |
| 33. | A | B | C | D |
| 34. | E | F | G | H |
| 35. | A | B | C | D |
| 36. | E | F | G | H |
| 37. | A | B | C | D |
| 38. | E | F | G | H |
| 39. | A | B | C | D |
| 40. | E | F | G | H |
| 41. | A | B | C | D |
| 42. | E | F | G | H |
| 43. | A | B | C | D |
| 44. | E | F | G | H |
| 45. | A | B | C | D |
| 46. | E | F | G | H |
| 47. | A | B | C | D |
| 48. | E | F | G | H |
| 49. | A | B | C | D |
| 50. | E | F | G | H |
| 51. | A | B | C | D |
| 52. | E | F | G | H |
| 53. | A | B | C | D |
| 54. | E | F | G | H |
| 55. | A | B | C | D |
| 56. | E | F | G | H |
| 57. | A | B | C | D |

### MATHEMATICS

| | | | | |
|---|---|---|---|---|
| 63. | E | F | G | H |
| 64. | A | B | C | D |
| 65. | E | F | G | H |
| 66 | A | B | C | D |
| 67. | E | F | G | H |
| 68. | A | B | C | D |
| 69. | E | F | G | H |
| 70. | A | B | C | D |
| 71. | E | F | G | H |
| 72. | A | B | C | D |
| 73. | E | F | G | H |
| 74 | A | B | C | D |
| 75. | E | F | G | H |
| 76. | A | B | C | D |
| 77. | E | F | G | H |
| 78. | A | B | C | D |
| 79. | E | F | G | H |
| 80. | A | B | C | D |
| 81. | E | F | G | H |
| 82. | A | B | C | D |
| 83. | E | F | G | H |
| 84 | A | B | C | D |
| 85. | E | F | G | H |
| 86. | A | B | C | D |
| 87. | E | F | G | H |
| 88. | A | B | C | D |
| 89. | E | F | G | H |
| 90. | A | B | C | D |
| 91. | E | F | G | H |
| 92. | A | B | C | D |
| 93. | E | F | G | H |
| 94. | A | B | C | D |
| 95. | E | F | G | H |
| 96. | A | B | C | D |
| 97. | E | F | G | H |
| 98. | A | B | C | D |
| 99. | E | F | G | H |
| 100. | A | B | C | D |
| 101. | E | F | G | H |
| 102. | A | B | C | D |
| 103. | E | F | G | H |
| 104. | A | B | C | D |
| 105. | E | F | G | H |
| 106. | A | B | C | D |
| 107. | E | F | G | H |
| 108. | A | B | C | D |
| 109. | E | F | G | H |
| 110. | A | B | C | D |
| 111. | E | F | G | H |
| 112. | A | B | C | D |
| 113. | E | F | G | H |
| 114. | A | B | C | D |

### MATHEMATICS (GRID IN)

58

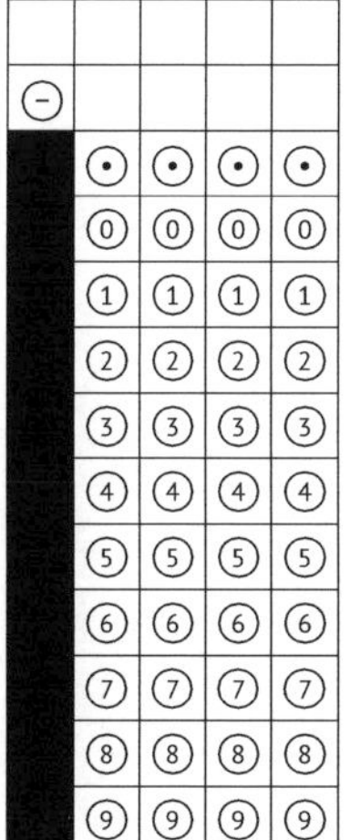


59

60

61

62

ARGOPREP
ARGOPREP.COM/SHSAT

**DIRECTIONS:** For questions 1 to 5, you will be asked to recognize and correct errors in sentences or short paragraphs.

**1.** Read this sentence.

> Try not to become a man of success Einstein said, but rather try to become a man of value.

Which revision uses proper punctuation to format the quotation?

**A.** "Try not to become a man of success" Einstein said, "but rather try to become a man of value.

**B.** "Try not to become a man of success Einstein said," but rather "try to become a man of value."

**C.** "Try not to become a man of success" Einstein said, "but rather try to become a man of value."

**D.** "Try not to become a man of success," Einstein said, "but rather try to become a man of value."

---

**2.** Read this sentence.

> Although he was considered handsome and athletic in his youth, King Henry VIII of England become overweight because he enjoyed huge meals of many courses made from exotic ingredients.

Which edit should be made to correct the sentence?

**E.** Change **was considered** to **is considered**

**F.** Change **become** to **became**

**G.** Change **enjoyed** to is **enjoying**

**H.** Change **made from** to **make from**

---

**3.** Read this paragraph.

> (1) Sir Isaac Newton made a number of key discoveries in the seventeenth century that earned him a reputation as the father of modern physics. (2) In 1687, he publishes his three laws of motion, which formed the foundation for the study of mechanics. (3) His first law stated that an object at rest will tend to stay at rest until acted upon by an outside force, while an object in motion will tend to stay in motion until acted upon by an outside force. (4) Newton's second law explained for the first time how to calculate the amount of force an object generates. (5) The often-quoted third law established that for every action, there is an equal and opposite reaction.

Which sentence in the paragraph should be revised for verb tense consistency?

**A.** Sentence 1

**B.** Sentence 2

**C.** Sentence 3

**D.** Sentence 4

CONTINUE ON TO THE NEXT PAGE ➡

**4.** Read this paragraph.

(1) The tale of Grover Cleveland's secret surgery is one of the most notorious stories about any American president. (2) Shortly after beginning his second term, Cleveland took a fishing trip on a private boat from New York to Cape Cod with a group of friends. (3) A secret kept from almost the entire country, Cleveland had a cancerous tumor in his mouth that needed to be removed. (4) A team of six surgeons worked to excise the mass below the deck of the moving ship. (5) Although the procedure was a total success, most Americans didn't hear the true reason for Cleveland's bizarre fishing trip for more than twenty years.

Which sentence in the paragraph should be revised to correct a dangling modifier?

**E.** Sentence 1
**F.** Sentence 2
**G.** Sentence 3
**H.** Sentence 4

**5.** Read this sentence.

The fifteenth century Danish astronomer Tycho Brache was famous for both the accuracy of his planetary observations and his artificial nose, which he needed because of a dueling injury.

Which revision of this sentence eliminates the use of "to be" verbs?

**A.** The fifteenth century Danish astronomer Tycho Brahe was well known for both the accuracy of his planetary observations and his artificial nose, which he needed because of a dueling injury.
**B.** The fifteenth century Danish astronomer Tycho Brache was famous for the accuracy of his planetary observations as well as his artificial nose, which he needed because of a dueling injury.
**C.** Fifteenth century Danish astronomer Tycho Brahe's accurate planetary observations and artificial nose, which he needed because of a dueling injury, both made him a well-known figure.
**D.** Fifteenth century Danish astronomer Tycho Brahe's accurate planetary observations and artificial nose, which he needed because of a dueling injury, were both features that made him a well-known figure.

**CONTINUE ON TO THE NEXT PAGE ➞**

**DIRECTIONS:** Read the passage below to answer questions 6 to 11. The questions will focus on improving the writing quality of the passage to follow the conventions of standard written English.

---

**William Shakespeare**

(1) Even though he's been dead more than 400 years, William Shakespeare remains one of the most famous Englishmen in history. (2) He also remains one of the most widely read authors in the world, and his plays are still performed regularly. (3) Although much of the details of his personal life are lost to history, his 38 plays and 154 sonnets suggest that Shakespeare was a sensitive, witty man filled with love for life and language. (4) Many of his most famous plays and poems are still taught in schools around the world, so most people have at least some experience reading Shakespeare.

(5) Shakespeare's comedies often dealt with cases of mistaken identity, including situations where poor characters were mistaken for rich characters and female characters were mistaken for male characters. (6) To Shakespeare's audience, these storylines were funny because the social structure of the time was very rigid, and there was a common belief that people needed to know and stay in their place. (7) Shakespeare also explored how human flaws and weaknesses can create sadness and misery in his tragedies. (8) The main characters in Shakespeare's tragedies were generally short-sighted, vain, jealous, or mean-spirited, and those traits most often lead to their death or ruin. (9) Shakespeare's histories told romanticized versions of the lives of the English monarchs, which gave his audience a sense of history and national pride at a time when many common people could not read.

(10) Many of Shakespeare's plays were originally performed for the first time in London's Globe Theatre, which was built in 1599. (11) The Globe was one of the few places in England where people of different social classes were entertained together. (12) Middle and upper class patrons could buy cushioned seats that were protected from the rain, while the poor could afford to stand on the floor under the stage. (13) Even Queen Elizabeth I, arguably the most powerful figure of Shakespeare's time, enjoyed his plays. (14) Out of respect to his wide audience, Shakespeare ensured there were jokes and situations in his plays that people of all social classes and professions could relate to. (15) This ability to reach people of all different backgrounds and circumstances is one of the qualities that has kept Shakespeare's work relevant for so many centuries.

CONTINUE ON TO THE NEXT PAGE ➡

6. What is the best way to combine sentences 1 and 2 to avoid repetition?

   E. Even though he's been dead more than 400 years, William Shakespeare remains one of the most famous Englishmen in history, and he also remains one of the most widely read authors in the world, and his plays are still performed regularly.
   F. Even though he's been dead more than 400 years, William Shakespeare remains one of the most famous Englishmen in history; he also remains one of the most widely read authors in the world, and his plays are still performed regularly.
   G. Even though he's been dead more than 400 years, William Shakespeare remains one of the most famous Englishmen in history as well as one of the most widely read authors in the world, with plays that are still performed regularly.
   H. Even though he's been dead more than 400 years, William Shakespeare remains one of the most famous Englishmen in history, and in spite of the fact that he is dead, he is one of the most widely read authors in the world, and his plays are still performed regularly.

---

7. Which edit is needed to correct sentence 3?

   A. Change **much** to **many**
   B. Change **are** to **is**
   C. Change **suggest** to **suggests**
   D. Change **was** to **is**

---

8. Which revision of sentence 4 eliminates the use of passive voice?

   E. Many of his most famous plays and poems are still taught in schools around the world, so most people have read Shakespeare.
   F. Most people have at least some experience reading Shakespeare because his plays and poems are still taught in schools around the world.
   G. Most people have at least some experience reading Shakespeare because his most famous plays and poems are staples of high school literature classes.
   H. Most people have at least some experience reading Shakespeare because they are taught his most famous plays and poems in school.

---

9. Which sentence would best precede sentence 5 to serve as a topic sentence?

   A. Shakespeare's comedies are regarded as some of the funniest plays of all time.
   B. Throughout his career, Shakespeare wrote many different plays.
   C. All of Shakespeare's plays are widely regarded as works of genius.
   D. Shakespeare focused on three different kinds of plays: comedies, tragedies, and histories.

**CONTINUE ON TO THE NEXT PAGE ➞**

**10.** How could sentence 7 best be revised to clarify ideas and prevent reader confusion?

**E.** Shakespeare explored how human flaws and weaknesses can create sadness and misery throughout his tragic plays.
**F.** In his tragedies, Shakespeare explored how human flaws and weaknesses can create sadness and misery.
**G.** At the same time, Shakespeare explored how human flaws and weaknesses can create sadness and misery in his tragedies.
**H.** Another group of Shakespeare plays explored how human flaws and weaknesses can create sadness and misery: the tragedies.

---

**11.** Which edit is needed to correct sentence 8?

**A.** Change **were** to **are**
**B.** Change **those** to **these**
**C.** Change **lead** to **led**
**D.** Change **their** to **they're**

---

CONTINUE ON TO THE NEXT PAGE ➞

**DIRECTIONS:** Read the passage below to answer questions 12 to 20. The questions will focus on improving the writing quality of the passage to follow the conventions of standard written English.

---

**Excerpt from "The Lumber Room" by H.H. Munro**

Often and often Nicholas had pictured to himself what the lumber-room might be like, that region that was so carefully sealed from youthful eyes and concerning which no questions were ever answered. It came up to his expectations. In the first place it was large and dimly lit, one high window opening onto the forbidden garden being its only source of illumination. In the second place it was a storehouse of unimagined treasures. The aunt-by-assertion was one of those people who think that things spoil by use and consign them to dust and damp by way of preserving them. Such parts of the house as Nicholas knew best were rather bare and cheerless, but here there were wonderful things for the eye to feast on. First and foremost there was a piece of framed tapestry that was evidently meant to be a fire-screen. To Nicholas it was a living, breathing story; he sat down on a roll of Indian hangings, glowing in wonderful colours beneath a layer of dust, and took in all the details of the tapestry picture. A man, dressed in the hunting costume of some remote period, had just transfixed a stag with an arrow; it could not have been a difficult shot because the stag was only one or two paces away from him; in the thickly growing vegetation that the picture suggested it would not have been difficult to creep up to a feeding stag, and the two spotted dogs that were springing forward to join in the chase had evidently been trained to keep to heel till the arrow was discharged. That part of the picture was simple, if interesting, but did the huntsman see, what Nicholas saw, that four galloping wolves were coming in his direction through the wood? There might be more than four of them hidden behind the trees, and in any case would the man and his dogs be able to cope with the four wolves if they made an attack? The man had only two arrows left in his quiver, and he might miss with one or both of them; all one knew about his skill in shooting was that he could hit a large stag at a ridiculously short range. Nicholas sat for many golden minutes revolving the possibilities of the scene; he was inclined to think that there were more than four wolves and that the man and his dogs were in a tight corner.

But there were other objects of delight and interest claiming his instant attention; there were quaint twisted candlesticks in the shape of snakes, and a teapot fashioned like a china duck, out of whose open beak the tea was supposed to come. How dull and shapeless the nursery teapot seemed in comparison! And there was a carved sandalwood box packed tight with aromatic cotton-wool, and between the layers of cotton-wool were little brass figures, hump-necked bulls, and peacocks and goblins, delightful to see and to handle. Less promising in appearance was a large square book with plain black covers; Nicholas peeped into it,

CONTINUE ON TO THE NEXT PAGE →

and, behold, it was full of coloured pictures of birds. And such birds! In the garden, and in the lanes when he went for a walk, Nicholas came across a few birds, of which the largest were an occasional magpie or wood-pigeons here were herons and bustards, kites, toucans, tiger-bitterns, brush turkeys, ibises, golden pheasants, a whole portrait gallery of undreamed-of creatures.

---

**12.** Based on the passage, what is a "lumber-room?"

- **E.** A secret garden
- **F.** A storage room
- **G.** An area for storing wood and other heavy supplies
- **H.** A playroom

---

**13.** Based on the passage, how is the lumber-room different from the rest of the house?

- **A.** The lumber-room is messy and disorganized, whereas the rest of the house is extremely clean and well decorated.
- **B.** The lumber-room is filled with natural light, whereas the rest of the house uses gas or electric lights.
- **C.** The lumber-room is filled with birds and dogs, whereas there are no animals allowed in the rest of the house.
- **D.** The lumber-room is filled with exotic and exciting objects, whereas the rest of the house is decorated in a very boring manner.

---

**14.** What does the author mean when he writes, "The aunt-by-assertion was one of those people who think that things spoil by use and consign them to dust and damp by way of preserving them?"

- **E.** The character in question believes that leaving nice things out where people can see and handle them will lead to them being ruined.
- **F.** The character in question believes that storing objects in damp, dusty areas will ruin them.
- **G.** The character in question believes it is important to preserve family heirlooms and important treasures for future generations.
- **H.** The character in question believes that family heirlooms and important treasures should be on display for everybody to see.

---

**15.** What attracts Nicholas to the fire screen tapestry?

- **A.** It is the most colorful object in the lumber-room
- **B.** It is the only object in the room that contains pictures of people or animals
- **C.** It tells a visual, action-packed story
- **D.** He recognizes that it is depicting a story he is already familiar with

---

**CONTINUE ON TO THE NEXT PAGE ➞**

**16.** How does the description of the tapestry reveal aspects of Nicholas' personality?

- **E.** The violence depicted in the tapestry reveals that Nicholas is a deeply troubled child.
- **F.** The descriptions of the number of arrows and difficulty of the hunt being depicted display Nicholas' knack for observation and sense of humor.
- **G.** The subject matter of the tapestry displays Nicholas' love for animals and nature.
- **H.** The subject matter of the tapestry displays Nicholas' love for hunting and shooting.

---

**17.** What is the best definition for "transfixed" as it is used in Paragraph 1?

- **A.** Transformed
- **B.** Repaired
- **C.** Located
- **D.** Pierced

---

**18.** What critical observation does Nicholas make about the hunter in the tapestry?

- **E.** His dogs are remarkably well-trained
- **F.** He is a very good marksman
- **G.** He has no way to bring the stag out of the forest
- **H.** He could soon be overcome by wolves

**19.** Which is the safest inference about the previous owners of the house in which this story takes place?

- **A.** They believed all the family treasures should be kept in the lumber-room.
- **B.** They traveled extensively around the world.
- **C.** They were wealthy and enjoyed collecting art.
- **D.** They would have disagreed with keeping all the family treasures hidden in the lumber-room.

---

**20.** How is the bird book Nicholas finds thematically similar to the lumber-room itself?

- **E.** The lumber-room used to be an indoor aviary for birds.
- **F.** It appears to be ordinary on the outside, but it is actually filled with incredible wonders.
- **G.** There are several other descriptions of bird-like objects in the lumber-room, including a duck-shaped teapot.
- **H.** The birds in the book are colorful and exciting, as is the lumber-room.

**CONTINUE ON TO THE NEXT PAGE ➡**

## Sonnet 18
### By William Shakespeare

Shall I compare thee to a summer's day?
Thou art more lovely and more temperate:
Rough winds do shake the darling buds of May,
And summer's lease hath all too short a date;

Sometime too hot the eye of heaven shines,
And often is his gold complexion dimm'd;
And every fair from fair sometime declines,
By chance or nature's changing course untrimm'd;

But thy eternal summer shall not fade,
Nor lose possession of that fair thou ow'st;
Nor shall death brag thou wander'st in his shade,
When in eternal lines to time thou grow'st:

So long as men can breathe or eyes can see,
So long lives this, and this gives life to thee.

---

**21.** What is the central metaphor of this poem?

- **A.** Comparing the destructive power of time to the changing of the seasons
- **B.** Comparing the power of the sun to that of celestial gods
- **C.** Comparing someone's beauty to that of summer
- **D.** Comparing the heat of summer to the pain of death

**22.** What is the best definition for "lease" as it is used in Line 4?

- **E.** A term or span of time
- **F.** An agreement to rent a building or parcel of land
- **G.** Enthusiasm or zest
- **H.** Having the smallest amount of something

---

**23.** What is "the eye of heaven" (Line 5) that's described in the poem?

- **A.** God
- **B.** The sun
- **C.** Gold
- **D.** Summer

---

**24.** What distinction does the speaker make between the beauty of summer and the beauty of the person to whom the poem is addressed?

- **E.** The speaker says the beauty of summer is hot like the sun, but the beauty of the person to whom the poem is addressed is cool like shade.
- **F.** The speaker says the beauty of summer is bright like the sun, but the beauty of the person to whom the poem is addressed is dark and mysterious.
- **G.** The speaker says the beauty of the person to whom the poem is addressed is fleeting, but the beauty of summer is eternal.
- **H.** The speaker says that the beauty of summer is fleeting, but the beauty of the person to whom the poem is addressed is eternal.

**CONTINUE ON TO THE NEXT PAGE ➞**

**25.** According to the speaker, what makes the sun inferior to the person about whom the poem is written?

- **A.** The sun's hot rays are painful, but the person about whom the poem is written always makes the speaker feel comfortable
- **B.** The sun's warmth can be undone by rough winds, but nothing can stop the beauty of the person about whom the poem is written
- **C.** The sun is not as consistently lovely as the person about whom the poem is written
- **D.** The sun is unreachable up in the heavens, but the person about whom the poem is written feels close to the speaker

---

**26.** Which poetic or literary device does the speaker use in Line 11?

- **E.** Personification
- **F.** Alliteration
- **G.** Irony
- **H.** Paradox

---

**27.** Which of these other words or phrases the speaker uses means the same thing as "poem?"

- **A.** Eye of heaven (Line 5)
- **B.** Nature's changing course (Line 8)
- **C.** Eternal summer (Line 9)
- **D.** Eternal lines (Line 12)

**28.** What favor does the speaker believe he or she has done for the person about whom the poem is written?

- **E.** The speaker has saved the person about whom the poem is written from death
- **F.** The speaker has given the person about whom the poem is written a legacy that will last forever
- **G.** The speaker has exposed the person about whom the poem is written to a much wider audience
- **H.** The speaker has made each day of the person about whom the poem is written's life as joyous and beautiful as summer

---

**29.** Which of these patterns best describes the rhyme scheme of the poem?

- **A.** ABAB CDCD EFEF GG
- **B.** AABB CCDD EEFF GG
- **C.** ABCD EFGA BCDE FG
- **D.** ABBA CDDC EFFE GG

**CONTINUE ON TO THE NEXT PAGE ➞**

# READING COMPREHENSION
## Practice Test 2

**DIRECTIONS:** Analyze the passages below, and answer the commensurate questions. Only use information provided within the passage for your answers. There is only one answer for each question.

### The Communist Manifesto

It's hard to argue that any publication was more influential or talked-about than *The Communist Manifesto* between 1850 and 2000. At under 50 pages, the text of the *Manifesto* is brief, but it contains ideas so powerful and controversial that much of the twentieth century became a struggle between those who agreed and disagreed with what it said. Its authors, the German philosophers Karl Marx and Friedrich Engels, wrote the *Manifesto* to reflect the beliefs of the Communist League, a European political party they both belonged to that rejected the traditional social and governmental order of the world.

Essentially, *The Communist Manifesto* had two main themes: class struggle and proper land usage. The former is better remembered today, but the latter was also crucial to Marx and Engels' original vision. The *Manifesto* claimed that all history was a series of cycles of struggle related to social class. Marx and Engels essentially believed that every society or form of government to date had been about establishing a social order in which a few people had all the wealth, status, and property at the expense of the masses, who had to do most of the real work with minimal reward. Eventually, the masses would organize and overthrow these oppressive regimes, but a new one would rise just as quickly.

Although many at the time believed the growth of capitalism had eliminated or lessened these inequalities, Marx and Engels believed it was just the same game of haves and have-nots under a new name. Instead, they sought to propose a different way of doing things. *The Communist Manifesto* was their way of articulating how they believed a perfect society that valued equality, fairness, and the common good would function. One of the key pillars of their proposed society was the abolition of private property. They believed all land and materials should belong to the group as a whole and be distributed in a way that ensured everyone's needs were met. In short, there would be no rich people and no poor people.

Marx and Engels also wanted to ensure that land was put to use in a way that benefitted all, not just some. They believed that large, government-run farms should grow food to feed all the people in a way that make sure everyone could eat and no stores were over-charging people for food. They also thought the government should build factories and other facilities that would provide people with work and a way to contribute meaningfully to their society.

Basically, the Communist League believed that nobody should be born powerful through inheritance or able to obtain enough money to use it to create an unfair advantage or manipulate

**CONTINUE ON TO THE NEXT PAGE ➡**

people. This was one of the most controversial ideas in the entire *Manifesto* because Europe (and much of the rest of the world) had traditionally been ruled by aristocrats and successful business owners, neither of whom were eager to suddenly have less money or influence. Marx and Engels were essentially calling for regular working class people, who had formed a silent global majority for millennia, to rise up and take power away from the elites who had traditionally run the world. The *Manifesto's* final line, "Workers of the world, unite!" was a scary call to action for the rich and powerful of the late nineteenth century.

Throughout the twentieth century, many countries became Communist states. In 1917, there was an uprising in Russia, which would eventually lead to the creation of the Soviet Union or U.S.S.R. The Soviet Union, which was built on the ideals of *The Communist Manifesto,* would grow into one of the great super powers of the 1900s. China, Cuba, and Vietnam all became Communist countries as well, although in each case, there were bloody revolutions where many people lost their lives. Ultimately, all these countries failed to accomplish the perfectly fair, equal society outlined by Marx and Engels. The challenge of using public land and communal farms to feed the entire population, for example, proved challenging in almost every attempt, and there were frequently famines in Communist countries. Even though the vision of *The Communist Manifesto* was never fully realized, it remains one of the most important texts in recent history.

**30.** Based on the text, which of these statements is most likely to be true?

**E.** The Communist League was created after the publication of *The Communist Manifesto*
**F.** The Communist League existed before *The Communist Manifesto*
**G.** Marx and Engels created The Communist League when they wrote *The Communist Manifesto*
**H.** The Communist League was a fictional political party Marx and Engels created to describe their ideals.

---

**31.** In what ways did Marx and Engels see history as a "series of cycles?"

**A.** They believed history repeated itself in that people were always seeking power, money, and influence in ways that harmed or ignored the majority of society.
**B.** They believed each era was markedly different from the one before it, but eventually things would return to being the way they were in the past.
**C.** They believed history was a series of different attempts to create a perfect society, each of which had failed so far.
**D.** They believed those who were poor would gradually become the rich and powerful over time.

**CONTINUE ON TO THE NEXT PAGE ➞**

**32.** Which of these statements would a member of the Communist League most likely agree with?

- **E.** Some people will always be rich and some people will always be poor.
- **F.** If you work hard, you can become wealthy no matter how poor you started out.
- **G.** All societies are flawed in similar ways, but if we have patience and belief in ourselves as people, things will work out over time.
- **H.** The excess of wealth and property that the very rich have is directly connected to the lack of wealth and property that most working class people have.

---

**33.** What was Marx and Engels' relationship to capitalism?

- **A.** They recognized capitalism as an improvement over monarchy and other forms of hereditary aristocracy but felt it didn't go far enough.
- **B.** They believed there was some validity to the principles of capitalism but wanted to improve upon it.
- **C.** They rejected capitalism completely because they saw it as the same oppressive social order with a new coat of paint.
- **D.** They were open minded about capitalism but believed the playing field needed to be leveled or reset first by abolishing private property.

**34.** Why was the abolition of private property a controversial idea?

- **E.** *The Communist Manifesto* didn't provide any explanation of where food or jobs would come from if there were no private farms or businesses.
- **F.** People who were used to possessing a great deal of land, property, and money wouldn't want to give those things up and become like everybody else.
- **G.** If private property were abolished, average people would have even less than they had before.
- **H.** Marx and Engels were rich themselves, so people thought they were being hypocrites by proposing that people should have to give up their wealth.

---

**35.** Which of these would not be a reason the slogan "Workers of the world unite!" might have inspired fear in global elites?

- **A.** It could be interpreted as a call for workers to organize to negotiate better pay and benefits from their employers.
- **B.** It could be interpreted as a call for the working class to rise up and overthrow their governments.
- **C.** It could be interpreted as a call for workers to recognize they were all on the same side of a crucially important "us-them" conflict.
- **D.** It could be interpreted as a call for the working class to try to ascend the social ladder through aggressive business tactics.

**CONTINUE ON TO THE NEXT PAGE ➞**

## Brewing

One of the most misunderstood and misused products in this country is beer. It's hard to watch a sports game or late night TV show without seeing several commercials for various brands of beer. Beer, however, is so much more than a drink for adults at cookouts; it's a beverage that was crucial to human history and the development of the way we live today. The process of creating beer, known as brewing, has been handed down and refined for more than 6,000 years. This makes brewing a fascinating combination of science, art, and social impact.

For millennia, brewers have made beer using the same basic steps, although technology and innovation have refined the process over time. Beer has four basic ingredients: water, malted grain, yeast, and hops. First, brewers boil the grain in the water to extract starches and sugars. This creates a sweet liquid known as "wort." Hops, which look like small green pinecones, are added to the wort to mellow out the sweetness and add piney or citrusy bitter flavors. Then, the wort is cooled to room temperature and the brewers add yeast, which begins the process of fermentation.

Brewer's yeast contains millions of single-celled microscopic fungi that consume the sugar and oxygen within the wort and convert them into alcohol and carbon dioxide. This process goes on for several days, gradually transforming the wort into something known as "green beer." Green beer is almost finished but often contains bizarre off-flavors like bubble gum or cotton candy. To clean up these undesirable tastes, brewers cool the green beer to begin a process known as "conditioning." During conditioning, most of the yeast goes dormant and falls to the bottom of the tank, where it can be poured off. Meanwhile, the small amount of very strong yeast that survived the temperature drop goes to work reconsuming the off-flavors. After several more days, the beer can be filtered and placed into bottles, kegs, or cans for storage.

Today, most people associate beer with adults having a barbecue or watching a sports game, but brewing has been vitally important to civilization in many different ways throughout history. Brewing was one of the innovations that made it safer for people to populate in cities around shared water sources. Drinking downstream from a bustling, over-populated town or drawing water from a village well people threw trash into could easily make someone deathly ill. Beer, however, was free from most of the bacteria and germs within the water because the wort had been boiled. The completed product stayed fresh and safe to consume for weeks because of the natural preservative quality of alcohol. In this way, beer was actually crucial to public health.

In medieval Europe, for example, sanitation was so poor and water-borne disease so prevalent that the Catholic Church actively discouraged their monks, priests, and nuns from drinking water. In response, the monasteries and abbeys where these religious communities lived became some of the first large-scale brewing operations. Initially, the brewer monks created just enough beer for their own needs and those of the religious communities around them, but soon they learned they could support their lifestyle financially and aid the health their flocks by selling their beer to taverns and alehouses where local laypeople could drink safe, nourishing beer as well.

CONTINUE ON TO THE NEXT PAGE ➞

Today, tens of millions of people of diverse cultures around the world enjoy beer each day. Unfortunately, however, our society often fails to contextualize beer properly, which has led to many people over-indulging or acting irresponsibly or dangerously as a result. If more folks understood the complex, artisanal process of brewing and beer's true origins as a means to preserve clean water, perhaps there would be more respect for the process and less emphasis on the intoxicating qualities of alcohol.

**36.** Which of these best describes the purpose of the passage?

- **E.** To convince readers to drink less beer
- **F.** To explain and contextualize beer to provide readers with a deeper understanding
- **G.** To describe how beer is connected to the development of cities
- **H.** To clarify the science behind brewing

---

**37.** Which of these is the best definition for "wort" as it is used in Paragraph 2 of the passage?

- **A.** Young beer that has not been fermented yet
- **B.** A bump that you get on your hand or finger
- **C.** An ingredient that makes the beer less sweet
- **D.** An off-flavor that must be removed from the beer during conditioning

**38.** Based on the passage, which of these would be most likely to happen if brewers did not cool their green beer properly?

- **E.** Off-flavors such as cotton candy or bubblegum would remain
- **F.** The yeast would not convert the sugar from the grain into alcohol
- **G.** The beer would spoil more quickly
- **H.** The beer would be impossible to store in bottles, cans, or kegs

---

**39.** How was brewing important to the ability of people to live in cities?

- **A.** When people first started gathering in cities, there were few jobs. Brewing was one of the first industries that began providing people with work.
- **B.** Brewing was a complex process that helped people think about principles of science. This led to cultures developing faster.
- **C.** Living in large groups often led to fouling crucial water sources. Brewing that water into beer made it drinkable again.
- **D.** People had not yet developed the technology to dig proper wells. Therefore, water was in short supply and people needed to drink beer instead.

CONTINUE ON TO THE NEXT PAGE →

**40.** Which of these is the best definition for "flock" as it is used in Paragraph 5 of the passage?

- **E.** A collection of sheep or similar herding animals
- **F.** To cover something in artificial snow
- **G.** A group of monks or nuns
- **H.** A group of religious followers or congregants

---

**41.** Based on the passage, why might people drink more responsibly if they understood the true origins of beer?

- **A.** They would understand that brewing is an artisanal process that's been passed down for millennia.
- **B.** They would understand that people originally brewed beer as a means of survival, not to have a good time.
- **C.** They would understand that beer is actually made from grain and fungus.
- **D.** They would understand that beer had been important to the survival of religious communities in the middle ages.

---

**42.** What is the main purpose of Paragraph 4's first sentence?

- **E.** To explain to the reader how beer is used today
- **F.** To introduce the historical connection between beer and sports
- **G.** To connect the content of the passage to experiences the reader might recognize
- **H.** To help the reader understand that beer is more than just a drink for adults

**43.** Which other word in the passage is used to mean the same thing as "undesirable" (Line 33)?

- **A.** Conditioning
- **B.** Green
- **C.** Bizarre
- **D.** Dormant

---

**44.** Which of these is the most reasonable assumption about the author of this passage?

- **E.** He or she is probably a brewer
- **F.** He or she is probably a historian
- **G.** He or she probably disapproves of people drinking beer
- **H.** He or she believes beer, enjoyed responsibly, is a key part of our history and culture.

**CONTINUE ON TO THE NEXT PAGE ➡**

## Classifying Soil Types

Many people mistakenly assume that dirt is dirt. However, if you're attempting to farm, garden, or maintain a beautiful yard, understanding your soil type is fundamental. Different soil types have different strengths, present different challenges, and demand different techniques. Understanding the soil in your yard or garden could be the difference between seeing bountiful, beautiful growth and feeling like you can't grow anything.

The best way to understand soil in general is to understand what the ideal soil is like. The best type of soil for growing most plants, flowers, and crops is loamy soil. Loamy soil is very dark in color (even appearing black when freshly tilled) and has a flaky or crumbly appearance, but if you press it together in your hands when it's crumbly, it should form a clump that holds its shape. That means that there's enough structure below ground to keep the plant safely anchored and provide structure for its root system but also enough plasticity to allow roots to spread out to find more water and nutrients.

On the other hand, sandy soil presents some challenges for plants and gardeners. As its name implies, sandy soil is made of big, dry, grainy particles. That means that water filters down through sandy soil extremely quickly, carrying it away from plants and their roots before they can get their fill. On the plus side, warming sunlight penetrates sandy soil more quickly than other types, which means that many of the first flowers and greens of the spring grow nicely in sandy soil.

Clay soil lies at the exact opposite end of the spectrum. It's tight, clumpy, and damp by nature. Its moisture-holding qualities make clay soil an extremely nutritious environment for plants, but its density means a short growing season, as spring and autumn frosts make the soil cold, hard, and uninviting for roots. If you wait too late into the summer to till your clay soil and allow it to dry out, though, getting your plants in the ground will be an incredible workout.

If you live in a desert-adjacent climate or near the ocean, you might have saline soil. Saline soil has a lot of salt in it, and salt's disagreeable relationship with water means that saline salt will make it tough for your plants and their roots to achieve full potential. Some plants won't even grow in saline soil! Unless you're satisfied to cultivate plants that naturally grow in desert-like environments, growing in a saline-rich environment means amending your soil with nutrients.

Silty soil is usually found near rivers, streams, ponds, swamps, and other bodies of fresh water. The consistency of silty soil is between that of sand and clay, which gives it a clumpy but slick feel. Plants can grow rapidly in silty soil because it is so rich in water and nutrients, but that often means shallow root systems that can cause plants to collapse easily under their own weight as they grow. Plants that grow in silty soil are also prone to getting washed out when the soil gets overly wet.

Finally, there's peat. Peat is somewhat similar to loam in that it is dark, holds water well, and is naturally loaded with nutrients. Peat contains the remains of ancient plants that were destroyed by glaciers, so it's almost like supporting your plants by feeding them concentrated plant food. However, peat is extremely prone to fluctuations in acidity that can suddenly kill even healthy-looking plants. That means that gardening with peat requires careful pH monitoring and frequent check-ins.

**CONTINUE ON TO THE NEXT PAGE ➞**

| Specifications/Growing Conditions for a Variety of Mystery Plants | | | | | | |
|---|---|---|---|---|---|---|
| | Root Length | Root Width | Above Ground Height | Water Needs | Susceptibility to Heat | Peak Growing Season |
| Vegetable A | Long | Wide | Very Low | Very High | Medium | Late Spring or Early Fall |
| Vegetable B | Medium | Narrow | Low | Medium-Low | Medium-High | Summer |
| Flower C | Medium | Medium | Medium | Low | Low | Year-round |
| Flower D | Shallow | Wide | Tall | High | Medium-High | Late Spring or Early Summer |
| Shrub E | Long | Medium | Medium | Medium | Low | Year-round |

**45.** Why does the author begin the body of the passage by describing loamy soil?

- **A.** To start by explaining what good soil is like so the reader can easily identify if they have bad soil
- **B.** The author finds it easiest to write about loamy soil because it is his or her favorite
- **C.** To introduce the reader to the qualities of soil by describing how good soil functions and supports a plant
- **D.** The author describes each soil type one at a time; there is no significance to the order in which they are presented

---

**46.** Which quality of clay soil described in Paragraph 4 supports the idea that "getting your plants in the ground [can be] an incredible workout"?

- **E.** It is damp by nature
- **F.** It has a short growing season
- **G.** It is an extremely nutritious environment
- **H.** It is dense

**47.** What does the author mean when he or she writes, "salt's disagreeable relationship with water" in Paragraph 5?

- **A.** The author means that salt tends to absorb or eliminate moisture
- **B.** The author is personifying salt and water like argumentative cartoon characters
- **C.** The author means that people can't agree whether water or salt levels in soil are more important
- **D.** The author is using the analogy of salt and water being in a bad relationship to show why saline soil is bad

---

**48.** Why is it especially problematic that silty soil is prone to over-watering?

- **E.** Plants in silty soil have shallow root systems
- **F.** Silty soil has qualities of both clay and sand
- **G.** Plants in silty soil can collapse under their own weight
- **H.** Silty soil is usually located near bodies of water

**CONTINUE ON TO THE NEXT PAGE ➡**

**49.** Which "Mystery Plant" from the table would most likely be found in silty soil?

- **A.** Vegetable A
- **B.** Vegetable B
- **C.** Flower C
- **D.** Flower D

---

**50.** Why would Vegetable A not be a great fit for clay soil?

- **E.** Vegetable A requires a lot of water, but clay soil is susceptible to drying out
- **F.** Vegetable A has wide roots, and clay soil is very dense, which may impede or slow their growth
- **G.** Vegetable A grows best in the spring and fall, and clay soil is easiest to work with in the summer
- **H.** Vegetable A is very low to the ground, which means it will be closer to the potentially frosty temperatures of the cold clay soil

CONTINUE ON TO THE NEXT PAGE ➞

## Epic Poetry

These days, the word "epic" is used to mean "really cool" or "exciting and memorable," but until recently, the word had a very specific, scholarly meaning. In the world of literature and academia, an "epic" is an especially long poem that contains a grandiose story. An epic is written in verse and meter, like traditional poetry, but follows the adventures and evolution of a main character, as we would expect from a novel. Many of the earliest recorded stories we know about are in the form of epics, such as *The Epic of Gilgamesh*, which was written about 4,000 years ago and may be the earliest recorded long form story.

The most famous creator of epics is undeniably Homer, a bard who wandered throughout what is now Greece and Turkey at some point between the twelfth and eighth centuries BC. Homer combined existing myths with narratives about famous warriors and kings to create a new form of literature, which we now refer to as the epic. The father of the epic wasn't just a writer, though; he was a performer who knew his incredibly long poems by heart and could recite them from memory over the course of hours. Some historical texts even suggest Homer may have been blind. On the other hand, however, other scholars believe the name "Homer" was a collective pseudonym used by a variety of ancient storytellers and no single author is responsible for the ancient Greek epics.

Homer's most famous works are *The Iliad* and *The Odyssey*, which are known as the "Homeric Epics." *The Iliad* tells the story of the Trojan War, in which the Greeks and their allies sailed to Troy (in modern Turkey) to reclaim their kidnapped queen, Helen. *The Iliad* isn't just a cut-and-dried battle story though, it involves serious reflections on the purpose of warfare and the need for diplomacy between enemies. *The Iliad* also established one of the conventions of epic poetry: the constant intercession of gods or other higher beings. In the epic, the Greek gods divide into two teams, one supporting the Greeks and one supporting the Trojans. The gods are portrayed not just as creators or observers, but active participants in the war. The second Homeric Epic, *The Odyssey* is effectively a sequel to *The Iliad* and follows the long journey of Odysseus, a Greek king who fought in the Trojan War, as he tries to make his way back home after fighting. Due to some strategic mistakes early in his voyage, Odysseus must wander the seas for ten years before finally returning home.

In the subsequent millennia, Homer has served as an inspiration to many authors and poets. For example, the English author and politician John Milton crafted two major epics, *Paradise Lost* and *Paradise Regained*, in the 1600s, both of which were highly imitative of Homer's style. Although few people are sitting around writing epic poems today, the tradition of the epic is still on display in many great movies and television shows. Any time you see a main character who faces impossible challenge after impossible challenge each episode, that's an example of epic storytelling. When characters must seek revenge for wrongs done against their family or friends, that's epic storytelling. The next time you hear something described as "epic," think about how that experience, story, or event connects to the legacy of Homer and the genre he made legendary.

**CONTINUE ON TO THE NEXT PAGE →**

**51.** What is the main purpose of Paragraph 1?

**A.** To define the term "epic" as it is used throughout the remainder of the text
**B.** To provide an introduction or overview for the rest of the passage
**C.** To convince the reader that epics are an important form of literature
**D.** To show the reader the difference between the formal definition of a word and how it is used in everyday life

---

**52.** Which of these is the best definition for "bard" as it is used in Paragraph 2?

**E.** An accomplished author
**F.** A warrior-king
**G.** A traveling storyteller
**H.** A person suffering from a disability such as blindness

---

**53.** Based on the passage, which of these is the single most important biographical detail about Homer?

**A.** He is regarded as "the father of the epic"
**B.** He was a wandering storyteller
**C.** He combined pieces of existing myths and narratives with history to innovate a new genre
**D.** He may be a mythological figure himself

**54.** Based on the passage, which of these is a similarity between Milton and Homer?

**E.** Homer and Milton were both poets and politicians.
**F.** Homer and Milton are both famous for writing two closely-related epic poems.
**G.** Homer and Milton both may have been pseudonyms for collections of writers rather than individual people.
**H.** Homer and Milton were both traveling bards.

---

**55.** According to the author, how is Homer's work still relevant today?

**A.** Students around the world still read *The Iliad* and *The Odyssey* in school.
**B.** Many authors still imitate Homer's style by writing modern epics.
**C.** Homer's style of epic storytelling is still used in many movies and TV shows.
**D.** People still use the term "epic," which is associated primarily with Homer, in daily life.

---

**56.** Based on the passage, approximately when was *The Epic of Gilgamesh* written?

**E.** Around 1 AD
**F.** Around 1000 AD
**G.** Around 4000 BC
**H.** Around 2000 BC

**CONTINUE ON TO THE NEXT PAGE ➡**

**57.** Based on the passage, how is *The Odyssey* a "sequel" to *The Iliad*?

- **A.** They were both written by the same poet, Homer
- **B.** *The Iliad* tells the story of the Trojan War, and *The Odyssey* tells the story of the next great war that followed.
- **C.** *The Iliad* tells the story of the Trojan War, and *The Odyssey* tells the story of a key figure from the Trojan War returning home.
- **D.** *The Iliad* was the first epic poem ever written, and *The Odyssey* was the second epic poem ever written.

CONTINUE ON TO THE NEXT PAGE ➡

MATHEMATICS
INSTRUCTIONS

90 MINUTES • 57 QUESTIONS

Select the best answer from the choices given by carefully solving each problem. Bubble the letter of your answer on the answer sheet. Please refrain from making any stray marks on the answer sheet. If you need to erase an answer, please erase thoroughly.

**Important Notes:**

1. There are no formulas or definitions in the math section that will be provided.
2. Diagrams may or may not be drawn to scale. Do not make assumptions based on the diagram unless it is specifically stated in the diagram or question.
3. Diagrams are not in more than one plane, unless stated otherwise.
4. Graphs are drawn to scale, therefore, you can assume relationships according to the graph. If lines appear parallel, then you can assume the lines to be parallel. This is also true for right angles and so forth.
5. Simplify fractions completely.

## Practice Test 2

**GRID IN PROBLEMS (Questions 58-62)**

*Directions: The following five questions are grid-in problems. On the answer sheet, please be sure to write your answer in the boxes at the top of the grid. Start on the left side of each grid.*

**58.** If $A$, $B$, $C$, $D$, and $E$ are points on a plane such that line $CD$ bisects $\measuredangle ACB$ and line $CB$ bisects right angle $\measuredangle ACE$, then $\measuredangle DCE$ = ?

| | | | | |
|---|---|---|---|---|
| | | | | |
| ⊖ | | | | |
| | ⊙ | ⊙ | ⊙ | ⊙ |
| | 0 | 0 | 0 | 0 |
| | 1 | 1 | 1 | 1 |
| | 2 | 2 | 2 | 2 |
| | 3 | 3 | 3 | 3 |
| | 4 | 4 | 4 | 4 |
| | 5 | 5 | 5 | 5 |
| | 6 | 6 | 6 | 6 |
| | 7 | 7 | 7 | 7 |
| | 8 | 8 | 8 | 8 |
| | 9 | 9 | 9 | 9 |

**59.** A truck traveled 130 miles using 4 gallons of diesel fuel. What distance would the same truck cover using 6.7 gallons of diesel fuel? (Round your answer to the nearest whole number)

| | | | | |
|---|---|---|---|---|
| | | | | |
| ⊖ | | | | |
| | ⊙ | ⊙ | ⊙ | ⊙ |
| | 0 | 0 | 0 | 0 |
| | 1 | 1 | 1 | 1 |
| | 2 | 2 | 2 | 2 |
| | 3 | 3 | 3 | 3 |
| | 4 | 4 | 4 | 4 |
| | 5 | 5 | 5 | 5 |
| | 6 | 6 | 6 | 6 |
| | 7 | 7 | 7 | 7 |
| | 8 | 8 | 8 | 8 |
| | 9 | 9 | 9 | 9 |



CONTINUE ON TO THE NEXT PAGE ➡

**60.** $||-10 - 18| - 20| =$

**61.** What is the perimeter of a rectangular garden that is 16 units wide and has the same area as a rectangular garden that is 10 units wide and 32 units long?

**62.** For the equation: $-1 - \frac{2}{5} \cdot \frac{5m - 10}{2 + 3m} = 1$, solve for $m$. Enter your answer in the grid below, rounded to the nearest whole number.

**CONTINUE ON TO THE NEXT PAGE ➞**

## MULTIPLE CHOICE PROBLEMS (Questions 63-114)

**63.** $(\sqrt{100})(\sqrt{64})$

**E.** 10
**F.** 18
**G.** 80
**H.** 164

---

**64.** 7.2 aliens = 1 monster
1 monster = 15.5 oranges

Using the conversion above, how many oranges are equal to 1 alien?

**A.** 0.46
**B.** 1.95
**C.** 2.15
**D.** 22.7

---

**65.** What is the greatest common factor of 147 and 98?

**E.** 3
**F.** 7
**G.** 14
**H.** 49

---

**66.** If $x = 7$ and $y = 0$, what is the value of $\frac{11x}{x-y}$?

**A.** 0
**B.** 7
**C.** 10
**D.** 11

**67.** Lucy scored a 85, 64 and 76 on her math exams. What score must Lucy obtain on the next math test to have an average of exactly 80?

**E.** 93
**F.** 97
**G.** 94
**H.** 95

---

**68.** Helga has 4 dogs, 3 cats and 2 birds. If she closes her eyes and picks one animal, what is the probability that it does not have 4 legs?

**A.** $\frac{2}{7}$

**B.** $\frac{7}{9}$

**C.** $\frac{2}{9}$

**D.** $\frac{4}{7}$

---

**69.** If $y = x^2 \bullet x^x$, what is $y$ when $x = 2$?

**E.** 16
**F.** 8
**G.** 4
**H.** 32

**CONTINUE ON TO THE NEXT PAGE →**

**70.** Train *A*, traveling at 200mph, leaves station *A* at 1P. M. Train *B*, traveling at 300mph, leaves station *B* at 3P.M. Both stations are directly across from each other and *X* miles away. If the trains meet at 4P.M., what is *X?*

**A.** 900mi
**B.** 700mi
**C.** 600mi
**D.** 400mi

---

**71.** Bernard is now *y* years old. Luis is 8 years older than Bernard. In terms of *y*, how old was Luis 5 years ago?

**E.** $8y - 5$
**F.** $y + 3$
**G.** $y + 13$
**H.** $y - 5$

---

**72.**

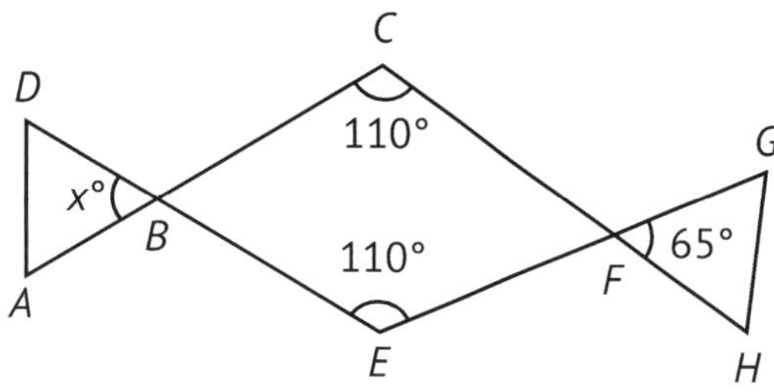


In the figure above, *ABC, DBE, EFG* and *CFH* are straight line segments. What is the value of *x?*

**A.** 45°
**B.** 65°
**C.** 70°
**D.** 75°

**73.** Which of the following shows the fraction $\frac{13}{3}$, $\frac{37}{8}$ and $\frac{19}{4}$ in order from greatest to least?

**E.** $\frac{37}{8}, \frac{19}{4}, \frac{13}{3}$
**F.** $\frac{37}{8}, \frac{13}{3}, \frac{19}{4}$
**G.** $\frac{19}{4}, \frac{13}{3}, \frac{37}{8}$
**H.** $\frac{19}{4}, \frac{37}{8}, \frac{13}{3}$

---

**74.** If *x* and *y* are integers, which is always even?

**A.** $\frac{x + y}{2}$
**B.** $2(\frac{x + y}{x})$
**C.** $2(x + y)$
**D.** $x^2 + y^2$

CONTINUE ON TO THE NEXT PAGE ➡

**75.**

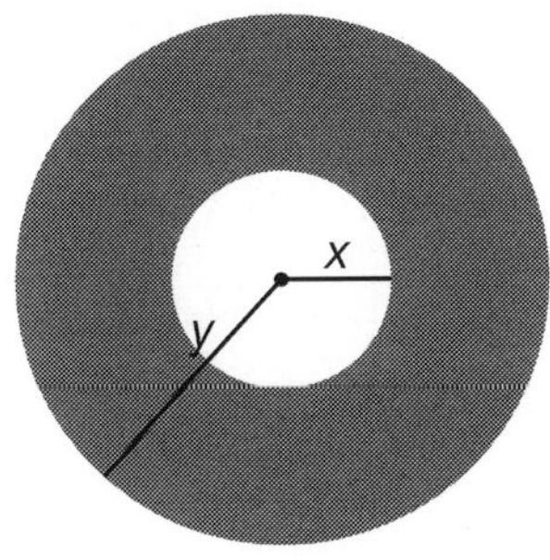


What is the probability that a point chosen will be in the shaded region?

**E.** $\frac{y^2}{x^2}$

**F.** $\frac{(x+y)^2}{y^2}$

**G.** $\frac{x^2}{y^2 - x^2}$

**H.** $\frac{y^2 - x^2}{y^2}$

---

**76.** If $q = x + y$ and $x = y + z$, what is $z$ in terms of $y$ and $q$?

**A.** $q - 2x$
**B.** $q - 2y$
**C.** $2x - q$
**D.** $2y + q$

---

**77.** What is $\frac{(5!)!}{5!}$?

**E.** 1
**F.** 5
**G.** 120
**H.** None of the above

---

**78.** What is $\frac{a^2 + 2ab + b^2}{(a+b)^3}$?

**A.** $(a + b)$

**B.** $a^2 + b^2$

**C.** $\frac{1}{a+b}$

**D.** $\frac{1}{(a+b)^2}$

---

**79.** It takes 3 cats 3 minutes to catch 3 mice. How many cats are needed to catch 99 mice in 99 minutes?

**E.** 3
**F.** 11
**G.** 33
**H.** 99

---

**80.** The sum of seven consecutive odd integers is 749, what is the largest of the seven integers?

**A.** 101
**B.** 103
**C.** 113
**D.** 115

**CONTINUE ON TO THE NEXT PAGE ➞**

**81.** $V = \pi r^2 h$
Using the formula above, if $r$ is doubled and $h$ is divided by 2, what is the ratio of the original volume to the new volume?

**E.** 1:4
**F.** 1:2
**G.** 1:1
**H.** 2:1

---

**82.** A yellow cab has a base fare of $3.50 per ride plus $0.20 for each $\frac{1}{4}$ of mile ridden. If a yellow cab costs $22.50, how many miles long was the ride?

**A.** 23.75 miles
**B.** 42.5 miles
**C.** 47.5 miles
**D.** 112.5 miles

---

**83.** John works 40 hours a week, and his monthly salary in June was $4,000. In the month of July, John got a 4% raise on his monthly salary. In the month of July, what was John's hourly rate? (Note: Assume there are four weeks in July)

**E.** $25
**F.** $26
**G.** $40
**H.** $100

**84.** If $8{,}575 = 5^x \bullet 7^y$, what is $(xy) - 5$?

**A.** 1
**B.** 3
**C.** 6
**D.** 7

---

**85.** When $d$ is divided by 8, the remainder is 3. What is the remainder when $d + 3$ is divided by 8?

**E.** 1
**F.** 3
**G.** 4
**H.** 6

---

**86.** Tommy is making a 6 Letter password using only the letters *A*, *B*, C, *D*, *E* and *F*. How many different codes can Tommy make, if every letter can only be used once in each code?

**A.** 6
**B.** 120
**C.** 720
**D.** 46,656

---

**87.** $-5(x - 3) \geq 20$
What is the solution to the inequality shown above?

**E.** $x \geq -1$
**F.** $x \geq 7$
**G.** $x \leq -1$
**H.** $x \geq 1$

CONTINUE ON TO THE NEXT PAGE ➡

**88.** Which number line below shows the solution to the inequality $-2 < \frac{x}{3} \leq 2$?

**A.** 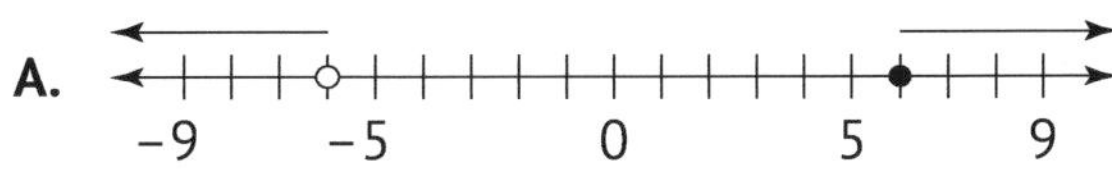


**B.**  −9 −5 0 5 9

**C.**  −9 −5 0 5 9

**D.**  −9 −5 0 5 9

---

**89.**

Favorite Genres of Movies amongst Teens

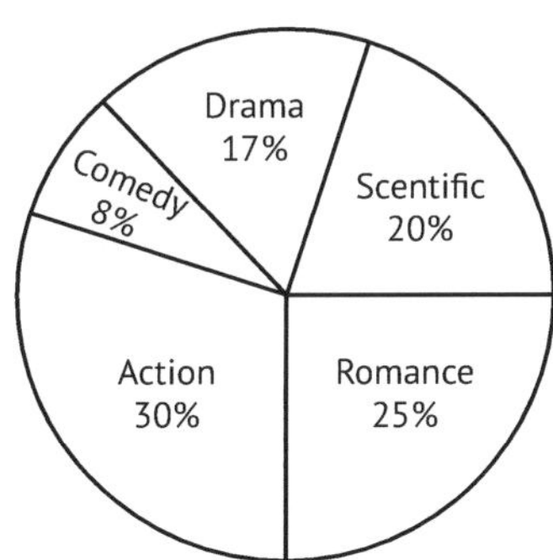


There are 15,000 teens whose favorite genre is comedy. How many teens have a favorite genre of action?

**E.** 30
**F.** 41,250
**G.** 52,500
**H.** 56,250

**90.** A computer originally priced at $550.50 is on sale for 20% off. Jamie used a 5% discount coupon which was applied to the sales price. How much did Jamie pay for the computer? (Assume there is no tax.)

**A.** $412.88
**B.** $418.38
**C.** $440.40
**D.** $522.98

---

**91.** Given the following value 4,760.

Solve the following, $\frac{x^2}{y}$, if $x$ represents the smallest prime factor of the given value, and $y$ represents the greatest prime factor of the given value.

**E.** $\frac{119}{4}$
**F.** $\frac{4}{17}$
**G.** $\frac{2}{119}$
**H.** $\frac{4}{119}$

---

**92.** An adult male Diptera has a mass of 11.5 milligrams. What is the Diptera's mass in grams?

**A.** 0.0115 g
**B.** 0.115 g
**C.** 1.15 g
**D.** 11.5 g

**CONTINUE ON TO THE NEXT PAGE ➡**

**93.** Michael has a project due in exactly 83 hours. It is currently 8:30 on a Monday morning. What time is his project due?

**E.** 6:30 PM Friday
**F.** 7:30 PM Friday
**G.** 7:30 AM Thursday
**H.** 7:30 PM Thursday

---

**94.** $(\frac{2}{3} + \frac{1}{4}) \div 2 =$

**A.** $\frac{22}{12}$
**B.** $\frac{1}{12}$
**C.** $\frac{11}{24}$
**D.** $\frac{1}{3}$

---

**95.** Michelle bought a dress that costs \$103.00, a pair of shoes that costs \$73.00 and a bag that costs \$111.00. There is a 7% sales tax on all items priced at \$90.00 and higher. There is no sales tax on items under \$90.00. How much did Michelle spend on the following items, including tax?

**E.** \$287.00
**F.** \$295.49
**G.** \$300.60
**H.** \$301.98

**96.** How many terms are in the sequence, 0, 3, 6, ... , 57, 60?

**A.** 20
**B.** 21
**C.** 23
**D.** 60

---

**97.** The larger of two consecutive even integers is two times the smaller. What is their sum?

**E.** 2
**F.** 3
**G.** 4
**H.** 6

---

**98.** $3^x = 27^{a+b}$ and $\frac{a^2 - b^2}{(a - b)} = 5$. What is $x$?

**A.** 6
**B.** 9
**C.** 12
**D.** 15

---

**99.** In Mr. Farmer's class there are 30 kids. If there are twice as many boys as there are girls in the English club, then what percentage of the English club are boys?

**E.** 33.3%
**F.** 30%
**G.** 20%
**H.** 66.6%

**CONTINUE ON TO THE NEXT PAGE ➞**

**100.** $a \star b = a^3 - 3a^2b + 3ab^2 - b^3$

$a \oplus b = (a - b)(a - b)$

What is $\dfrac{a \star b}{a \oplus b}$

A. $a^2 + b^2$
B. $(a - b)$
C. $a^2 + 3b^2 + 3ab$
D. $a^2 - b^2$

---

**101.** What is the prime factorization of 752?

E. $2^3 \bullet 48$
F. $2^3 \bullet 49$
G. $2^4 \bullet 47$
H. $3^4 \bullet 47$

---

**102.** If $x$ can be any integer, what is the least possible value of the expression $4x^2 - 10$?

A. $-10$
B. $-4$
C. 4
D. $\infty$

---

**103.** There are a total of 5 bicycles and tricycles in a park. There are 12 wheels. How many tricycles are there?

E. 2
F. 3
G. 6
H. 7

---

**104.** What is least possible value of $\dfrac{x^2 - 1}{x^2}$ if $x \geq 1$

A. $-1$
B. 0
C. 3
D. $\dfrac{3}{4}$

---

**105.** What is the maximum number of points in which a circle and triangle can intersect?

E. 3
F. 5
G. 6
H. $\infty$

---

**106.**

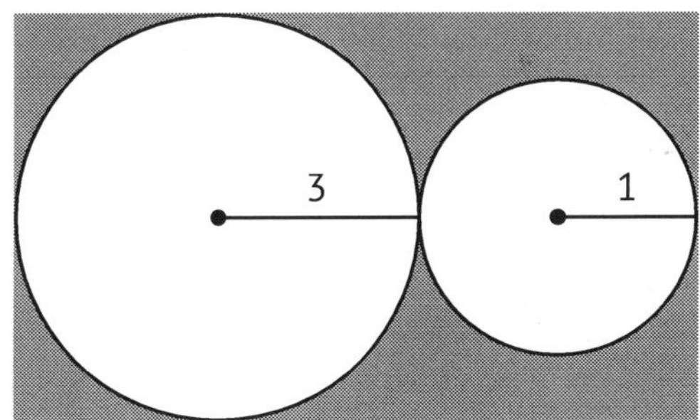


Figure not drawn to scale.

What is the area of the shaded region?

A. $48 - 10\pi$
B. $64 - 22\pi$
C. $48 - 6\pi$
D. $16\pi$

CONTINUE ON TO THE NEXT PAGE ➡

**107.** There are 45 plastic ducks in a bag. If there are black, green, blue, and purple plastic ducks and $\frac{1}{3}$ of the plastic ducks are black, $\frac{1}{5}$ of the plastic ducks are blue, one third of the number of black plastic ducks are green, then how many purple plastic ducks are in the bag?

**E.** 6
**F.** 15
**G.** 16
**H.** 21

---

**108.**

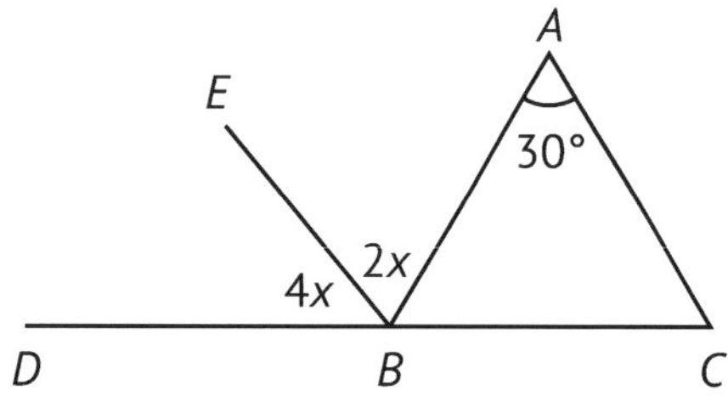


Figure not drawn to scale.

In the figure above, point *B* is on line segment *DC*. If *AB* = *BC*, what is the measure of angle *ABE?*

**A.** 20°
**B.** 40°
**C.** 80°
**D.** 90°

**109.**

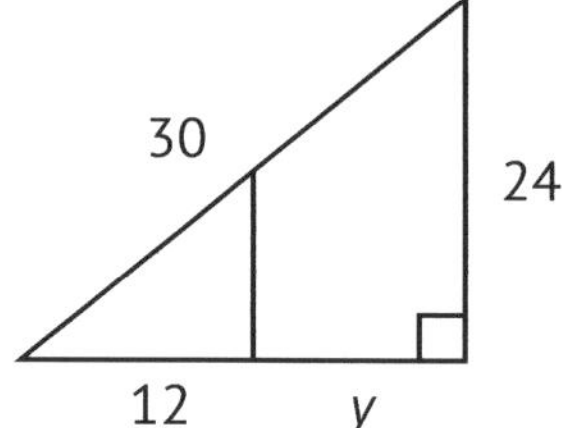


According to the figure above, what is the value of *y?*

**E.** 3
**F.** 6
**G.** 12
**H.** 15

---

**110.** A painter needs 4 gallons of paint to paint each room. If a house has 8 rooms in total, how many quarts of paint is he going to need?

**A.** 12
**B.** 32
**C.** 128
**D.** 200

---

**111.** A rectangle is inscribed in a circle. The rectangle is tangent at the points *A, B, C* and *D.* If the diagonal of the rectangle is 20 inches long, what is the area of the circle?

**E.** $10\pi$
**F.** $15\pi$
**G.** $20\pi$
**H.** $100\pi$

**CONTINUE ON TO THE NEXT PAGE ➡**

**112.**

| Gas Prices | |
|---|---|
| Regular | \$2.00 |
| Premium | \$2.25 |
| Unloaded | \$2.50 |

The prices in the table above show the different types of gas offered at a gas station and the prices of the gas per gallon. If Emily has \$50, what is the least amount of gas, in gallons, she can purchase subtracted from the greatest amount of gas, in gallons, she can purchase?

**A.** 2 gallons
**B.** 3 gallons
**C.** 5 gallons
**D.** 20 gallons

---

**113.** A survey was conducted to determine the age at which the members of the Youth Advisory Committee started their first job.

Age at First Job

| Age | Frequency |
|---|---|
| 14 | 1 |
| 15 | 3 |
| 16 | 3 |
| 17 | 4 |
| 18 | 1 |
| 19 | 2 |
| 21 | 1 |

What was the median age reported by the Youth Advisory Committee?

**E.** 15.5
**F.** 16
**G.** 17.5
**H.** 17

**114.** Use the following frequency chart to answer the following question.

| Item | Cost | Number |
|---|---|---|
| Oatmeal Cookies | \$1.76 | 4 |
| Whole Milk | \$3.99 | 2 |
| Sugar Cured Ham | \$4.54 | 2 |
| 7 Grain Bread | \$3.27 | 3 |
| CFL Light bulbs | \$2.00 | 5 |
| Ginger Soda | \$0.67 | 6 |
| Chocolate Candy Bar | \$1.15 | ? |

How many Chocolate Candy Bars must Cindy purchase in order to end up with a median price of \$1.88?

**A.** 0
**B.** 1
**C.** 2
**D.** 3

**THIS IS THE END OF THE TEST. IF THERE IS TIME REMAINING, YOU MAY CHECK YOUR ANSWERS TO PART 1 OR PART 2.**

**CONTINUE ON TO THE NEXT PAGE ➞**

**You can find detailed video explanations to each problem in the book by visiting: ArgoPrep.com**

# SHSAT PRACTICE TEST 2
## ANSWER KEY

### PART 1 (ENGLISH LANGUAGE ARTS)

**Revising/Editing**

1. **D**
2. **F**
3. **B**
4. **G**
5. **C**
6. **G**
7. **A**
8. **G**
9. **D**
10. **F**
11. **C**

**Reading Comprehension**

12. **F**
13. **D**
14. **E**
15. **C**
16. **F**
17. **D**
18. **H**
19. **C**
20. **F**
21. **C**
22. **E**
23. **B**
24. **H**
25. **C**
26. **E**
27. **D**
28. **F**
29. **A**
30. **F**
31. **A**
32. **H**
33. **C**
34. **F**
35. **D**
36. **F**
37. **A**
38. **E**
39. **C**
40. **H**
41. **B**
42. **H**
43. **C**
44. **H**
45. **C**
46. **H**
47. **A**
48. **H**
49. **D**
50. **F**
51. **A**
52. **G**
53. **D**
54. **F**
55. **C**
56. **H**
57. **C**

### PART 2 (MATHEMATICS)

**Math**

58. **67.5°**
59. **218 miles**
60. **8**
61. **72**
62. **0**
63. **G**
64. **C**
65. **H**
66. **D**
67. **H**
68. **C**
69. **E**
70. **A**
71. **F**
72. **D**
73. **H**
74. **C**
75. **H**
76. **B**
77. **H**
78. **C**
79. **E**
80. **C**
81. **F**
82. **A**
83. **F**
84. **A**
85. **H**
86. **C**
87. **G**
88. **D**
89. **H**
90. **B**
91. **F**
92. **A**
93. **H**
94. **C**
95. **H**
96. **B**
97. **H**
98. **D**
99. **H**
100. **B**
101. **G**
102. **A**
103. **E**
104. **B**
105. **G**
106. **A**
107. **G**
108. **A**
109. **F**
110. **C**
111. **H**
112. **C**
113. **H**
114. **C**

# Practice Test 2 (Answers and Explanations)

**1. D** Answer D is correct because it correctly punctuates both halves of the sentence. First, "Try not to become a man of success" must go into quotation marks because it is part of what Einstein is saying. Similarly, "but rather try to become a man of value" also requires quotation marks because it is part of what is being said. Each half of the quotation also requires a comma for formatting. In the first half of the sentence, the comma goes inside the quotation mark before the attribution. In the second half of the sentence, the comma comes after the attribution and before the second set of quotation marks. Answer A is incorrect because there is no closing quotation mark at the end of the sentence. Answer B is incorrect because there is no comma following "rather." Answer C is incorrect because there is no comma following "success."

**2. F** This sentence is consistently written in the past tense and talks about historical events, so using the past tense verb "became" is the best correction that can be made to this sentence, making Answer F correct. Answers E, G, and H are all incorrect because each of them would introduce an inconsistent, confusing present tense verb to the sentence.

**3. B** Sentences 1, 3, 4, and 5 are written consistently in the past tense, which is appropriate because they discuss events from the historical past (as indicated by "...in the seventeenth century..." and "In 1687..."). Answer B is correct because Sentence 2 contains the present tense verb "publishes." This should be corrected to "published" to correctly indicate when the action occurred (in the past) and to make Sentence 2 consistent with the tense of the rest of the paragraph.

**4. G** A dangling modifier occurs when a sentence begins with a modifier whose subject is unclear or easily mistaken. "A secret kept form almost the entire nation," which comes at the beginning of Sentence 3, is a dangling modifier, making Answer G correct. "A secret kept..." is a dangling modifier because at point those words appear on the page, it's unclear what the secret is. The reader could mistakenly infer that the fishing trip itself was the secret rather than the cover story for the actual secret (the surgical procedure). Sentence 3 should be revised to clarify the relationship between these ideas.

**5. C** "To be" verbs (is, am, are, was, were, will be, etc.) are generally discouraged from use in formal writing. In this sentence, the only "to be" verb is "was" in the phrase "...was famous for..." Answer C is correct because it rearranges the sentence to eliminate the need for the "to be" verb. Answer choice A is incorrect because it maintains "was" and simply substitutes "well known" for "famous." Answer choice B is incorrect because it substitutes "as well as" for "and" without addressing the "to be" verb issue. Answer choice D is incorrect because it removes the "to be" verb was, but inserts the equally incorrect "were."

**6. G** Answer G is the best combination of the two sentences because it includes all relevant information without repeating key phrases. Answers E and F cannot be correct because both repeat the verb "remains," which is unnecessary. Similarly, Answer H is repetitive because it states the fact that Shakespeare is dead twice. Only Answer G communicates that Shakespeare has been dead for more than 400 years, is one of history's most famous Englishmen, and is still widely read and performed without repeating phrases.

**7.** **A** The adjective "much" is used to describe singular nouns. The adjective "many" is used to describe plural nouns. (For example, you have "much electricity" but "many light bulbs.") Since the adjective in question is modifying the plural noun "details," then "many" must be used. Answer B cannot be correct because the plural noun "details" takes the plural verb "are," so "is" would be incorrect. Answer C cannot be correct because the plural nouns "plays" and "sonnets" take the plural verb "suggest." Answer D cannot be correct because it's already been established that Shakespeare is dead, so he cannot exist in the present tense.

**8.** **G** Passive voice occurs when the subject of a sentence or clause is having action performed on them rather than performing the action themselves. The original sentence states that Shakespeare's plays and poems "are still taught," which is a passive voice construction because the plays and poems are not the ones doing the teaching. Answers E, F, and H do not correct this error and are therefore all incorrect. Only Answer G creates an active voice construction by stating that the "plays and poems are staples."

**9.** **D** Answer D provides the best topic sentence because it provides a clear preview of the paragraph's main ideas (the three types of plays Shakespeare focused on). Answer A would not make a good topic sentence because it only focuses on comedies. Answer B provides a relevant topic sentence for the paragraph, but it is somewhat vague and non-specific, so it cannot be the "best" answer. While Answer C makes tangential reference to Shakespeare having written a variety of plays, it is focused more on judgment or appraisal of his work than describing it.

**10.** **F** As written, sentence 7 waits until its last word to identify that it is talking about the tragedies. Readers could easily become confused and think that Shakespeare "explored how human flaws and weaknesses can create sadness and misery" in his comedies, based on the fact that the comedies were the topic of the previous two sentences. Answer F eliminates this issue by providing a clear, signposted transition to discussing the tragedies. Answer E cannot be correct because it is simply a rewording of the original sentence with the same confusing structure intact. Answer G attempts to provide a transition from one idea to the next by using the phrase "At the same time," but the concept of tragedy is still not introduced until the last word of the sentence, leaving the reader to wonder whether the early content of the sentence is referring to the comedies or something else. Answer H attempts to create a transition towards the tragedies, but it is not the best answer because it still waits until the end of the sentence to name the tragedies, using the colon for a "dramatic reveal" rather than using clear signposting.

**11.** **C** Paragraph 2 is consistently written using past tense verbs (dealt, were, was, explored, told, etc.). Answer C is correct because "lead" is a present tense verb, so it must be replaced for consistency. Answer A cannot be correct because "are" is a present tense verb, and therefore also inconsistent with the rest of the paragraph. Answer B is incorrect because either "these" or "those" would be acceptable in the sentence, so neither is wrong. Answer D is incorrect because "they're" is a contraction of "they are," which would not make sense in the sentence.

**12.** **F** Answer F is the best choice because the passage describes the lumber-room as a place where many different objects that are not on display in the public parts of the house are stored. In Paragraph

1, the text says, "It was the storehouse of unimagined treasures." Answer E is incorrect, although it does show the reader focusing on the correct portion of the text. The garden, however, is outside the lumber-room and provides the light, which enters through the room's window. It would be incorrect to say the lumber-room and the garden were the same place, though. Answer G is incorrect and has no basis in the text, as the materials stored in the lumber-room are described as fragile (like a china teapot) or works of art (like the tapestry). Answer H is incorrect because the lumber-room is specifically described in the opening sentences as a place that's kept secret or forbidden for the children. Nicholas has fun in the lumber-room, but it's not specifically a playroom; it's a storage room.

**13. D** In Paragraph 1, the author writes, "Such parts of the house as Nicholas knew best were rather bare and cheerless, but here there were wonderful things for the eyes to feast one," clearly establishing that Answer D is the correct choice. All the other answer choices represent a failure by the reader to identify this key sentence. Answer A is incorrect because it assumes the rest of the house is "well decorated," which is inconsistent with the narrator's description of it as "bare and cheerless." Answer B is incorrect because we do not have enough information to confirm whether it is a true statement or not. The story says that light only enters the lumber-room through the window to the garden, but there's no mention at all of how the other rooms are lit. Answer C is incorrect and represents a major misunderstanding of the text, as there are not literal birds and dogs in the lumber-room, but rather artistic depictions of them.

**14. E** Answer E is the best choice because it represents an understanding of the language in the quoted sentence as well as the overall tone and inferential meaning of the passage. The sentence itself could be translated to mean "The so-called aunt thought things would get ruined if people could see or touch them, so she hid them away where no one could see them." The overall tone of the passage confirms this conclusion, as the objects in the lumber-room are described as some of the most fascinating objects in the house, and they are intentionally kept away from the people who could enjoy them most. Answer F is incorrect because it actually inverts the meaning of the quoted sentence. According to the passage, the aunt believes storing objects in dust and damp is preferable to people seeing them. Answer G is incorrect because we don't have enough information in the passage to determine the aunt-by-assertion's motivates. She could have a strong desire to preserve the objects in the lumber-room for posterity, but that's never explicitly stated or explored, making Answer E still the stronger answer. Answer H is incorrect as well because it completely flips the meaning of the sentence to suggest the aunt-by-assertion wants people to see the items, which we know cannot be the case, as they are intentionally hidden away in the lumber-room.

**15. C** Answer C is the best choice as it reflects the best understanding of Paragraph 1, particularly the line, "To Nicholas it was a living, breathing story." The narrator's detailed description of the hunt, the arrow, and the lurking wolves shows that Nicholas is enthralled by the narrative that the tapestry tells. Answer A is incorrect because the passage makes it clear that there are many colorful objects in the room, and the narrator never specifically mentions that the tapestry is the most colorful. If anything, the bird book is portrayed as containing more vibrant colors than the tapestry. Answer B is incorrect because the bird book also contains pictures of animals. Answer D is incorrect because there is no suggestion in the passage that the picture portrays any story that Nicholas knows; rather, it is suggested that Nicholas is fascinated to the tapestry because of the uniqueness of the narrative it presents, making Answer A a better overall choice.

**16. F** Answer F is the best choice because, throughout the description of the tapestry, Nicholas' powers of observation and knack for humor are on display. He notices somewhat sarcastically that "it could not have been a difficult shot as the stag was only one or two paces away from him," and the narrator later jokes that "all [Nicholas] knew about [the hunter's] skill in shooting was that he could hit a large stag at ridiculously short range," once again suggesting that Nicholas sees the silly side of the tapestry. However, he also makes some very keen, serious observations about the number of arrows in the quiver and the number of wolves in the woods, which show that his observations go beyond the simply humorous. Answer E is incorrect because there's nothing in the passage to suggest that Nicholas is a troubled child (he may be presented as a somewhat mischievous boy, but he's not violent or bad), and the violence on the tapestry is almost presented as cartoonish in his eyes, which again points back to Answer F. Answer G is incorrect because Nicholas' love for animals is reflected in many of the lumber-room objects (the duck tea pot and bird book, especially), not just the tapestry. Answer F remains a better choice as it gives a more specific insight about Nicholas that other objects in the room do not provide. Answer H is incorrect because there's nothing else in the passage that shows that Nicholas is a hunter himself or has extensive knowledge about hunting.

**17. D** Answer D is the best choice because the word "transfixed" is used in Paragraph 2 to describe what has just happened to a stag with an arrow in it. The key sentence states, "A man, dressed in the hunting costume of some remote period, had just transfixed a stag with an arrow." Since "Pierced" is the only choice that describes what an arrow might do to an animal, Answer D is the correct answer. Answers A, B, and C are all incorrect because they fail to identify the context clues in the sentence ("arrow," "hunting," "stag") and the overall description of the tapestry ("quiver," "shooting," etc.) that point to "transfixed" being closely related to the idea of being shot by an arrow.

**18. H** Answer H is the best choice because it reflects the most complete understanding of the final sentences of Paragraph 1. The passage says, "That part of the picture was simple, if interesting, but did the huntsman see, what Nicholas saw, that four galloping wolves were coming in his direction through the wood? There might be more than four of them hidden behind the trees, and in any case would the man and his dogs be able to cope with the four wolves if they made an attack? The man had only two arrows left in his quiver, and he might miss with one or both of them; all one knew about his skill in shooting was that he could hit a large stag at a ridiculously short range. Nicholas sat for many golden minutes revolving the possibilities of the scene; he was inclined to think that there were more than four wolves and that the man and his dogs were in a tight corner." The sentences clearly establish that Nicholas observes a detail many people might not notice in the tapestry: that the hunter could be in big trouble. Answer E is incorrect, although the passage does describe the dogs as "trained to keep to heel," because Answer H contains a much more specific, insightful observation about the tapestry. For one thing, the threat of the wolves is a detail other people might miss, and the idea that the central figure in the tapestry might be in a position of weakness rather than power is a key observation that potentially affects the meaning of the artwork. Answer F is incorrect because, if anything, Nicholas suggests the huntsman might be a bad shot by saying, "...he could hit a large stag at a ridiculously short range." Answer G is incorrect because Nicholas never mentions anything at all about removing the stag from the woods.

**19. C** Answer C is the best choice because the objects in the lumber-room, which vary from European tapestries to Chinese dishes and sculptures from around the round, all suggest that the people who have owned the house over the years have been wealthy and shared a passion for collecting fascinating works of art. Answer A is incorrect because we only know for certain that the aunt-by-assertion thinks that way. We have no way of confirming whether previous generations felt the same way. Answer B is incorrect because we have no way of specifically knowing whether someone acquired these objects for themselves during their travels or simply bought them from other people or merchants who had imported them from foreign lands. Answer D is incorrect because, again, we do not have any details in the text on which to base the conclusion that previous generations would have agreed or disagreed with storing all the beautiful objects in the lumber-room.

**20. F** Answer F is the best choice because both the lumber-room and the bird book are seemingly boring, uncomplicated ideas (a storage closet and a book with "plain black covers"), but they actually wind up providing a world of joy for Nicholas. In that way, one could say that both the lumber-room and the bird book illustrate that "you can't judge a book by its cover." Answer E is incorrect because there are no literal birds in the lumber-room; rather, there is a book that contains many detailed pictures of birds. Answer G is incorrect, although it is a true statement, because it doesn't discuss a thematic similarity, but rather a shallow, surface-level similarity. Answer F is still the best choice because it dives into deeper, symbolic meaning, not just a visual coincidence. Finally, Answer H is incorrect for the exact same reason as Answer G: it provides a shallow, visual similarity between the lumber-room and the book, not a thematic similarity, as the working of the question calls for.

**21. C** Answer C is the correct choice as it reflects the best understanding of Line 1: "Shall I compare thee to a summer's day?" The opening line of the poem establishes the central metaphor that the speaker is comparing the person the poem is written for to a summer's day. The phrase "more lovely" in Line 2 should be a major hint to the reader that the poet is especially focused on beauty. Answer A is incorrect because no season but summer is mentioned in the poem, so it would be unfair to say the poem reflects changing seasons. Answer B is incorrect because, while the sun is described as being "the eye of heaven," there is no other specific religious language or imagery in the poem, and no mention of gods. Answer D is incorrect because it fails to recognize that the poet is discussing the beauty of the person to whom the poem is addressed.

**22. E** Answer E is the best choice because it correctly decodes Line 4 of the text. The phrase "hath all too short a date" should have been a major indicator to the reader that the speaker is using "lease" to talk about a term or amount of time. Essentially, in Line 4, the poet is saying "Summer isn't long enough." Answer F is incorrect because it fails to use the context clues to choose the best definition for "lease" in the poem. Answer F represents a legitimate definition, but not the appropriate one based on context. Answer G is incorrect and probably indicates the reader is connecting "lease" to the term "new lease on life," which is acceptable usage, but not the way the word is being used in Line 4.

Answer H is incorrect and most likely represents the reader conflating the word "lease" with "least."

**23. B** Answer B is the correct choice because it uses the context clues to determine the meaning of the phrase. The words "hot" and "shines" in Line 5 should be major indicators to the reader, as should "gold complexion" in Line 6. All those words (as well as the overall context of the poem) point to "the eye of heaven" being the sun. Answer A is incorrect because there's no explicit mention of god or gods anywhere in the poem. Answer C is incorrect because "gold" is an adjective used to describe the "complexion" (color) of the sun rather than a noun. Answer D is incorrect as well because it is not specific enough, focusing on the general themes of the poem rather than diving into the details of Lines 5 and 6.

**24. H** Answer H is the correct choice and represents a strong understanding of Lines 6-9. Line 9, in particular, states, "But thy eternal summer shall not fade," clearly stating that the beauty of the person to whom the poem is addressed is eternal. Answer G identifies the distinction between the two ideas but mistakenly flips the relationship, making it incorrect. Answers E and F are both incorrect because they each fail to identify the main distinction the speaker makes in Line 9, instead focusing on details about the sun and summer from earlier lines in the poem.

**25. C** Answer C is the best choice because the author frequently uses imagery to communicate that the sun's inconsistency is its major flaw compared to the person about whom the poem is written. In Lines 5-8, the speaker explains how sometimes the sun is too hot, too bright, or too dark which contrasts with the "eternal summer" (Line 9) of the person about whom the poem is written, which Stanza 3 describes in depth. Throughout the poem, the speaker repeats that the sun and summer are both inconsistently beautiful and enjoyable, but the person about whom the poem is written is much more stable. Answer A is incorrect because the sun's variable temperature is just one example of how it is not as "temperate" (Line 2) and wonderful as the person about whom the poem is written, making Answer C a better choice. Answer B is incorrect because the specific example of rough winds impairing the sun's beauty is simply an example of how the sun can be inconsistent, again pointing back to Answer C. Answer D is incorrect because physical distance between the speaker, the sun, or the person about whom the poem is written is never mentioned in the poem, meaning Answer D has no textual basis.

**26. E** Answer E is the best choice because Line 11 of the poem treats "death" as a person or character rather than a concept or event, which is a textbook example of personification. The best context clue is the verb "brag," which is certainly something that death cannot do in real life. Answer F is incorrect because alliteration involves repeating the opening letter or sound of words, and that does not occur at all in Line 11 ("shade" and "shall" both begin with "sh" sounds, but those are the only examples of similarity in the line and the two words are not located near each other at all). Answer G is incorrect because nothing in Line 11 is presented as contrary to expectations, so there cannot be any irony occurring. Finally, Answer H is incorrect because no facts in Line 11 seem to contradict each other, so there is no use of paradox.

**27. D** Answer D is the best choice because in Line 12, the speaker explains that the person to whom the sonnet is written will live forever because his or her beauty has been memorialized in "eternal lines." Essentially, the speaker is saying, "I wrote this great poem about you, so people will know about you forever." The word "lines" should be a major hint to the reader, as poetry is written in lines. Answer A is incorrect because the "eye of heaven" is the sun, which can be deduced using the context clues "hot" and "shines." Answer B is incorrect because "nature's changing course" is simply describing how things change over time, and it's not reflecting on the nature of the poem in any self-aware way. Answer C is also incorrect because the "eternal summer" represents the person about whom the poem is written's immortal beauty, not the power of the poem to make him or her an immortal beauty.

**28.** **F** Answer F is the best choice because it represents the best understanding of Lines 9-14, particularly the closing couplet, Lines 13-14. The speaker believes the "eternal lines" (Line 12) of the poem will give the person about whom the speaker is written a legacy of beauty that will last forever. We also see this reflected in Line 14, where it says, "So long lives this, and this gives life too thee." The "this" in Line 14 is referring to the poem (Sonnet 18) itself, meaning that as long as the poem exists, people will learn about how beautiful and wonderful the person about whom the poem is written was. Answer E is incorrect because it mistakes the metaphorical protection from death that the speaker offers to literal protection from death. There is nothing in the poem that suggests anybody has literally saved anybody else's life. Answer G is incorrect because it suggests the person about whom the poem is writing is seeking attention or fame, while there is nothing in the text at all to suggest this is the case. Finally, Answer H is incorrect as well because it fails to identify the themes of legacy and eternal life that are introduced in Lines 9-14.

**29.** **A** Answer A is the best choice because it accurately breaks the poem into three quatrains (sets of four lines) and one couplet (set of two lines). Each of the three quatrains has a rhyme scheme in which the first and third lines rhyme, as do the second and fourth. This pattern is repeated three times before the final couplet, which contains two rhyming lines. This is the standard format of Shakespearean sonnets, but it can also be deduced by examining the poem's structure on the page. Answer B is incorrect and can quickly be proven so by looking at the first two lines of the poem. "Day" and "temperate" do not rhyme; therefore, B cannot be correct. Similarly, Answer C can be proven incorrect because Lines 1 and 3 do rhyme, which Answer C suggests is not the case. Finally, Answer D can also quickly be proven incorrect because "temperate" (Line 2) and "May" (Line 3) do not rhyme, as Answer D suggests. Only Answer A correctly recognizes the rhyme scheme of the poem.

**Passage 3 ("The communist manifesto"):**

**30.** **F** Answer F is the best choice because Paragraph 1 states: "Its authors, the German philosophers Karl Marx and Friedrich Engels, wrote the *Manifesto* to reflect the beliefs of the Communist League, a European political party they both belonged to..." which indicates both authors were already members of the Communist League at the time *The Manifesto* was published. Answers E and G are both incorrect because they fail to recognize the sequence of events established in Paragraph 1. First, Marx and Engels were members of the Communist League, then they codified the Leagues' beliefs in *The Communist Manifesto*. Answer G is incorrect because it fails to recognize

that the passage deals entirely with nonfiction subject matter.

**31. A** Answer A is the best choice because it reflects the content of Paragraph 2, which states that Marx and Engels saw history as a series of situations in which small groups of elites exploited the masses only to be overthrown and then replaced with a new group of exploitative elites. Answer A is incorrect because Marx and Engels emphasized the similarities and repetitive nature of historical eras, not the differences between them. Answer C is incorrect because the text strongly suggests that Marx and Engels believed the powerful cared little about creating a perfect society for the masses. Rather, *The Communist Manifesto* asserts that elites have consistently acted in their own interests with little regard for society as a whole. Answer D is incorrect because Marx and Engels believed the poor were constantly being used and exploited; only through uniting and toppling the order could the poor improve their situation, according to *The Communist Manifesto*.

**32. H** Answer H is the best choice because a member of the Communist League would strongly believe that the wealthy and powerful are inherently exploitative are succeed at the expense of the working class. Answer E is incorrect because the Communists sought to create a society in which no one was rich or poor, so they would optimistically disagree that the social order was immovable. Answer F is incorrect because it reflects a capitalist way of thinking rather than a communist one. Answer G is incorrect as well because it emphasizes patience, whereas the members of the Communist League wanted to take decisive action to change the world significantly.

**33. C** Answer C is the best choice because it reflects the content of Paragraph 3, which describes that Marx and Engels believed capitalism was "the same game of haves and have-nots." Answers A, B, and D are incorrect because they all suggest that Marx and Engels admired capitalism to some degree, which is never stated in the passage. On the contrary, the passage only suggests the idea that Marx and Engels' beliefs differed significantly from those of capitalism.

**34. F** Answer F is the best choice because it reflects the content of Paragraphs 3 and 5 and demonstrates the reader's understanding of the main ideas of *The Communist Manifesto*. Answer E is incorrect because Paragraph 4 clearly states that there were plans to grow food using communal farms and create jobs for workers present in *The Communist Manifesto*. Answer G is incorrect because the abolition of private property would generally affect those who had a great deal. For most average or working-class people, the communist approach provided a chance to maintain or slightly improve their position. It would be the upper classes who had less. Answer H is incorrect with no textual basis, since no biographical details are ever provided about Marx and Engels in the passage, other than the fact that they were members of the Communist League.

**35. D** Answer D is the best choice because Answers A, B, and C all reflect ways "Workers of the world unite!" was an aggressive or intimidating call to action. Answer A is incorrect because workers organizing to demand better conditions or pay would have been a threat to the existing capitalist order. Answer B is incorrect because Paragraph 6 confirms violent revolutions often occurred when countries converted to communism. Answer C is also incorrect because Paragraph 2 clearly states that Marx and Engels viewed history as a series of "us-them" conflicts between haves and have-nots. Only Answer D fails to describe a way in which "Workers of the world unite!" could've inspired fear in elites. The slogan was not about calling workers to better their lives within the system but rather calling them to topple that system.

**Passage 4 ("Brewing")**

**36. F** Answer F is the best choice because the passage seeks to clear up the fact that beer is "misunderstood" by describing both its long history and the complex process behind making it. Answer E is incorrect because, while the author clearly believes alcohol should be enjoyed in a respectful and responsible manner, there are no explicit arguments against drinking beer anywhere in the passage. Answer G is incorrect because it represents only part of the passage and not the whole. The connection between beer and the development of cities is certainly a main idea, but Answer G ignores the passage's equally heavy emphasis on the brewing process. On the other hand, Answer H is incorrect because it mentions only the brewing process while leaving out the importance of beer to the development of cities. The wording of Answer F gives voice to both these ideas, making it the best choice.

**37. A** Answer A is the best choice because Paragraph 2 describes wort as "a sweet liquid" to which hops is added before the fermentation process begins. Answer A shows that the reader understands the sequence of events laid out in Paragraphs 2 and 3. Answer B is incorrect and instead provides a definition for "wart," which has nothing to do with the passage. Answer C is incorrect and instead provides a definition for "hops," which is one of the ingredients added to the wort. Answer C shows the reader is looking in the correct portion of the text but failing to read closely enough. Answer D is incorrect because the portion of the text about "off-flavors" is related to parts of the process that occur after fermentation (in Paragraph 3), whereas "wort" refers to the beer prior to fermentation.

**38. E** Answer E is correct because it displays the clearest understanding of Paragraph 3. Answer E displays that the reader sees the connection between cooling the green beer and conditioning to remove off-flavors. Answer F is incorrect because a close reading of Paragraphs 2 and 3 reveals the green beer is fully fermented by this point in the process. Answer G is incorrect and has no basis in the text because there is nothing in the passage related to conditions that might cause beer to spoil. Answer H is incorrect because, while bottling comes after conditioning in the sequence of steps, there is no cause-and-effect relationship between the two. Hypothetically, a beer that had not been cooled could still be put in bottles; it would just be filled with off-flavors.

**39. C** Answer C is the correct answer because it reflects the best understanding of Paragraph 4. The paragraph clearly describes fouled water sources, including wells and streams and explains how brewing removed most of the dangerous bacteria from the water. Answer A is incorrect with no basis in the text because the passage never mentions job creation or economic development as results of brewing. Answer B is also incorrect, although it at least shows the reader attempting to think critically and connect the topic of brewing to cultural development. Although the passage does mention the connection between brewing and science, Answer C is still a much better, more specific answer that makes direct connections between large concentrations of people near water sources and the need for brewing. Answer D is incorrect as well, although it does show the reader examining Paragraph 4 and recognizing the importance of wells. However, the paragraph states

that people throwing trash into wells was the problem, not the integrity of the wells themselves.

**40. H** Answer H is the best choice because the text of Paragraph 5 clearly connects the use of "flock" to a religious community. The paragraph clearly shows that the "flock" the monks and nuns were sharing their beer with was the "local laypeople" mentioned in the final sentence. Answer E is incorrect, although it is an accurate definition for "flock," because it fails to recognize the context-specific use of the word in the passage. Answer F is also hypothetically an accurate definition for "flock" (i.e. "a flocked Christmas tree"), but like Answer E, it totally ignores the clearly religious context of the word in Paragraph 5. Answer G is incorrect because, while it recognizes the word is related to religious communities, it mistakenly assumes the "flock" is the made up of the monks and nuns themselves, not the common people they live near.

**41. B** Answer B is the best choice because it reflects both the reader's understanding of the text and their understanding of the author's point of view. By selecting Answer B, a reader shows they understand that the passage emphasizes beer's importance to public health in the past. Answer B also shows that the reader understands that the author believes beer is "misunderstood and misused" as laid out in Paragraphs 1 and 6. Answers A and D both reflect important takeaways from the passage but neither offers an explanation of why people might have an increased respect for beer and be encouraged to drink responsibly. Understanding that beer was necessary to the survival of communities, which is expressed in Answer B, on the other hand, provides information that actually might lead people to examine their motivations when they drink beer. Answer C is incorrect because, while somewhat true, it does not sum up the overall content of the passage as well as Answer B.

**42. H** Answer H is the best choice because the main goal of Paragraph 4's first sentence is to help the reader prepare to see past their contemporary understanding of beer and gain important historical context for brewing. The rest of the paragraph discusses in detail how beer was much more than just a drink for barbecues at key moments in history, and the first sentence primes the reader to understand and make sense of those details by inviting them to extend their thinking beyond their own personal context. Answer E is incorrect because beer is relatively commonplace in our society, and readers probably have a general idea of how and when people consume beer. Answer Gis similarly incorrect because the contemporary use of beer is not what the author is trying to explain to the reader; rather, the author is inviting them to think beyond their own personal understanding of beer and consider its importance to civilization in general. Answer F is incorrect because sports are only mentioned briefly in the sentence and the topic is never expanded upon further in the passage.

**43. C** Answer C is the best choice because "undesirable" and "bizarre" are both words used in Paragraph 3 to discuss flavors that must be removed from beer before it is finished. Answer A is incorrect because "conditioning" is the process by which undesirable/bizarre flavors are removed. Answer B is incorrect because "Green" is the term used to describe the beer before it has been conditioned, not to describe the flavors that must be conditioned out (as "undesirable" and "bizarre" both do). Answer D is incorrect because "dormant" describes the condition of the majority of the yeast once the conditioning period has been begun; not the flavors that need to be removed during conditioning.

**44. H** Answer H is the best choice based on the passage as a whole. All six paragraphs show that the author believes beer is culturally and historically significant. The content of Paragraphs 1, 4 and 6 in particular emphasizes the importance of responsibility and appreciation of beer's true historic importance. Answers E and F are both incorrect because they both make assumptions we can't possibly confirm without actually learning more about the author and his or her specific occupation. Answer G is incorrect because, while the author believes beer should be respected and contextualized, never says anything directly about disapproving of drinking responsibly.

**Passage 5 ("Classifying Soil Types"):**

**45. C** Answer C is the best choice because it reflects the most complete understanding of Paragraph 2. The opening or topic sentence of the paragraph should have been a major indicator, as it says, "The best way to understand soil in general is to understand what the ideal soil is like," to introduce the concept of loamy soil. The author describes how loamy soil supports roots and helps plants access water and minerals to establish a basis for comparison with the other soil types that follow later. Answer A is incorrect because the author isn't trying to show anybody they have "bad soil" but rather explaining what very good soil is like to establish a basis for comparison and show people what they should be trying to achieve. There is no negative or judgmental tone displayed at any point in the passage. Answer B is incorrect because, while the author clearly has some passion about the topic of soil, there is no explicit indication that he or she has a "favorite." Rather, loamy soil is presented as ideal and therefore established as a basis for comparison, making Answer C a better choice. Answer D is incorrect because it ignores the fact that loamy soil is established as a basis for comparison. While it's true that Paragraphs 3-7 could have come in any order, there is significance to loam being established and explained first.

**46. H** Answer H is the correct choice because, if something is very dense, then tilling it and digging into it would logically be very difficult. Paragraph 4 establishes that the density of clay soil is the direct cause of many of its pros and cons (both its nutritious nature, and sensitivity to temperature changes, for example), so the reader can reasonably infer that the density of clay soil is what makes it uniquely challenging. Answer E is incorrect because, while the dampness of clay soil would make it heavier, the density of the soil is identified within the paragraph as the main characteristic of clay soil, making Answer H the better choice. Answer F is incorrect because the short growing season is actually a result of the soil's density, making Answer H a better choice. Answer G is incorrect because the nutritious nature of the soil is in no way directly connected to how difficult it is to till.

**47. A** Answer A is the best choice because, as many empirical tests in daily life can show, salt tends to reduce or eliminate moisture. Paragraph 5 characterizes saline soil as occurring in "desert-adjacent" conditions and being suitable for "plants that grow naturally in desert-like environments," which should have indicator to the reader that the problem with saline soil is its dryness. Answer B is incorrect because there is no extended example of personification in the passage, and salt and water are not presented as having any particularly human-like traits. Answer C is incorrect because the author is using the word "disagreeable" to portray that salt and water have difficulty coexisting, not implying that any groups of people are actually disagreeing about the relative importance of salt and water. Answer D is incorrect as well because, as with Answer B, there is no extended personification of salt and water as "characters" and they are never portrayed in being in a "relationship" in either the platonic or romantic sense. The author simply means salt dries water out, making Answer A the best choice.

**48. H** Answer H is the best choice because Paragraph 6 begins by explaining that silty soil is typical found near "bodies of water" but ends by saying that the composition of the soil leaves plants susceptible to washout. This is especially problematic because it means that silty soil naturally occurs in areas where its worst quality can easily be observed or brought out. Answer E is incorrect because, while shallow root systems make plants susceptible to washout, the presence of a great deal of water nearby (such as a stream or pond) makes that potential washout exponentially more likely to occur, making Answer H a better choice, based on the passage. Answer F is incorrect because, while it makes an accurate observation, that observation has no bearing on why the threat of over-watering is especially bad in silty environments. Answer G is incorrect because the collapse of plants is the result of shallow roots and potential washouts, making Answer H (nearby water) the root cause and therefore the better overall answer.

**49. D** Answer D is the best choice because Flower D has shallow roots, requires a great deal of water, and grows quite tall. This aligns with the characteristics of plants in silty soil that are laid out in Paragraph 6 of the passage. Answer A is incorrect because Vegetable A has long roots, and the passage suggests that silty soil is generally the best fit for plants with shallow root systems. Answer B is incorrect because Vegetable B has Medium-Low water needs, and silty soil is generally found near bodies of water, which means Vegetable B could get too much moisture there. Answer C is incorrect because Flower C also has Low water needs and Medium roots, both of which suggest it is not a great fit for silty soil. Only Flower D is a natural fit, due to its shallow roots and love for water.

**50. F** Answer F is the best choice because Paragraph 4 repeatedly states that the density of clay soil is its most important and potentially most challenging characteristic. Since Vegetable A grows a very long, wide root (like a carrot, for example), that plant would have a difficult time growing in a tight-packed clay environment. Answer E is incorrect because clay soil's moisture-holding capabilities are mentioned in Paragraph 4, and while the passage says that clay soil can dry out in the summer, its water- and nutrient- holding capabilities in the other seasons are well-established. On the other hand, Answer G is incorrect because it is completely contrary to the content of the passage. Paragraph 4 actually states that clay soil can be "a workout" in the summer. Answer H is incorrect as well because, while clay soil is prone to frosts, there's nothing in the passage about how the height of a plant might impact its susceptibility to frost. Since the reader is not provided with any information that might support Answer H, Answer F is a much better choice.

**Passage 6 ("Epic poetry"):**

**51. A** Answer A is the best choice because Paragraph 1 introduces and defines the term "epic," which is used consistently throughout the rest of the passage. Answer B is incorrect because Paragraph 1 does little to preview or predict the rest of the passage (for example, it makes no mention of Homer). Answer C is incorrect because there is no clear attempt to persuade anybody of anything in the first paragraph. Rather, this part of the passage serves to introduce the key term "epic." Answer D is incorrect as well, although the paragraph does differentiate between "epic" as it's commonly used and "epic" in academic settings. Although this element is present in the paragraph, Answer A is still a better choice because it focuses on the main goal of the section, which is defining the topic.

**52. G** Answer G is the best choice because Paragraph 2 establishes that Homer was a traveling storyteller. The phrase, "a bard who wandered throughout what is now Greece and Turkey at some point between the twelfth and eighth centuries BC" should have been a major hint to the reader, as should, "The father of the epic wasn't just a writer, though; he was a performer who knew his incredibly long poems by heart and could recite them from memory over the course of hours." Answer E is incorrect because an "author" is simply a writer, whereas the paragraph takes pains to say Homer performed the poems as well. Answer F is incorrect because Homer was not a warrior-king, but rather a poet who wrote about warrior-kings. Answer H is incorrect because it simply focuses on the one detail about Homer's blindness and fails to pay attention to the other descriptions of his activities throughout the paragraph.

**53. D** Answer D is the best choice because it reflects a complete understanding of the paragraph. The sentence, "On the other hand, however, other scholars believe the name 'Homer' was a collective pseudonym used by a variety of ancient storytellers and no single author is responsible for the ancient Greek epics" should have been a major hint for the reader. The phrases "collective pseudonym" and "no single author" clearly communicate that it is possible that no biographical Homer ever existed. The very nature of someone's existence (or lack thereof) would clearly be the most important biographical fact about that them and would trump any other details. Answers A, B, and C are all incorrect, even though they represent legitimate details from the passage, because they all ignore the crucially important fact that Homer may not have lived at all.

**54. F** Answer F is the best choice because it reflects a strong understanding of the content of Paragraphs 3 and 4. Paragraph 3 states that Homer wrote both *The Iliad* and its sequel, *The Odyssey*. Paragraph 4 states that Milton wrote *Paradise Lost* and *Paradise Regained*, which, based on their similar titles, the reader can infer are closely related. Answer E is incorrect because the passage never says Homer was a politician. Answer G is incorrect because the author of the passage never suggests Milton was not a single author. Answer H is incorrect because Milton is never described as traveling at any point in the passage.

**55. C** Answer C is the best choice and reflects the best understanding of Paragraph 4. The phrase, "the tradition of the epic is still on display in many great movies and television shows" should have been a major indicator to the reader. Answer A is incorrect, although somewhat true, because the author never mentions school or students in the passage. Answer B is incorrect because the paragraph clearly states, "few people are sitting around writing epic poems today." Answer D is incorrect because it focuses on a weak correlation from the text (the use of the word "epic" to mean "cool") rather than the strong one (the clear link between today's entertainment and epic storytelling).

**56. H** Answer H is correct because it uses the information in Paragraph 1 to contextualize *The Epic of Gilgamesh* in time. Paragraph 1 states, "Many of the earliest recorded stories we know about are in the form of epics, such as The Epic of Gilgamesh, which was written about 4,000 years ago and may be the earliest recorded long form story." Since it is approximately 2000 AD now, the reader simply needs to do a little mental math and determine what year it was 4,000 years ago. Since 2000 – 4000 = (-2000), the reader should conclude 2000 BC is the correct choice. Answer E is incorrect because it is approximately two thousand years off. Answer F is incorrect because it is approximately three thousand years off. Answer G is incorrect because it is also approximately two thousand years off.

**57. C** Answer C is correct because it reflects the best overall understanding of Paragraph 3, which briefly summarizes the plots of both epics and explicitly states the connection between the two. Answer A is incorrect because the fact that the same author wrote two stories doesn't necessarily make one the sequel to the other. An author can write two completely self-contained works, and the second is only a sequel if it directly follows the story or themes of the first. Answer B is incorrect because Paragraph 3 clearly explains that *The Odyssey* follows Odysseus' journey home, not another war. Finally, Answer D is incorrect because Paragraph 1 mentions *The Epic of Gilgamesh* as an earlier epic, which means Answer D can't be true.

ARGOPREP
ARGOPREP.COM/SHSAT

**58. 67.5°**

You are given that $CB$ bisects the right-angle $\measuredangle ACE$. So, $\measuredangle ACB = \measuredangle BCE = \frac{\measuredangle ACE}{7.2} = \frac{90°}{2} = 45°$.

Since $CD$ bisects $\measuredangle ACB$, $\measuredangle ACD = \measuredangle DCB = \frac{\measuredangle ACB}{2} = \frac{45°}{2} = 22.5°$.

Since $\measuredangle DCE = \measuredangle DCB + \measuredangle BCE = 22.5° + 45° = 67.5°$.

**59. 218** This problem tests your ability to set up a ratio equation. Given the distance of 130 miles travelled on 4 gallons of fuel, you are to find the number of miles the same truck could travel on 6.7 gallons of fuel. Write the equation:

$\frac{130}{4} = \frac{x}{6.7}$ the given ratio

$\frac{130(6.7)}{4} = x$ multiply both sides by 6.7

$217.75 = x$ calculate

The nearest whole number is 218, which is the correct answer.

**60. 8** Solve the innermost absolute value expression first, then solve the outmost absolute value expression:

$|-10 - 18| = |-28| - 20 = 8$.

**61. 72** This problem tests your ability to set up a word problem, as well as your understanding of the perimeter of a rectangle. You are asked to find the perimeter of a garden with a width of 16 units and an area equal to that of a 10-unit × 32-unit garden. Start by calculating the area of the second garden: 10 × 32 = 320. Next, divide the width of the first garden into the area of the second. This will give you the depth of the first garden: 320 ÷ 16 = 20. Now find the perimeter by substituting this value into the formula for Perimeter:

$2 \times (width + depth) = Perimeter$ Perimeter Formula

$2 \times (16 + 20) = 72 = Perimeter$ subtitute and calculate

The perimeter is 72.

**62. 0** This problem asks you to solve a single variable equation:

$-1 - \frac{2}{5} \cdot \frac{5m - 10}{2 + 3m} = 1$ given

$-\frac{10m - 20}{10 + 15m} = 2$ add 1 to both sides and simplify the fraction

$-(10m - 20) = 2(10 + 15m)$ multiply both sides by $(10 + 15m)$

$-10m + 20 = 20 + 30m$ simplify

$-40m = 0$ simplify

$m = 0$ solve for $m$

The value of $m$ is 0.

**63.** **G** $(\sqrt{100})(\sqrt{64}) = (10)(8) = 80$

**64.** **C** 7.2 aliens = 1 monster = 15.5 oranges

$(\frac{1}{7.2})$ monster = 1 alien = $(\frac{15.5}{7.2})$ oranges

= 2.15 oranges.

**65.** **H** Factor each value, then chose all copies of the factors and multiply.

147: 3 • 7 • 7
98: 2 • 7 • 7
GCF: 7 • 7 = 49

**66.** **D** $\frac{11x}{x-y} = \frac{11(7)}{7-0} = \frac{77}{7} = 11$

**67.** **H** Lucy's average is the sum of all of her test scores divided by the total number of tests which is 4.

$$\frac{85 + 64 + 76 + x}{4} = 80$$

$$\frac{225 + x}{4} = 80$$

$320 = 225 + x$
$x = 95$

**68.** **C** There are 7 animals that have 4 legs out of 9 animals. So, there are 2 animals that do not have 4 legs out of 9.

$\frac{2}{9}$

**69.** **E** $y = (x^2)(x^x) = x^{2+x}$
if $x = 2$, then $y = 2^{2+2} = 2^4 = 16$

**70.** **A** By 4pm, train *A* has been traveling at 200 mph for 3 hours. Train *A* has traveled 600 miles. By 4pm, train *B* has been traveling 300 mph for 1 hour. Train *B* traveled 300 miles.

600 miles + 300 miles = 900 miles

**71.** **F**

| Present Age | Age 5 years ago |
|---|---|
| Bernard: $y$ | $y - 5$ |
| Luis: $y + 8$ | $y + 3$ |

**72.** **D** $\measuredangle CBE = \measuredangle DBA$ due to vertical angles.

The sum of the integer angles of *BCFE* is 360° and $\measuredangle CBE$ can be found as followed.

Knowing that $\measuredangle CFE = \measuredangle GFH$, it follows

$360° - (110° + 110° + 65° + \measuredangle CBE) = 0$
$360° - 285° = \measuredangle CBE = x°$
$x° = 75°$

**73.** **H** $(\frac{19}{4})(\frac{2}{2}) = \frac{37}{8}$. This means $\frac{19}{4} > \frac{37}{8}$

Using cross multiplication, for $\frac{13}{3}$ and $\frac{37}{8}$, it follows

(8)(13) < (3)(37)

104 < 111, so $\frac{13}{3} < \frac{37}{8}$

Therefore: $\frac{19}{4} > \frac{37}{8} > \frac{13}{3}$

**74.** **C** Two times any integer is even always. Thus, this leaves our choices to probably **B** or **C.**

Since $(\frac{x+y}{x})$ is not always an integer, and $x + y$ is, the answer is C.

**75.** **H** The probability of a point being chosen if the shaded region is

$$\frac{\text{Average of shaded region}}{\text{Total Area}} = \frac{\pi y^2 - \pi x^2}{\pi y^2}$$

This simplifies to $\frac{y^2 - x^2}{y^2}$

**76.** **B** $q = x + y$ and $x = y + z$
so, $q = y + z + y = 2y + z$
$q - 2y = z$

**77.** **H** Let $x = 5!$; $\frac{(5!)!}{5!} = \frac{x!}{x} = (x - 1)!$
$(x - 1)! = (5! - 1)!$ This answer is huge relative to the rest of the answers, therefore the answer is non of the above.

**78.** **C** $(a + b)(a + b) = a^2 + 2ab + b^2 = (a + b)^2$

$$\frac{a^2 + 2ab + b^2}{(a+b)^3} = \frac{(a+b)^2}{(a+b)^3} = \frac{1}{a+b}$$

**79.** **E** If it takes 3 cats 3 minutes to catch 3 mice, then it will take 3(1) cats $3x$ minutes to catch $3x$ mice, as long as x is an integer.

$3x = 99$

$x = 33$. Since $x$ is an integer, it will take 3(1) = 3 cats.

**80.** **C** Seven consecutive odd integers may be expressed as:

$$\underset{1^{st}}{x} + \underset{2^{nd}}{(x + 2)} + \underset{3^{rd}}{(x + 4)} + \underset{4^{th}}{(x + 6)} + \underset{5^{th}}{(x + 8)} + \underset{6^{th}}{(x + 10)} + \underset{7^{th}}{(x + 12)} = 7x + 42 = 749$$

$7x = 707$
$x = 101$

The largest is $x + 12$ or
$101 + 12 = 113$

**81.** **F** Original Volume= $\pi r^2 h$

New Volume = $\pi(2r)^2(\frac{h}{2}) = \pi(4r^2)(\frac{h}{2})$
$= 2\pi r^2 h$

$\pi r^2 h : 2\pi r^2 h$
1:2

**82.** **A** \$3.50 + \$0.20(4$x$) = \$22.50
Where $x$ is the number of miles ridden.

Solving for $x$:
\$0.20(4$x$) = \$19
$4x = 95$
$x = 23.75$ miles

**83.** **F** Assuming there are 4 weeks in July, John's hourly rate can be calculated as follows:

$$\frac{\$(1.04)(4000)}{4\text{ weeks}} = \frac{\$1040}{\text{week}}$$

$$\frac{\$1040}{\text{week}} \bullet \frac{1\text{ week}}{40\text{ hours}} = \frac{\$26}{\text{hours}}$$

**84.** **A** $8575 = 5^2 \bullet 7^3$
$x = 2, y = 3; (xy) - 5 = (6) - 5 = 1$

**85.** **H** Since $d$ is not specified, the value can be chosen to be 43.

When 43 is divided by 8, there is a remainder of 3.

$d + 3 = 46$.

When 46 is divided by 8, there is a remainder of 6.

**86.** **C** Permutations can be used. For 6 letters,
$6! = 6 \bullet 5 \bullet 4 \bullet 3 \bullet 2 \bullet 1 = 720$

**87.** **G** $-5(x - 3) \geq 20$
$(x - 3) \leq -4$
$x \leq -1$

**88.** **D** $-2 < \frac{x}{3} \leq 2$
$-6 < x \leq 6$

**89.** **H** If there are $x$ teens in total, then
$15{,}000 = 0.08x$
$x = 187{,}500$

Now, to find the number of teens whose favorite genre is action:
(.30)(187,500) = 56,250

**90.** **B** With the 20% sale, the price becomes (0.8)(\$550.50) = \$440.40

Applying the 5% coupon: (0.95)(\$440.4) = \$418.38

**91.** **F** $4760 = 2^3 \bullet 5 \bullet 7 \bullet 17$
$x = 2, y = 17$
$\frac{x^2}{y} = \frac{4}{17}$

**92.** **A** 11.5 milligrams = $(\frac{11.5}{1000})$ grams = 0.0115 grams

**93.** **H** 83 hours = (24 + 24 + 24 + 11) hours
Each 24 hours is a full day. So three days and eleven hours passes. Thus, this leaves the project due at 7:30PM Thursday.

**94.** **C** $(\frac{2}{3} + \frac{1}{4}) \div 2 = (\frac{8}{12} + \frac{3}{12}) \bullet \frac{1}{2}$
$\frac{11}{12} \bullet \frac{1}{2} = \frac{11}{24}$

**95.** **H** The dress and the bag are the only items taxed with 7% sales tax. All the items cost:
1.07($103 + $111) + ($73)
$228.98 + $73 = $301.98

**96.** **B** There are $(\frac{60 - 0}{3}) + 1$ numbers.

**97.** **H** The two numbers are $x$ and $(x + 2)$.
$x + (x + 2)$.The larger is $(x + 2)$.
So, $(x + 2) = 2x$
$x = 2$
$x + (x + 2) = 2 + (2 + 2) = 6$

**98.** **D** $3^x = 27^{a+b} = (3^3)^{a+b} = 3^{3a+3b}$
$x = 3a + 3b$ and $\frac{a^2 - b^2}{(a - b)} = \frac{(a - b)(a + b)}{(a - b)}$
$= a + b = 5$
$x = 3(a + b) = 3(5) = 15$

**99.** **H** Let $x$ = # of boys
Let $y$ = # of girls
$x = 2y; x + y = 2y + y = 30$
$3y = 30$
$y = 10$
The percentage of boys is
$\frac{x}{30} = \frac{2y}{30} = \frac{2(10)}{30} = \frac{20}{30} = \frac{2}{3} = 66.66\%$

**100.** **B** $a \star b = (a - b)^3$
$a \oplus b = (a - b)^2$
$\frac{a \star b}{a \oplus b} = \frac{(a - b)^3}{(a - b)^2} = a - b$

**101.** **G** $752 = 2^4 \bullet 47$

**102.** **A** Squaring any integer results in a positive integer.
The least value of $4x^2 - 10$ occurs when $4x^2$ is the lowest it can be, which happens at $x = 0$.
Then $4(0)^2 - 10 = -10$

**103.** **E** Let $x$ = # of bicycles
Let $y$ = # of tricycles
$x + y = 5$
$2x + 3y = 12$
$x = 5 - y$
$2(5 - y) + 3y = 10 - 2y + 3y = 12$
$10 + y = 12$
$y = 2$.
So, there are 2 tricycles.

**104. B** $x^2$ can never be negative for $x \geq 1$

So, the lowest value of $x^2$ is chosen, to make $\frac{x^2 - 1}{x^2}$ the lowest.

That occurs at $x = 1$

$\frac{x^2 - 1}{x^2} = \frac{1^2 - 1}{1^2} = \frac{1 - 1}{1} = 0$

**105. G**

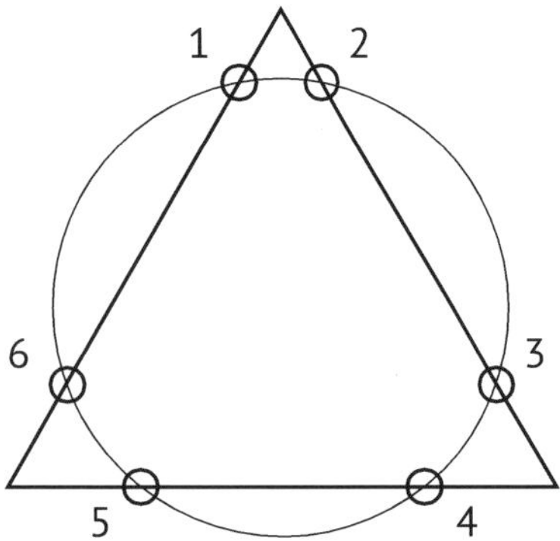


**106. A** The area of the rectangle is

$(3 + 3 + 1 + 1) \bullet (3 + 3) = 48$

Length Width

The area of the two circles is

$9\pi + \pi = 10\pi$

The area of the shaded region is

$48 - 10\pi$

**107. G** There are $\frac{1}{3}(45) = 15$ black ducks

and $\frac{1}{5}(45) = 9$ blue ducks

and $\frac{1}{3}(15) = 5$ green ducks.

45 = 15 + 9 + 5 + purple, where purple = # of purple ducks.

purple = 16.

**108. A** $\measuredangle ABC + 2x + 4x = \measuredangle ABC + 6x$,

then $6x + \measuredangle ABC = 180°$.

$\measuredangle ABC = 180° - 120° = 60°$,

since $\Delta ABC$ is isosceles.

So, $4x + 2x + 120° = 180°$

$6x = 180° - 120°$

Solve for $x$ and you get $x = 10°$

So $2x = 2(10°) = 20°$

**109. F** This is a triangle with a 3, 4, 5 special right triangle proportion.

$\frac{30}{6} = 5, \frac{24}{6} = 4$

$\frac{12 + y}{6} = 3$

$12 + y = 18$

$y = 6$

**110. C** 1 gallon = 4 quarts

The painter needs

(4 gallons)(8 rooms) = 32 gallons

of paint= $32 \cancel{\text{gallons}} \bullet \frac{4 \text{ quarts}}{1 \cancel{\text{gallon}}}$

= 128 quarts.

**111. H**

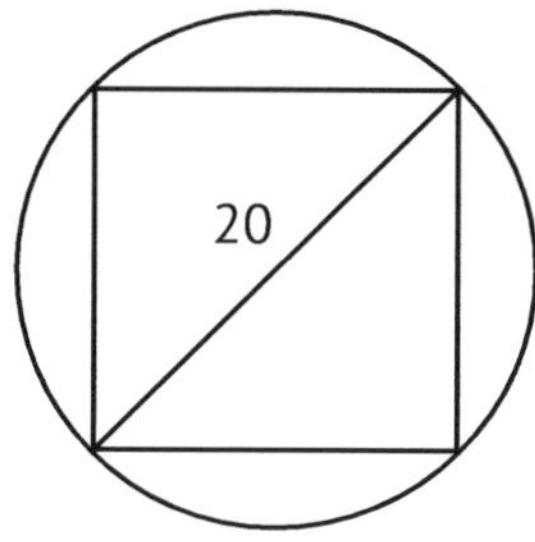


The radius is half of the diagonal length.

Circle Area = $\pi(r)^2 = \pi(10)^2 = 100\pi$

**112. C** Divide $50 by the unloaded price and regular price respectively.

Thus, this comes out to 20 gallons and 25 gallons, which gives a difference of 5 gallons.

**113. H** This problem tests your understanding of median value. First, organize the data in numerical order, remembering to put in each value the number of times it is listed in the frequency column.

Your data set will be: {14,15,15,15,16, 16,16,17,17,17,17,18,19,19,21}

The median is 17.

**114. C** This problem asks you to add Chocolate Candy Bars to the table in order to achieve a median price of $1.88. Recall that the median value is dependent on the count of entries in a set: it will be the value of the middle item by count. If there is an even number of entries in the set, then the median value will be the average of the two middle values. Looking over the chart, you can see that there are no items in the data set with a value of $1.88. This tells you that the median must be an average of two values. You can see that $1.88 lies between $1.76 (Oatmeal Cookies) and $2.00 (CFL Light Bulbs). Sort the set of values from lowest to highest, remembering to have an entry for each count of each value. Your data set will look like this:

{.67, .67, .67, .67, .67, .67, 1.76, 1.76, 1.76, 1.76, 2, 2, 2, 2, 2, 3.27, 3.27, 3.27, 3.99, 3.99, 4.54, 4.54}

Count the number of entries greater than $1.88 and the number of entries lower than $1.88. In this case you find 12 entries above $1.88 and 10 entries below. So you will need to add 2 entries below $1.88. Chocolate Candy Bars are $1.15 so you will need to add 2 Chocolate Candy Bars in order to reach a median value of $1.88. The correct answer choice is C.

ARGOPREP
ARGOPREP.COM/SHSAT

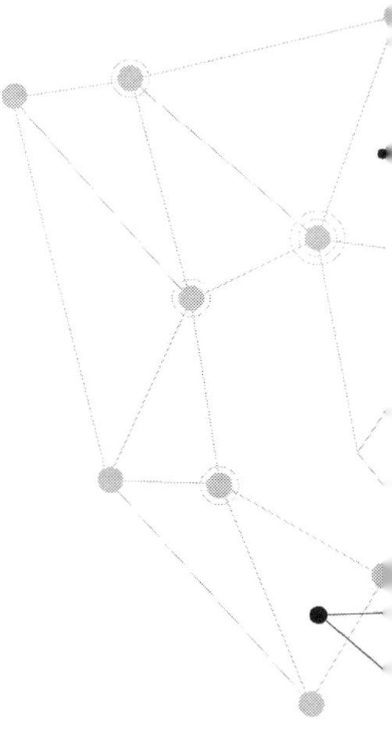

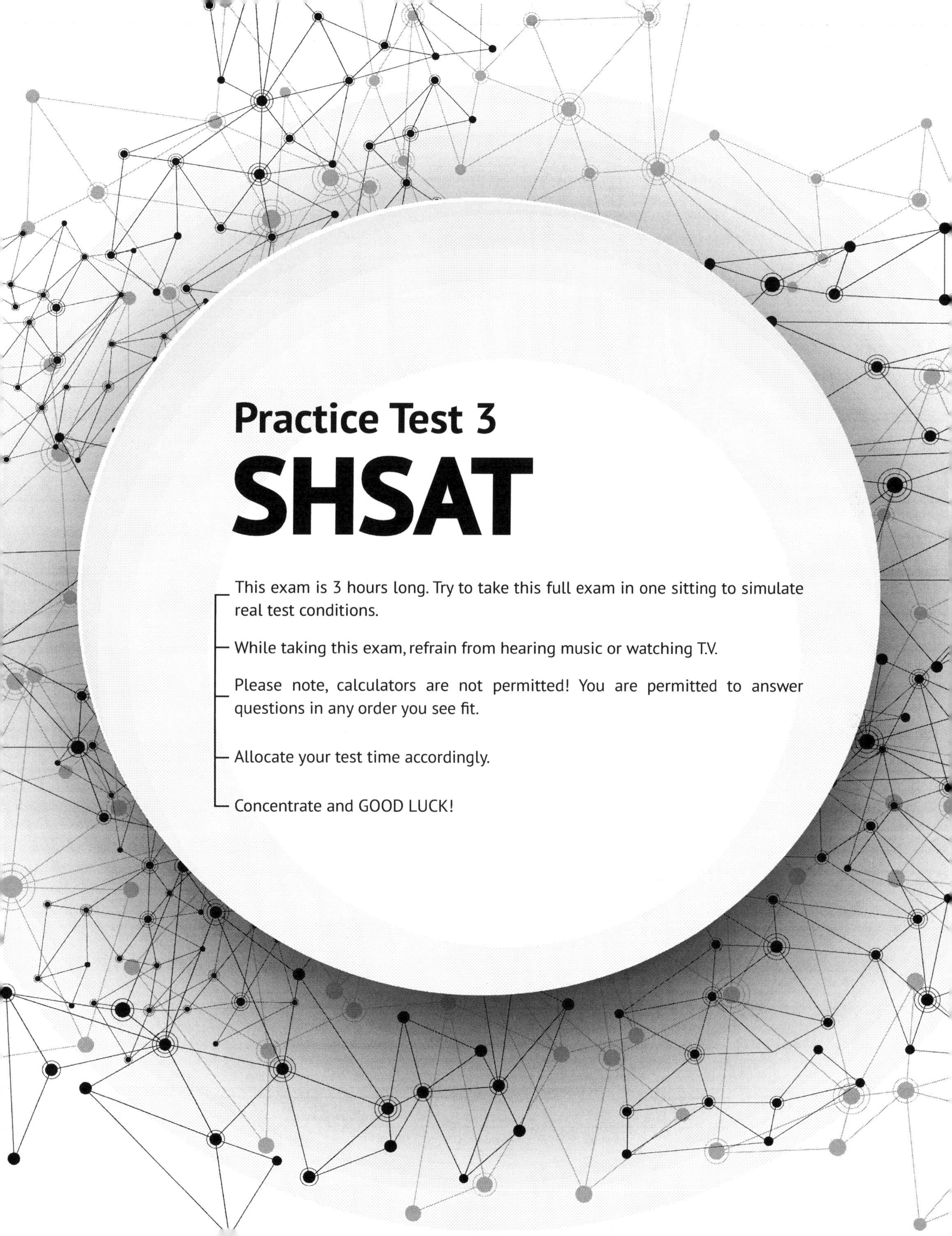

# Practice Test 3

# SHSAT

- This exam is 3 hours long. Try to take this full exam in one sitting to simulate real test conditions.
- While taking this exam, refrain from hearing music or watching T.V.
- Please note, calculators are not permitted! You are permitted to answer questions in any order you see fit.
- Allocate your test time accordingly.
- Concentrate and GOOD LUCK!

**You can find detailed video explanations to each problem in the book by visiting: ArgoPrep.com**

# SHSAT PRACTICE TEST 3
## ANSWER SHEET

### ENGLISH LANGUAGE ARTS

1. Ⓐ Ⓑ Ⓒ Ⓓ
2. Ⓔ Ⓕ Ⓖ Ⓗ
3. Ⓐ Ⓑ Ⓒ Ⓓ
4. Ⓔ Ⓕ Ⓖ Ⓗ
5. Ⓐ Ⓑ Ⓒ Ⓓ
6. Ⓔ Ⓕ Ⓖ Ⓗ
7. Ⓐ Ⓑ Ⓒ Ⓓ
8. Ⓔ Ⓕ Ⓖ Ⓗ
9. Ⓐ Ⓑ Ⓒ Ⓓ
10. Ⓔ Ⓕ Ⓖ Ⓗ
11. Ⓐ Ⓑ Ⓒ Ⓓ
12. Ⓔ Ⓕ Ⓖ Ⓗ
13. Ⓐ Ⓑ Ⓒ Ⓓ
14. Ⓔ Ⓕ Ⓖ Ⓗ
15. Ⓐ Ⓑ Ⓒ Ⓓ
16. Ⓔ Ⓕ Ⓖ Ⓗ
17. Ⓐ Ⓑ Ⓒ Ⓓ
18. Ⓔ Ⓕ Ⓖ Ⓗ
19. Ⓐ Ⓑ Ⓒ Ⓓ
20. Ⓔ Ⓕ Ⓖ Ⓗ
21. Ⓐ Ⓑ Ⓒ Ⓓ
22. Ⓔ Ⓕ Ⓖ Ⓗ
23. Ⓐ Ⓑ Ⓒ Ⓓ
24. Ⓔ Ⓕ Ⓖ Ⓗ
25. Ⓐ Ⓑ Ⓒ Ⓓ
26. Ⓔ Ⓕ Ⓖ Ⓗ
27. Ⓐ Ⓑ Ⓒ Ⓓ
28. Ⓔ Ⓕ Ⓖ Ⓗ
29. Ⓐ Ⓑ Ⓒ Ⓓ
30. Ⓔ Ⓕ Ⓖ Ⓗ
31. Ⓐ Ⓑ Ⓒ Ⓓ
32. Ⓔ Ⓕ Ⓖ Ⓗ
33. Ⓐ Ⓑ Ⓒ Ⓓ
34. Ⓔ Ⓕ Ⓖ Ⓗ
35. Ⓐ Ⓑ Ⓒ Ⓓ
36. Ⓔ Ⓕ Ⓖ Ⓗ
37. Ⓐ Ⓑ Ⓒ Ⓓ
38. Ⓔ Ⓕ Ⓖ Ⓗ
39. Ⓐ Ⓑ Ⓒ Ⓓ
40. Ⓔ Ⓕ Ⓖ Ⓗ
41. Ⓐ Ⓑ Ⓒ Ⓓ
42. Ⓔ Ⓕ Ⓖ Ⓗ
43. Ⓐ Ⓑ Ⓒ Ⓓ
44. Ⓔ Ⓕ Ⓖ Ⓗ
45. Ⓐ Ⓑ Ⓒ Ⓓ
46. Ⓔ Ⓕ Ⓖ Ⓗ
47. Ⓐ Ⓑ Ⓒ Ⓓ
48. Ⓔ Ⓕ Ⓖ Ⓗ
49. Ⓐ Ⓑ Ⓒ Ⓓ
50. Ⓔ Ⓕ Ⓖ Ⓗ
51. Ⓐ Ⓑ Ⓒ Ⓓ
52. Ⓔ Ⓕ Ⓖ Ⓗ
53. Ⓐ Ⓑ Ⓒ Ⓓ
54. Ⓔ Ⓕ Ⓖ Ⓗ
55. Ⓐ Ⓑ Ⓒ Ⓓ
56. Ⓔ Ⓕ Ⓖ Ⓗ
57. Ⓐ Ⓑ Ⓒ Ⓓ

### MATHEMATICS

63. Ⓔ Ⓕ Ⓖ Ⓗ
64. Ⓐ Ⓑ Ⓒ Ⓓ
65. Ⓔ Ⓕ Ⓖ Ⓗ
66 Ⓐ Ⓑ Ⓒ Ⓓ
67. Ⓔ Ⓕ Ⓖ Ⓗ
68. Ⓐ Ⓑ Ⓒ Ⓓ
69. Ⓔ Ⓕ Ⓖ Ⓗ
70. Ⓐ Ⓑ Ⓒ Ⓓ
71. Ⓔ Ⓕ Ⓖ Ⓗ
72. Ⓐ Ⓑ Ⓒ Ⓓ
73. Ⓔ Ⓕ Ⓖ Ⓗ
74 Ⓐ Ⓑ Ⓒ Ⓓ
75. Ⓔ Ⓕ Ⓖ Ⓗ
76. Ⓐ Ⓑ Ⓒ Ⓓ
77. Ⓔ Ⓕ Ⓖ Ⓗ
78. Ⓐ Ⓑ Ⓒ Ⓓ
79. Ⓔ Ⓕ Ⓖ Ⓗ
80. Ⓐ Ⓑ Ⓒ Ⓓ
81. Ⓔ Ⓕ Ⓖ Ⓗ
82. Ⓐ Ⓑ Ⓒ Ⓓ
83. Ⓔ Ⓕ Ⓖ Ⓗ
84 Ⓐ Ⓑ Ⓒ Ⓓ
85. Ⓔ Ⓕ Ⓖ Ⓗ
86. Ⓐ Ⓑ Ⓒ Ⓓ
87. Ⓔ Ⓕ Ⓖ Ⓗ
88. Ⓐ Ⓑ Ⓒ Ⓓ
89. Ⓔ Ⓕ Ⓖ Ⓗ
90. Ⓐ Ⓑ Ⓒ Ⓓ
91. Ⓔ Ⓕ Ⓖ Ⓗ
92. Ⓐ Ⓑ Ⓒ Ⓓ
93. Ⓔ Ⓕ Ⓖ Ⓗ
94. Ⓐ Ⓑ Ⓒ Ⓓ
95. Ⓔ Ⓕ Ⓖ Ⓗ
96. Ⓐ Ⓑ Ⓒ Ⓓ
97. Ⓔ Ⓕ Ⓖ Ⓗ
98. Ⓐ Ⓑ Ⓒ Ⓓ
99. Ⓔ Ⓕ Ⓖ Ⓗ
100. Ⓐ Ⓑ Ⓒ Ⓓ
101. Ⓔ Ⓕ Ⓖ Ⓗ
102. Ⓐ Ⓑ Ⓒ Ⓓ
103. Ⓔ Ⓕ Ⓖ Ⓗ
104. Ⓐ Ⓑ Ⓒ Ⓓ
105. Ⓔ Ⓕ Ⓖ Ⓗ
106. Ⓐ Ⓑ Ⓒ Ⓓ
107. Ⓔ Ⓕ Ⓖ Ⓗ
108. Ⓐ Ⓑ Ⓒ Ⓓ
109. Ⓔ Ⓕ Ⓖ Ⓗ
110. Ⓐ Ⓑ Ⓒ Ⓓ
111. Ⓔ Ⓕ Ⓖ Ⓗ
112. Ⓐ Ⓑ Ⓒ Ⓓ
113. Ⓔ Ⓕ Ⓖ Ⓗ
114. Ⓐ Ⓑ Ⓒ Ⓓ

### MATHEMATICS (GRID IN)

58

⊖ ⊙ 0 1 2 3 4 5 6 7 8 9

59

⊖ ⊙ 0 1 2 3 4 5 6 7 8 9

60

⊖ ⊙ 0 1 2 3 4 5 6 7 8 9

61

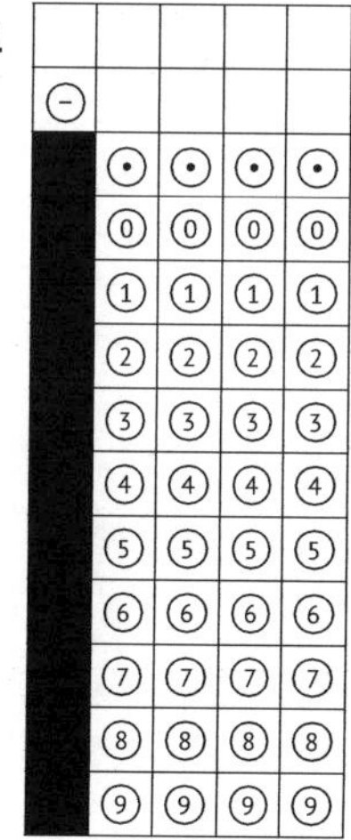

62

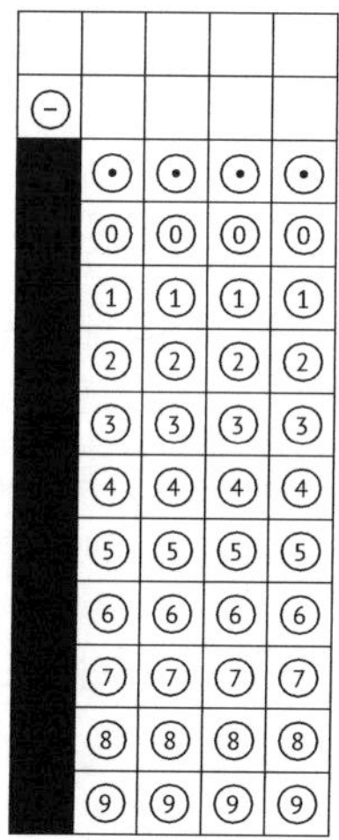

ARGOPREP
ARGOPREP.COM/SHSAT

**DIRECTIONS:** For questions 1 to 5, you will be asked to recognize and correct errors in sentences or short paragraphs.

**1.** Read this paragraph.

> (1) The Academy Awards, informally known as the Oscars, have taken place in Hollywood, California every year since 1929. (2) The goal of the yearly ceremony is to distribute awards for the best movies, greatest performances by actors, and most impressive technical achievements. (3) The Academy of Motion Picture Arts and Sciences presents awards for each of 24 different categories, ranging from "Best Actress in a Leading Role" to "Best Sound Mixing." (4) Elaborate, often memorable acceptance speeches are given by the winners of each award.

Which sentence in the paragraph should be revised to correct the use of passive voice?

**A.** Sentence 1
**B.** Sentence 2
**C.** Sentence 3
**D.** Sentence 4

**2.** Read this sentence.

> In tennis, the ball is hit back and forth across the net by two players trying to score points.

How could this sentence be rewritten to eliminate the use of passive voice?

**E.** In tennis, two players hit a ball back and forth across a net to score points.
**F.** In tennis, the ball is hit by two players, who knock it back and forth to try and score points.
**G.** In tennis, the ball is hit by two players who try to score points by knocking the ball back and forth.
**H.** In tennis, points are scored when players hit the ball back and forth across the net.

**CONTINUE ON TO THE NEXT PAGE ➞**

**3.** Read this paragraph.

(1) George Gershwin was arguably the most influential American composer of the twentieth century. (2) Gershwin broke into the music industry in 1913 as a "song plugger," a public performer and salesman who promoted new music. (3) By the age of 20 Gershwin had written several hit songs. (4) Throughout his twenties, Gershwin wrote songs for Broadway musicals as well, partnering with his brother Ira, who was a lyricist. (5) Later in his career, Gershwin began focusing more on classical arrangements and opera. (6) Although he only lived 38 years, Gershwin left behind an impressive catalogue of songs, musicals, and film scores.

Which sentence in the paragraph should be revised to correct comma use?

**A.** Sentence 2
**B.** Sentence 3
**C.** Sentence 4
**D.** Sentence 5

---

**4.** Read this sentence.

A secret government program known as the Manhattan project developed the nuclear weapons that helped end World War II.

Which revision is most necessary to correct the sentence?

**E.** Change **government** to **Government**
**F.** Change **project** to **Project**
**G.** Change **nuclear weapons** to **Nuclear Weapons**
**H.** Change **World War II** to **world war II**

**5.** Read this paragraph.

(1) One of my happiest childhood memories is baking pies with my grandmother every fall. (2) My mother also baked, but I always felt a strong connection to the pies my grandma and I would make with the apples from her back yard. (3) The process would start with us picking the sweetest, most delicious-looking apples from their Golden Delicious tree. (4) Then, I would wash and peel the apples while my grandmother made the dough for our crust. (5) When the pie was ready to be filled, my grandmother would always let me put the cinnamon on top of the apples, which was my favorite part.

Which sentence is least relevant and should be removed from the paragraph?

**A.** Sentence 2
**B.** Sentence 3
**C.** Sentence 4
**D.** Sentence 5

**CONTINUE ON TO THE NEXT PAGE ➞**

**DIRECTIONS:** Read the passage below to answer questions 6 to 11. The questions will focus on improving the writing quality of the passage to follow the conventions of standard written English.

---

**The Early Years of Baseball**

(1) Baseball is hailed as a uniquely American sport, even though it is truly an international game. (2) One of the most fascinating aspects of baseball is its long, complex history. (3) Baseball evolved gradually from European bat-and-ball games, particularly cricket and rounders, which were popular schoolyard games in England during the colonial period. (4) People first began calling a variation of bat-and-ball "base-ball" or "bass-ball" in the south of England in the 1740s. (5) American colonists put their own spin on the games they brought with them from Europe and by the 1790s baseball had become popular throughout the United States.

(6) Early American baseball was a game of local variations. (7) The number of bases, the construction of the ball, and the methods of making outs could be different from town to town. (8) In 1845, Alexander Cartwright, a member of the New York Knickerbocker Club, created "The Knickerbocker Rules," the closest direct ancestor of the modern game. (9) The Knickerbocker Rules introduce the modern concept of a "force play," meaning the fielders could make an out by throwing the ball to the base a runner was approaching. (10) Previously, fielders had to "soak," or hit the runner with a thrown ball. (11) The Knickerbocker rules were significantly different from today's baseball in several key ways, however. (12) These official rules were used to play the earliest professional baseball games, beginning a long American tradition.

(13) For many years, these historical origins of baseball were clouded in myth. (14) In 1905, a group called the Mills Commission declared that Civil War General Abner Doubleday had invented baseball in Cooperstown, New York in 1839, which the commission most likely knew wasn't entirely true, but they wanted to provide baseball with a uniquely American back-story to distance the game from its European origins. (15) This kind of dishonesty provides a significant challenge to historians trying to discover the truth. (16) Furthermore, Doubleday was a decorated war hero, which made the game's invention seem more grandiose. (17) Over 100 years later, the Doubleday myth is still told by some historians, obscuring the incredible true history of baseball.

---

**6.** Which sentence could be eliminated from the first paragraph without detracting from the main ideas of the paragraph?

**E.** Sentence 2
**F.** Sentence 3
**G.** Sentence 4
**H.** Sentence 5

**CONTINUE ON TO THE NEXT PAGE →**

7. Which revision of sentence 5 makes proper use of commas?

   A. American colonists put their own spin on the games they brought with them, from Europe, and by the 1790s baseball had become popular throughout the United States.
   B. American colonists put their own spin on the games they brought with them from Europe, and by the 1790s baseball had become popular throughout the United States.
   C. American colonists put their own spin on the games they brought with them from Europe and by the 1790s, baseball had become popular throughout the United States.
   D. American colonists put their own spin on the games they brought with them from Europe, and by the 1790s, baseball had become popular throughout the United States.

---

8. What is the best way to combine sentences 6 and 7 to clarify the relationship between ideas and reduce wordiness?

   E. Early American baseball was a game of local variations because the number of bases, the construction of the ball, and the methods of making outs could be different from town to town.
   F. The number of bases, the construction of the ball, and the methods of making outs could all be different from town to town, making early American baseball a game of variations.
   G. Early American baseball was a game of town-to-town variations, including the number of bases, the construction of the ball, and the methods of making outs.
   H. Early American baseball was different from town to town, making it a game of variations.

---

9. Which transition word should be added to sentence 8?

   A. However
   B. Consequently
   C. Moreover
   D. Unfortunately

---

10. Which edit is needed to correct sentence 9?

   E. Change **Rules** to **Rule**
   F. Change **introduce** to **introduced**
   G. Change **meaning** to **meant**
   H. Change **approaching** to **approached**

---

11. Which of these would best follow sentence 11 to provide support?

   A. There was no such thing as a “strikeout,” and the ball had to be pitched underhand.
   B. Alexander Cartwright is often referred to as “the Father of Modern Baseball.”
   C. There are recreational leagues around the country today in which people still play Knickerbocker Rules games.
   D. The rules introduced the concept of a foul ball, which is still used in today’s game.

**CONTINUE ON TO THE NEXT PAGE ➡**

**DIRECTIONS:** Read the passage below to answer questions 6 to 13. The questions will focus on improving the writing quality of the passage to follow the conventions of standard written English.

---

**Excerpt from Chapter 5 of "Frankenstein"**
By Mary Shelley

It was on a dreary night of November that I beheld the accomplishment of my toils. With an anxiety that almost amounted to agony, I collected the instruments of life around me, that I might infuse a spark of being into the lifeless thing that lay at my feet. It was already one in the morning; the rain pattered dismally against the panes, and my candle was nearly burnt out, when, by the glimmer of the half-extinguished light, I saw the dull yellow eye of the creature open; it breathed hard, and a convulsive motion agitated its limbs.

How can I describe my emotions at this catastrophe, or how delineate the wretch whom with such infinite pains and care I had endeavoured to form? His limbs were in proportion, and I had selected his features as beautiful. Beautiful! Great God! His yellow skin scarcely covered the work of muscles and arteries beneath; his hair was of a lustrous black, and flowing; his teeth of a pearly whiteness; but these luxuriances only formed a more horrid contrast with his watery eyes, that seemed almost of the same colour as the dun-white sockets in which they were set, his shrivelled complexion and straight black lips.

The different accidents of life are not so changeable as the feelings of human nature. I had worked hard for nearly two years, for the sole purpose of infusing life into an inanimate body. For this I had deprived myself of rest and health. I had desired it with an ardour that far exceeded moderation; but now that I had finished, the beauty of the dream vanished, and breathless horror and disgust filled my heart. Unable to endure the aspect of the being I had created, I rushed out of the room and continued a long time traversing my bedchamber, unable to compose my mind to sleep. At length lassitude succeeded to the tumult I had before endured, and I threw myself on the bed in my clothes, endeavouring to seek a few moments of forgetfulness. But it was in vain; I slept, indeed, but I was disturbed by the wildest dreams. I thought I saw Elizabeth, in the bloom of health, walking in the streets of Ingolstadt. Delighted and surprised, I embraced her, but as I imprinted the first kiss on her lips, they became livid with the hue of death; her features appeared to change, and I thought that I held the corpse of my dead mother in my arms; a shroud enveloped her form, and I saw the grave-worms crawling in the folds of the flannel. I started from my sleep with horror; a cold dew covered my forehead, my teeth chattered, and every limb became convulsed; when, by the dim and yellow light of the moon, as it forced its way through the window shutters, I beheld the wretch– the miserable monster whom I had created. He held up the curtain of the bed; and his eyes, if eyes they may be called, were

CONTINUE ON TO THE NEXT PAGE →

fixed on me. His jaws opened, and he muttered some inarticulate sounds, while a grin wrinkled his cheeks. He might have spoken, but I did not hear; one hand was stretched out, seemingly to detain me, but I escaped and rushed downstairs. I took refuge in the courtyard belonging to the house which I inhabited, where I remained during the rest of the night, walking up and down in the greatest agitation, listening attentively, catching and fearing each sound as if it were to announce the approach of the demoniacal corpse to which I had so miserably given life.

---

**12.** Which of these best describes the mood of the passage?

**E.** Ominous
**F.** Adventurous
**G.** Ironic
**H.** Melancholy

---

**13.** Based on Paragraph 1 of the text, how does Dr. Frankenstein bring his creation to life?

**A.** By using electricity from the storm
**B.** By using special chemicals
**C.** By using fire from the candle
**D.** The text does not specify

---

**14.** Which of these is the best definition for "wretch" as it is used in Paragraph 2 of the text?

**E.** To gag or vomit
**F.** An unfortunate person
**G.** A forceful, violent twisting
**H.** An intimidating figure

**15.** What does Dr. Frankenstein find to be the most freakish or off-putting aspect of the creature that he has created?

**A.** The watery and off-color appearance of its eyes
**B.** The way muscles and arteries can be seen bulging through its flesh
**C.** The way the creature is somehow ugly even though it's made with attractive pieces
**D.** The way the creature follows him around his house

---

**16.** Which of these is the best definition for "lassitude" as it is used in Paragraph 3?

**E.** Fear
**F.** Anger
**G.** Tiredness
**H.** Regret

---

**17.** Based on the text, Dr. Frankenstein's dream is most likely an example of:

**A.** Metaphor
**B.** Irony
**C.** Foreshadowing
**D.** Rising Action

**CONTINUE ON TO THE NEXT PAGE →**

**18.** Which of these best characterizes the change Dr. Frankenstein goes through in the passage?

**E.** He changes from being a man into being a monster
**F.** He changes from fearing his creation to devising a plan to stop it
**G.** He changes from being enthusiastic about his creation to regretting it
**H.** He changes from loving Elizabeth to realizing he no longer cares for her

---

**19.** How does Elizabeth initially appear to Dr. Frankenstein in his dream?

**A.** She is decomposing and being eaten by worms
**B.** She looks very similar to the creature Dr. Frankenstein created
**C.** She looks like his mother
**D.** She looks completely normal and healthy

**20.** Which phrase from Paragraph 1 best foreshadows the tone of the rest of the passage?

**E.** "It was on a dreary night..."
**F.** "...I beheld the accomplishment of my toils..."
**G.** "With an anxiety that almost amounted to agony..."
**H.** "...a convulsive motion agitated its limbs."

**CONTINUE ON TO THE NEXT PAGE ➞**

# READING COMPREHENSION
## Practice Test 3

**DIRECTIONS:** Analyze the passages below, and answer the commensurate questions. Only use information provided within the passage for your answers. There is only one answer for each question.

---

### Asthma

More than 350 million people around the world suffer from asthma, a disease that effects the ability to breathe. The severity and symptoms of asthma can vary a great deal from person to person, but generally, asthma causes the airways within the lungs to swell or fill with mucus, making it harder to fill and empty the lungs. This often results in coughing, wheezing, or shortness of breath. These symptoms can also lead to panic, irritability, and fatigue, all of which make the episodes more difficult to get over. For some patients, asthma presents daily challenges. For others, it remains dormant or managed via medication for long stretches of time until an acute episode presents itself.

There are multiple causes of asthma, and some of them may not be fully understood yet. Doctors and researchers do agree, however, that genetics play a major part in determining whether someone will develop asthma. If previous members of your family have had asthma, there's a much greater chance you will as well. It's currently believed that environmental factors are responsible for most other cases of asthma. Lower air quality due to pollution and the increased use of volatile chemicals in the household are often seen as major environmental risks, as are smoking (or being around smokers) and mold. Allergies are also connected to asthma, as there is a high coincidence of indoor allergies among asthmatics. The exact nature of this relationship has not been fully defined yet, however.

Regardless of the cause, when an asthma attack strikes, it can have effects that range from the annoying to the life-threatening. During a minor flare, an asthmatic might catch themselves making a high-pitching wheezing sound (especially when exhaling), breathing a little faster or shallower than usual, or coughing. If they have their rescue inhaler handy, these symptoms can be fought back with a few puffs of medicine and a few minutes to rest and recover, but without medication, even a minor asthma attack can leave the sufferer feeling disoriented and over-heated with a pounding heart, throbbing headache, and intense feelings of dread. In the case of a major asthma attack, someone may even feel that they are unable to breath due to heaviness or tightness in their chest. Unfortunately, the very worst asthma attacks can even be fatal, so even the slightest symptoms should be managed and paid attention to.

There are numerous effective treatments for asthma today, although that wasn't always the case. Dating back to ancient times, doctors have understood that clean air is crucial to minimizing asthma symptoms, but there were virtually no tools for managing acute asthma attacks until

**CONTINUE ON TO THE NEXT PAGE →**

very recently. In the late nineteenth and early twentieth centuries, there were a variety of quack medical treatments for asthma that included inhaling chemical vapors and smoking special cigarettes. Of course, listening to the salesmen and doctors who prescribed those treatments was generally catastrophic to patients. Now, however, there are a wide range of inhaled and oral steroids that asthma sufferers can rely on to give them daily comfort and peace of mind in the case of a major asthma attack.

Many patients actually use more than one steroid to treat their asthma. Just about anybody with asthma will have some form of a rescue inhaler which can be used in emergencies. Rescue inhalers clear the lungs quick, but they can also leave users feeling edgy with their hearts pounding out of their chests. These tools work to clear things up for the moment, but if they're used frequently, their effectiveness plummets quickly. That's why many patients also have a daily inhaler that they use each morning. Daily inhalers (also known as "maintenance inhalers") are designed to keep a lower dose of steroids in the body at all times to keep symptoms from presenting themselves in the first place. When symptoms are strong and persistent, a doctor might even prescribe oral steroids, in the form of pills, for a few days. All these medications just show that while asthma is common, it's still complex!

**21.** Which of these best describes the author's overall point of view?

**A.** Asthma is somewhat commonplace, but it is no longer dangerous thanks to modern medicine.
**B.** Asthma should be taken seriously, in spite of the effective treatments we have available, because it is widespread and episodes can escalate quickly.
**C.** In the past, asthma killed many people because there weren't effective medicines, but now we have mastered treatment.
**D.** People with asthma are often panicked and irritable because the disease is so bad.

---

**22.** Based on the passage, which of these things happens first when a person suffers from asthma?

**E.** They begin to wheeze
**F.** They become panicked or irritable
**G.** They have difficulty filling and emptying their lungs
**H.** They experience swelling or mucus build-up in their airways

---

**23.** Which is the best definition of "coincidence" as it is used in Paragraph 2?

**A.** A surprising, unexpected situation
**B.** Two separate but related incidents
**C.** A correlation
**D.** A medical term for multiple asthma symptoms

**CONTINUE ON TO THE NEXT PAGE ➡**

**24.** What is the main purpose of Paragraph 3 within the passage?

- **E.** To provide examples of how to successfully manage an asthma attack
- **F.** To help the reader understand how someone might feel while they're having an asthma attack
- **G.** To illustrate why people with asthma should always have their rescue inhaler with them
- **H.** To show the difference between minor, unimportant asthma symptoms and major, dangerous asthma symptoms

---

**25.** What is the best definition of "quack" as it is used in Paragraph 4?

- **A.** Unscientific or disreputable
- **B.** The sound made by a duck
- **C.** Traditional herbal remedies
- **D.** Outdated or old-timey

**26.** Which of these is not a reason most long-term asthma patients use a daily inhaler?

- **E.** The medication in rescue inhalers is short-acting and has undesirable side effects
- **F.** Asthma patients experience symptoms every day, so it's necessary to medicate every day
- **G.** Daily inhalers discourage symptoms from presenting themselves
- **H.** The effectiveness of rescue inhaler medication decreases rapidly

**CONTINUE ON TO THE NEXT PAGE ➡**

## Gravity

Most people know that a phenomenon called "gravity" keeps our feet fixed to the ground so we don't float away, but few truly understand how important gravity is to the existence of the universe. Gravity is what makes our planet habitable and what holds the cosmos together. Without gravity, there wouldn't be life on this planet – in fact, the planet might not exist at all. Gravity is the force that keeps objects close to each other. The rocks that came together to make our planet billions of years ago would never have combined and become a single sphere without gravity. In a universe without gravity, we wouldn't orbit the sun, either; we'd either float away from it, which would mean our planet would no longer have conditions suitable for life, or we would stay in a fixed position forever, meaning there would be no seasons, making much of the planet impossible to farm or live on.

In spite of all that, physicists actually consider gravity a fairly weak force. All objects exert some kind of gravitational pull on each other, but the effects are only really observable when you're dealing with incredible large objects. That's why your body (which only weights a few hundred pounds at most) doesn't have a gravitational pull that attracts objects from across the room, but the Earth (which is quite massive) can keep our moon in orbit. Similarly, the Sun is about 333,000 times bigger than Earth, which means its force of gravity determines our movement. This makes gravity fascinating because it's difficult to observe in daily life but vitally important to the larger workings of the universe.

One thing that's important to understand, though, is that gravity is not a one-way street. Even though a more massive object (like the Sun) will ultimately determine the orbit of a smaller object (like the Earth), the smaller object also attracts the bigger object. This can be hard to conceptualize, but thinking about a pair of magnets can help illustrate things. If you put one magnet, which represents the Sun, in a fixed position in the middle of a table and spiral another magnet, representing the Earth, around it, moving closer and closer, eventually, when you bring the moving magnet close enough to fixed one, the fixed magnet would move slightly to meet the other magnet. Obviously, magnetism is a different force than gravity, but this demonstration illustrates how the gravity of a smaller body can actually affect the bigger one, especially if the objects get close to each other. Of course, the force the Sun exerts on our Earth is much greater than that of the Earth on the Sun because of the tremendous difference in mass.

We understand what we do about gravity due to the work of some of history's most important and well-known scientists. During the sixteenth and seventeenth centuries, the Italian scientist Galileo discovered that all objects, dropped from any height, fall to the ground at a fixed rate of acceleration, unless they have an especially air-resistant shape. Prior to his work, it was assumed that heavier objects would fall to the Earth at a faster rate than light ones. After Galileo, the English scientist and philosopher Sir Isaac Newton continued exploring the mystery of gravity. Newton's study essentially gave birth to the field of physics, and his understanding of gravity persisted from the seventeenth century

CONTINUE ON TO THE NEXT PAGE ➡

through the twentieth. Newton's work was refined and expanded upon by Albert Einstein in the early 1900s. Without the work of these scientific giants, we would have absolutely no real idea how our world, and the universe around us, works.

**27.** Which of these works of gravity is the most crucial to our existence here on Earth?

**A.** Gravity keeps our feet attached to the ground and prevents things from floating away.
**B.** Gravity keeps the moon near the Earth, which creates our tides.
**C.** Gravity keeps the Earth near the Sun, which provides us with crucial light and warmth.
**D.** Gravity helped pull together all the materials that created our planet.

---

**28.** Based on the passage, why is gravity considered a "fairly weak force" even though it plays such a crucial role in the universe?

**E.** Gravity only attracts very small objects to each other.
**F.** Gravity is easy to eliminate or defy, so in spite of its importance to the universe, it's actually not a very impressive force.
**G.** Gravity is reliant on mass, so only really massive objects have appreciable gravity.
**H.** Other forces are more important to keeping the planets in orbit.

**29.** Which of these best describes the gravitational relationship between the Sun and the Earth?

**A.** The Sun exerts a gravitational pull on the Earth because it is much more massive, which keeps the Earth in its orbit.
**B.** The Sun and Earth exert gravitational pulls on each other, but the force of the Sun is much stronger, which keeps the Earth in its orbit.
**C.** The Sun and Earth exert gravitational pulls on each other, but the force of the Earth is stronger, which keeps the moon in its orbit.
**D.** The Sun exerts a gravitational pull on the Earth because it is very hot, which keeps the Earth in its orbit.

---

**30.** What does the author mean when he or she says that "gravity is not a one-way street?"

**E.** Gravity is an interaction between two objects, not just a smaller object being drawn to a bigger one.
**F.** Gravity can be reversed through specific scientific processes which reverse the attractive pull.
**G.** There isn't just one definition for the term "gravity."
**H.** There is more than one way to explain gravity using science.

**CONTINUE ON TO THE NEXT PAGE →**

**31.** What does the example of the two magnets in Paragraph 3 illustrate about gravity?

- **A.** Gravity and magnetism work the same way in that they cause attraction between different objects.
- **B.** The gravitational pull of a smaller object on a more massive one is present but only observable when they are very close to each other.
- **C.** Gravity is gradually causing the Earth to spiral closer and closer to the sun.
- **D.** Magnetism is a much stronger force than gravity, which is why we can observe it on a tabletop scale.

---

**32.** Based on the passage, if you dropped a tennis ball and a bowling ball from the top of the Empire State Building at the same time, what would happen?

- **E.** The tennis ball would hit the ground first because it is lighter.
- **F.** The bowling ball would hit the ground first because it is more massive.
- **G.** The bowling ball would hit the ground first because it has a greater gravitational pull.
- **H.** The two balls would hit the ground at the same time because the acceleration of gravity is constant.

CONTINUE ON TO THE NEXT PAGE ➡

**Henry VIII**

Henry VIII is one of the most important monarchs in the history of Europe, but most of his notoriety today is based on his horrific personal life. Henry's reign was crucial to history because he broke hundreds of years of European tradition by splitting from the Pope and the Catholic Church in Rome. For centuries, the Church and monarchies across Europe had essentially partnered to provide supplies, infrastructure, spiritual support, and law and order to subjects in the cities and farm towns that dotted the continent at the time. Henry, however, upended this order and asserted that a monarch should be the supreme leader of his or her country, with final say on all issues – including religion. It was one of many crucial straws on the back of an already-burdened camel as the Protestant Reformation began to gather steam and an important step on the road toward the modern era of independent, self-determining states.

By any measure, this should've been a legacy-making accomplishment, but Henry's motives were deeply problematic. He simply wanted absolute power in his kingdom so he could treat his wives any way he wanted. He originally split from the Catholic Church because they would not annul his marriage to his first wife, Catherine of Aragon. That meant that if he left her for another woman, any sons he had with his future wife would not have legitimate claim to being the king of England. Once the Pope made it clear he wouldn't dissolve Henry's marriage, Henry split from the Catholic Church and started the Church of England, which, unsurprisingly, granted him his annulment. His break from the Catholic Church wasn't really about high-minded ideals after all; he simply wanted to remove the Church's oversight in order to do whatever he wanted.

Women were disposable in Henry VIII's worldview because the goal of all European kings at the time was to produce male heirs. Henry felt his first wife Catherine was incapable of producing a boy, so he wanted her out of the way. Of course, our modern understanding of genetics tells us that it is in fact the male whose genetic material determines the sex of a baby, which makes Henry even more of a vain monster in hindsight. After he started the Church of England and got his way, Henry married Anne Boleyn, who he ultimately had executed just three years later. His third wife, Jane Seymour, died in childbirth, finally providing Henry with a son, but then Henry continued his wicked ways by annulling his fourth marriage and executing his fifth wife.

This gruesome story has evolved over the centuries, transforming Henry into a bloviating, over-eating monster that threw turkey legs across the room and bellowed, "Off with their heads!" This depiction of Henry VIII as a megalomaniacal cartoon villain isn't exactly accurate either. In spite of his capacity for cruelty, Henry was admired in his time as an accomplished athlete and musician. With that said, Henry's despicable behavior makes it hard for us to appreciate the philosophical importance of his split from the Catholic Church.

In the ultimate ironic victory, Henry VIII's daughter Elizabeth rose to the throne 11 years after his death. Although she was not the male heir he had plotted, schemed, and murdered so gleefully to get, Elizabeth became one of the highest renowned monarchs in English history, overseeing an age of exploration, a renaissance of English literature, and the expansion of England as a naval power in the Atlantic.

**CONTINUE ON TO THE NEXT PAGE ➞**

**33.** Based on the passage, which of these most closely aligns with the viewpoint of the author?

**A.** Henry VIII's great accomplishments are overshadowed by our over-emphasis on his personal life.
**B.** Henry VIII's split from the Roman Catholic Church was a crucial moment in time, but his motivation was so twisted that it's hard to appreciate his accomplishments.
**C.** Henry VIII shouldn't be regarded as an important historical figure because he was so cruel in his personal life.
**D.** Henry VIII's split from the Roman Catholic Church was one of the worst mistakes in history, and it's easy to tell he had bad judgement because of the way he treated his wives.

---

**34.** Which of these best describes the relationship between the Catholic Church and European monarchs prior to the time of Henry VIII?

**E.** Generally, monarchs shared some of their power with the Church and relied on them help govern their kingdoms.
**F.** The Church actually controlled Europe and allowed monarchs to manage certain areas for them.
**G.** Each monarch was the supreme leader of his or her country, with final say on all issues – including religion.
**H.** There was full separation of church and state throughout Europe.

**35.** How was Henry VIII's work "an important step in the road toward the modern era?"

**A.** Henry's daughter Elizabeth I made England a true world power, which has lasted up to today.
**B.** Henry made it easier for married couples to get annulments and divorces, which are commonplace in today's world.
**C.** Henry championed the idea that countries should be able to govern and control themselves rather than having to constantly consult with religious leaders in faraway lands.
**D.** Henry abolished religion, creating the kind of secular country we see around the world today.

---

**36.** Which is the best definition for "problematic" as it is used in Paragraph 2?

**E.** Noble and worthy
**F.** Trivial and unimportant
**G.** Confusing and nuanced
**H.** Complex and controversial

---

**37.** What is the best definition for "bloviating" as it is used in Paragraph 4?

**A.** Self-important and loud
**B.** Greedy and stupid
**C.** Nauseous and sickly
**D.** Handsome and smart

CONTINUE ON TO THE NEXT PAGE →

**38.** What does the author mean when he or she says that Elizabeth I's reign was "the ultimate ironic victory" in Paragraph 5?

**E.** The author finds it amusing that Elizabeth I actually undid most of Henry's accomplishments, essentially destroying his legacy.

**F.** The author finds it amusing that, in spite of his desperation to have a male heir, Henry VIII ultimately had only daughters.

**G.** The author finds it amusing that, in spite of Henry VII's obsession with having a son and general disregard for female life, it was actually his daughter who became known as one of the greatest English monarchs of all time.

**H.** The author finds it amusing that, in spite of his many accomplishments, Henry VIII is mostly remembered for being Elizabeth I's father.

**CONTINUE ON TO THE NEXT PAGE ➞**

**Ozymandias**
By Percy Bysshe Shelley

I met a traveller from an antique land
Who said: "Two vast and trunkless legs of stone
Stand in the desert . . . Near them, on the sand,
Half sunk, a shattered visage lies, whose frown,
And wrinkled lip, and sneer of cold command,
Tell that its sculptor well those passions read
Which yet survive, stamped on these lifeless things,
The hand that mocked them, and the heart that fed:
And on the pedestal these words appear:
'My name is Ozymandias, king of kings:
Look on my works, ye Mighty, and despair!'
Nothing beside remains. Round the decay
Of that colossal wreck, boundless and bare
The lone and level sands stretch far away."

---

**39.** Which of these is the best definition for "visage," as it is used in Line 4?

**A.** Statue
**B.** Face
**C.** Artifact
**D.** King

---

**40.** Which of these best describes the statue of Ozymandias, as the "traveller" in Line 1 describes it to the speaker?

**E.** The statue looms over the entire desert and can be seen from a great distance.
**F.** The statue has been repaired repeatedly over time, which gives the legs a characteristically strange look.
**G.** The statue has been toppled and fallen onto its side.
**H.** The statue is broken and lies in ruins.

**41.** To whom do the "vast and trunkless legs" (Line 2) belong?

**A.** Ozymandias
**B.** The traveler
**C.** Shelley
**D.** The statue

---

**42.** How did the narrator or speaker of the poem first learn about Ozymandias?

**E.** By finding the statue in the desert
**F.** By reading the pedestal inscription in an old book
**G.** By talking to a traveler who had found the statue in the desert
**H.** By taking an ancient history class

---

**43.** What are the "lifeless things" mentioned in Line 7?

**A.** Pieces of the statue of Ozymandias
**B.** Dead warriors from ancient history
**C.** The dust and sand of the desert
**D.** The pedestal and the inscription that is written upon it

---

**44.** Based on the passage, which of these is the safest conclusion about the sculptor who created the statue being described?

**E.** The sculptor was among the most skilled of his time
**F.** The sculptor wanted to flatter Ozymandias with the statue
**G.** The sculptor found Ozymandias to be very intimidating
**H.** The sculptor was killed for not producing a good enough statue

**CONTINUE ON TO THE NEXT PAGE →**

**45.** Who are the "Mighty" described in Line 11?

- **A.** Gods
- **B.** Other monarchs and rulers
- **C.** Warriors
- **D.** Forces of nature

---

**46.** What poetic/literary device does Shelley use in Lines 9-14 to highlight the final lines of the poem?

- **E.** Irony
- **F.** Personification
- **G.** Metaphor
- **H.** Onomatopoeia

---

**47.** Shelley uses the image of the statue in the desert to communicate the message that...

- **A.** Kingdoms come and go over time, but monarchs have always been obsessed with power
- **B.** No king will ever truly be all-powerful
- **C.** Time destroys all things and all people
- **D.** We often forget how different the world used to be

**CONTINUE ON TO THE NEXT PAGE ➡**

**The Six Basic Biomes**

If you've travelled even a little bit, you've probably observed that different plants and animals are native to different parts of the country. For example, the trees, fish, plants, and animals that are abundant in New England are extremely rare in the American Southwest. That's because, in each region, climate and geography create certain conditions that make it easy for some species to thrive while others can barely survive. These distinct climatic and geographic are known as biomes.

Researchers, biologists, and ecologists around the world identify different numbers of biomes, but just about everybody agrees on these six: desert, grassland, rain forest, deciduous forest, taiga, and tundra. These distinctions represent different climates, geographic features, specific flora and fauna, and unique challenges for those organisms that make their home in that environment.

Desert is one of the most straightforward biomes to understand. A desert is any place in which less than 9.75 inches of liquid rain falls annually. Deserts generally see very high temperatures during daylight hours but also experience violent temperature swings after dark. Some deserts, like the Gobi in Asia, see snowfall, which contradicts many people's preconceptions about deserts. Desert life is very challenging and requires plants and animals to make specific adaptations to find adequate food, water, and shelter to survive.

The second major biome is grassland, which, as its name implies, constitutes areas in which the most common plants are grasses. Rainfall in grasslands is sporadic, which is why plants and trees bigger than grass cannot reliably grow there. Grasslands are generally populated by small, herbivorous animals and larger hunting carnivores that prey upon them.

Next is the rainforest, which, as its name implies, is a biome that includes areas with large, dense foliage and a large amount of rainfall. In stark contrast to deserts and grasslands, rainforests get more than six feet of rain per year. This bounty of water means that trees can grow much taller and faster than they can in other biomes. The availability of water, food, and shelter created by these conditions means that rainforests can support a great deal of plant and animal diversity.

Deciduous forests are similar to rainforests in that they contain large trees, but deciduous forests face much colder winters than their rainforest cousins. That means that the trees in deciduous forests often lose their leaves after they change color in the autumn and winter due to the cold conditions. Plants and animals in deciduous forests live very seasonal lives, which means they must develop a wider range of abilities and strategies than organisms that live in more consistent climates.

The taiga biome represents another kind of forest that is less well-known (at least in the United States) than rainforests or deciduous forests. Found primarily in the northern parts of Europe and Asia, taiga represents forests with exceptionally cold, harsh winters. Evergreen or fir trees are the most common plants in the taiga biome, which sees large-scale precipitation, both in the form of rain during warm months and snow during cold months. Animals that live in the taiga biome must ensure they stay warm during the winter without becoming overheated during the more temperate months.

**CONTINUE ON TO THE NEXT PAGE ➞**

Finally, the last basic biome is tundra. Tundra is extremely cold and barren land, generally found around the north and south poles. Growing seasons for plants in the tundra are exceptionally short, which can leave this biome looking barren and blasted. Animals that choose to live in the tundra face daily struggle when it comes to finding water to drink, food to eat, and warmth to stay alive. It is every bit as harsh, if not harsher, than the desert.

| | Annual Rainfall (inches) | Are there tall trees? | Do leaves change? | Does it snow in the winter? | Are there major seasonal changes? |
|---|---|---|---|---|---|
| LOCATION A | 70 | Yes | No | No | No |
| LOCATION B | 8.75 | No | No | Yes | No |
| LOCATION C | 37 | Yes | Yes | Yes | Yes |
| LOCATION D | 21 | No | No | Yes | Yes |
| LOCATION E | 11 | No | No | Yes | No |

**48.** Based on the passage, why did the author select the title "The Six Basic Biomes?"

- **E.** To emphasize that this is only base-level information and the topic is much more complex
- **F.** To emphasize that some scientists recognize more than six biomes
- **G.** To emphasize that biomes are conceptually simple to understand
- **H.** To emphasize that the reader must do additional reading to fully understand the concepts in the passage

**49.** Why does the author choose to use the seemingly repetitive "liquid rain" in Paragraph 3?

- **A.** To differentiate the rain being described from acid rain, which is common in areas that have become over-developed by humans
- **B.** To differentiate the rain being described from water vapor, which often forms in very hot places like deserts.
- **C.** To differentiate the rain being described from snow, which the paragraph explains can occur in some deserts
- **D.** To differentiate the rain being described from the heavier rains seen in rainforest and deciduous forest biomes

**50.** Which of these is the best definition for "sporadic," as it's used in Paragraph 5?

- **E.** Inconsistent or unpredictable
- **F.** Violent and uncontrolled
- **G.** Insufficient or weak
- **H.** Impossible to measure accurately

**51.** Based on the passage and the information in the data table, which biome is Location A most likely to belong to?

- **A.** Desert
- **B.** Deciduous Forest
- **C.** Rainforest
- **D.** Taiga

CONTINUE ON TO THE NEXT PAGE ➡

**52.** Based on the passage and the information in the data table, is Location C in a deciduous forest or a taiga, and how can you be certain?

**E.** Location C must be in a deciduous forest because it experiences major seasonal changes.
**F.** Location C must be in a deciduous forest because the leaves on the trees change color.
**G.** Location C must be a taiga because it receives both liquid rainfall and a great deal of snow in the winter.
**H.** Location C must be a taiga because the leaves on the trees do not lose their leaves.

---

**53.** Why is the category "Do leaves change?" fundamental to interpreting the data table?

**A.** Because leaves changing colors is a sign of cold temperatures, which strongly suggest deciduous forest, taiga, or tundra
**B.** Because there have to be tall trees for leaves to change color, so if the answer is "no," you can assume the table is describing a desert or tundra
**C.** Because leaves changing colors is a sign of inadequate liquid water, which strongly suggests a desert or tundra
**D.** Because leaves changing colors is a distinct sign of deciduous forests in temperate climates

**54.** Based on the passage and the information in the data table, which biome is Location D most likely to belong to?

**E.** Grassland
**F.** Taiga
**G.** Desert
**H.** Deciduous Forest

---

**55.** Which is the clearest indicator that Location B is a desert biome?

**A.** There are minimal seasonal changes throughout the year
**B.** The fact that there are no tall trees
**C.** The annual rainfall of 8.75 inches
**D.** The fact it can snow in the winter

---

**56.** Based on the passage and the information in the data table, which biome is Location E most likely to belong to?

**E.** Grassland
**F.** Taiga
**G.** Rainforest
**H.** Tundra

---

**57.** Based on the passage, which column would be most useful to add to the data table?

**A.** Can people live there?
**B.** Is life a major challenge for plants and animals?
**C.** Is there a bounty of water?
**D.** What strategies must animals use for survival?

**CONTINUE ON TO THE NEXT PAGE ➞**

ARGOPREP
ARGOPREP.COM/SHSAT

# MATHEMATICS
## INSTRUCTIONS

## 90 MINUTES • 57 QUESTIONS

Select the best answer from the choices given by carefully solving each problem. Bubble the letter of your answer on the answer sheet. Please refrain from making any stray marks on the answer sheet. If you need to erase an answer, please erase thoroughly.

**Important Notes:**

1. There are no formulas or definitions in the math section that will be provided.
2. Diagrams may or may not be drawn to scale. Do not make assumptions based on the diagram unless it is specifically stated in the diagram or question.
3. Diagrams are not in more than one plane, unless stated otherwise.
4. Graphs are drawn to scale, therefore, you can assume relationships according to the graph. If lines appear parallel, then you can assume the lines to be parallel. This is also true for right angles and so forth.
5. Simplify fractions completely.

# Practice Test 3

**GRID IN PROBLEMS (Questions 58-62)**

*Directions: The following five questions are grid-in problems. On the answer sheet, please be sure to write your answer in the boxes at the top of the grid. Start on the left side of each grid.*

**58.** If Sarah scored an 80, 95, 75 and an 90 on her first four tests, what must she score on her fifth test if she wants an average of 88?

**59.** Solve for $x$

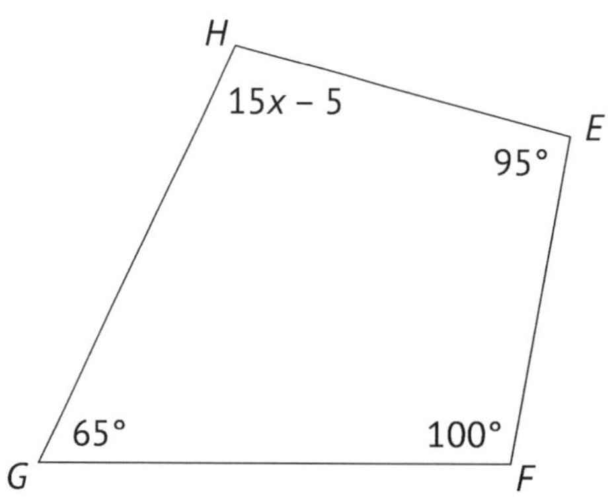


CONTINUE ON TO THE NEXT PAGE ➡

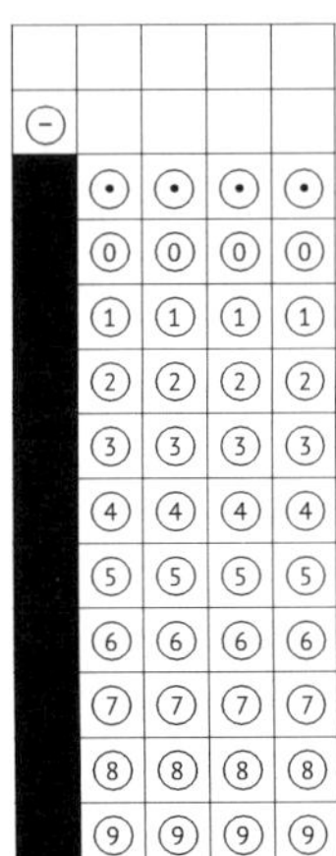

**60.** Lea's school is selling tickets for the upcoming choral performance. On the first day of ticket sales, the school sold 10 adult tickets and 10 child tickets for a total of $200. On the second day, the school sold 13 adult tickets and 2 child tickets for a total of $172 dollars. How much did each child ticket cost?

**61.** In a population of 10,000 geese the growth rate is 4% per year. What is the total increase in population over 4 years? Round your answer to the nearest whole number.

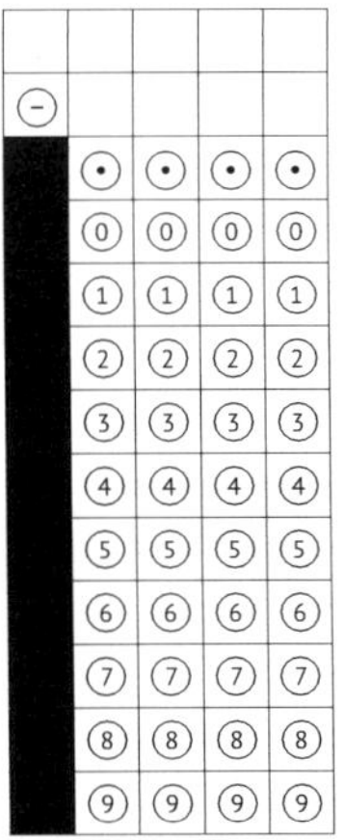

**62.** $\frac{5.5}{0.1} \times .20$

CONTINUE ON TO THE NEXT PAGE ➡

## MULTIPLE CHOICE PROBLEMS (Questions 63-114)

**63.** $3[9 \div (-3)] + (-3 - (-8)] =$

**E.** $-20$
**F.** $-4$
**G.** $-2$
**H.** $2$

---

**64.** If $\frac{2{,}000}{2x} = 10$, then what is $\sqrt{x}$

**A.** $\sqrt{10}$
**B.** $10$
**C.** $\sqrt{1{,}000}$
**D.** $100$

---

**65.** If $x = 9$, $y = -9$ and $z = -1$, what is the value of $yz + \sqrt{x} + yz - \sqrt{x}$ ?

**E.** $-24$
**F.** $-18$
**G.** $0$
**H.** $18$

**66.**

1 dollar = 0.5 pillets
4 coss = 1 dollar

Lindsey has $20 to spend. She needs to buy exactly 2 pillets. She spends the remaining amount buying coss. How many coss does Lindsey purchase?

**A.** 4
**B.** 5
**C.** 64
**D.** 72

---

**67.** $\sqrt{100} \div \sqrt{25} =$

**E.** $\sqrt{2}$
**F.** $2$
**G.** $4$
**H.** $10$

---

**68.** If $x = -8$, what is the value of $\frac{1}{2}|4x - 4|$?

**A.** $-18$
**B.** $-14$
**C.** $14$
**D.** $18$

CONTINUE ON TO THE NEXT PAGE ➞

**69.**

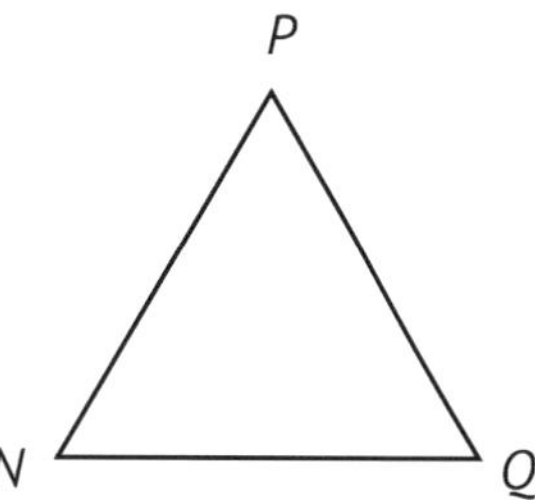


Triangle *NPQ* is an equilateral triangle. If its perimeter is 27, what is the length of *NP* + *NQ*?

**E.** 16
**F.** 18
**G.** 4
**H.** 32

---

**70.** If 40% of $x$ is 160, what is $x$?

**A.** .0025
**B.** 64
**C.** 360
**D.** 400

---

**71.** When $d$ is divided by 7, the remainder is 5. What is the remainder when $d + 1$ is divided by 7?

**E.** 0
**F.** 1
**G.** 5
**H.** 6

**72.**

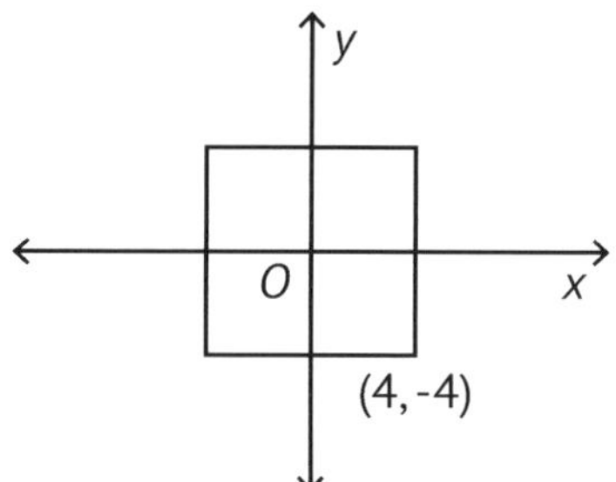


In the figure above, *O* is the center of the square. What is the area of the square?

**A.** 8
**B.** 16
**C.** 32
**D.** 64

---

**73.**

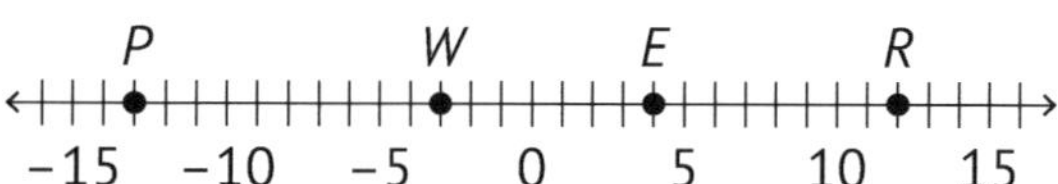


If *O* is the midpoint of $\overline{PW}$, then what is the distance of $\overline{OE}$?

**E.** 10
**F.** 11
**G.** 12
**H.** 13

CONTINUE ON TO THE NEXT PAGE ➡

**74.** The average of 7 consecutive even integers is 20. What is the median?

**A.** 18
**B.** 20
**C.** 20.5
**D.** 22

---

**75.** What is 0.003815 in scientific notation?

**E.** $3815 \times 10^{-2}$
**F.** $3.815 \times 10^{-3}$
**G.** $0.03815 \times 10$
**H.** $0.003815 \times 10^{2}$

---

**76.**

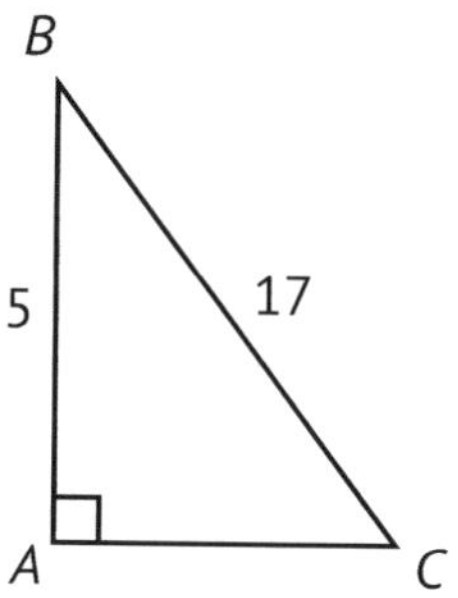


In the figure above, what is the length of $\overline{AC}$?

**A.** 8
**B.** 12
**C.** $2\sqrt{66}$
**D.** $2\sqrt{289}$

**77.** What time will it be 53 hours after 3:30 P.M. on Thursday?

**E.** 8:30 A.M. Saturday
**F.** 7:30 P.M. Saturday
**G.** 8:30 P.M. Saturday
**H.** 8:30 P.M. Sunday

---

**78.**

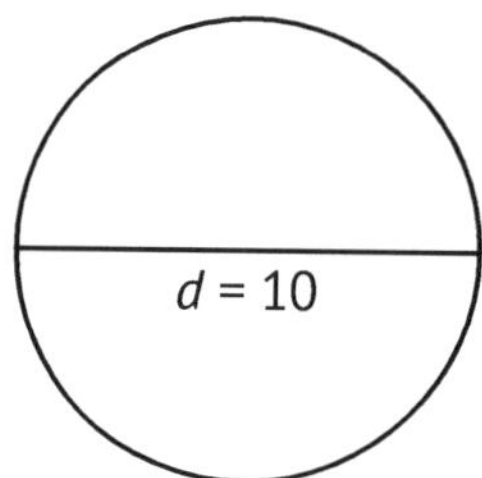


If $x$ represents the circumference of the above figure, and $y$ represents the area, what is $\frac{x}{y}$?

Note: $d$ is the diameter of the circle above.

**A.** $\frac{10}{25}\pi$
**B.** $\frac{5}{2}$
**C.** $\frac{2}{5}$
**D.** $\frac{25}{10}\pi$

CONTINUE ON TO THE NEXT PAGE ➡

**79.** A certain substance has a mass of 98 milligrams. What is the mass of this substance in kilograms?

**E.** $9.8 \times 10^{5}$ kg
**F.** $9.8 \times 10^{3}$ kg
**G.** $9.8 \times 10^{-3}$ kg
**H.** $9.8 \times 10^{-5}$ kg

---

**80.** Samuel scored a 72, 92 and 80 on his first three exams. What is the minimum score he needs to get on his next exam to get an average of 85?

**A.** 85
**B.** 90
**C.** 93
**D.** 96

---

**81.** Five out of 10 marbles in a bag are red. What percentage of the marbles are **not** red?

**E.** 50%
**F.** 55%
**G.** 60%
**H.** 75%

---

**82.**

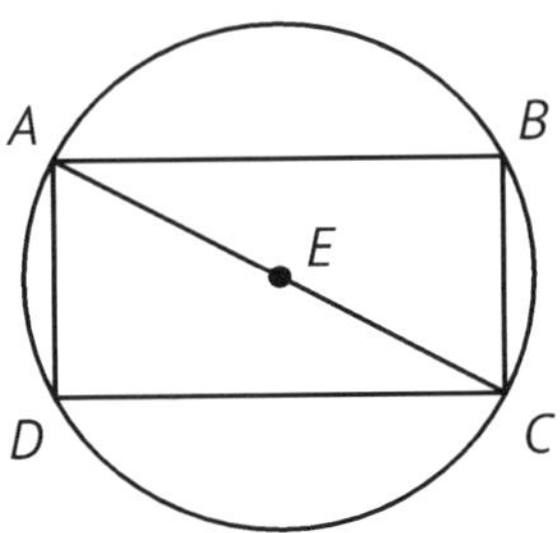


Figure not drawn to scale.

In the figure above, the rectangle *ABCD* is inscribed in the circle. Where *E* is the center and the radius is 5. If the length of *AD* is 6, what is the area of rectangle *ABCD?*

**A.** 30
**B.** 48
**C.** 60
**D.** $25\pi$

---

**83.** $(\sqrt{81})(\sqrt{25}) + \sqrt{16} =$

**E.** 5
**F.** 40
**G.** 49
**H.** 56

---

**84.** It takes George 3 minutes to read 300 words. If each page in a book that he is reading has 750 words, how long will it take George to read 6 pages?

**A.** 30 minutes
**B.** 45 minutes
**C.** 60 minutes
**D.** 90 minutes

**CONTINUE ON TO THE NEXT PAGE ➞**

**85.** $(\frac{1}{2} - \frac{3}{4})^2 + \frac{5}{10} =$

**E.** $\frac{9}{16}$
**F.** $\frac{1}{2}$
**G.** $\frac{1}{16}$
**H.** $\frac{3}{4}$

---

**86.** If $x = 2^5 \bullet 3^2 \bullet 7$, then what is the value of $x$?

**A.** 1150
**B.** 2000
**C.** 2015
**D.** 2016

---

**87.**

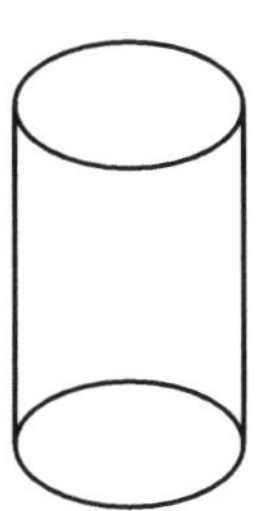

A right cylyndrical can is being filled with water. At 1 P.M. it is half full. At 2 P.M. it is $\frac{3}{4}$ th full. At this rate, when was it empty?

**E.** 11:00 A.M.
**F.** 11:30 A.M.
**G.** 12:00 P.M.
**H.** 12:30 P.M.

**88.** If $x^8 = (2^2)^4$, what is $x^2$?

**A.** 2
**B.** 4
**C.** 8
**D.** 64

---

**89.** James has yard work to finish. He finishes $\frac{1}{8}$ of the total work on the first day. What fraction of the work is left?

**E.** $\frac{1}{8}$
**F.** $\frac{3}{8}$
**G.** $\frac{7}{8}$
**H.** $\frac{3}{4}$

---

**90.**

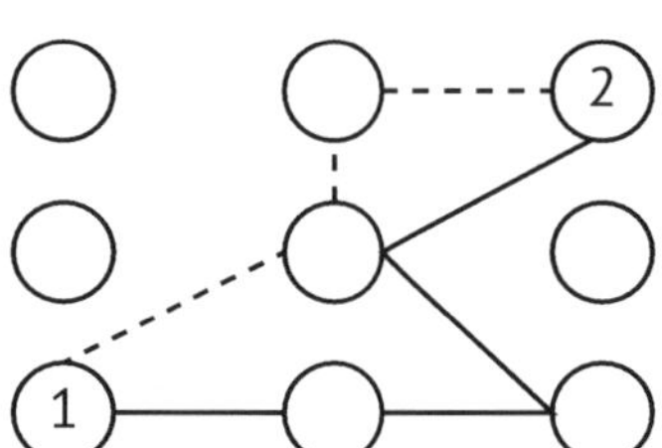


There are two different pathways connecting ① and ②. How many fewer steps is the solid-line path than the dotted-line path. (A step is defined as a line segment connecting 2 circles)?

**A.** −4
**B.** −1
**C.** 1
**D.** 4

CONTINUE ON TO THE NEXT PAGE ➡

**91.** Jackie and Jesse each solve the same problem a different way.

Problem: $\sqrt{a + b} = ?$
Jackie 's way: $\sqrt{a + b} = \sqrt{a} + \sqrt{b}$
Jesse's way: $\sqrt{a + b} = \sqrt{a + b}$

If $a = 9$ and $b = 25$, how much bigger is Jackie's way than Jesse's way?

**E.** 0
**F.** 2
**G.** $\sqrt{36}$
**H.** $8 - \sqrt{34}$

---

**92.** If $\theta\,(a, b, c, d, e, f, g, h, i) =$

$$\frac{(a)(b) - (c)(d) + (ef)^2(gh)^2}{i}$$

which cannot be a value of $\theta$?

**A.** $\theta(0, 0, 0, 0, 0, 0, 0, 0, 1)$
**B.** $\theta(1, 1, 1, 1, 1, 1, 1, 1, 0)$
**C.** $\theta(2, 2, 2, 2, 2, 2, 2, 2, 10)$
**D.** $\theta(2, 3, 1, 4, 5, 6, 7, 0, 10)$

---

**93.** If James grows by 20 inches every day starting Monday, what is the difference in his height between Wednesday and Monday?

**E.** 0 inches
**F.** 20 inches
**G.** 30 inches
**H.** 40 inches

**94.** $(\frac{1}{2} - \frac{3}{4}) \div \frac{1}{2} =$

**A.** $\frac{1}{2}$

**B.** $\frac{3}{2}$

**C.** $\frac{-1}{2}$

**D.** $\frac{-3}{4}$

---

**95.**

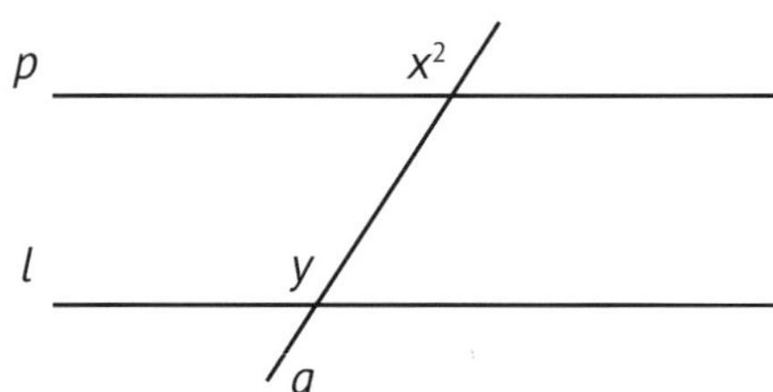


Line $q$ intersects the parallel lines $p$ and $l$.

What is $\frac{y^3}{3}$?

**E.** $\frac{x^4}{3}$

**F.** $x^9$

**G.** $\frac{x^4}{9}$

**H.** $\frac{x^6}{3}$

CONTINUE ON TO THE NEXT PAGE ➞

**96.** Given the arithmetic sequence $x, y, 30, z, f$ find $x + y + z + f$?

**A.** 60
**B.** 80
**C.** 120
**D.** 130

---

**97.** If $(-1)^2 = 1$, then the value of $(-1)^{2023}$ is

**E.** −2023
**F.** −1
**G.** 0
**H.** 1

---

**98.** Caroline has two times as many marbles as Jake. Jake has 12 less than 7 times as many marbles James has. James has 14 marbles. How many marbles does Caroline have?

**A.** 54
**B.** 86
**C.** 98
**D.** 172

---

**99.** John is trying to escape a ditch. Every time he jumps 10 meters, he falls back 5 meters right after. The ditch is 19 meters long. What is the minimum number of jumps he needs to make to escape?

**E.** 3
**F.** 4
**G.** 5
**H.** 7

**100.** What is the largest number of digits the product of a 3 digit and a 2 digit number has?

**A.** 4 digits
**B.** 5 digits
**C.** 6 digits
**D.** 7 digits

---

**101.** If $F_n = 2F_{n-1} + 3F_{n-2}$, then what is $F_3$ if $F_1 = F_2 = 1$?

**E.** 2
**F.** 3
**G.** 4
**H.** 5

---

**102.** Sam walks 3m to the West, then 4m South, then 4m North. How far is he from his original location?

**A.** 3m
**B.** 5m
**C.** 7m
**D.** 8m

---

**103.** If $a = 3$, and $b = 5$, what is the value of $\frac{9a}{b-a} = ?$

**E.** 9
**F.** 27
**G.** $\frac{13}{5}$
**H.** $\frac{27}{2}$

**CONTINUE ON TO THE NEXT PAGE ➡**

**104.** The perimeter of a square is **four** times the circumference of a circle with radius of 1m. What is the area of the square?

**A.** $4\pi$
**B.** $8\pi$
**C.** $4\pi^2$
**D.** $8\pi^2$

---

**105.** If [trapezoid with $a$, $b$ on top and $c$, $d$ on bottom] means $bc + ad$, then what is the value of [trapezoid with 4, 5 on top and 7, 8 on bottom]

**E.** 24
**F.** 66
**G.** 67
**H.** 68

---

**106.** Convert $\frac{3}{40}$ to a decimal.

**A.** 0.0075
**B.** 0.075
**C.** 0.06
**D.** .75

---

**107.** For what value of $q$ is $6(q + 3) = 2(q + 4)$?

**E.** $\frac{-1}{2}$

**F.** $\frac{-4}{9}$

**G.** $\frac{-5}{2}$

**H.** $-3$

**108.**

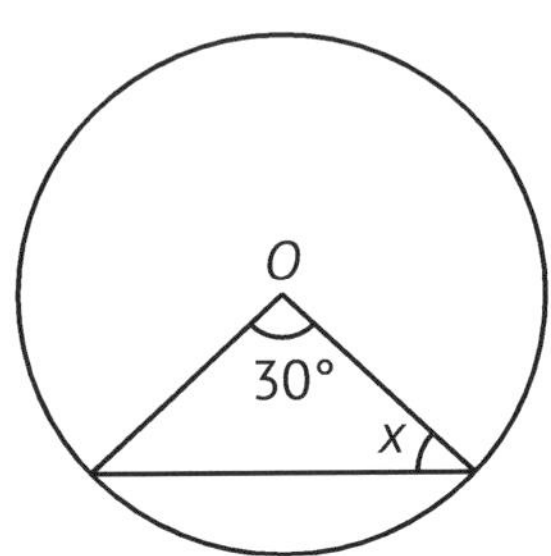


What is $\measuredangle x$ if point $O$ is the center of the above circle?

**A.** 45°
**B.** 60°
**C.** 75°
**D.** $\frac{\pi}{2}$

---

**109.** For how many values of $x$ is, $\frac{-3x^2}{4} > 0$ ?

**E.** 0
**F.** 1
**G.** 3
**H.** 5

---

**110.** $x$ is 40% of $y$ and $y$ is the square of $x$. What is the value of $x$?

**A.** $\sqrt{x}$
**B.** $0.4\sqrt{x}$
**C.** $0.4x^2$
**D.** $0.4x$

**CONTINUE ON TO THE NEXT PAGE ➞**

**111.** If $x = 7$; and $4x(3y - 2x) = 112$; what is the value of $y$?

**E.** 4
**F.** 6
**G.** 7
**H.** 28

---

**112.** If $x \partial y = \dfrac{x + y}{x - y}$, what is $a \partial (a - b)$?

**A.** $\dfrac{2a}{b}$

**B.** $\dfrac{2a - b}{2a}$

**C.** $\dfrac{2a - b}{b}$

**D.** $\dfrac{2a - b}{2b}$

---

**113.** A newly cleared tract of land has been designated for reforestation. The commission responsible for the project decided to plant 30 trees. 12 of the trees will be oak trees, one-fifth of the trees will be pine trees, 3 are weeping willows, and the rest of the trees will be fruit-bearing trees of a various types. What is the ratio of weeping willows to fruit-bearing trees?

**E.** 1:3
**F.** 1:2
**G.** 3:1
**H.** 3:12

**114.** The chart below reflects the total record sales (in thousands) for six major labels: Petra, Jams, AudioPro, Keynote, GSharp, and Lumia.

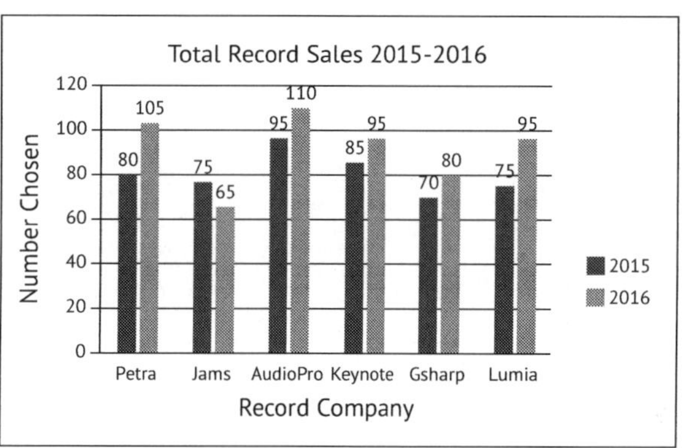


Which company experienced the greatest percentage increase in sales from 2015 to 2016?

**A.** Petra
**B.** Audiopro
**C.** Keynote
**D.** Lumia

**THIS IS THE END OF THE TEST. IF THERE IS TIME REMAINING, YOU MAY CHECK YOUR ANSWERS TO PART 1 OR PART 2.**

**CONTINUE ON TO THE NEXT PAGE ➞**

**You can find detailed video explanations to each problem in the book by visiting: ArgoPrep.com**

# SHSAT PRACTICE TEST 3
## ANSWER KEY

### PART 1 (ENGLISH LANGUAGE ARTS)

**Revising/Editing**

1. **D**
2. **E**
3. **B**
4. **F**
5. **A**
6. **E**
7. **D**
8. **G**
9. **A**
10. **F**
11. **A**

**Reading Comprehension**

12. **E**
13. **D**
14. **F**
15. **C**
16. **G**
17. **C**
18. **G**
19. **D**
20. **G**
21. **B**
22. **H**
23. **C**
24. **F**
25. **A**
26. **F**
27. **D**
28. **G**
29. **B**
30. **E**
31. **B**
32. **H**
33. **B**
34. **E**
35. **C**
36. **H**
37. **A**
38. **G**
39. **B**
40. **H**
41. **D**
42. **G**
43. **A**
44. **G**
45. **B**
46. **E**
47. **C**
48. **F**
49. **C**
50. **E**
51. **C**
52. **F**
53. **D**
54. **E**
55. **C**
56. **H**
57. **B**

### PART 2 (MATHEMATICS)

**Math**

58. **100**
59. **7**
60. **$8**
61. **1,699**
62. **11**
63. **F**
64. **B**
65. **H**
66. **C**
67. **F**
68. **D**
69. **F**
70. **D**
71. **H**
72. **D**
73. **G**
74. **B**
75. **F**
76. **C**
77. **G**
78. **C**
79. **H**
80. **D**
81. **E**
82. **B**
83. **G**
84. **B**
85. **E**
86. **D**
87. **E**
88. **B**
89. **G**
90. **B**
91. **H**
92. **B**
93. **H**
94. **C**
95. **H**
96. **C**
97. **F**
98. **D**
99. **E**
100. **B**
101. **H**
102. **A**
103. **H**
104. **C**
105. **G**
106. **B**
107. **G**
108. **C**
109. **E**
110. **C**
111. **F**
112. **C**
113. **E**
114. **A**

**You can find detailed video explanations to each problem in the book by visiting: ArgoPrep.com**

## Practice Test 3 (Answers and Explanations)

**1.** **D** Passive voice occurs when the subject of a sentence is having action done to it rather than performing the action of the sentence. Answer D is correct because Sentence 4 contains the passive voice construction "acceptance speeches are given." Sentence 4 should be revised to say, "The winners of each award give elaborate, often memorable acceptance speeches." All the other sentences in the paragraph are written in active voice, so answers A, B, and C are all incorrect.

**2.** **E** Passive voice occurs when the main subject of a sentence is having action done to it rather than performing the action. The sample sentence is written in the passive voice because the subject "the ball" is being "hit" rather than hitting anything. Answer E corrects this error by restructuring the sentence to create a new subject ("two players") who are performing the action "hit," creating an active voice construction. Answer choices F and G both fail to correct the passive voice error, as both sentences still begin "the ball is hit..." Answer H restructures the sentence but is still incorrect because it contains the phrase "points are scored," which is a new example of passive voice in the sentence.

**3.** **B** Answer B is correct because Sentence 3 requires a comma to separate the introduction phrase "By the age of 20" from the rest of the sentence. Introductions that provide context such as this one should always be separated in this way. The sentence should read, "By the age of 20, Gershwin had written several hit songs." Answers A, C, and D are all incorrect because each of those sentences uses commas as appropriate to separate lists, introduction phrases, and nonessential clauses.

**4.** **F** Proper nouns (people, places, things, and ideas with specific names) are always capitalized. Answer F is correct because "Manhattan Project" was the specific name of the research in question, so both words in the name are capitalized. Answer H is incorrect because it takes a proper noun (World War II) and incorrectly reduces it to a common noun by removing its capital letters. Answers E and G are also incorrect because "government" and "nuclear weapons" are both common nouns with no specific names, so they do not need to be capitalized.

**5.** **A** Answer A is correct because Sentence 2 is the least thematically connected to the other sentences in the paragraph. Sentences 1, 3, 4, and 5 all deal specifically with memories of the author making a pie with his or her grandmother. Sentence 2 introduces the author's mother, who is not mentioned otherwise throughout the paragraph and whose involvement does little to enhance the main story. While this sentence could be the jumping-off point for a following paragraph, it is far less connected to this paragraph than any of the other sentences. Answers B, C, and D are all incorrect because each of those answers connects directly to the topic of the grandmother's pie making process.

**6.** **E** Sentence 2 is unnecessary because it is an expositional, declarative sentence that does little to develop the main ideas from Sentence 1 or transition into Sentence 3. If Sentence 2 is removed, the idea of baseball being an "international game" at the end of Sentence 1 transitions seamlessly into the discussion of Europe in Sentence 3. Answer F is incorrect because Sentence 3 introduces the concept of baseball's European origins, which is central to the rest of the paragraph. Answer G is incorrect because Sentence 4 provides a key link in the logic that brings baseball from Europe to England in the time of colonization to the Americas. Answer H is incorrect because it introduces the idea of baseball in America, which is the main idea explored in Paragraph 2.

**7.** **D** This sentence requires two commas: one to indicate the fact that it's a compound sentence, and one to separate the introductory phrase "by the 1790s." Answer choice D includes both these commas and is therefore correct. Answer choice A is incorrect because it separates off the phrase "from Europe" as though it is parenthetical or nonessential information, which it is not. Answer choice B is incorrect because, while it correctly identifies the sentence as a compound sentence, it does not separate the introductory phrase from the second half of the sentence. Answer choice C is incorrect because it separates the introductory clause "by the 1790s" from the clause that follows but does not correctly place the comma before the conjunction that forms the compound sentence.

**8.** **G** Answer G is the best choice because it communicates the main ideas of both sentences (first, that early baseball was a game of local variations, and second, by providing some examples of those variations) while reducing the overall length of both. Answer choice E provides a solid effort to combine the sentences, but it does not adequately reduce wordiness by including both the phrases "local variations" and "different from town to town," which are redundant. Answer choice F is incorrect because the sentence is logically backwards, providing examples to support the point before making the point itself. This can create potential confusion for the reader. Answer choice H, while concise, is incorrect because it leaves out one of the important main ideas by not providing examples.

**9.** **A** The fact that Cartwright created a unified set of rules is contrary to the preceding idea (that the game had been built on local variation), so "However" (Answer A) is the best transition. Answer B is incorrect because "consequently" implies a causal relationship between the two ideas that is inaccurate. Answer choice C is incorrect because "moreover" implies that the content of sentence 8 is reinforcing the content of sentence 7, which it is not. Answer choice D is incorrect because there is nothing in the passage to suggest there were negative consequences to the creation of Cartwright's rules, so "unfortunately" would not be appropriate.

**10.** **F** From sentence 3 to sentence 16, the passage is consistently written in the past tense, so the sentence should read "The Knickerbocker Rules introduced the modern concept..." Also, since the content of the sentence refers to history, the past tense should be used to provide clarity for the reader, to prevent them from incorrectly assuming these events occurred very recently. Answer choice E is incorrect because, throughout the passage, the Knickerbocker Rules are referred to only in plural form. Answer choice G is incorrect because even though the rule change was made in the past, the author's explanation/interpretation of it is current and ongoing, so a progressive verb is appropriate. Answer choice H is also incorrect because "approaching" is a participle taking the role of an adjective in this sentence rather than a verb, so it cannot be put into the past tense.

**11. A** Answer A is the best choice to support sentence 11 because it provides two concrete examples of ways in which the Knickerbocker Rules differ from today's game (the main idea of sentence 11). Answer choice D is incorrect because it does the exact opposite, providing an example of a way the Knickerbocker Rules are similar to today's baseball. Answer choice D would better support sentences 8 and 9. Answer choices B and C are interesting facts that could fit in this passage, but they do not provide any material support to the idea laid out in sentence 11.

**12. E** Answer E is the best choice because the term "ominous" aligns with the dark, foreboding, and overall threatening tone of the passage. The narrator's tone in the opening paragraphs introduces a dark mood, which is reinforced by the nightmare that Dr. Frankenstein experiences in Paragraph 3. Answer F is incorrect because "adventurous" implies that the protagonist is on an exciting and uplifting journey. On the contrary, this passage is quite dark, making Answer E a much better choice. Answer G is incorrect because, while it's ironic that the creature is ugly even though it's made from beautiful parts, irony is not a major feature of the passage on the whole. Answer H is also incorrect, although there are certainly melancholy aspects to the passage, because Answer E is better, more focused choice. Dr. Frankenstein isn't just experiencing sadness or regret in this passage, he is also anticipating how things could get much worse, making Answer E the best choice.

**13. D** Answer D is the best choice because it reflects the best understanding of Paragraph 1. The text states, "I collected the instruments of life around me" without ever specifying what those instruments are. Answer A is incorrect and probably shows the reader relying on prior knowledge of the plot of the Frankenstein movies. Answer B is incorrect because there is no mention of chemicals in the passage. Answer C is incorrect because, while the light of the candle is mentioned just before the creature comes to life, there is no causal link between the two ideas. Only Answer A reflects a full understanding of Paragraph 1.

**14. F** Answer F is the best choice because the text of Paragraph 2 shows Dr. Frankenstein expressing pity and disgust for the creature. He describes it as a "catastrophe" and introduces the unattractive qualities of the creature in detail, displaying that he feels the creature is malformed and not meant for this world. Therefore, the reader can conclude that a "wretch" is an unfortunate, unlucky, or pitiable person. Answer E is incorrect and mistakenly conflates the noun "wretch" with the verb "retch." Answer G is incorrect because it mistakenly assumes "wretch" is a verb rather than a noun as well. Answer H is incorrect because Paragraph 2 clearly describes that, while the creature is scary and intimidating, Frankenstein's initial feelings are disgust and pity.

**15. C** Answer C is the best choice because it reflects the most complete understanding of Paragraph 2. In Paragraph 2, Dr. Frankenstein says, "...I had selected his features as beautiful. Beautiful! Great God!" before describing the ugliness of the monster. This juxtaposition of beauty and ugliness is primarily what disturbs the doctor as he describes the creature's hair as "lustrous black" and teeth as "pearly white." While those features are generally associated with good looks, they take on a much darker meaning in the passage. Answers A and B are both incorrect, although they are both features of the creature described in the passage. Answer A and Answer B both ignore the quoted lines in which Frankenstein draws attention to the monster's intended beauty, however. Answer D also represents a factually accurate textual detail but shows the reader searching in Paragraph 3, rather than Paragraph 2 where the answer can most clearly be found.

**16. G** Answer G is the best choice because, using the context clues available in the surrounding sentences, it is clear that Dr. Frankenstein is tired and trying to sleep. The previous sentence identifies that Frankenstein is in his "bedchamber, unable to...sleep" The sentence before that also states that the doctor had "deprived [himself] of rest and health," implying he is very worn down and near exhaustion. Finally, the phrase "I slept, indeed" should communicate to the reader that lassitude is tiredness. Answers E, F, and H are all incorrect, although they do voice emotions that Dr. Frankenstein experiences in the passage, because they fail to identify all the words associated with sleep in the sentences surrounding "lassitude."

**17. C** Answer C is the correct choice because the Doctor's dream of his love becoming a corpse clearly shows his fear that things will go badly, especially in light of the monster he has just created. Dreams are frequently used in literature for the purpose of foreshadowing. Answer A is incorrect because, while the dream has metaphoric significance, its main purpose is still to reflect the doctor's regret and show his concern that his actions might ruin everything he loves, making Answer C a better choice. Answer B is incorrect because the dream doesn't emphasize any sense of irony in the passage. Answer D is incorrect because "rising action" is a feature of plot structure in which the protagonist faces increasingly difficult challenges. Obviously that is not the case in the passage, as it represents just one episode in Dr. Frankenstein's story. Overall, Answer C is the best choice because the dream shows Frankenstein's concern that things are about to get much worse.

**18. G** Answer G is the best choice because it correctly identifies that in Paragraph 1, Dr. Frankenstein is eager to create the creature (he describes that he is very anxious to complete the project), but by the end of Paragraph 3, his dream clearly reveals that he regrets the decision and is deeply concerned about what will happen next. Answer E is incorrect because the monster is Dr. Frankenstein's creation; he does not become the monster himself. Answer F is incorrect because the passage does not contain any plotting or planning by Frankenstein to eliminate the creature. Answer H is incorrect because the passage clearly establishes Elizabeth as Frankenstein's love and never says anything about his feelings for her fading. Only Answer G reflects true comprehension of the passage as a whole.

**19. D** Answer D is the correct choice because the question is phrased to ask how Elizabeth appears "initially" (i.e. at first). The text of Paragraph 3 clearly states, "I thought I saw Elizabeth, in the bloom of health," displaying that she appears fine at first. Answers A, B, and C are all true of the horrific imagery of Dr. Frankenstein's nightmare, but only Answer D gives voice to how Elizabeth looks at the very beginning of the dream. Answer A is incorrect because the image of the worms comes at the very end of the dream, not the beginning. Answer B is a reasonable inference based

on the imagery of the dream, but it fails to focus on the "initial" description of Elizabeth. Similarly, Answer C is incorrect because it does not zero in on the very first appearance of Elizabeth in the scene.

**20. G** Answer G is the best choice because the remainder of the passage contains a great amount of anxiety on Dr. Frankenstein's part and shows his emotional and psychological agony. Answer E isn't the best choice because it focuses on the weather or atmosphere of the night, which is far from the most important feature of the passage. Dr. Frankenstein's work and psychological journey are far more relevant to the content of the passage than the weather outside. Answer F is also incorrect because the word "accomplishment" has a strong positive connotation. Throughout Paragraphs 2 and 3, Dr. Frankenstein displays shame, fear, and agony, which are not words generally associated with feelings of "accomplishment." Finally, Answer H is incorrect as well because it focuses on the simple physical descriptions of the scene rather than the tonal and thematic details that the question asks for.

---

**Passage 2 ("Asthma")**

**21. B** Answer B is the best choice because it reflects the overall content and tone of the passage. In Paragraphs 1 and 3, the author describes the seriousness of asthma and the fact that it has effects that go far beyond a little coughing and wheezing. Paragraph 3 in particular shows how asthma can escalate in a quick and dangerous manner. Answer A is incorrect because the author describes how asthma can still be quite dangerous, especially when someone doesn't have their medicine available. Answer C is similarly incorrect because it implies we have mastered treatment, whereas the passage clearly says, "There are multiple causes of asthma, and some of them may not be fully understood yet" at the beginning of Paragraph 2. That clearly shows we have not mastered treatment. Finally, D is incorrect as well because, while the author emphasizes these secondary side effects multiple times throughout the passage, they are far from the "overall point of view" the question asks for. Answer B reflects the general message much more clearly.

**22. H** Answer H is the best choice because it is the only one that accurately reflects Paragraph 1 and displays and understanding of the cause-and-effect relationships described in the paragraph. The swelling and mucus build-up in airways are the root causes of the other symptoms, and therefore, they are the first step in the process. Answer G is incorrect because it fails to recognize that asthmatics have difficulty filling and emptying their lungs *because* their airways are swollen or filled with mucus. Similarly, Answer E is incorrect because it fails to recognize that wheezing is a result of swelling and mucus build-up. Answer F is also incorrect because panic and irritability are described as secondary symptoms, rather than the root cause, of asthma.

**23. C** Answer C is the best choice because, in the text, the term "coincidence" is used to denote the fact that many people with asthma also have allergies. Therefore, it could be said there's a "correlation" between the two. Answer A is incorrect, although it is a definition for "coincidence." In this context, however, the term is used to describe a correlation, not the kind of coincidence we think of in daily life (like wearing the exact same outfit to school as your classmate). Answer B is incorrect because "coincidence" implies that two things are in fact somehow related. Finally, Answer D is incorrect as well because "coincidence" is not medical jargon at all and has nothing specifically to do with asthma.

**24. F** Answer F is the best choice because Paragraph 3 walks the reader through the process of an asthma attack starting and progressing, describing how the person with asthma could be thinking and feeling at each step of the way. Answer E is incorrect because, other than advising people to use their inhaler, there are no specific examples of strategies in the paragraph. Answer G is incorrect because, while it's true that asthmatics should always have their inhaler, the paragraph's true role is to show the reader what it's like to be in the midst of an asthma attack. Answer H is incorrect as well because the paragraph specifically mentions that even small, minor symptoms can easily progress and build into a bigger, dangerous asthma attack, especially without medication.

**25. A** Answer A is the best choice because the ideas of inhaling chemicals and smoking cigarettes were established as causes or risk factors for asthma in Paragraph 2. Therefore, any treatment that involved using such means would be unscientific. The phrase "listening to the salesmen and doctors who prescribed those treatments was generally catastrophic" in the following sentence should be a major clue to the reader that "quack" medicine is bad. Answer B is incorrect because "quack" is not used to describe an animal in any way, and there is no reference to ducks at any point in the passage. Answer C is incorrect, because the sentence details that the so-called "quack" treatments often involved inhaling chemicals, which would be far from traditional herbal medicine. Answer D is incorrect because it does not provide a specific, clear enough definition. Although outdated medical practices could in some contexts be described as "quack medicine," the term "quack" specifically refers to unscientific or fraudulent pseudo-medical practices.

**26. F** Answer F is the best choice because it's the only answer not supported by the text. In fact, it directly contradicts the line from the first paragraph that states, "For others, it remains dormant or managed via medication for long stretches of time until an acute episode presents itself." Answer E is incorrect because Paragraph 5 clearly says rescue inhalers are short-acting and describes the "edginess" and pounding heart that can accompany rescue inhaler use. Answer G is incorrect because Paragraph 5 states that daily inhalers are "designed to keep a lower dose of steroids in the body at all times to keep symptoms from presenting themselves in the first place." Finally, Answer H is incorrect as well because Paragraph 5 states, "These tools work to clear things up for the moment, but if they're used frequently, their effectiveness plummets quickly."

**Passage 3 ("Gravity"):**

**27. D** Answer D is the best choice because, if gravity had not played a role in creating our planet, then we (or the planet) never would've existed. Answers A, B, and C all represent valid important roles gravity plays in our existence, but Answer D is by far the most fundamental issue because, if not for the formation of the planet, none of the other choices would even exist.

**28. G** Answer G is the best choice and reflects the best understanding of Paragraph 2. The sentences "All objects exert some kind of gravitational pull on each other, but the effects are only really observable when you're dealing with incredible large objects. That's why your body (which only weights a few hundred pounds at most) doesn't have a gravitational pull that attracts objects from across the room, but the Earth (which is quite massive) can keep our moon in orbit" from Paragraph 2 should serve as major hints to the reader. Answer E is incorrect because it's backwards – only large objects have appreciable gravity. Answer F is incorrect because the passage makes no reference to defying gravity and, if anything, suggests gravity is always present. Answer H is incorrect because the passage presents gravity as the force responsible for keeping the planets in orbit. Other, stronger forces might exist, but keeping the planets near the Sun is squarely the job of gravity.

**29. B** Answer B is the best choice because it shows the clearest understanding of Paragraphs 2 and 3. Answers A and D are both incorrect because they ignore that the Earth and Sun both have some degree of a gravitational pull on each other (as explained in Paragraph 3). The sentence, "Even though a more massive object (like the Sun) will ultimately determine the orbit of a smaller object (like the Earth), the smaller object also attracts the bigger object" should have been a major indicator to the reader. Answer C is incorrect because it mentions the moon, whereas the question is only concerned with the relationship between the Earth and the Sun.

**30. E** Answer E is the best choice because it reflects the best understanding of Paragraph 3. The sentence "Even though a more massive object (like the Sun) will ultimately determine the orbit of a smaller object (like the Earth), the smaller object also attracts the bigger object" should be a major indicator to the reader, as should the example of the magnets. Answer F is incorrect because, again, there is nothing in the passage about defying or eliminating gravity. If anything, gravity is presented as always present. Answer G is incorrect, while it may be a somewhat true statement, because it has nothing to do with the idea of a "two-way street," which implies some sort of reciprocal relationship. Answer H is incorrect as well because, again, while it might be true, it has nothing to do with a reciprocal relationship, which is what the term "one- way" or "two-way street."

**31. B** Answer B is the best choice because it points back at the early sentences of Paragraph 3 to explain what the magnet example is demonstrating. The sentences "One thing that's important to understand, though, is that gravity is not a one-way street. Even though a more massive object (like the Sun) will ultimately determine the orbit of a smaller object (like the Earth), the smaller object also attracts the bigger object. This can be hard to conceptualize, but thinking about a pair of magnets can help illustrate things" should be a major signpost to the reader. Answer A is incorrect because the passage takes pains to say "Obviously, magnetism is a different force than gravity," which establishes that they are not the same, although we're using the example of one to visually illustrate the other. Answer C is incorrect because the spiraling of the magnet is only to simulate what happens as objects get closer together. It is not actually meant to mirror the orbit of the Earth "toward" the Sun. Finally, Answer D is incorrect as well, although it is a somewhat true statement, because it fails to describe what the example is actually illustrating about gravity.

**32. H** Answer H is the best choice and reflects the best understanding of Galileo's work as it is described in Paragraph 4. The sentences, "Galileo discovered that all objects, dropped from any height, fall to the ground at a fixed rate of acceleration, unless they have an especially air-resistant shape. Prior to his work, it was assumed that heavier objects would fall to the Earth at a faster rate than light ones" should have served as a major hint to the reader. Answers E and F are incorrect because they misunderstand the fact that gravity has "a fixed rate of acceleration." Similarly, Answer G is incorrect because it mistakenly believes the greater mass of the bowling ball would create additional gravity, which would speed up the process.

**Passage 4 ("Henry VIII"):**

**33. B** Answer B is the best choice because, throughout the passage, the author emphasizes that Henry's accomplishments, while impressive, were born out of bad motivations. Paragraph 2 describes his motives as "deeply problematic," and Paragraph 4 states, "Henry's despicable behavior makes it hard for us to appreciate the philosophical importance of his split from the Catholic Church." Answer A is incorrect because the content of Paragraphs 3 – 5 reveals that the author clearly feels Henry's horrific personal life is worth emphasizing. Answer C is incorrect because the author never denies that Henry VIII is an important historical figure and even praises his accomplishments somewhat in Paragraph 1. Answer D is incorrect as well because the author never says that the split with the Church was a mistake in any way.

**34. E** Answer E is the best choice and reflects a full understanding of Paragraph 1. The sentence, "For centuries, the Church and monarchies across Europe had essentially partnered to provide supplies, infrastructure, spiritual support, and law and order to subjects in the cities and farm towns that dotted the continent at the time" should be especially helpful to the reader in making this determination. Answer F is incorrect because Paragraph 1 clearly states that the monarchs and Church had "partnered" to control Europe, denoting the monarchs had an equally important role. Answer G is incorrect and reflects the reality Henry VIII wanted to create rather than the reality of the world he was born into. Answer H is incorrect as well because Paragraph 1 clearly states that monarchs and the Church worked hand-in-hand during the time prior to Henry.

**35. C** Answer C is the best choice because it clearly identifies Henry's ideals (that countries should be ruled by their own governments without outside interference) to the way our world is different from the world that Henry was born into. Since the Catholic Church does not play a strong role in the governments of powerful countries around the world today, the reader can infer that Henry was a part of that shift. Answer A is incorrect because the English Renaissance was an accomplishment of Elizabeth's, not her father Henry. Answer B is incorrect as well because it mistakes Henry's motivations (to annul his first marriage) with his accomplishment (separating England from the influence of the Roman Catholic Church). Answer D is incorrect because Henry never abolished religion. Paragraph 2 clearly states: "Henry split from the Catholic Church and started the Church of England, which, unsurprisingly, granted him his annulment," which shows that there was a religion in England after Henry's split, it just wasn't the Roman Catholic Church anymore.

**36. H** Answer H is the best choice because Paragraph 2 goes on to describe Henry VIII's self-centered motivations, while Paragraph 3 provides details into the ordeals he put his wives through, which would certainly be controversial. Answer E is incorrect because it implies the author has unabashed admiration for Henry, which is clearly not true throughout the passage. Answer F is incorrect because Paragraph 1 establishes that Henry's impact on history was, in fact, quite important. Answer G is incorrect as well because it fails to recognize the many negative aspects of Henry's plans and actions that are explored in Paragraphs 2 and 3.

**37. A** Answer A is the best choice because the other details in Paragraph 4 provide context that point to Henry being portrayed as both loud and self-important. Paragraph 4 describes the stereotyped portrayal of Henry as "bellowing, 'Off with their heads!'" which demonstrates his loudness, while the phrase "megalomaniacal cartoon villain" shows he is often portrayed as self-important. Answer B is incorrect because there is nothing in the passage to suggest Henry was stupid, although it is certainly a reasonable inference he was greedy. Answer C is incorrect and probably reflects the reader attempting to interpret the fact that the text says Henry was an over-eater. Answer D is incorrect as well because, while Paragraph 4 does say that Henry was considered athletic and musical, the portrayal being described in the early sentences of the paragraph is that of Henry as a disgusting, negative caricature.

**38. G** Answer G is the best choice because it demonstrates that the reader understands what exactly the author finds ironic: that, in spite of Henry's disregard for women, his daughter ultimately wound up being one of history's most celebrated rulers. Answer E is incorrect because there's nothing in the passage about Elizabeth undoing Henry's work. Answer F is incorrect because Paragraph 3 clearly states Henry did, in fact, have a son (he just didn't turn out to be a famous monarch). Answer H is incorrect as well because the author stresses Henry's own individual accomplishments in Paragraph 1. The issue is not that Elizabeth is more famous; it's the fact that she was extremely accomplished in spite of having a father who is known as one of history's great misogynists.

**Passage 5 ("Ozymandias"):**

**39. B** Answer B is the best choice because the details of the following lines provide context to show the reader that the "visage" being described is a face. Line 4 mentions a "frown," while Line 5 introduces a "wrinkled lip" and a "sneer." All of these words are describing a facial expression, reinforcing that Answer B is correct. Answer A is not the best choice because it isn't nearly specific enough. The speaker isn't simply describing the statue; he is focusing on the statue's face. Similarly, Answer C focuses on the statue without recognizing the specific language pointing to the statue's face and facial expression. Answer D is also incorrect because it fails to focus in on what specific part of the king's body is being described.

**40. H** Answer H is the best choice because it reflects the best understanding of the poem's visual imagery. The statue is described as "half-sunken" and "shattered" (Line 4) as well as being called a "colossal wreck" (Line 13). All of these context clues point to the statue lying in ruins. Answer E is incorrect because Line 2 clearly describes the "trunkless legs" of the statue, which implies it is not standing any longer. Answer F is incorrect because there is no evidence of repairs to the statue; rather, the statue is presented as being beyond repair. Answer G is incorrect because it is not as specific as Answer H. While it's true that the statue has fallen, it's more correct to say it has broken into many pieces, making Answer H a better choice.

**41. D** Answer D is the best choice because the legs being described are those of the statue of Ozymandias which lies ruined in the desert. The term "legs of stone" (Line 2) should have made that distinction clear to the reader. Answer A is incorrect because the real Ozymandias died in ancient times, and the legs being described are those of a statue that was created to resemble him, making Answer D the better, more specific choice. Answer B is incorrect because the traveler (or "traveller" in the poem) is describing the stone legs that he saw during his journey in the desert (Lines 1-2), which clearly shows that they are not his legs. Answer C is incorrect because Shelley is simply the poet, and there is no evidence that he is a character in the poem or even the narrator.

**42. G** Answer G is the correct answer because Line 1 clearly opens the poem by stating that he narrator/ speakers only knows about the statue and Ozymandias second-hand through "a traveller from an antique land." Everything from that point forward is description of something the narrator has no personal knowledge of. Answer E is incorrect because the narrator has never been to the desert where the statue is located, as far as the poem states; only the traveler is confirmed to have been there. Answer F is incorrect because the pedestal inscription only exists out in the middle of the desert and has been seen by very few people. Answer H is incorrect as well because the poem strongly implies that the name Ozymandias is lost to history and that he is not a king that is known to many people (perhaps just the traveler and the people he has told about the statue).

**43. A** Answer A is the best choice because Lines 6-7 reveal that the sculptor who created the statue put great effort into reflecting how truly awful and powerful Ozymandias was. The preceding lines mention the king's "visage," "frown," and "sneer," and the proceeding line mentions "the hand." All of these descriptions show that the "lifeless things" are pieces of the fallen statue. Answer B is incorrect because there are is no mention of warriors or direct reference to battle anywhere in the passage. Answer C is incorrect because it fails to recognize that Lines 6-7 directly connect the "lifeless things" to the statue. Answer D is incorrect because the pedestal is not mentioned until Line 9, which means that the details about the statue appear closer in the text to the phrase in question, making it much more likely that they are connected.

**44. G** Answer G is the best choice because Lines 2-8 clearly reveal that the sculptor took pains to portray Ozymandias as a powerful and unpleasant figure. The sneering, "cold" facial expression described in Lines 4-5 reinforces the idea that the sculptor found Ozymandias intimidating, as does the description of "the hand that mocked them" in Line 8. Answer E is incorrect because the passage provides no other sculptures or sculptors against which to compare the statue described in the poem. Answer F is incorrect because a flattering statue would've probably looked a little nicer or more inviting rather than cold and intimidating, as the statue is described in the poem. Answer H is incorrect because it has no textual basis. We as readers have no way of knowing if the sculptor was killed or not.

**45. B** Answer B is the best choice because the plaque described in Lines 9-14 is clearly directed as a message to others who believe themselves to be powerful rulers. The phrase "king of kings" (Line 10) supports this conclusion well. The purpose of the statue is clearly to communicate that Ozymandias is the most powerful king in the world and serve as a warning to others who would challenge him. Answer A is incorrect because there is no mention of religion anywhere in the poem, and the phrase "king of kings" points to Ozymandias' rivals being primarily human. Answer C is incorrect because it ignores the phrase "king of kings" and fails to recognize that the king's natural rivals would be other kings, not simply warriors. Answer D is incorrect because Ozymandias is clearly concerned with other humans knowing about his greatness. Additionally, the forces of nature are what has destroyed the statue, so the forces of nature have had no need to "despair" (Line 11). Overall, only Answer B shows the reader thinking beyond the text in a logical, focused manner.

**46. E** Answer E is the correct choice because the pedestal inscription claims that Ozymandias is almighty and to be looked upon for all time. Clearly, the image of the broken, ruined statue stands in direct, ironic contrast to that message. Through this use of irony, Shelley is able to illustrate his point that time destroys all things and all people are eventually forgotten. Answer F is incorrect because the statue is simply described as a fallen statue, not personified as though the king were still living or somehow accessible. Answer G is incorrect because, while the entire poem serves as a metaphor in some way, Lines 9-14 specifically focus on the irony of Ozymandias' hubris and ambition. Answer H is incorrect because there are no words in the selected lines which form onomatopoetic sounds (like "buzz" or "boom").

**47. C** Answer C is the best choice because it reveals both a strong understanding of the poem and an ability to think beyond the text on the page and apply the poem to real life. The greatness of Ozymandias introduced in Lines 10-11 has clearly been negated by "the lone and level sands" (Line 14), showing that even someone who was the "king of kings" (Line 10) has been leveled and forgotten over time. Answer A represents a clear understanding of the text but fails to identify the destroying power of time as the poem's main feature. Answer B is incorrect because it ignores the role of time and nature in the poem (the word "antique" and the phrase "nothing beside remains" both show that the passage of time is crucial to the meaning of the poem). Answer D is incorrect because it fails to recognize the significance of the inscription on the pedestal, which points to the idea that time destroys all things – even those which people think are indestructible.

**Passage 6 ("The Six Basic Biomes"):**

**48. F** Answer F is the correct choice because it reflects a complete understanding of Paragraph 2. The first sentence of that paragraph states, "Researchers, biologists, and ecologists around the world identify different numbers of biomes, but just about everybody agrees on these six." That strongly implies that some scientists recognize more than six biomes. Answer E is incorrect because the term "basic" in the title is not describing the information in the passage; rather, it's describing the "biomes." Answer G is incorrect because the term "basic" is not used to suggest that biomes are simple information to understand, but rather to communicate that this is the most simplified way to look at biomes. Answer H is incorrect because the text is written in a way to give a general overview. The reader could do additional research to deepen his or her understanding, but the passage also stands on its own without the need to reference another text to ensure comprehension.

**49. C** Answer C is the best choice because Paragraph 3 emphasizes that deserts get very little liquid precipitation; however, some deserts like the Gobi do see snow. The term "liquid" is used to differentiate rain from snow. Answer A is incorrect because there is no mention of acid rain (or humans generally) in Paragraph 3, and the impact of humanity on ecosystems is not mentioned anywhere in the passage. Answer B is incorrect because there is nothing in the passage about evaporation of water in the desert, which means Answer B has no connection to the text. Answer D is incorrect because heavy rain is still in liquid form; the term "liquid" is only used to differentiate rain from snow.

**50. E** Answer E is the best choice because the rain in grasslands is presented as being inconsistent. The fact that trees and large plants have difficulty growing should suggest a lack of consistent water (especially when contrasted with the content about rainforests, which is mentioned in the following paragraph). Answer F is incorrect because there is nothing about out-of-control weather in the paragraph; the text simply suggests that rainfall is unreliable. Answer G is similarly wrong

because the text never says the rainfall is weak; it simply suggests it isn't consistent enough for trees to grow, making Answer E a better choice. Finally, Answer H is incorrect as well because measuring rainfall is presented as achievable throughout the text, and the author gives no reason for the reader to believe that measuring rainfall would be any more difficult in a grassland than in another climate.

**51. C** Answer C is the best choice because the annual rainfall, presence of tall trees, and lack of major seasonal changes all point to Location A being a rainforest. These qualities of rainforests are all laid out in Paragraph 5. Answer A is incorrect because Location A gets far too much rain to be a desert (based on information from Paragraph 3). Answer B is incorrect because the leaves in Location A do not change colors, which is one of the major features of a deciduous forest (based on information from Paragraph 6). Answer D is incorrect because Location A does not get snow or see major seasonal changes, both of which are features of the taiga biome (as described in Paragraph 7). Based on the content in the passage and data table, only Answer C makes sense.

**52. F** Answer F is correct because Paragraph 6 establishes that the leaves on trees in deciduous forests change color during colder seasons. Since that is not an established feature of any other biome, the presence of changing leaves strongly suggest a deciduous forest. Answer E is incorrect because there are major seasonal changes in taigas as well. Answer G is incorrect because deciduous forests also receive both rain and snowfall; that is not an exclusive trait of the taiga biome. Answer H is incorrect as well because it completely misinterprets the data table. The table clearly says that Location C does experience seasonal leaf changes.

**53. D** Answer D is the best choice because, based on the passage, the only biome in which leaves changing is specifically mentioned is the deciduous forest. If any location added to the table had changing leaves, it would be a solid inference to suggest it was a deciduous forest. Answer A is incorrect because, while it's true that leaves changing colors is a sign of dropping temperatures, it's untrue to say that you would see that kind of change in a taiga or tundra. The text clearly states that the taiga biome contains almost exclusively fir or evergreen trees, and also suggests that it's very difficult for large trees of any kind to grow in tundra conditions. Answer B is incorrect because there are plenty of tall trees on which the leaves do not change color (such as in a rainforest or a taiga), so Answer B is not a reliable conclusion. Answer C is also incorrect because Paragraph 6 clearly links the changing of leaves to temperature, not water levels.

**54. E** Answer E is the best choice because Location D experiences decent rainfall and does not have tall trees. Based on the content of the passage, only grassland makes sense. Answer F is incorrect because the taiga biome has tall trees. Answer G is incorrect because Location D experiences far more than the 9 inches of rain associated with deserts. Answer H is incorrect because Location D does not have tall trees or leaves that change color, eliminating deciduous forest. Based on the evidence in the data table and the descriptions in the passage, Location D must be a grassland.

**55. C** Answer C is the best choice because Paragraph 3 clearly states,"A desert is any place in which less than 9.75 inches of liquid rain." By that definition, rainfall should always be the clearest indicator of whether or not a biome is a desert. Answer A is incorrect because other biomes like tundra have minimal seasonal changes. Answer B is incorrect because, again, a lack of tall trees could also indicate a tundra or grassland. Answer D is incorrect because, while it can snow in the desert according to Paragraph 3, there are many better indicators (principally rainfall) to determine whether or not something is a desert.

**56. H** Answer H is the best choice because Location E's lack of liquid rain, lack of tall trees, and minor seasonal differences all align with what was described about the tundra biome in Paragraph 9. Answer E is incorrect because a grassland has noticeable seasonal changes, whereas it is cold, icy, and barren almost all of the year in a tundra (as expressed by the lack of seasonal change for Location E). Answer F is incorrect because a taiga would have tall trees, which Location E does not. Answer G is incorrect for the same reason: a rainforest would have tall trees (as well as much more liquid rain), so Location E cannot be a rainforest.

**57. B** Answer B is the best choice because each paragraph in the passage devotes at least a little time to explaining whether getting food, water, etc. is a major challenge for plants and animals in the area. Adding that category to the table might help readers more easily determine which biome a given location was based in. Answer A is not the best choice because there is minimal mention of humans in the passage, and humans can make most environments at least somewhat livable using technology, so the answer would probably be "Yes" in most situations, making the question less useful for categorizing purposes. Answer C is incorrect because the issue of water is already addressed in the "rainfall" column. The phrase "bounty of water" is simply taken from the paragraph describing the rainforest. Answer D is also incorrect because it is not a yes or no question or an easily quantifiable number (like rainfall). Because it is so open-ended and has so many possible responses, it wouldn't be a useful column for people who were trying to distinguish between different biomes at a glance.

**58. 100** This problem tests your ability to set up an average calculation. In order to find the average of the test scores, use the formula:

$$\frac{\text{sum of test scores}}{\text{number of tests}} = \text{test score average}$$

The number of tests is 5 and the desired average is 88. You have 4 of the test scores, and are asked to find the fifth to achieve this average. So let $x$ be the fifth test score.

Now write your equation:

$$\frac{80 + 95 + 75 + 90 + x}{5} = 88$$

Cross multiply and solve for $x$.

$80 + 95 + 75 + 90 + x = 88(5)$

$340 + x = 440$

$x = 100$

**59. 7** This problem tests your knowledge of geometry and your ability to set up a single variable equation. You are given three interior angles of a four-sided figure. The fourth side is defined by the expression $15x - 5$. First, find the value of the missing angle. Remember that the sum of the interior angles of a four-sided figure will always total 360. The missing angle calculates as $360 - 95 - 65 - 100 = 100$. Now solve the given expression using the missing angle:

| | |
|---|---|
| $15x - 5 = 100$ | write equation |
| $15x = 105$ | add 5 to each side |
| $x = \frac{105}{15} = 7$ | calculate |

$x$ is 7.

**60. $8** The school made $200 the first day by selling 10 adult tickets and 10 child tickets. Create an equation to solve.

$10a + 10c = 200$

$10c = 200 - 10a$

$c = 20 - a$

Now, you can plug in the value for $c$ in terms of $a$.

$13a + 2(20 - a) = 172$

$13a + 40 - 2a = 172$

$11a = 132$

$a = 12$

Therefore, an adult ticket is $12 and a child ticket is $8.

**61. 1,699**

If the population is 10,000 and the growth rate is 4% per year, to find the population after the first year, you simply multiply 10,000 × .04 to get 400. The population grew by 400 and therefore the total population at the end of the year was 10,400. The question asks you for the population increase over a period of 4 years. Second year the population increases by 416. Third year population increased by 432.64. Fourth year population increased by 449.95. The question asks for the total population increase over the span of four years, so add 400 + 416 + 432.64 + 449.95 = 1,698.59. The question asks you to round your answer to the nearest whole number which is 1,699.

**62.** **11** To make this computation easier, manipulate the denominator into a whole number. You can multiple the fraction by 10 to the numerator and denominator to get $\frac{55}{1}$. Now simply multiple 55 × .20 to get 11.

**63.** **F** We must perform the operations inside the parentheses first and follow the order of operations:

**P**arentheses
**E**xponentiation
**M**ultiplication
**D**ivision
**A**ddition
**S**ubtraction

3[−3] + [5] = −9 + 5 = −4, which is answer choice F.

**64.** **B** Simplify the expression to $\frac{1000}{x} = 10$, which when we solve, gives us, $x = 100$. If $x = 100$, then, $\sqrt{100} = 10$, which is the answer choice B.

**65.** **H** Plug in the values for *x*, *y* and *z*: $9 + \sqrt{9} + 9 - \sqrt{9} = 18$, which is answer choice H.

**66.** **C** If she needs to buy 2 pillets, that will cost $(\frac{2}{0.5})$ dollars = 4 dollars.

So, she will have $20 – $4 left, or $16.

With 16 dollars, she can buy (16 • 4) coss, or 64 coss, which is answer choice C.

**67.** **F** Simplifying gives us:

$$\frac{\sqrt{100}}{\sqrt{25}} = \frac{10}{5} = 2,$$

which is answer choice F.

**68.** **D** If $x = -8$, then $(4 \cdot -8) - 4 = -36$. Since we have an absolute value sign, we must take the positive of whatever number we have inside, which in this case, is −36.

So we have:
$(\frac{1}{2})(36) = 18$, which is answer choice D.

**69.** **F** Triangle *NPQ* is an equilateral triangle, which means all sides are equal. If the perimeter is 27, then the length of each side must be a third of the perimeter, or 9. Side lengths *NP* and *NQ* must add to 2(9) = 18, which is answer choice F.

**70.** **D** 40% is equivalent to $(\frac{2}{5})$, so our expression is $(\frac{2}{5})(x) = 160$, and solving for *x* gives us 400, which is answer choice D.

**71.** **H** We know that the statement must hold for all numbers. We can substitute a number of our choosing such as 40. When 40 is divided by 7, we get a remainder of 5. Adding 1 to 40, we get 41, which when divided by 7, gives us a remainder of 6, which is answer choice H.

**72. D** The vertical distance (parallel to the y-axis) from the origin to a point on the square must be 4. Doubling that would give us the side Length of the square, which is 8. The area of the square is just the side length squared. 8 = 64, which is answer choice D.

**73. G** The points we are concerned with here are *P*, *W*, *O* and *E*. It is helpful to state the coordinates of those points. *O* is the midpoint of *P* and *W*. To find the midpoint , all we need to do is take the difference between points *P* and *W*, divide by 2, and subtract it from point *P*.

$P(-13)$
$W(-3)$
$O(-8)$
$E(4)$

So, therefore, the distance between *O* and *E* is $|-8 - 4| = 12$, which is answer choice G.

**74. B** The median of an odd number of even consecutive integers is actually just the average of those numbers. For example:

{2, 4, 6}

The mean of those numbers is 4, and the median is 4. So the answer here is 20, which is answer choice B.

**75. F** $3.815 \times 10^{-3}$ is the answer since we moved the decimal point three places to the right.

**76. C** Applying the Pythagorean Theorem, we get that the Length of *AC* is:

$(-17^2 - 5^5)^{\frac{1}{2}} = 2\sqrt{66}$,

which is answer choice C.

**77. G** 53 hours from 3:30PM on a Thursday is composed of 2 sets of 24 hour days and 5 extra hours. This gives us Saturday at 8:30PM, which is answer choice G.

**78. C** The ratio of the circumference to the area of any circle is $(\frac{2}{r})$, where *r* is the radius. The radius of this circle is half of the diameter, which gives us 5.

The answer is $(\frac{2}{5})$, which is answer choice C.

**79. H** To convert from milligrams to grams, we must divide by 1000. To convert from grams to kilograms, we must divide by 1000. So, to convert between milligrams to kilograms, we must divide by 1,000,000, which would give us, $9.8 \times 10^{-5}$, which is answer choice H.

**80. D** Let *x* be the minimum score he must get to get the desired average. The average equation can be expressed as:

$\frac{244 + x}{4} = 85$,

and solving for *x*, we get $x = 96$, which is answer choice D.

**81. E** If 5 out of 10 marbles in a bag are red, then 5 are not red, making the percentage 50%, which is answer choice E.

**82. B** If the radius is 5, then the diameter or length *AC* is 10 units. We know that length *AD* is 6, so then we must also know that length *DC* is 8 (3, 4, 5 special right triangle), which gives the rectangle an area of 6 • 8 = 48, which is answer choice B.

**83. G** (9 • 5) + (4) = 49

**84. B** If it takes him 3 minutes to read 300 words, then it will take him 7.5 minutes to read 750 words. If there are 6 pages, each with 750 words, then it will take him (6 • 7.5) minutes to read the 6 pages.

(7.5 • 6) = 45 minutes, which is answer choice B.

**85. E** If we simplify what is in the parentheses first, we get $(-\frac{1}{4})$.

$(-\frac{1}{4})^2 + (\frac{5}{10}) = (\frac{1}{16}) + (\frac{1}{2}) =$

$(\frac{1}{16}) + (\frac{8}{16}) = (\frac{9}{16})$, which is answer choice E.

**86. D** The only answer choice that is divisible by 7, is 2016, which is answer choice D.

**87. E** We can tell that each consecutive hour adds $\frac{1}{4}$ th to the amount.

Let's say the units is gallons. So, if we work backwards, we can tell that the cylinder was empty 2 hours ago. So, the answer is 11AM, which is answer choice E.

**88. B** After simplifying, we get $x^8 = 2^8$, so we know that $x = 2$ and therefore $x^2 = 4$, which is answer choice B.

**89. G** If James finished $\frac{1}{8}$ of his total work, you can set up the following computation to solve for this problem. $\frac{8}{8} - \frac{1}{8} = \frac{7}{8}$

**90. B** The solid line path takes 4 steps. The dotted line path takes 3 steps. So the solid line path is −1 steps fewer than the dotted line path, which is answer choice B.

**91. H** Jackie's way: $\sqrt{34}\sqrt{9} + \sqrt{25} = 8$
Jesse's way : $= \sqrt{9} + 25 = \sqrt{34}$

$8 - \sqrt{34}$, the answer choice is H.

**92. B** We need theta to be a real value. Since *i*, is in the denominator, if *i* ever equals to 0, it will make the value undefined. Answer choice B gives *i* the value of 0, and therefore using the values in answer choice B cannot give us a value for theta. Therefore, the answer choice is B.

**93. H** Every day, James grows by 20 inches. There is a difference of 2 days between Monday and Wednesday, which means the answer is 2(20) = 40 inches, which is answer choice H.

**94. C** Simplify and you will get $(-\frac{1}{2})$, which is answer choice C.

**95. H** We can tell that $x^2 = y$ since they are corresponding angles. So, $y^3 = x^6$, and $x^2$ and $y$ are corresponding angles, meaning that they are equal.

*Note: Make sure you know the difference between corresponding, alternate interior, alternate exterior, and consecutive interior angles to help you with these types of problems.

Since $x^2$ and $y$ are equal, and the question asks what is $\frac{y^3}{3}$, replace the $y$ is $x^2$.

This gives you $\frac{x^{2^{(3)}}}{3}$, simplify to get $\frac{x^6}{3}$, which is answer choice H.

**96. C** Let, $d$, be the difference between consecutive terms. Each consecutive term differs by $d$. The values of $x$, $y$, $z$ and $f$ in terms of the differenced, is:

$x = 30 - 2d$
$y = 30 - d$
$z = 30 + d$
$f = 30 + 2d$

so when we add $x$, $y$, $z$ and $f$, we get, 120, which is answer choice C.

**97. F** If a negative number in parentheses is raised to an even exponent, then the answer will always be positive. However, 2023 is an odd exponent, making the value of this expression −1, which is answer choice F.

**98. D** If Jake has $X$ marbles, then Caroline has $2X$ marbles. If James has $Y$ marbles, then:

$X = 7Y - 12$.

We know that James has 14 marbles, so $Y = 14$, so $X = 86$. Therefore, Caroline has $2X$ marbles or 172, which is answer choice D.

**99. E** The first jump he makes, he goes up 10 meters. Then he falls back 5 meters. Then he jumps again, reaching the 15 meter mark, then falls back 5 meters to the 10 meter mark. He only has to jump one last time to reach the 20 meter mark, which is past the 19 meter mark. In total, he jumped 3 times, so the answer is E.

**100. B** We can take the highest 3 digit number, 999, and the highest 2 digit number, which is 99. When we multiply them, we get a 5 digit number, 98901. The answer is B.

**101. H** We can plug in the initial values into the formula to get $F_3$.

$F_3 = 2 \bullet F_2 + 3 \bullet F_1 = 2 \bullet 1 + 3 \bullet 1 = 5$.

The answer is H.

**102. A** Sam moves 3 meters to the West. Since Sam walked 4 meters North after walking 4 meters South, he undid his vertical movement, making him end up 3 meters from his original location. The answer is A.

**103. H** Plugging in for the values of $a$ and $b$, we get:

$\frac{9(3)}{5-3} = \frac{27}{2}$,

which is answer choice H.

**104. C** The circumference of a circle with a radius of 1m is $2\pi$, which equals 4 times the perimeter of the square. The perimeter of a square is 4 times the length of one of its sides. If $s$ is the side length of the square, then we can write:

$4s = 8\pi$, which means $s = 2\pi$ and the area is $s^2 = 4\pi^2$.

The answer is C.

**105. G** Following the pattern in the question, we know that $a = 4$, $b = 5$, $c = 7$ and $d = 8$. The question is asking what is the value of $be + ad$. Plug in the values, and you get $(4)(8) + (7)(5) = 32 + 35 = 67$, which is answer choice G.

**106. B** We know that $(\frac{3}{4})$ equates to 0.75 as a decimal. We simply multiply the denominator by 10 to get $(\frac{3}{40})$, which gives us 0.075 as a decimal, which is answer choice B.

**107. G** This requires us to solve for $q$.

$6(q + 3) = 2(q + 4)$
$3(q + 3) = (q + 4)$
$3q + 9 = q + 4$
$2q = -5$
$q = -\frac{5}{2}$

The answer is G.

**108. C** The two sides of the triangle that are adjacent to the angle of 30 degrees are equal since they make up two radii of the circle. All radii are equal. Therefore, the remaining two angles must be equal and must add up to 150° (180° – 30°).

This means that angle $x$ is 75°, which is answer choice C.

**109. E** For this expression to be true, we must find a value of $x$ that makes $\frac{-3x^2}{4}$ positive, which is impossible for real values of $x$ since we are squaring $x$. When we square $x$, we return a positive value. So the answer is 0, which is answer choice E.

**110. C** We must equate the sentence into mathematical terms. We know that,

$x = 0.4y$ and
$y = x^2$ so,
$x = 0.4x^2$

which is answer choice C.

**111. F** Plugging in 7 for $x$ in the equation, we get,

$4(7)(3y - 2(7)) = 112$, which gives us $28(3y - 14) = 112$ and solving for $y$, we get,
$(3y - 14) = 4$
$3y = 18$ so,
$y = 6$, which is answer choice F.

**112. C** Using the formula, we get,

$$\frac{a + (a - b)}{a - (a - b)} = \frac{2a - b}{b}$$

which is answer choice C.

**113. E** This problem tests your ability to understand fractional ratios as part of a whole. There are 30 trees in total, and you must find the ratio between fruit-bearing tress and weeping willows. There are 12 oak trees, while one-fifth are pine trees. This can be calculated: $\frac{30}{5} = 6$ pine trees. There are 3 weeping willows. The remainder must then be fruit-bearing.

Calculate: $30 - 12 - 6 - 3 = 9$ fruit-bearing trees.

The ratio of weeping willows to fruit-bearing is therefore 3:9 or 1:3.

**114. A** You are asked to find the company which has experienced the greatest percentage increase in sales from 2015 to 2016. The strategy here is to use some reasoning to eliminate some choices so you do not waste time calculating each percentage. The percentage increase will use the difference in sales between the years divided by the sales in 2015.

$$\frac{\text{sales year 2016} - \text{sales year 2015}}{\text{sales in 2015}} =$$

Percentage Increase

Keeping this in mind, you can save time by performing quick estimates without calculating the percentages. First start with Petra. Petra sold 80 units in 2015 and 105 in 2016, for an increase of 25. Set up the fraction $\frac{25}{80} = \frac{5}{16}$.
Now compare this fraction with that of each company:

• AudioPro increased by 15 units while selling 95 units in 2015. $\frac{15}{95} = \frac{3}{19} < \frac{5}{16}$.
Eliminate B.

• Keynote increased by 10 units while selling 85 units in 2015. $\frac{10}{85} = \frac{2}{17} < \frac{5}{16}$.
Eliminate C.

• GSharp increased only 10 units but started from 70 units. $\frac{10}{70} = \frac{2}{14} < \frac{5}{16}$.
Eliminate D.

• Lumia had an increase of 20 units and sold 75 units in 2015. $\frac{20}{75} = \frac{4}{15} ? \frac{5}{16}$.
This ratio is close enough to that or Petra to justify calculating in order to verify.

If you are quick with fractions, you can see that $\frac{4}{15} < \frac{5}{16}$. Petra shows the greatest percentage increase, therefore the correct answer choice is A.

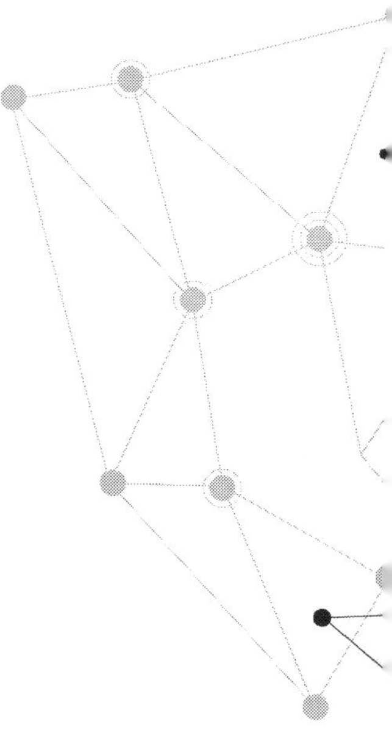

ARGOPREP
ARGOPREP.COM/SHSAT

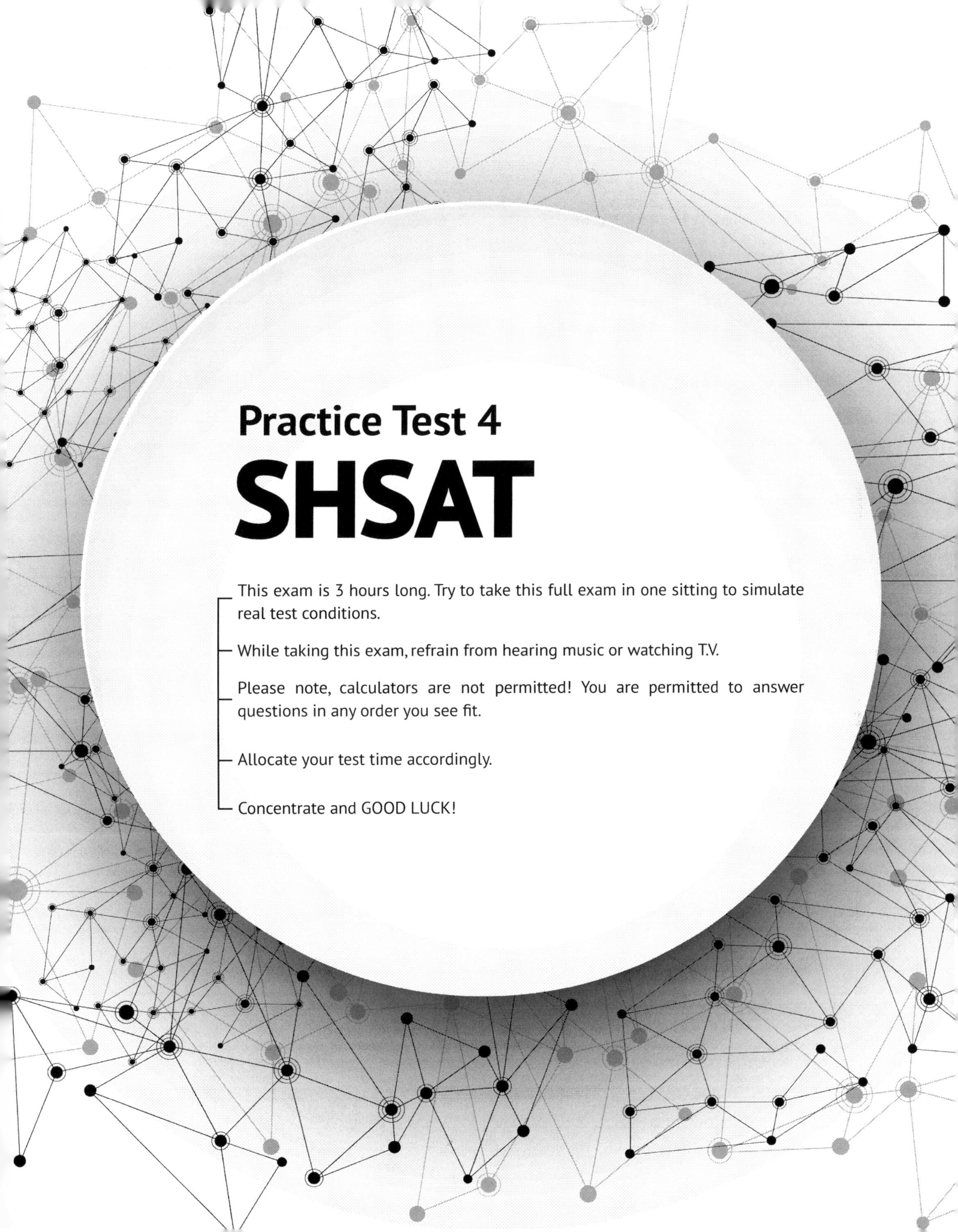

# Practice Test 4

# SHSAT

- This exam is 3 hours long. Try to take this full exam in one sitting to simulate real test conditions.
- While taking this exam, refrain from hearing music or watching T.V.
- Please note, calculators are not permitted! You are permitted to answer questions in any order you see fit.
- Allocate your test time accordingly.
- Concentrate and GOOD LUCK!

**You can find detailed video explanations to each problem in the book by visiting: ArgoPrep.com**

# SHSAT PRACTICE TEST 4
## ANSWER SHEET

### ENGLISH LANGUAGE ARTS

1. Ⓐ Ⓑ Ⓒ Ⓓ
2. Ⓔ Ⓕ Ⓖ Ⓗ
3. Ⓐ Ⓑ Ⓒ Ⓓ
4. Ⓔ Ⓕ Ⓖ Ⓗ
5. Ⓐ Ⓑ Ⓒ Ⓓ
6. Ⓔ Ⓕ Ⓖ Ⓗ
7. Ⓐ Ⓑ Ⓒ Ⓓ
8. Ⓔ Ⓕ Ⓖ Ⓗ
9. Ⓐ Ⓑ Ⓒ Ⓓ
10. Ⓔ Ⓕ Ⓖ Ⓗ
11. Ⓐ Ⓑ Ⓒ Ⓓ
12. Ⓔ Ⓕ Ⓖ Ⓗ
13. Ⓐ Ⓑ Ⓒ Ⓓ
14. Ⓔ Ⓕ Ⓖ Ⓗ
15. Ⓐ Ⓑ Ⓒ Ⓓ
16. Ⓔ Ⓕ Ⓖ Ⓗ
17. Ⓐ Ⓑ Ⓒ Ⓓ
18. Ⓔ Ⓕ Ⓖ Ⓗ
19. Ⓐ Ⓑ Ⓒ Ⓓ
20. Ⓔ Ⓕ Ⓖ Ⓗ
21. Ⓐ Ⓑ Ⓒ Ⓓ
22. Ⓔ Ⓕ Ⓖ Ⓗ
23. Ⓐ Ⓑ Ⓒ Ⓓ
24. Ⓔ Ⓕ Ⓖ Ⓗ
25. Ⓐ Ⓑ Ⓒ Ⓓ
26. Ⓔ Ⓕ Ⓖ Ⓗ
27. Ⓐ Ⓑ Ⓒ Ⓓ
28. Ⓔ Ⓕ Ⓖ Ⓗ
29. Ⓐ Ⓑ Ⓒ Ⓓ
30. Ⓔ Ⓕ Ⓖ Ⓗ
31. Ⓐ Ⓑ Ⓒ Ⓓ
32. Ⓔ Ⓕ Ⓖ Ⓗ
33. Ⓐ Ⓑ Ⓒ Ⓓ
34. Ⓔ Ⓕ Ⓖ Ⓗ
35. Ⓐ Ⓑ Ⓒ Ⓓ
36. Ⓔ Ⓕ Ⓖ Ⓗ
37. Ⓐ Ⓑ Ⓒ Ⓓ
38. Ⓔ Ⓕ Ⓖ Ⓗ
39. Ⓐ Ⓑ Ⓒ Ⓓ
40. Ⓔ Ⓕ Ⓖ Ⓗ
41. Ⓐ Ⓑ Ⓒ Ⓓ
42. Ⓔ Ⓕ Ⓖ Ⓗ
43. Ⓐ Ⓑ Ⓒ Ⓓ
44. Ⓔ Ⓕ Ⓖ Ⓗ
45. Ⓐ Ⓑ Ⓒ Ⓓ
46. Ⓔ Ⓕ Ⓖ Ⓗ
47. Ⓐ Ⓑ Ⓒ Ⓓ
48. Ⓔ Ⓕ Ⓖ Ⓗ
49. Ⓐ Ⓑ Ⓒ Ⓓ
50. Ⓔ Ⓕ Ⓖ Ⓗ
51. Ⓐ Ⓑ Ⓒ Ⓓ
52. Ⓔ Ⓕ Ⓖ Ⓗ
53. Ⓐ Ⓑ Ⓒ Ⓓ
54. Ⓔ Ⓕ Ⓖ Ⓗ
55. Ⓐ Ⓑ Ⓒ Ⓓ
56. Ⓔ Ⓕ Ⓖ Ⓗ
57. Ⓐ Ⓑ Ⓒ Ⓓ

### MATHEMATICS

63. Ⓔ Ⓕ Ⓖ Ⓗ
64. Ⓐ Ⓑ Ⓒ Ⓓ
65. Ⓔ Ⓕ Ⓖ Ⓗ
66 Ⓐ Ⓑ Ⓒ Ⓓ
67. Ⓔ Ⓕ Ⓖ Ⓗ
68. Ⓐ Ⓑ Ⓒ Ⓓ
69. Ⓔ Ⓕ Ⓖ Ⓗ
70. Ⓐ Ⓑ Ⓒ Ⓓ
71. Ⓔ Ⓕ Ⓖ Ⓗ
72. Ⓐ Ⓑ Ⓒ Ⓓ
73. Ⓔ Ⓕ Ⓖ Ⓗ
74 Ⓐ Ⓑ Ⓒ Ⓓ
75. Ⓔ Ⓕ Ⓖ Ⓗ
76. Ⓐ Ⓑ Ⓒ Ⓓ
77. Ⓔ Ⓕ Ⓖ Ⓗ
78. Ⓐ Ⓑ Ⓒ Ⓓ
79. Ⓔ Ⓕ Ⓖ Ⓗ
80. Ⓐ Ⓑ Ⓒ Ⓓ
81. Ⓔ Ⓕ Ⓖ Ⓗ
82. Ⓐ Ⓑ Ⓒ Ⓓ
83. Ⓔ Ⓕ Ⓖ Ⓗ
84 Ⓐ Ⓑ Ⓒ Ⓓ
85. Ⓔ Ⓕ Ⓖ Ⓗ
86. Ⓐ Ⓑ Ⓒ Ⓓ
87. Ⓔ Ⓕ Ⓖ Ⓗ
88. Ⓐ Ⓑ Ⓒ Ⓓ
89. Ⓔ Ⓕ Ⓖ Ⓗ
90. Ⓐ Ⓑ Ⓒ Ⓓ
91. Ⓔ Ⓕ Ⓖ Ⓗ
92. Ⓐ Ⓑ Ⓒ Ⓓ
93. Ⓔ Ⓕ Ⓖ Ⓗ
94. Ⓐ Ⓑ Ⓒ Ⓓ
95. Ⓔ Ⓕ Ⓖ Ⓗ
96. Ⓐ Ⓑ Ⓒ Ⓓ
97. Ⓔ Ⓕ Ⓖ Ⓗ
98. Ⓐ Ⓑ Ⓒ Ⓓ
99. Ⓔ Ⓕ Ⓖ Ⓗ
100. Ⓐ Ⓑ Ⓒ Ⓓ
101. Ⓔ Ⓕ Ⓖ Ⓗ
102. Ⓐ Ⓑ Ⓒ Ⓓ
103. Ⓔ Ⓕ Ⓖ Ⓗ
104. Ⓐ Ⓑ Ⓒ Ⓓ
105. Ⓔ Ⓕ Ⓖ Ⓗ
106. Ⓐ Ⓑ Ⓒ Ⓓ
107. Ⓔ Ⓕ Ⓖ Ⓗ
108. Ⓐ Ⓑ Ⓒ Ⓓ
109. Ⓔ Ⓕ Ⓖ Ⓗ
110. Ⓐ Ⓑ Ⓒ Ⓓ
111. Ⓔ Ⓕ Ⓖ Ⓗ
112. Ⓐ Ⓑ Ⓒ Ⓓ
113. Ⓔ Ⓕ Ⓖ Ⓗ
114. Ⓐ Ⓑ Ⓒ Ⓓ

### MATHEMATICS (GRID IN)

58

59

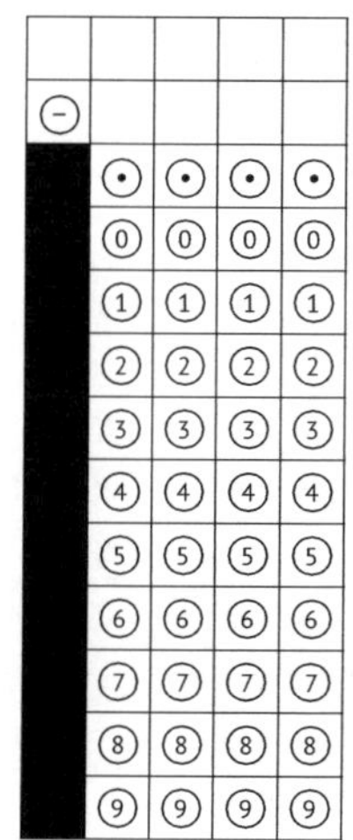

60

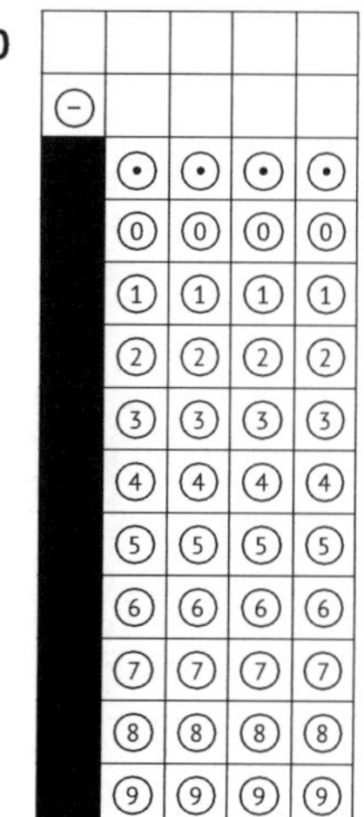

61

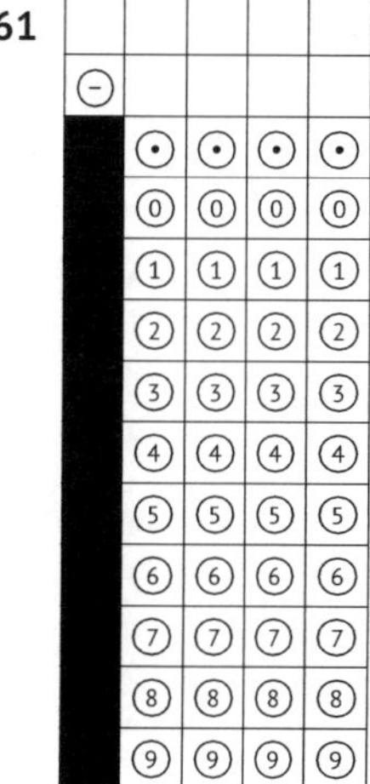

62

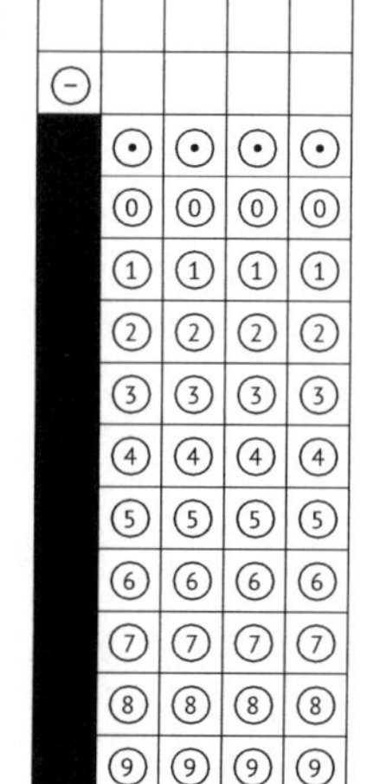

ARGOPREP
ARGOPREP.COM/SHSAT

**DIRECTIONS:** For questions 1 to 5, you will be asked to recognize and correct errors in sentences or short paragraphs.

**1.** Read this paragraph.

> (1) Most American students read F. Scott Fitzgerald's *The Great Gatsby* at some point in high school. (2) The book which is sometimes recognized as the "Great American Novel" tells the story of two star-crossed lovers Jay Gatsby and Daisy Buchanan. (3) Many students find the novel hard to connect with because all of the characters seem to be profoundly unhappy. (4) Although not everybody loves *The Great Gatsby*, the fact that is so widely taught in schools makes it a common touchstone for many Americans.

Which answer provides a correct revision of Sentence 2?

**A.** The book which is sometimes recognized as the "Great American Novel," tells the story of two star-crossed lovers Jay Gatsby and Daisy Buchanan.

**B.** The book, which is sometimes recognized as the "Great American Novel," tells the story of two star-crossed lovers Jay Gatsby and Daisy Buchanan.

**C.** The book, which is sometimes recognized as the "Great American Novel," tells the story of two star-crossed lovers, Jay Gatsby and Daisy Buchanan.

**D.** The book, which is sometimes recognized as the "Great American Novel" tells the story of two star-crossed lovers, Jay Gatsby and Daisy Buchanan.

**2.** Read this paragraph.

> (1) Stan Lee revolutionized the comic book world as a writer for Marvel Comics. (2) In 1961, Lee and his partner Jack Kirby created the Fantastic Four, a team of four radioactive heroes who changed the way comics were written. (3) Within three years, Lee had also created the Hulk Thor Spider-Man and the X-Men all of whom are still major characters for Marvel more than 50 years later. (4) Lee's signature was creating deeply flawed characters who seemed like real people with real problems, even though they were fictional heroes with incredible powers.

Which revision would correct the comma use in Sentence 3?

**E.** ...Lee had also created the Hulk, Thor, Spider-Man and the X-Men all of whom are still major characters for Marvel more than 50 years later.

**F.** ...Lee had also created the Hulk, Thor, Spider-Man, and the X-Men all of whom are still major characters for Marvel more than 50 years later.

**G.** ...Lee had also created the Hulk Thor Spider-Man, and the X-Men, all of whom are still major characters for Marvel more than 50 years later.

**H.** ...Lee had also created the Hulk, Thor, Spider-Man, and the X-Men, all of whom are still major characters for Marvel more than 50 years later.

**CONTINUE ON TO THE NEXT PAGE ➡**

3. Read this sentence.

> I have three uncles: Mike who is my mother's brother, Steve who is my father's brother, and Henry who is my mother's half-brother.

Which revision uses proper punctuation to format the sentence?

**A.** I have three uncles: Mike who is my mother's brother; Steve who is my father's brother; and Henry who is my mother's half-brother.
**B.** I have three uncles: Mike, who is my mother's brother; Steve, who is my father's brother; and Henry, who is my mother's half-brother.
**C.** I have three uncles: Mike; who is my mother's brother, Steve; who is my father's brother, and Henry; who is my mother's half-brother.
**D.** I have three uncles; Mike, who is my mother's brother; Steve, who is my father's brother; and Henry, who is my mother's half-brother.

4. Read this paragraph.

> (1) Historians often cite the Seneca Falls Convention of 1848 as the beginning of feminism in America. (2) Throughout the two-day convention, women's conditions and rights were discussed by as many as 300 attendees. (3) At the conclusion of the convention, 100 people signed the Declaration of Sentiments, a document that set goals for the feminist movement moving forward. (4) Elizabeth Cady Stanton, the author of the Declaration of Sentiments, modeled the document on the structure of the United States Declaration of Independence.

In what way is Sentence 2 inconsistent with the rest of the paragraph?

**E.** Subject matter
**F.** Verb tense
**G.** Passive voice
**H.** "To be" verb use

---

5. Read this sentence.

> After school Gerry walked down the road to the park and played with Stephanie and Hunter.

Which edit should be made to correct the sentence?

**A.** Add a **comma** after **school**
**B.** Add a **comma** after **road**
**C.** Add a **comma** after **park**
**D.** Add a **comma** after **Stephanie**

**CONTINUE ON TO THE NEXT PAGE ➡**

**DIRECTIONS:** Read the passage below to answer questions 6 to 11. The questions will focus on improving the writing quality of the passage to follow the conventions of standard written English.

---

**King Arthur**

(1) Although historians cannot be sure that the legendary ruler of England, King Arthur, ever existed, his mythic importance to the English identity is undeniable. (2) According to legend, Arthur ruled around 500 AD and is considered an extremely brave and honorable king. (3) By the twelfth century, mythical stories were already being told about Arthur assembling the bravest knights of all time to serve at his heroic Round Table.

(4) In most versions of the story Arthur the secret son of King Uther Pendragon pulls a magical sword from a stone to prove that he is the rightful ruler of England. (5) The wizard Merlin mentors Arthur and teaches him how to be an effective leader as he assembles his Round Table of the bravest and best knights in the land. (6) The Knights of the Round Table go on a variety of quests to gather sacred relics (including the Holy Grail) and protect England from a variety of invading armies and magical monsters. (7) The Round Table and Arthur's idealized rule both end when his wife, the beautiful Queen Guinevere, engages in a relationship with one of his most trusted knights, Sir Lancelot. (8) These general elements are present in almost all versions of the Arthur myth.

(9) The Arthur myth has been central to English culture for over a thousand years. (10) Arthur exists as an ideal for English government: he is fair-minded, stands up for the weak, and always chooses the path of righteousness. (11) His emphasis on assembling a team of the best and brightest provides an example for business leaders and managers all over the world. (12) The myth of Arthur has even guided England's military policy over the years, emphasizing participation in just causes and decisive action. (13) For England's royal family, he and his Round Table stand as pillars of trustworthiness, responsibility, and public adulation that they can also aspire to. (14) King Arthur is one of the key figures in English history, even if he wasn't real.

6. Which edit is needed to correct Sentence 2?
   - **E.** Change **ruled** to **rules**
   - **F.** Change **is** to **was**
   - **G.** Change **considered** to **considering**
   - **H.** Changed **honorable** to **honored**

---

7. What kind of error does Sentence 3 contain?
   - **A.** Subject-verb agreement
   - **B.** Spelling
   - **C.** Comma usage
   - **D.** Passive voice

CONTINUE ON TO THE NEXT PAGE ➞

8. Which sentence would best precede Sentence 4 to serve as a topic sentence for the second paragraph?
   - **E.** Although many versions of the Arthur myth have been told throughout history, most of them contain the same major characters and elements.
   - **F.** The story of Arthur is packed with action, adventure, and betrayal.
   - **G.** Arthur wields a mythical sword known as Excalibur.
   - **H.** The story has a variety of interesting characters.

---

9. Which revision makes proper use of commas in Sentence 4?
   - **A.** In most versions of the story, Arthur the secret son of King Uther Pendragon pulls a magical sword from a stone to prove that he is the rightful ruler of England.
   - **B.** In most versions of the story, Arthur, the secret son of King Uther Pendragon, pulls a magical sword from a stone to prove that he is the rightful ruler of England.
   - **C.** In most versions of the story Arthur, the secret son of King Uther Pendragon, pulls a magical sword from a stone to prove that he is the rightful ruler of England.
   - **D.** In most versions of the story, Arthur, the secret son of King Uther Pendragon, pulls a magical sword from a stone to prove that he is the rightful ruler, of England.

10. Which transition should be added to the beginning of Sentence 7?
   - **E.** Therefore
   - **F.** However
   - **G.** Ultimately
   - **H.** Subsequently

---

11. Which sentence is least relevant to the content of the rest of the passage and should be removed?
   - **A.** Sentence 9
   - **B.** Sentence 10
   - **C.** Sentence 11
   - **D.** Sentence 12

**CONTINUE ON TO THE NEXT PAGE ➡**

**DIRECTIONS:** Read the passage below to answer questions 12 to 20. The questions will focus on improving the writing quality of the passage to follow the conventions of standard written English.

---

**The Author to Her Book**
By Anne Bradstreet

Thou ill-formed offspring of my feeble brain,
Who after birth did'st by my side remain,
Till snatcht from thence by friends, less wise than true,
Who thee abroad exposed to public view,
Made thee in rags, halting to th' press to trudge,
Where errors were not lessened (all may judge).
At thy return my blushing was not small,
My rambling brat (in print) should mother call.
I cast thee by as one unfit for light,
The visage was so irksome in my sight,
Yet being mine own, at length affection would
Thy blemishes amend, if so I could.
I washed thy face, but more defects I saw,
And rubbing off a spot, still made a flaw.
I stretcht thy joints to make thee even feet,
Yet still thou run'st more hobbling than is meet.
In better dress to trim thee was my mind,
But nought save home-spun cloth, i' th' house I find.
In this array, 'mongst vulgars may'st thou roam.
In critic's hands, beware thou dost not come,
And take thy way where yet thou art not known.
If for thy father askt, say, thou hadst none;
And for thy mother, she alas is poor,
Which caused her thus to send thee out of door.

**12.** Who or what is the "offspring" mentioned in Line 1?

**E.** The speaker
**F.** The speaker's child
**G.** The speaker's book
**H.** The speaker's mental illness

---

**13.** Based on the text, what is the speaker's opinion of her friends who helped promote the book?

**A.** She is frustrated by their lack of support for the book and worries they don't believe it is worthy of being published.
**B.** She is flattered by their enthusiasm for the book and thankful that they have shared her work with others.
**C.** She is frustrated by their childlike behavior and wishes that they were better friends.
**D.** She is flattered by their enthusiasm for her book but frustrated that they think it's better than she does.

---

**14.** Which of these is not a specific objection the speaker has to the way her book was published?

**E.** The book was not effectively proofread
**F.** She was not paid for the story
**G.** The book was printed on cheap, unattractive paper
**H.** The book was rushed to print too fast

**CONTINUE ON TO THE NEXT PAGE ➡**

**15.** To what does the speaker consistently compare her book throughout the poem?

**A.** An ugly baby
**B.** A dirty face
**C.** Cheap clothes
**D.** A bad dream

---

**16.** What does the speaker mean when she says, "If for thy father askt, say, thou hadst none" (Line 22)?

**E.** She no longer loves the man who inspired her to write the book.
**F.** She is disowning the book because she is not proud of it
**G.** Her book was created entirely by a female author and therefore has only one parent, who is a mother.
**H.** She is ashamed of the identity of her baby's father

---

**17.** What is the best definition for "array" as it is used in Line 19 of the poem?

**A.** Configuration
**B.** Data set
**C.** Outfit
**D.** Display

---

**18.** According to the speaker, what was her principle reason for publishing her book?

**E.** She believed it was a great work of art and only saw its flaws after publication.
**F.** She needed the money badly.
**G.** Her friends were extremely enthusiastic about the book and wanted to share it with others.
**H.** She believes it is important for art to exist, even if it is ugly or low-quality.

**19.** Who is the speaker especially nervous will read her book?

**A.** Her parents
**B.** Her child
**C.** Low-class people
**D.** Literary critics

---

**20.** Based on the text, which of these is the safest inference about Anne Bradstreet?

**E.** She was a highly successful author and poet in her time
**F.** She was a harsh critic of her own work
**G.** She never had any children
**H.** She never published another book after the one described in "The Author to Her Book"

**CONTINUE ON TO THE NEXT PAGE ➡**

# READING COMPREHENSION
## Practice Test 4

**DIRECTIONS:** Analyze the passages below, and answer the commensurate questions. Only use information provided within the passage for your answers. There is only one answer for each question.

---

### Sports Champions

Every athlete who laces up a pair of cleats, puts on a jersey, or straps on a helmet wants to be a champion. Championships represent the highest level of achievement in sport and are accomplishments that athletes remember for the rest of their lives. However, there are many different paths to becoming a champion. Each sport or game has a unique championship history that dates back as long as the game has existed. For some fans, those histories are as enjoyable to study as the games themselves. That's because championships bring out the best in the greatest athletes and create truly memorable moments.

Each of the four predominant professional sports in the U.S. (football, baseball, basketball, and hockey) has a top-level championship with its own unique personality. For baseball, it's the World Series, which is sometimes called the October Classic. The World Series is famous for its long tradition, which dates back to 1903. Football's Super Bowl is a yearly spectacle that often draws the biggest TV viewing audience of the year across the country, as the game occurs on a Sunday in late winter, when most people are at home lounging on the couch and eating junk food. Hockey and basketball both peak in June, but their championships have very different flavors. For hockey, the Stanley Cup is known for intense, grinding games; whereas the NBA Finals are famous for thrilling, fast-paced action.

Of course, there are many other legendary sports titles outside of the few that we see on TV each year. For example, the World Heavyweight Championship of boxing was regarded as the richest prize in American sport for a century. Although its prominence has waned over the last few decades, World Heavyweight Champion boxers are still among the highest-earning and most-watched athletes around the world. Horse racing's three Triple Crown races also carry great prestige, and any horse who can win all three of them in a single year is bound to capture the attention and adulation of the entire nation. Similarly, golf and tennis each have a "Grand Slam," which is comprised of four major events. Winning one major is a career-making accomplishment, but winning the entire Grand Slam in a single year makes someone an all-time great.

For some athletes, however, the deepest satisfaction comes from international competition. Track and field athletes, skaters, fencers, skiers, judo practitioners, wrestlers, and many, many more test their mettle every four years on the Olympic stage. These national heroes rarely get rich playing high-level sports and chasing medals, but they dedicate their time and bodies to representing our nation and culture around

CONTINUE ON TO THE NEXT PAGE →

the world. Although they might not frequently attain the celebrity status that other professional athletes receive, international athletes compete with a higher sense of purpose, making those medals and championships even sweeter.

Clearly, there are thousands of different ways to be a sports champion, and no two of them look exactly alike. Just here in the U.S. alone, there are thousands of great achievements and accomplishments for athletes to chase. That's not even accounting for the for the dozens of championship soccer leagues throughout Europe or the unique,traditional sports played in countries around the world. In spite of the wide variety of championships out there, they all represent the same ideals: greatness, hard work, and pride.

**21.** What is the main purpose of Paragraph 1 in the passage?

- **A.** To help the reader understand how it feels to be an athlete
- **B.** To describe the traits of a championship athlete to the reader
- **C.** To make the reader excited to read about sports championships
- **D.** To convince the reader that sports championships are great accomplishments

---

**22.** Based on the passage, which professional sport's championship occurs first each year?

- **E.** Football
- **F.** Baseball
- **G.** Hockey
- **H.** Basketball

**23.** Which of these is the best definition for "flavors" as it is used in Paragraph 2?

- **A.** Tastes
- **B.** Personalities
- **C.** Tempos
- **D.** Rules

---

**24.** In what way does the author distinguish boxing from the other sports mentioned in the passage?

- **E.** The author claims that boxing is less reputable than other sports.
- **F.** The author mentions that boxing's championship is not a as prestigious as as it once was.
- **G.** The author qualifies that some sports fans are offended by the violence of boxing.
- **H.** The author states that boxing matches are highly profitable and widely watched.

---

**25.** If you added up the number of Triple Crown horse races and Grand Slam golf and tennis majors in a given year, how many events would you have in total?

- **A.** 7
- **B.** 9
- **C.** 11
- **D.** 13

**CONTINUE ON TO THE NEXT PAGE ➞**

**26.** Which of these is the best summary of Paragraph 4?

- **E.** Olympic medals are very different from American professional sports championships.
- **F.** There is a huge variety of sports at the Olympics, and each of those sports has a champion.
- **G.** Olympic athletes are especially impressive because they chase global championships without the rewards associated with sports stardom.
- **H.** Olympic athletes don't get as famous as other athletes because they're only on TV every four years.

**CONTINUE ON TO THE NEXT PAGE ➡**

### Trademarks

Have you ever noticed the letters "TM" or an "R" in a circle next to the name, slogan, or logo of your favorite toy or snack? Those letters indicate that the name, phrase, or logo you just saw is a trademark. Trademarks allow companies to utilize certain words or images to market their products while also preventing others from using them. Establishing, utilizing, and protecting trademarks is vitally important to many large businesses.

The goals of trademark law are to prevent confusion in the marketplace for consumers and allow companies to market themselves as having a distinct identity. Essentially, this means that once a company registers their name or logo as a trademark, their competitors cannot try to copy their style or message to leach off of their success. If an organization feels that somebody else is infringing on their trademark, they can send a warning letter urging them to cease or desist their use of the protected words or images. If the activity continues, the trademark holder can sue the offender to prevent their usage and recover any funds they feel they lost as a result of the infringement.

This means that holding a trademark on certain strategic words or images could make someone very powerful. However, before the U.S. Patent and Trademark Office grants a person or company a trademark, they consider whether the term or image the business is trying to register is specifically tied to their unique business or just a generic or generally descriptive term. For example, if a restaurant chain was trying to trademark the phrase "Delicious food!" to use in their advertising, the USPTO would reject that application because "food" is just the generic term for what is sold in restaurants, and "delicious" is a descriptive adjective that could easily be applied to the food that's made by any number of people or restaurants. Similarly, a florist couldn't just trademark a picture of a rose because many other businesses also sell roses.

The best and strongest trademarks are what's described as "arbitrary" or "fanciful." An arbitrary or fanciful mark is when a business registers a name or logo that has nothing obvious to do with their business. For example, if a chain of oil change businesses called themselves "Birdies," that name would be considered arbitrary because birds have absolutely nothing to do with oil changes. Arbitrary trademarks are considered strong because they show that a company is trying to create a unique brand identity for itself. If another oil change business came along and tried to call themselves "Birds," the owner of Birdies could claim that the name of the new business was too close to theirs, and therefore potentially confusing to customers. Furthermore, if a cell phone company had registered a fish as their logo, no other cell phone company could market their product using a fish.

Without trademarks, marketing products would be tough for businesses, and buying products would be tough for consumers. Imagine a store where the shelves are filled with paper towels that all have pictures of squirrels on them or cans of vegetables that all have blue labels with black text. Trademarks allow businesses to differentiate themselves from the competition and empower customers to choose the product they feel best fits their needs. When businesses don't protect their identity in this way, they're setting themselves up to lose.

**CONTINUE ON TO THE NEXT PAGE ➡**

**27.** Which of these best describes the author's goal for this passage?

**A.** To convince the company where he or she works to protect themselves using trademarks
**B.** To explain the difference between different kinds of trademarks
**C.** To describe the role the USPTO plays in the U.S. economy
**D.** To establish the goals and value of trademarks

---

**28.** Based on the passage, why is "establishing, utilizing, and protecting trademarks ...vitally important to many large businesses?"

**E.** Owning trademarks allows companies to sue their competitors, which can be very profitable and also hurts the competition financially.
**F.** Trademarks help companies connect with potential customers and protect them from competitors who use copycat tactics.
**G.** Once a business registers a trademark, the USPTO will go out of their way to monitor the market and make sure no one else infringes on that mark.
**H.** The strength of a company's trademarks is often more important than the quality of the product itself when it comes to sales.

**29.** Which of these is the best definition for "infringing" as it's used in Paragraph 2?

**A.** Violating someone's established legal right
**B.** Stealing with intent to defraud
**C.** Attacking in a court of law through a suit
**D.** Preventing something from being profitable

---

**30.** Which of these would be an example of an "arbitrary" or "fanciful" mark?

**E.** A logo of a dog's face for a dog rescue organization
**F.** The name "Wheat O's" for a ring-shaped cereal made of whole wheat
**G.** The catchphrase "Get your whippy wozzle on!" for a new slip-and-slide toy
**H.** The name "Soda" for a new brand of soft drink

---

**31.** Based on the passage, which of these statements is not true of trademarks?

**A.** In this country, trademarks are registered with and governed by the USPTO.
**B.** Trademarks are designed to protect both businesses and consumers.
**C.** "Arbitrary" or "fanciful" marks are considered the strongest and easiest to protect.
**D.** Trademarks prevent a company's competition from attempting to copy their brand or advertising style.

**CONTINUE ON TO THE NEXT PAGE ➡**

**32.** What does the author mean when he or she writes, "Imagine a store where the shelves are filled with paper towels that all have pictures of squirrels on them" in Paragraph 5?

**E.** Without trademark law, products would all have much simpler designs, which would make shopping less visually engaging

**F.** Without trademark law, the market could become so filled with imitators and copycats that it would be hard to tell the actual differences between good products and bad products.

**G.** Without trademark law, brands wouldn't try to differentiate themselves from the competition.

**H.** Without trademark law, there would be no actual differences between the different products at the store.

**CONTINUE ON TO THE NEXT PAGE ➞**

**Ralph Waldo Emerson**

Some years ago, in company with an agreeable party, I spent a long summer day in exploring the Mammoth Cave in Kentucky. We traversed, through spacious galleries affording a solid masonry foundation for the town and county overhead, the six or eight black miles from the mouth of the cavern to the innermost recess which tourists visit – a niche or grotto made of one seamless stalactite, and called, I believe, Serena's Bower. I lost the light of one day. I saw high domes and bottomless pits; heard the voice of unseen waterfalls; paddled three quarters of a mile in the deep Echo River, whose waters are peopled with the blind fish; crossed the streams "Lethe" and "Styx;" plied with music and guns the echoes in these alarming galleries; saw every form of stalagmite and stalactite in the sculptured and fretted chambers – icicle, orange-flower, acanthus, grapes, and snowball. We shot Bengal lights into the vaults and groins of the sparry cathedrals, and examined all the masterpieces which the four combined engineers, water, limestone, gravitation, and time, could make in the dark.

The mysteries and scenery of the cave had the same dignity that belongs to all natural objects, and which shames the fine things to which we foppishly compare them. I remarked, especially, the mimetic habit, with which Nature, on new instruments, hums her old tunes, making night to mimic day, and chemistry to ape vegetation. But I then took notice, and still chiefly remember, that the best thing which the cave had to offer was an illusion. On arriving at what is called the "Star-Chamber," our lamps were taken from us by the guide and extinguished or put aside, and, on looking upwards, I saw or seemed to see the night heaven thick with stars glimmering more or less brightly over our heads, and even what seemed a comet flaming among them. All the party were touched with astonishment and pleasure. Our musical friends sung with much feeling a pretty song, "The stars are in the quiet sky," etc., and I sat down on the rocky floor to enjoy the serene picture. Some crystal specks in the black ceiling high overhead, reflecting the light of a half-hid lamp, yielded this magnificent effect.

I own, I did not like the cave so well for eking out its sublimities with this theatrical trick. But I have had many experiences like it, before and since; and we must be content to be pleased without too curiously analyzing the occasions. Our conversation with Nature is not just what it seems. The cloud-rack, the sunrise and sunset glories, rainbows, and northern lights are not quite so absolute as our childhood thought them; and the part our organization plays in them is too large. The senses interfere everywhere and mix their own structure with all they report of. Once, we fancied the earth a plane, and stationary. In admiring the sunset, we do not yet deduct the rounding, coordinating, pictorial powers of the eye.

**33.** What is this passage mostly about?

**A.** The curiosity of man.
**B.** The ignorance of man concerning nature.
**C.** The importance of nature to man.
**D.** The way human senses interact with our understanding of nature.

**CONTINUE ON TO THE NEXT PAGE ➞**

**34.** What is implied about the "star-chamber?"

- **E.** It was the only natural phenomenon of its kind.
- **F.** The stars were very bright.
- **G.** There was a comet.
- **H.** There were no actual stars on display.

---

**35.** Why does Emerson describe water as an engineer?

- **A.** Water is necessary for engineering.
- **B.** Water is one of the forces that created the cave.
- **C.** Water is the only force that created the cave.
- **D.** Water is the most important force in the creation of the cave.

---

**36.** Why did the party start singing under the "star-chamber?"

- **E.** They were tired after a long day of hiking.
- **F.** It is tradition to sing under the "star-chamber."
- **G.** They were moved by the beauty of the "star-chamber."
- **H.** They were always singing.

**37.** Why does Emerson note that we once believed the earth was flat?

- **A.** It is an example of when the senses led us to an incorrect belief.
- **B.** To show that humans are not capable of understanding nature.
- **C.** To show that nature is never understood.
- **D.** To show that it is best to avoid deeply considering the nature of the world.

---

**38.** In what state did Emerson's adventure take place?

- **E.** Maine
- **F.** North Dakota
- **G.** South Dakota
- **H.** Kentucky

**CONTINUE ON TO THE NEXT PAGE ➞**

**Excerpt from "After Twenty Years"**
By O. Henry

The policeman on the beat moved up the avenue impressively. The impressiveness was habitual and not for show, for spectators were few. The time was barely 10 o'clock at night, but chilly gusts of wind with a taste of rain in them had well nigh depeopled the streets.

Trying doors as he went, twirling his club with many intricate and artful movements, turning now and then to cast his watchful eye adown the pacific thoroughfare, the officer, with his stalwart form and slight swagger, made a fine picture of a guardian of the peace. The vicinity was one that kept early hours. Now and then you might see the lights of a cigar store or of an all-night lunch counter; but the majority of the doors belonged to business places that had long since been closed.

When about midway of a certain block the policeman suddenly slowed his walk. In the doorway of a darkened hardware store a man leaned, with an unlighted cigar in his mouth. As the policeman walked up to him the man spoke up quickly.

"It's all right, officer," he said, reassuringly. "I'm just waiting for a friend. It's an appointment made twenty years ago. Sounds a little funny to you, doesn't it? Well, I'll explain if you'd like to make certain it's all straight. About that long ago there used to be a restaurant where this store stands--'Big Joe' Brady's restaurant."

"Until five years ago," said the policeman. "It was torn down then."

The man in the doorway struck a match and lit his cigar. The light showed a pale, square-jawed face with keen eyes, and a little white scar near his right eyebrow. His scarfpin was a large diamond, oddly set.

"Twenty years ago to-night," said the man, "I dined here at 'Big Joe' Brady's with Jimmy Wells, my best chum, and the finest chap in the world. He and I were raised here in New York, just like two brothers, together. I was eighteen and Jimmy was twenty. The next morning I was to start for the West to make my fortune. You couldn't have dragged Jimmy out of New York; he thought it was the only place on earth. Well, we agreed that night that we would meet here again exactly twenty years from that date and time, no matter what our conditions might be or from what distance we might have to come. We figured that in twenty years each of us ought to have our destiny worked out and our fortunes made, whatever they were going to be."

**39.** Based on the passage, which of these adjectives best describes the policeman character?

- **A.** Quick-tempered
- **B.** Smart
- **C.** Incredulous
- **D.** Reliable

---

**40.** Why was the policeman "trying doors as he went" in Paragraph 2?

- **E.** To check for criminals
- **F.** To see if any of the businesses were still open
- **G.** To ensure they were locked and secure
- **H.** To find the missing Jimmy

**CONTINUE ON TO THE NEXT PAGE ➞**

**41.** Which other word used in the passage is a synonym for "thoroughfare" as it is used in Paragraph 2?

**A.** Street (Paragraph 1)
**B.** Store (Paragraph 2)
**C.** Block (Paragraph 3)
**D.** Restaurant (Paragraph 4)

---

**42.** How many years after the two men made their agreement to meet was Big Joe Brady's restaurant torn down?

**E.** Twenty years
**F.** Ten years
**G.** Fifteen years
**H.** Five years

---

**43.** Which of these is the best definition for "straight" as it is used in Paragraph 4?

**A.** Not crooked
**B.** Directly to the point
**C.** Even
**D.** Legitimate

---

**44.** Why is it an important plot detail that the man in the doorway lights a cigar?

**E.** The act of smoking shows that he is an evil or untrustworthy character
**F.** The light allows the policeman (and reader) to see the man's face
**G.** The light reveals the man's expensive jewelry, which shows he is rich
**H.** The fact that he has matches is highly suspicious to the policeman

**45.** What distinction does the man in the doorway make between himself and Jimmy Wells?

**A.** He is adventurous, whereas Jimmy is a homebody
**B.** He is a homebody, whereas Jimmy is adventurous
**C.** He has become rich and successful, whereas Jimmy is still struggling financially
**D.** He is struggling financially, whereas Jimmy has become rich and successful

---

**46.** What earlier detail from the text makes the initial description of the man in the doorway in Paragraph 3 additionally suspicious?

**E.** The narrator mentions that there are chilly winds
**F.** The narrator mentions that there are open cigar stores nearby
**G.** The narrator mentions that the policeman is checking to make sure doors are locked
**H.** The narrator mentions that the man speaks up to the policeman quickly

---

**47.** Which of these best describes the mood of the passage?

**A.** Dark
**B.** Chaotic
**C.** Mysterious
**D.** Horrific

**CONTINUE ON TO THE NEXT PAGE ➡**

### Infrastructure in the United States

Even though the United States is considered to be one of the world's most advanced and prosperous countries, American infrastructure is consistently graded among the worst in the developed world. Part of the problem may lie in the fact that few Americans truly understand what "infrastructure" means. The term is broadly used to describe the roads, tunnels, bridges, power stations, and other buildings and structures that are fundamental to the operation of a city or society. Essentially, infrastructure is the stuff we need to make day-to-day life work.

So, why is America's infrastructure considered so bad? Well, in part, it was designed for a much smaller world. A great example of this is the American aviation system. US airports process more than two million passengers per day, as advances in communication, technology, and economics have made both domestic and international travel much more commonplace over the last thirty years. Not wanting to shut down or divert traffic in any major ways during necessary upgrades and expansions, most airports have elected to do piecemeal updates over the years, which has resulted in many airports with a wide range of modern and outdated facilities.

Another famous example of the woes of American infrastructure is the condition of our bridges. According to American Society of Civil Engineers, 40% of bridges in the United States are more than 50 years old and more than 9% of them are considered structurally deficient. Much like updates to airports, updating bridges is challenging because it requires fully or partially closing bridges in ways that disrupt the normal daily lives of thousands, if not millions, of people at a time. However, that inconvenience must be weighed against the potential short-term catastrophe and long-term impact of a bridge collapse.

The United States also lags behind other developed countries when it comes to providing adequate public transportation for its citizens. Most developed countries in Europe and Asia have thriving high-speed rail systems that help people get from place to place efficiently and affordably without the need for a car, but there are many places in the U.S. where train and bus services are extremely limited. The need for these services has never been higher, as more than 130 million American workers commute each day, and the expenses of automobile maintenance, gasoline, and insurance are all major expenditures that could be reduced or eliminated for many people with proper public transportation.

The United States is a global leader in many different ways, but the increasing age and declining quality of American infrastructure is beginning to affect citizens in more ways than they know. The price of constant repairs to outdated roads, bridges, and tunnels and the expense of replacing those structures quickly when they eventually fail creates an incredible tax burden on everyday Americans. On the other hand, the government's lack of proactive infrastructure improvements has made transportation less safe and less affordable for everyone. Unfortunately, over the last 50 years, infrastructure has become an area where the government pinches pennies to balance budgets, but if Americans don't start paying for infrastructure improvements now, they'll pay a much higher price later.

CONTINUE ON TO THE NEXT PAGE →

| A Selection of Historical Grades from the American Society of Civil Engineers' Infrastructure Report Card | | | | | |
|---|---|---|---|---|---|
| | 1988 | 1998 | 2005 | 2013 | 2017 |
| Aviation | B– | C– | D+ | D | D |
| Bridges | No Grade | C– | C | C+ | C+ |
| Transit | C– | C– | D+ | D | D– |
| Schools | D | F | D | D | D+ |
| GPA | C | D | D | D+ | D+ |

**48.** Which of these is the best definition for "graded" as it is used in Paragraph 1?

**E.** Enforced
**F.** Assessed
**G.** Mentioned
**H.** Included

---

**49.** Why does the author put "infrastructure" in quotation marks only once in Paragraph 1?

**A.** The author puts the word in quotation marks the first time it's used to show it's a new or key term.
**B.** The author puts the word in quotation marks because he or she is using it ironically or as part of a joke.
**C.** The author puts the word in quotation marks to show that he or she is discussing the word itself at that moment rather than concept of infrastructure.
**D.** The author puts the word in quotation marks to show that the term appears in many official government documents and reports.

**50.** Based on the text, which of these issues would you be likely to encounter in an airport that's had piecemeal updates done?

**E.** Over-crowding due to waiting rooms that were designed when fewer people flew
**F.** A lack of affordable public transportation to and from the airport
**G.** Fewer flights because insufficient infrastructure means fewer people than ever can travel
**H.** Inconsistent quality of services and facilities due to different parts of the airport being vastly different ages

---

**51.** Why does the author mention the American Society of Civil Engineers in Paragraph 3?

**A.** To provide examples of people who are experts when it comes to bridges
**B.** To show that his or her points are supported by the work of respected and knowledgeable professionals
**C.** To build notoriety for an important organization whose work not enough Americans know about
**D.** To explain which professionals infrastructure is most relevant to

---

**52.** Which other word in the text is a synonym for "weighed" as it is used in Paragraph 3?

**E.** Graded (Paragraph 1)
**F.** Designed (Paragraph 2)
**G.** Updating (Paragraph 3)
**H.** Developed (Paragraph 4)

**CONTINUE ON TO THE NEXT PAGE ➞**

**53.** Which other detail from the passage supports the assertion in Paragraph 2 that American infrastructure was "designed for a much smaller world?"

**A.** The fact that 40% of American bridges are more than 50 years old
**B.** The fact that the public transportation system is so inadequate relative to the size of the workforce
**C.** The fact that closing a bridge for temporary repairs would impact millions of people's lives and schedules
**D.** The fact that many airports have a variety of different facilities

---

**54.** Which information from the data table is surprising in light of the passage?

**E.** The grade for bridges has actually gone up over the last 20 years
**F.** The grade for aviation has gotten worse in spite of advances in technology
**G.** The current grade for schools is surprisingly good
**H.** The current grade for schools is surprisingly bad

---

**55.** Based on the table, in which area of infrastructure has progress stagnated most over the last 30 years?

**A.** Bridges
**B.** Aviation
**C.** Transit
**D.** Schools

**56.** Based on the table, in which area of infrastructure has the most improvement been made over the last 20 years?

**E.** Bridges
**F.** Aviation
**G.** Transit
**H.** Schools

---

**57.** Based on the GPA grades, what can we infer about the American Society of Civil Engineers' Infrastructure Report Card

**A.** The American Society of Civil Engineers is a fictitious organization
**B.** There were more graded categories on the report card than appear in this table
**C.** The American Society of Civil Engineers are harsher graders than most teachers
**D.** The report card contained only the graded categories that appear in this table

CONTINUE ON TO THE NEXT PAGE ➡

ARGOPREP
ARGOPREP.COM/SHSAT

# MATHEMATICS INSTRUCTIONS

## 90 MINUTES • 57 QUESTIONS

Select the best answer from the choices given by carefully solving each problem. Bubble the letter of your answer on the answer sheet. Please refrain from making any stray marks on the answer sheet. If you need to erase an answer, please erase thoroughly.

**Important Notes:**

1. There are no formulas or definitions in the math section that will be provided.
2. Diagrams may or may not be drawn to scale. Do not make assumptions based on the diagram unless it is specifically stated in the diagram or question.
3. Diagrams are not in more than one plane, unless stated otherwise.
4. Graphs are drawn to scale, therefore, you can assume relationships according to the graph. If lines appear parallel, then you can assume the lines to be parallel. This is also true for right angles and so forth.
5. Simplify fractions completely.

# Practice Test 4

### GRID IN PROBLEMS (Questions 58-62)

*Directions: The following five questions are grid-in problems. On the answer sheet, please be sure to write your answer in the boxes at the top of the grid. Start on the left side of each grid.*

**58.** If $f(x) = x^2 + \sqrt[3]{x}$ and $g(y) = \sqrt{(y - 2)}$, solve for $g(f(8))$.

**59.** The length of a rectangle is $3x - 1$ and the width is $3x + 9$, while the perimeter is 172. What is the area of the rectangle?

CONTINUE ON TO THE NEXT PAGE ➡

**60.** A fair coin is flipped 10 times. If the first 9 flips resulted in Heads, what is the chance the tenth flip will result in Heads? Make sure your answer is in decimal form.

| | | | | |
|---|---|---|---|---|
| ⊖ | | | | |
| | ⊙ | ⊙ | ⊙ | ⊙ |
| | 0 | 0 | 0 | 0 |
| | 1 | 1 | 1 | 1 |
| | 2 | 2 | 2 | 2 |
| | 3 | 3 | 3 | 3 |
| | 4 | 4 | 4 | 4 |
| | 5 | 5 | 5 | 5 |
| | 6 | 6 | 6 | 6 |
| | 7 | 7 | 7 | 7 |
| | 8 | 8 | 8 | 8 |
| | 9 | 9 | 9 | 9 |

**61.** A construction crane has a boom which extends 50 ft from the base. If the crane is stationed 30 ft from a building, how high up the building wall can the crane reach?

| | | | | |
|---|---|---|---|---|
| ⊖ | | | | |
| | ⊙ | ⊙ | ⊙ | ⊙ |
| | 0 | 0 | 0 | 0 |
| | 1 | 1 | 1 | 1 |
| | 2 | 2 | 2 | 2 |
| | 3 | 3 | 3 | 3 |
| | 4 | 4 | 4 | 4 |
| | 5 | 5 | 5 | 5 |
| | 6 | 6 | 6 | 6 |
| | 7 | 7 | 7 | 7 |
| | 8 | 8 | 8 | 8 |
| | 9 | 9 | 9 | 9 |

**62.** If $\frac{x-8}{x+3} = 12$, solve for $x$.

| | | | | |
|---|---|---|---|---|
| ⊖ | | | | |
| | ⊙ | ⊙ | ⊙ | ⊙ |
| | 0 | 0 | 0 | 0 |
| | 1 | 1 | 1 | 1 |
| | 2 | 2 | 2 | 2 |
| | 3 | 3 | 3 | 3 |
| | 4 | 4 | 4 | 4 |
| | 5 | 5 | 5 | 5 |
| | 6 | 6 | 6 | 6 |
| | 7 | 7 | 7 | 7 |
| | 8 | 8 | 8 | 8 |
| | 9 | 9 | 9 | 9 |

**CONTINUE ON TO THE NEXT PAGE ➡**

**MULTIPLE CHOICE PROBLEMS (Questions 63-114)**

**63.** What is the value of $\sqrt{25} + \sqrt{64}$ ?

**E.** 10
**F.** 13
**G.** 14
**H.** 89

---

**64.** What is the value of $r$ in the equation: $2r = 10^2$ ?

**A.** 10
**B.** 25
**C.** 50
**D.** 100

---

**65.** What is the area of a square with a perimeter of 16?

**E.** 8
**F.** 12
**G.** 16
**H.** 24

---

**66.** What is 10% of a number whose square is 81?

**A.** 0.81
**B.** 0.9
**C.** 8.1
**D.** 9

**67.** What is the range of the set $\{1, 2, 5, 10, 6, 12\}$?

**E.** −16
**F.** −11
**G.** 3
**H.** 11

---

**68.** Nancy found a formula for the area of a square in terms of its perimeter. Let A stand for the area and P for perimeter. What is the formula Nancy found?

**A.** $\frac{P^2}{8}$
**B.** $\frac{P^2}{4}$
**C.** $\frac{P^2}{16}$
**D.** $4P$

---

**69.** Anayet is driving to work from home and realizes he left his wallet at home when he is at his workplace. He turns back to retrieve his wallet. His workplace and home are 45 miles apart and it takes him twice as long to get to workplace from his home than the other way around. It is a 30 minute drive from his workplace to home. What is the average speed for the round trip in miles per minute?

**E.** 0.75
**F.** 1.5
**G.** 1
**H.** 2

**CONTINUE ON TO THE NEXT PAGE →**

**70.** Given that, $\overleftrightarrow{a} = a^2 + a$, what is $\overleftrightarrow{a} \div a$ ?

**A.** $a$
**B.** $a + 2$
**C.** 1
**D.** $a + 1$

---

**71.** Sarah has a trick coin that has heads on both sides. She asks her friend John, who believes the coin is fair, to guess what face it will land on. If they flip the coin 100 times, how many times bigger is Sarah's expected probability of the coin landing on heads than John's expected probability of the coin landing on heads?

**E.** 0.25
**F.** 0.5
**G.** 1
**H.** 2

---

**72.** What is the square of a number that when added to any number does not change that number's value?

**A.** 0
**B.** 0.5
**C.** 1
**D.** undefined

---

**73.** How many nonzero numbers are between 3 and 5?

**E.** 1
**F.** 2
**G.** 3
**H.** $\infty$

---

**74.** The circle that is inscribed in the square below has a radius of 2. What is the length of the diagonal of the square?

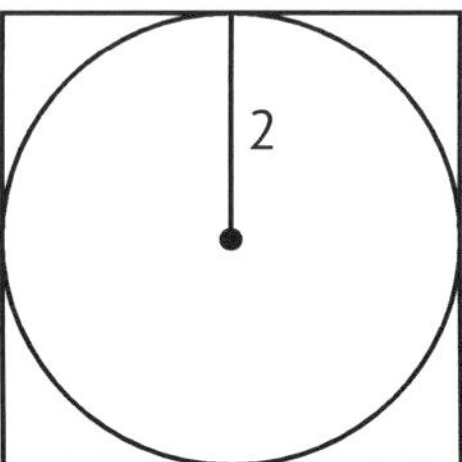


**A.** 4
**B.** 16
**C.** $4\sqrt{2}$
**D.** $2\sqrt{2}$

---

**75.** What is the absolute value of the difference between the number of integers between 0 and 5 inclusive and the number of integers between 1 and 6 exclusive?

**E.** 0
**F.** 1
**G.** 2
**H.** 3

---

**76.** Corey is walking on a path. Every three steps he takes, he makes a 30 degree rotation to counterclockwise. If he took 18 steps in total, how many full revolutions was he able to make all together?

**A.** 0.25
**B.** 0.5
**C.** 1
**D.** 2

**CONTINUE ON TO THE NEXT PAGE ➡**

**77.** What is 20% of 20% of 20?

**E.** 0.2
**F.** 0.8
**G.** 2
**H.** 8

---

**78.** What is the difference between the largest and lowest integer in the sequence of consecutive odd integers whose sum is 15?

**A.** 2
**B.** 4
**C.** 5
**D.** 9

---

**79.** The half life of a substance is the time it takes for a substance to decrease to half its initial amount. John has a pile of goo that decreases in amount at a constant rate. If John initially had 100 pounds of goo, and ten days later, he only had 25 pounds of goo, what is the half life of the goo?

**E.** 10 days
**F.** 5 days
**G.** 7.5 days
**H.** 20 days

---

**80.** What is the value of $\frac{9^4 - 8^4}{9^2 + 8^2}$?

**A.** 1
**B.** 16
**C.** 17
**D.** 18

**81.** Jackie fills a jug with water continuously. It takes her 2 minutes to fill up 50% of the empty space in the jug with water. After every 2 minutes, she puts a penny into a jar to celebrate. How many pennies will she have in the jar at the instant the jug has less than 30% empty space left?

**E.** 0
**F.** 1
**G.** 2
**H.** 3

---

**82.**

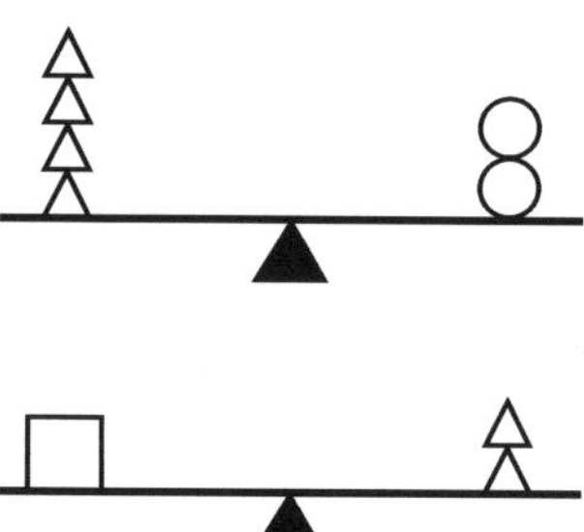

In the figure above, there are two balance beams that have triangles, circles and squares on them. Both beams are fully balanced. How many circles are needed to balance 70 squares?

**A.** 10
**B.** 12
**C.** 35
**D.** 70

CONTINUE ON TO THE NEXT PAGE ➞

**83.** $.\overline{7} + \frac{2}{9} = .\overline{6} + $ ___

E. $\frac{1}{2}$
F. $\frac{1}{3}$
G. $\frac{2}{9}$
H. $\frac{4}{9}$

---

**84.** The prime factors of 232 are

A. 2, 2, 2, 29
B. 116, 2
C. 2, 29
D. 2, 2, 58

---

**85.** If the pattern continues, what will be the 438th symbol?

□ ↻ ← ↑ → ↖ □ ↻ ← ↑ → ↖ □ ↻

E. □
F. ↑
G. ↖
H. ↻

---

**86.** Find the value of $t$ if $\frac{t}{32} = \frac{x}{p}$

A. $\frac{32p}{x}$
B. $\frac{32}{px}$
C. $\frac{32x}{p}$
D. $32px$

---

**87.** What is the least integer greater than $\frac{52}{3}$?

E. 16
F. 17
G. 18
H. 19

---

**88.** If $5^5 + 5^5 + 5^5 + 5^5 + 5^5 = 5^{a+1}$, what is $a$?

A. 3
B. 4
C. 5
D. 6

---

**89.** If $(x + y)^2 = x^2 + y^2$, then what condition must be true?

E. $x + y = 0$
F. $2x = 0$
G. $2y = 0$
H. $xy = 0$

**CONTINUE ON TO THE NEXT PAGE ➡**

**90.** What is the maximum number points that two distinct circles can intersect at?

**A.** 2
**B.** 3
**C.** 4
**D.** $\infty$

---

**91.** A cumulative product of a set $\{a, b, c, ...\}$ is the sequence, $a$, $ab$, $abc$, ... What is the mean of the terms in the cumulative product of $\{1, 2, 3, 0\}$?

**E.** 0
**F.** 2
**G.** 2.25
**H.** 3.5

---

**92.** How many integers are in the set of nonpositive, nonnegative integers?

**A.** 0
**B.** 1
**C.** 2
**D.** $\infty$

**93.** How many chords are in the circle below?

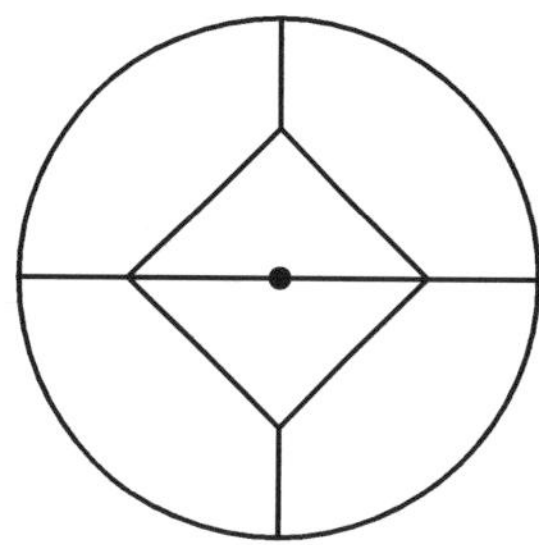

**E.** 1
**F.** 2
**G.** 3
**H.** 7

---

**94.** In the figure below, there is a function plotted and there are 5 points labeled $A$ through $E$ drawn. For how many points is $y(x)$ equal to 0?

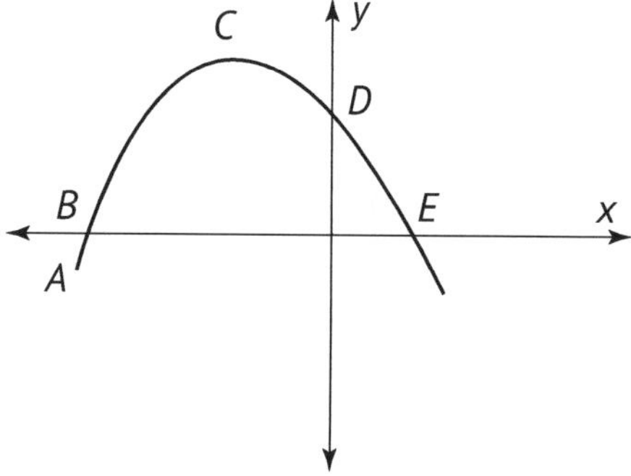


**A.** 0
**B.** 1
**C.** 2
**D.** 3

CONTINUE ON TO THE NEXT PAGE ➡

**95.** At what time on a clock will the hands form an acute angle formed of 60°?

**E.** 1:00 PM
**F.** 2:00 PM
**G.** 2:30 PM
**H.** 3:00 PM

---

**96.** A jar contains only red and blue marbles. The probability of picking a red marble is 20%. One blue marble is added to the jar. What is the probability of picking a blue marble?

**A.** $\frac{1}{2}$

**B.** $\frac{4}{5}$

**C.** $\frac{1}{6}$

**D.** Cannot be determined from the information given.

---

**97.** If $a$ = 35, what is, $(-6)^2(-6)(-6) + 6(-6)$ in terms of $a$?

**E.** $a + 1$
**F.** $a^2$
**G.** $a^2 + 1$
**H.** $a^2 + a$

**98.** A circle and an octagon share the same perimeter (circumference for the circle). If the side length of the octagon is, $a$, and the radius of the circle is, $r$, then what is the radius in terms of the side length of the octagon?

**A.** $\frac{a}{\pi}$

**B.** $\frac{4}{\pi}$

**C.** $\frac{4a}{\pi}$

**D.** $4\pi$

---

**99.** What is the least integer greater than the greatest integer less than 1.5?

**E.** 2
**F.** 1.5
**G.** 0.5
**H.** 1

---

**100.** What is the area of a semicircle in terms of tau ($\tau$) with a radius of $r$. Tau is double the value of $\pi$.

**A.** $\tau^2 r$

**B.** $\tau r^2$

**C.** $\frac{\tau r^2}{4}$

**D.** $\frac{\tau r}{2}$

CONTINUE ON TO THE NEXT PAGE ➡

**101.** If $F = -kx$ and greater than 0, then what happens to the value of $k$ if $F$ triples in value and $x$ remains constant

**E.** Increases
**F.** Doubles
**G.** Decreases
**H.** Cannot be determined from the information given.

---

**102.** If the length of the side of a square is, $7^a$, what is the area?

**A.** $7^a$
**B.** $49^a$
**C.** $7^{2a}$
**D.** $7a^a$

---

**103.** What is the circumference of the dotted section of the circle whose center is $O$ below?

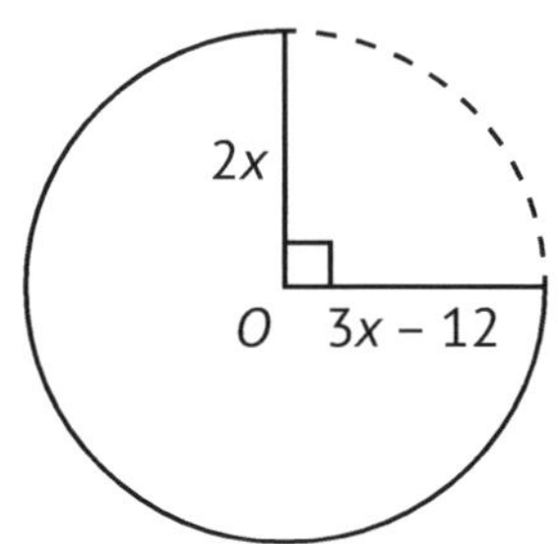


**E.** $6\pi$
**F.** $12\pi$
**G.** $24\pi$
**H.** $48\pi$

**104.** Given that $0 < x < 1$, and set $A = \{x, x^2, x^3, x^4\}$, what is the smallest value in set $A$?

**A.** $x^2$
**B.** $x^3$
**C.** $x^4$
**D.** Cannot be determined from the information given.

---

**105.** Sammy has a faulty clock. Every 15 degrees that one of the hands moves, 5 minutes passes. If a hand is initially 5:35 PM, in how long will the hand be at that same position?

**E.** 65 minutes
**F.** 2 hours
**G.** 1 hour
**H.** 45 minutes

---

**106.** If $(x - 2)(x + 2) = ax^2 + bx + c$, what is the sum of $a$, $b$ and $c$?

**A.** $-4$
**B.** $-3$
**C.** 0
**D.** 1

**CONTINUE ON TO THE NEXT PAGE ➡**

**107.** Natalie walks in a special way. After every 2 steps, she takes 1 step in the opposite direction. She starts at point *A* and walks forward. When she is 7 steps away from point *A*, she has reached her destination, point *B*. How many steps in total did she take to get from point *A* to *B*?

**E.** 7
**F.** 8
**G.** 17
**H.** 15

---

**108.** If, $C_{m,n} = C(m + n)$, for what value of $n$ is $C_{m,n}$ neither positive nor negative?

**A.** $-C$
**B.** $-m$
**C.** $2m$
**D.** 0

---

**109.** Two sides of a triangle are 6 and 8. What is the length of the third side?

**E.** 2
**F.** 4
**G.** 5
**H.** Cannot be uniquely determined.

**110.** $2 + \frac{1}{3} = \frac{14}{b}$, what is $b$?

**A.** 3
**B.** 6
**C.** 7
**D.** 9

---

**111.** In the formula $V = r^2h$, if $h$ is doubled and $r$ triples, then $V$ is multiplied by?

**E.** 6
**F.** 9
**G.** 12
**H.** 18

---

**112.** Max *A* returns the largest value in the set A. Min *A* returns the lowest value in the set A. For example, max{1, 2, 3} = 3 and min{0, 4, 5} = 0.

What is $\max\{\min\{x, 2x, 3x\}, \max\{\frac{x}{2}, \frac{x}{4}, \frac{x}{8}\}\}$?

**A.** $2x$
**B.** $\frac{x}{2}$
**C.** $3x$
**D.** Cannot be uniquely determined.

**CONTINUE ON TO THE NEXT PAGE ➞**

*Use the graph below to answers questions 51 and 52.*

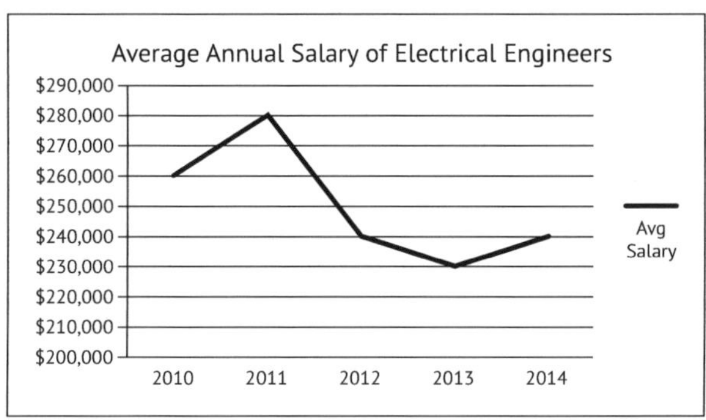


---

**113.** What was the approximate percentage decrease in average annual salary from 2011 to 2012?

**E.** 14.3%
**F.** 15.2%
**G.** 50%
**H.** 25%

---

**114.** What was the average salary in 2015 if it was 10% greater than the median salary for the previous five years?

**A.** $253,000
**B.** $264,000
**C.** $275,000
**D.** $286,000

**THIS IS THE END OF THE TEST. IF THERE IS TIME REMAINING, YOU MAY CHECK YOUR ANSWERS TO PART 1 OR PART 2.**

**CONTINUE ON TO THE NEXT PAGE ➞**

# SHSAT PRACTICE TEST 4
## ANSWER KEY

### PART 1 (ENGLISH LANGUAGE ARTS)

**Revising/Editing**

1. **C**
2. **H**
3. **B**
4. **G**
5. **A**
6. **F**
7. **D**
8. **E**
9. **B**
10. **G**
11. **C**

**Reading Comprehension**

12. **G**
13. **D**
14. **F**
15. **A**
16. **G**
17. **C**
18. **F**
19. **D**
20. **F**
21. **C**
22. **E**
23. **B**
24. **F**
25. **C**
26. **G**
27. **D**
28. **F**
29. **A**
30. **G**
31. **D**
32. **F**
33. **D**
34. **H**
35. **B**
36. **G**
37. **A**
38. **H**
39. **D**
40. **G**
41. **A**
42. **G**
43. **D**
44. **F**
45. **A**
46. **F**
47. **C**
48. **F**
49. **C**
50. **H**
51. **B**
52. **E**
53. **B**
54. **E**
55. **B**
56. **H**
57. **B**

### PART 2 (MATHEMATICS)

**Math**

58. **8**
59. **1824**
60. **0.5**
61. **40**
62. **-4**
63. **F**
64. **C**
65. **G**
66. **B**
67. **H**
68. **C**
69. **G**
70. **D**
71. **H**
72. **A**
73. **H**
74. **C**
75. **G**
76. **B**
77. **F**
78. **B**
79. **F**
80. **C**
81. **F**
82. **D**
83. **F**
84. **A**
85. **G**
86. **C**
87. **G**
88. **C**
89. **H**
90. **A**
91. **G**
92. **B**
93. **E**
94. **C**
95. **F**
96. **D**
97. **H**
98. **C**
99. **E**
100. **C**
101. **H**
102. **C**
103. **F**
104. **C**
105. **F**
106. **B**
107. **G**
108. **B**
109. **H**
110. **B**
111. **H**
112. **D**
113. **E**
114. **B**

You can find detailed video explanations to each problem in the book by visiting:
**ArgoPrep.com/SHSAT**

# Practice Test 4 (Answers and Explanations)

**1.** **C** Answer C is correct because it inserts the three necessary commas into the sentence. The phrase "...which is sometimes recognized as the 'Great American Novel,'" needs a comma on each side of it because it is a nonessential clause. Nonessential clauses in the middle of a sentence are separated from the main text with two commas to provide clarity to the reader. The names of the two lovers at the end of the sentence are also technically nonessential information, which should also be preceded by a comma. Answer A is incorrect because it fails to insert commas to indicate the beginning of the first nonessential clause (after "book") as well as the second one (after "lovers"). Answer B correctly separates the first nonessential clause but not the second, making it incorrect overall. Answer D is incorrect because it neglects to indicate the end of the first nonessential clause by not putting a comma after "Novel."

**2.** **H** Answer H is correct because it separates all the items in the list using commas and separates the list from the nonessential clause "...all of whom are still major characters..." Answer E is incorrect because, while it puts commas between list items correctly, it fails to separate the end of the list from the nonessential modifier that follows. Answer F is incorrect because, while it puts commas between list items correctly (including the optional Oxford comma), it also fails to separate the list from the nonessential clause at the end. Answer G is incorrect because it does not put commas between Hulk, Thor, and Spider-Man.

**3.** **B** Semicolons can be used to separate list items that already contain commas. Since the description of each uncle contains a comma, the writer of this sentence can use semicolons to compartmentalize the sections of the sentence about each one of them. Answer B punctuates the sentence correctly, putting a comma after each name and a semicolon at the end of each section. Answer choice A is incorrect because it lacks the commas that separate each uncle's name from his describing clause. Answer choice C is incorrect because it incorrectly reverses the placement of commas and semicolons. Answer choice D is incorrect because it introduces the list which a semicolon, which is the job of a colon (as can be seen in the original sentence).

**4.** **G** Answer G is correct because Sentence 2 contains the passive voice construction "women's conditions and rights were discussed." Passive voice occurs when the subject of a sentence is having the action of the verb performed on it rather than being the actor in the sentence. Passive voice is generally discouraged in formal writing. Sentence 2 should be revised to create an active voice construction (for example: "Throughout the two-day convention, as many as 300 attendees discussed women's conditions and rights."). Answer E is incorrect because Sentence 2 is clearly about the Seneca Falls Convention, as are all the other sentences. Answer F is incorrect because the entire paragraph is consistently written in the historical past tense. Answer H is incorrect the "to be" verb "were" in the sentence is acting primarily as a helping verb as part of the passive voice construction. By correcting the passive voice, the author also eliminates the need for the "were" in the sentence, making Answer G a much better answer.

**5.** **A** "After school" should be separated from the rest of the sentence with a comma because it is an introductory phrase that only serves to provide context, making Answer A correct. Answers B, C, and D are all incorrect because they place commas at inappropriate places in the sentence. A comma after road (Answer B) would incorrectly break up the phrase "down the road to the park," reducing the clarity of the sentence. A comma after park (Answer C) would incorrectly identify the sentence as a compound sentence, which it is not since there is no second subject. A comma after Stephanie (Answer D) would incorrectly suggest a list at the end of the sentence, when there are only two names mentioned.

**6.** **F** The first verb of Sentence 2, "ruled," establishes that the events of this sentence occur in the past. Therefore, to prevent reader confusion, the present tense verb "is" later in the sentence should be made consistent by changing it to "was," making Answer F correct. Answer E is incorrect because a date of 500 AD is given in the sentence, demonstrating that Arthur could not possibly be ruling today and cementing the need for the past tense verb "ruled." Answer G is also incorrect because, again, the main verb of the sentence and date provided both establish that this sentence deals with events of the past. Answer H is incorrect because "honorable" and "honored" are two completely different adjectives with separate meanings. Substituting "honored" would change the fundamental meaning of the sentence, and is therefore incorrect.

**7.** **D** Passive voice occurs when the subject of the sentence is having action performed on or to it rather than being the actor of the main verb. Answer D is correct because Sentence 3 contains the passive voice construction "...mythical stories were already being told..." Sentence 3 should be revised to eliminate this use of passive voice. One example of a correct revision would be, "By the twelfth century, storytellers were already telling tales about Arthur assembling the bravest knights of all time to serve at his heroic Round Table." Answer A is incorrect because the given subject of the sentence ("stories") agrees in number with the verb. Answer B is incorrect because the sentence contains no spelling errors. Answer C is incorrect because the only necessary comma in the sentence (the one that separates the introduction "By the fifteenth century,") is placed correctly.

**8.** **E** Paragraph 2 contains a summary of the major features that most Arthur stories contain. This idea is summarized in the final (conclusion) sentence of the paragraph as well. Answer E is correct because it previews the main content of the paragraph and has a strong connection to Sentence 8, the conclusion. Answer F is incorrect because it is overly general and fails to address the idea of variation between different tellings of the story. Answer G is a relevant detail, but not a topic sentence because Sentences 4-8 do not all focus on Excalibur. Finally, Answer H is also incorrect because it is overly general and could be used at the beginning of a discussion of any story.

**9.** **B** Answer B is correct because it separates the introduction using a comma (by placing one after "story') and correctly separates out the nonessential modifier "the secret son of King Uther Pendragon"). Answer A is incorrect because, while it separates the introduction using a comma, it does not separate out the nonessential information. Answer C is also incorrect because it fails to separate the introduction phrase, even though it correctly identifies the nonessential modifier in the middle of the sentence. Answer D is incorrect because even though it identifies all the necessary commas, it also adds a completely unnecessary one at the end (after "ruler").

**10. G** Sentence 7 tells what happens at the end of a story, having skipped a large number of specific details and events. "Ultimately" is the best transition to indicate that the author is skipping to the end or conclusion of an idea, making Answer choice G correct. Answer E is incorrect because "Therefore" implies there is a clear, causal relationship between two events or ideas, which is not the case in this paragraph. Answer F is incorrect because "However" implies that the content of Sentence 7 is directly contrary to Sentence 6, which it is not. Answer H is incorrect because "Subsequently" is not the best answer choice. "Subsequently" implies that the events of Sentence 7 happened later after the events of Sentence 6, but "Ultimately" is still the best answer because it clearly communicates to the reader that many specific steps or events are being skipped over in order to discuss the end of the story.

**11. C** Sentences 9, 10, 12, and 13 all connect clearly to Arthur's relevance to English culture and government. Sentence 11, however, is not thematically connected to the rest of the paragraph because it talks generally about businesspeople "all over the world," a phrase that should be a hint to the reader. Answer C is correct because removing Sentence 11 would not detract from the overall meaning of the paragraph and would create a clearer link between the other sentences. Answers A, B, and D are all incorrect because each of those sentence is tied directly to ways in which the Arthur myth is still culturally relevant in England today.

**12. G** Answer G is the best choice because the entire poem focuses on an author's mixed feelings about the publication of her book. The title of the poem should be a major indicator to the reader. Additionally, the poem is filled with language that is directly indicative of the publishing world ("errors," "press," "in print," etc.). Answer E is incorrect because the speaker is clearly referring to an entity separate from herself. She clearly states that the offspring was "snatcht" and taken away from her "abroad," which means she cannot be speaking of herself. Answer F is incorrect because there are no literal children in the poem. The image of a child is used as an extended metaphor for the book, which the speaker sees as the "offspring of [her] feeble brain." Answer H is incorrect because it mistakenly interprets "offspring of my feeble brain" to be describing mental illness. The book is "offspring" of the speaker's "brain" because she created it, which is metaphorically compared to giving birth throughout the poem.

**13. D** Answer D is the best choice because it is the only answer that captures both the fact that she appreciates her friends' support but also thinks there enthusiasm is slightly misguided. When the speaker describes her friends as "less wise than true," she acknowledges that they are very loyal to her and think highly of her work, even when she does not. The fact that her friends enthusiastically spread her work abroad also demonstrates their confidence in her, but she balances her gratitude for their friendship with her frustration that they made sure a book she considered unfinished was published. Answer A is incorrect because there is nothing in the text to say her friends were unsupportive; if anything, they took extreme pains to make sure people found out about her work. Answer B is incorrect because, while she is flattered by their enthusiasm, the speaker expresses some frustration that they shared her book so freely before she was fully satisfied with it. Answer C is incorrect as well because she never accuses her friends of childlike behavior, but rather accuses her book of being childlike.

**14. F** Answer F is the correct choice because it is the only frustration that was not voiced in the poem. In fact, the speaker specifically says she was paid in Lines 23 and 24, and that payment was her only real motivation for publication. Answer E is incorrect because Line 6 clearly states that errors were left in the book. Answer G is incorrect because Line 5 states that the printers "made [the book] in rags" and Line 10 goes on to say that the book's "visage" (face) is unattractive. Answer H is incorrect as well because the poem specifically says the book was distributed to would-be publishers in an enthusiastic but haphazard manner (Lines 4-6).

**15. A** Answer A is the best choice because Lines 8-24 of the poem primarily feature an extended metaphor in which the speaker compares her ambivalence toward to her poem to that someone would feel toward an ugly, annoying child. She calls the book a "brat" (Line 8) and describes its ugly face (Line 11), uneven limbs (Line 15-16), and unattractive clothes (Lines 17-19). Answer B is incorrect because the dirty face is only part of the large metaphor for a baby, making Answer A the best choice. Similarly, Answer C is incorrect because the cheap clothes are also part of the larger metaphor of an unattractive child, making Answer A a better choice. Answer D is incorrect because there is no mention of dreams anywhere in the passage.

**16. G** Answer G is the best choice because from the very first line ("...offspring of my feeble brain..."), the speaker identifies the book as her child. Since the child was created in her brain and not through the typical reproductive process, it has no biological father. As a female writer, she is the sole parent of her work. Answer E is incorrect because there is no mention of any specific men or father figures anywhere in the poem. Answer F is incorrect because, while she is not especially proud of her work, she does not intend to disown it. Answer H is incorrect because the speaker is not describing a literal baby at any point in the poem but rather using a baby as an extended metaphor for her relationship with her book.

**17. C** Answer C is the best choice because the lines being referenced are describing the shabby clothes the speaker imagines her book/baby wearing. The words terms "better dress" (Line 17) and home-spun cloth" (Line 18) should have been valuable context clues to communicate that the lines are describing clothing. Answer A is incorrect because the poem never describes how anything is set up or organized. Answer B is incorrect because there is no math or statistical data being presented in the poem. Answer D is incorrect because it is not describing a visual display (like a computer monitor) but rather the combination of clothes the book/baby is wearing, making Answer C a better choice.

**18. F** Answer F is the best choice because the closing lines of the poem (Lines 23-24) specifically state, "And for thy mother, she alas is poor, / Which caused her thus to send the out the door," meaning that she published her work because she desperately needed money. Answer E is incorrect because the speaker is clearly well-aware of her book's flaws throughout the passage. Answer G is incorrect because, while it's true her friends promoted her book enthusiastically, Lines 23-24 still make Answer F a much better, more specific answer. Answer H is incorrect because the speaker does not hold any illusions about her book being a work of art but instead views it as a decent paycheck.

**19. D** Answer D is the choice because in Line 20, the speaker states, "In critic's hands, beware thou dost not come," specifically expressing concern of the potential critical reaction to her book. Answer A is incorrect because the speaker does not mention her parents at any point in the poem. Answer B is incorrect because the author never mentions a literal child anywhere in the poem, only her book which she metaphorically sees as a child. Answer C is incorrect because the speaker actually goes out of her way to say that she's comfortable with low-class people reading the book when she writes, "In this array, 'mongst vulgars may'st thou roam" (Line 19).

**20. F** Answer F is the best choice because, based on the content of the poem, the reader can infer that Bradstreet held her work to a high standard and was never satisfied with it just because other people told her it was good. The entire story told in Lines 3-8 describes how the poem's speaker is uncomfortable with the condition her book is published in, and the rest of the poem details how distraught and exposed the author feels. The reader can infer that Bradstreet is writing from experience. Answer E is incorrect because there is nothing specific in the poem to suggest financial success; in fact, the only mention of money is that the author "alas is poor" (Line 23), pointing the reader in the exact opposite direction. Answer G is incorrect because, while the speaker compares the book to a child, there is no reference made to literal children anywhere in the poem. In reality, Bradstreet had many children, but there is no way to know one way or the other based on the poem. Answer H is similarly incorrect because we have no specific evidence one way or the other.

---

### Passage 2 ("Sports Champions")

**21. C** Answer C is the best choice because Paragraph 1 introduces the topic of championships and uses a lot of exciting language to try and engage the reader. The sentences "Championships represent the highest level of achievement in sport and are accomplishments that athletes remember for the rest of their lives" and "That's because championships bring out the best in the greatest athletes and create truly memorable moments" are designed to entice the reader and assure them they are about to read about an interesting, memorable subject. Answer A is incorrect because, while the author states that athletes want to win championships, he or she does little to explain the actual athletic mindset. Answer B is incorrect because Paragraph 1 never provides qualities of a champion;

rather, it discusses the importance of championships generally. Answer D is incorrect because the author never makes any explicit effort to "sell" skeptics on the importance of championships. Rather, the author seeks to describe the variety of great achievements that are possible.

**22. E** Answer E is the best choice because it represents the best understanding of Paragraph 2. The paragraph clearly states that the Super Bowl takes place in "late winter," which would place it toward the beginning of the calendar year. Answer F is incorrect because baseball's championship is referred to as "the October Classic" in the paragraph, which suggests it takes place in the fall, toward the end of the year. Finally, Answers G and H are both incorrect because Paragraph 2 clearly states that hockey and basketball both have their championships in June, which falls in the middle of the year.

**23. B** Answer B is the best choice because when the author distinguishes between the "flavors" of championship hockey and basketball, he or she is discussing their different tones, styles, or personalities. The sentence, "Each of the four predominant professional sports in the U.S. (football, baseball, basketball, and hockey) has a top-level championship with its own unique personality" at the beginning of the paragraph should be a major indicator to the reader, as should the fact that each championship is followed by a brief statement about its individual tone or tradition. Answer A is incorrect, although it is a conventional definition for "flavor," but since the passage has nothing to do with food, it cannot possibly be the correct answer. Answer C is incorrect as it fails to connect "flavors" to use of the word "personalities" earlier in the passage and instead assumes the concept must be related to pace of place, which is explored in the next sentence. Answer D is incorrect as well with no textual basis, as there is no reference made to rules anywhere in the passage.

**24. F** Answer F is the best choice because all the other sports in the passage are discussed as great achievements in the present tense, whereas the author takes pains to point out that boxing's "prominence has waned over the last few decades." The author states that boxing champions are still well-paid and widely watched, but the text makes it clear that being a boxing champion used to be a bigger deal than it is today. Answer E is incorrect because the author never calls boxing's reputation (or that of any sport) into question. Answer G is incorrect with no textual basis because the author never mentions violence or moral objections to boxing whatsoever. Answer H is incorrect because the Super Bowl was also described as drawing "the biggest TV viewing audience of the year across the country" in Paragraph 2, which would make it even more widely watched and profitable than boxing.

**25. C** Answer C is the best choice because it reflects the best understanding of Paragraph 3. The paragraph states that horse racing has "three Triple Crown races" each year and that "golf and tennis each have a 'Grand Slam,' which is comprised of four major events." Therefore, the reader knows there are three races, four tennis tournaments, and four golf tournaments. $3 + 4 + 4 = 11$. Answers A, B, and D are all incorrect because they fail to quantify the number of specific events the author is discussing.

**26. G** Answer G is the best choice because it accesses the paragraph's two main ideas: (1) that the passion of Olympic athletes is especially strong and (2) Olympic athletes are not often compensated as richly as the kinds of professional athletes mentioned in Paragraphs 2 and 3. Answer E is incorrect because Paragraphs 1 and 5 stress that all championships are built around the same ideals and feelings. Since Paragraph 4 is in the same essay as those paragraphs, it would not make sense to suddenly begin explaining how some championships are markedly different from others. Answer F is incorrect, although it represents a true statement, because it ignores the repeated point that Olympic athletes don't often get as rich and famous as other sports stars. Finally, Answer H is incorrect because the author never directly states or even suggests that the Olympic schedule has anything to do with the athletes being less famous or financially compensated.

**Passage 3 ("Trademarks")**

**27. D** Answer D is the best choice because all five paragraphs of the passage are squarely focused on either the goals of trademark law or the value of trademarks to businesses and consumers. Answer A is incorrect because there is nothing to suggest this text is written to a personal audience known by author. Additionally, if this text were intended to convince particular people at a certain company to embrace trademarks, it would most likely include specific examples of what that company did or manufactured. Answer B is incorrect because, while the passage does delve into different levels of trademark distinctiveness, it also focuses on the role of trademarks and their importance to businesses and consumers, which Answer B ignores. Answer C is incorrect as well because, while the USPTO is mentioned in the passage, the activities of the organization itself are not the main focus of the passage. Instead, the passage focuses on the value of trademarks, not the trademark office itself.

**28. F** Answer F is correct because it reflects the best overall understanding of the passage. Paragraph 5 describes how trademarks are crucial to connecting with customers, and Paragraph 4 describes how trademarks protect businesses from competitors, using the example of Birdies Oil Change. Answer E is incorrect because it mistakenly assumes that the point of filing a trademark infringement lawsuit is simply to make money through suing, whereas the true goal of trademark law (as reflected in Paragraphs 2, 4, and 5) is to protect one's own project or image, not hurt that of the competition. Answer G is incorrect because Paragraph 2 establishes that when a business feels their marks are being infringed upon, it's their responsibility to identify and contact the offender, not that of the USPTO. Finally, H is incorrect as well because it has no basis in the text. Product quality is never actually discussed one way or the other in the passage, so it would be an unsupported assumption to infer that quality has no value.

**29. A** Answer A is the best choice because Paragraph 2 establishes that trademarks offer businesses the legal right to "market themselves as having a distinct identity." When competitors use copycat tactics, they are infringing on that company's legally registered trademarks. Answer B is incorrect because "stealing" implies that a product or object is being taken away, whereas "infringing" refers more directly to violating a company's right to its established identity. Answer C is incorrect because it mistakes "infringing" (the offense) with a court proceeding (which is the result or consequence of the offense). Answer D is incorrect as well because, while infringement may hurt profits, the two terms are not direct synonyms.

**30. G** Answer G is the best choice because "Get your whippy wozzle on!" has nothing to do with toys or slip-and-slides and is simply a unique statement used to market the product. "Arbitrary" and "fanciful" marks are defined and explained in Paragraph 4 of the text. Answer E is incorrect because a dog's face directly reflects what a dog rescue organization does, and is therefore simply descriptive or generic (as defined in Paragraph 3). Answer F is incorrect because "Wheat O's" essentially describes what the product is (an "O" made of wheat), making it a descriptive mark. Finally, Answer H is incorrect because, as in the previous question, the term "Soda" is simply a generic term used to refer to soft drinks.

**31. D** Answer D is the best choice because, while registered trademarks allow businesses to stop their competition from infringing on their brand identity or marketing style, they don't prevent the competition from attempting to imitate a great product or advertising strategy. It is up to the trademark holder to keep a watchful eye on the market and protect their trademarks once they've been established (as described in Paragraph 2). Answer A is incorrect because Paragraph 3 establishes the USPTO's role as overseers of the trademark process here in the United States. Answer B is incorrect because the passage repeatedly stresses that trademarks are designed to protect companies as well as provide clarity for consumers. Answer C is incorrect as well because Paragraphs 3 and 4 describe the hierarchy of distinctiveness for trademarks and clearly state, "The best and strongest trademarks are what's described as 'arbitrary' or 'fanciful...'"

**32. F** Answer F is the correct answer because, as Paragraph 5 later states, trademarks allow companies and products to "differentiate themselves from the competition." The example of paper towels illustrates that if a brand that was regarded as "the best" used an image of a squirrel, then, in a world without trademark laws, all other paper towel companies could easily use a picture of a squirrel to try to confuse customers as to what product they were buying in order to leach off of the original "squirrel towel's" success. Answer A is incorrect because it prioritizes the visual aspect of trademarks over the business aspect. That is to say, the goal of trademarks is not to ensure visual variety in the grocery store; it is to ensure that no company can copy another's design or campaign outright. Answer G is incorrect because, even without trademarks, the best and most competitive companies would always be working to set their product apart from others. Finally, Answer H is also incorrect because, even in a world with no trademarks, the products could be totally different, it would just be harder for consumers to identify competing products from each other.

**Passage 4 ("Some years ago, in company with...")**

**33. D** Answer D is the best choice because Emerson's sensory experience of nature is a feature of each paragraph of the passage. Lines 53-63 establish Emerson's main thoughts on this topic, stating,

"Our conversation with Nature is not just what it seems... The senses interfere everywhere, and mix their own structure with all they report of." Answer A is incorrect because, while Emerson clearly views man as curious, the answer fails to take nature, which is one of the key features of the passage, into account. Answer B is not the best answer either because, although Emerson certainly believes man is in some ways ignorant towards nature (Lines 59-63), he mostly puts the blame on mankind's sensory experience of nature (Lines 58-59), making Answer D a better choice. Answer C is also incorrect because, while the connection between man and nature is clearly key to the passage, Answer D still represents a more complete, specific explanation of the passage by including the senses, which are also a key feature of the text.

**34. H** Answer H is correct because Emerson's repeated use of "seemed" (Lines 37 & 39) reinforces that what they are seeing is not in fact a starry sky, but rather a natural illusion that looks very much like the night sky. Emerson also describes the sight as a "magnificent effect" in Line 47, suggesting again that it's not a real sky. Answer E cannot be correct because Emerson never states whether or not the star-chamber was the only one of its kind. Answers F and G cannot be correct either because Emerson explicitly states that what "seemed" like stars and a comet appeared bright, but since both effects were illusions, Answer H remains the best choice.

**35. B** Answer B is the best choice because, in Lines 22-24, Emerson describes "four combined engineers, water, limestone, gravitation, and time," clearly establishing that water is one of the four main forces that created the cave. Answer A is incorrect because it is not tied to the text in any way. Answer C cannot be correct because Lines 22-24 establish that there were four engineers of the cave, not just water. Answer D is also incorrect because Emerson does not rank or grade the four engineers, he simply states what they are, so the reader has no way of knowing which (if any) was most important.

**36. G** Answer G is the best choice because Lines 40-45 state that "All the party were touched with astonishment and pleasure... I sat down on the rocky floor to enjoy the serene picture," indicating to the reader that the group was overcome by the beauty of the star-chamber. Answer E is incorrect because exhaustion is never mentioned and, if anything, Lines 40-45 suggest that the party members were energized by the beauty of the star-chamber. Answer F cannot be correct because Emerson never establishes how many people have been in the star-chamber or any traditions associated with it. Answer H cannot be correct because the Emerson makes no mention of the party singing in any other circumstances and says they "sung with much feeling," suggesting that they had just begun.

**37. A** Answer A is the best choice because Lines 58-63 focus on how the senses' perception of nature cannot necessarily be trusted. Emerson provides "Once, we fancied the earth a plane and stationary" (Lines 59-60) as an example of how "The senses interfere everywhere" (Line 58). Answer B is incorrect because humans eventually realized that the earth was spherical, meaning that nature can be comprehended, at least on some level, eventually. Answer C is incorrect because people eventually understood the world was spherical, so the example of a flat earth is not proof that nature will never be understood. Answer D has no textual basis because, throughout the text, Emerson makes it clear that he believes people should deeply consider the nature of the world, so Answer D is completely contrary to his point.

**38. H** Answer H is correct because, in Lines 2-3, Emerson clearly identifies that he "spent a long summer day in exploring the Mammoth Cave in Kentucky." Answers E, F, and G are all incorrect with no textual basis because Maine and the Dakotas are never mentioned in the passage.

**Passage 5 ("Excerpt from "After Twenty Years")**

**39. D** Answer D is the best choice because Paragraphs 1 and 2 describe the policeman as being competent and consistent. The opening sentence says he walks up the avenue "impressively," and the second paragraph describes how he checks the doors dutifully. Paragraph 2 also describes him as "a fine picture of a guardian of the peace." All these details point to him being a reliable police officer. Answer A is incorrect because the policeman never loses his temper or talks about getting angry anywhere in the passage. Answer B is incorrect because, while we know he is good as his job, there is nothing specific in the text about the policeman being smart, making Answer D a better choice. Answer C is incorrect as well because, while the policeman expresses some skepticism at what the man is doing in the doorway, he is not especially suspicious of or befuddled by the situation. Overall, the passage depicts him as a good policeman, making Answer D the best choice.

**40. G** Answer G is the best choice because Paragraph 2 describes that he is checking the doors in his role as a "guardian of the peace" and that he is checking with his "watchful eye." Both of these point to him checking the doors out of security. Answer E is incorrect because he isn't especially looking for criminals as far as we know; rather, he is simply performing his standard duties as a night policeman. Answer F is incorrect because the paragraph clearly states that a few well-lit businesses are open but the majority of places have "long since been closed." Answer H is incorrect because the policeman has not yet heard the story about "Jimmy" at the point in the story when he is checking doors.

**41. A** Answer A is the best choice because Paragraph 2 describes the "thoroughfare" as something the policeman walks down, "turning now and then to cast his watchful eye." Answers B and D are both incorrect because the stores and restaurants being described are businesses on the thoroughfare, not the thoroughfare itself. Answer C is incorrect because the text specifically says that the policeman "cast[s] his watchful eye down the thoroughfare," which communicates that the thoroughfare is a straight line, not a block with corners. The words "avenue" (Paragraph 1) and "streets" (Paragraph 1) should have been major hints.

**42. G** Answer G is correct because it communicates the best understanding of Paragraphs 5-7. Paragraph 7 clearly states that the friends made their agreement "twenty years ago to-night," while Paragraph 5 states that the restaurant was torn down "five years ago." 20 – 5 = 15, so that means that they made their agreement fifteen years before the restaurant was torn down.

Answers E, F, and H are all incorrect because they misunderstand the way the numbers are being communicated and fail to recognize the question as a simple subtraction problem based on the numbers given in the text.

**43. D** Answer D is the best choice because the man in the doorway uses the word "straight" to reassure the policeman that everything is alright, suggesting that "straight" means "legitimate" or "above board." The man in the doorway contrasts things being "straight" with things "seeming funny," which should be another hint to the reader. Answer A is incorrect because he does not mean straight as in a straight line; rather he is using "straight" to describe a situation. Answer B is incorrect because he does not mean that he is "talking straight" with him in that he is telling the truth, but rather he's trying to assure the police officer that his presence in that dark doorway is legitimate, making Answer D a better choice. Answer C is incorrect because the man in the doorway is not talking about "getting straight" as in "getting even" with someone, but again using the term to defend the legitimacy of his presence in the dark street.

**44. F** Answer F is the best choice because it recognizes the fact that the author attracts attention to the way the light illuminates the man's face in Paragraph 6. Immediately after the man strikes a match, the text describes his "square-jawed face" and distinctive scar, which were previously obscured by the darkness of the night and doorway. Answer E is incorrect because, while it is true that smoking is unhealthy, there is no direct connection between smoking and evilness. Answer G is incorrect because the detail of the diamond pin is mentioned after the more in-depth description of the man's face, suggesting that the face is a much more important detail and reinforcing Answer F as the best choice. Answer G is incorrect as well because neither the policeman nor the author makes any dangerous mention of fire or suggestion of arson at any point.

**45. A** Answer A is the best choice because it represents the most complete understanding of Paragraph 7. The man in the doorway states that he "was to start for the West to make [his] fortune, whereas "you couldn't have dragged Jimmy out of New York." Answer B is incorrect because it reverses the order described in the text. Answer C is incorrect because, while we know the man in the doorway has a diamond pin, the text does not yet provide an indication of how successful Jimmy has been. Answer D is incorrect because there are no details to suggest the man in the doorway is poor and, if anything, his diamond pin suggests he has access to money.

**46. F** Answer F is the best choice because the description in Paragraph 3 clearly states the man has an "unlighted cigar in his mouth." This is strange because Paragraph 2 clearly states that there are cigar stores open in the area. If the man's objective was to smoke a cigar, then he easily could've done so at one of the open stores, where he would've had light and shelter. His unlit cigar in an empty doorway suggests he is waiting for something more than a late-night smoke. Answer E is incorrect because, while chilly winds would discourage many people from standing outside, the fact that someone is caught outside in bad weather isn't inherently suspicious or odd. Answer G is incorrect because there is nothing in the description of the man in the doorway that suggests he is trying to rob the hardware store. If that were his goal, he probably would've run from the police officer rather than greeting him in a friendly manner. Answer H is incorrect because the fact that the man speaks to the police officer suggests he has little to hide and therefore does not contribute to the suspiciousness of the situation. Answer F remains the best choice because there would be much more comfortable places to smoke a cigar than where the man was in that moment.

**47. C** Answer C is the best choice because there are many features within the passage that create a sense of mystery. The image of the policeman patrolling in the dark suggests mystery, as does the man standing in the doorway with an unlit cigar. The man's strange story, facial scar, and large diamond jewelry all suggest that something larger and unseen is at work and serve to make the reader (and policeman) wonder what is going on. Answer A is incorrect because, while the street is physically dark, there is nothing especially threatening or evil-feeling anywhere in the passage. Answer B is incorrect because there is nothing crazy or disordered in the story. While the man's story about meeting his friends after 20 years is out-of-the-ordinary, there's nothing chaotic about it. Finally, Answer D is incorrect as well. While the passage has mysterious qualities, there is nothing outwardly scary, threatening, or graphically violent about it, making Answer C a better choice.

### Passage 6 ("Infrastructure in the United States")

**48. F** Answer F is the best choice because when the passage says "American infrastructure is consistently graded among the worst..." it means that it has been scored or assessed, as a teacher does to students. This comparison is reinforced in Paragraph 4, when the author directly compares American public transportation to the rest of the world. Answer E is incorrect because there are no rules being enforced, only assessments being made. Answer G and H are both incorrect for the same reason: neither one of them is as specific and context-specific in its meaning as "assessed." It isn't just that people think of or talk about America when it comes to poor infrastructure, it's important to distinguish that people are making direct comparisons and actually grading or assessing the infrastructure of different countries head-to-head. Therefore, Answer F is the best choice.

**49. C** Answer C is the best choice because the author uses quotation marks to reinforce that "infrastructure" is a complex, potentially scary word that not many people know the actual definition to. By putting the term in quotation marks, the author communicates that he or she is talking about the word itself rather than the concept. Answer A is incorrect because the term has already appeared several times in the passage before it is used in quotation marks. Answer B is incorrect because the overall tone of the passage is serious and there are no jokes being made in Paragraph 1. Answer D is incorrect because the author does not name or reference any particular text or report that he or she is quoting in Paragraph 1; therefore, it makes little sense to assume that the single word is quoted material.

**50. H** Answer H is the best choice because it displays the most complete understanding of Paragraph 2. The final phrase of the paragraph ("...which has resulted in many airports with a wide range of modern and outdated facilities.") encapsulates this idea clearly, explaining that the desire to keep airports open without service interruptions has led to some sections appearing quite updated while others are outdated. Answer E is incorrect because the over-crowding issue is not directly connected to piecemeal additions and updates but rather to the increased volume of air traffic, which is also mentioned in Paragraph 2. Answer F is incorrect because, while public transportation is a major topic in the passage, the issue is not directly connected to over-crowding in airports. Answer G is incorrect because the passage clearly states that more people than ever travel, so Answer G is a factually inaccurate statement.

**51. B** Answer B is the best choice because, by citing a professional organization of highly qualified experts, the author reinforces that the points he or she makes about infrastructure are not just his or her own opinions, but instead conclusions reached by informed professionals. Using data is one of the best and strongest ways to support a viewpoint and make it seem more like fact than opinion. Answer A is incorrect because the author isn't just trying to identify people who know about bridges but rather trying to strengthen his or her own point by relying on the supporting knowledge and opinions of the organization. Answer C is incorrect because, while the author would agree that people should generally have more knowledge about infrastructure, his or her purpose is not to create publicity for this professional organization. Rather, the author uses their grades and opinions as support. Answer D is incorrect because, like Answer A, it fails to recognize the manner in which the author uses the work of others to support his or her writing.

**52. E** Answer E is the correct choice because "weighed" and "graded" are both used to mean "assessed" in the passage. "Graded" is used in Paragraph 1 to explain how experts assess American infrastructure, while "weighed" is used in Paragraph 3 to explain that people must assess whether they want to risk long-term catastrophe over short-term inconvenience. Answers F, G, and H are all incorrect because none of those terms reflect the spirit of assessment, ranking, and critical decision making that are encapsulated in "grade" and "weigh" in the passage.

**53. B** Answer B is the best choice because the information about commuting in Paragraph 4 echoes the concept that the American population and workforce has outgrown its infrastructure that was introduced in Paragraph 2. Both systems show that there are more people than ever who need these services, but the scope of the services has not adequately grown along with the demand. Answer A is incorrect because the age of the bridges has nothing to do with the world being "small;" it just communicates that the bridges are quite old. Answer C is incorrect because the number of people impacted by bridge repairs has nothing to do with the adequacy of the bridge itself. While more people than ever are driving over bridges, the increase in population isn't the issue. Answer D is incorrect because the variety of facilities at airports is the result of piecemeal updates, according to the passage, and has nothing to do with the "smaller world" of the past.

**54. E** Answer E is the best choice because the passage portrays the state of bridges in America as woeful, but the table actually shows that the grade for bridges has gone up over the last 30 years. This revelation is somewhat contrary to the tone of the preceding passage. Answer F is incorrect because Paragraph 2 clearly explained why that aviation grade has gone down (inadequate or piecemeal updates), meaning that the aviation grade actually supports what is written in the passage. Answers G and H are both incorrect for the same reason: schools are never explicitly mentioned in the passage, so the reader has no way of knowing whether those numbers are aligned with or contrary to expectations.

**55. B** Answer B is the best choice because a look at the table reveals that aviation has fallen from a B- to a D+ over the last 30 years. Answer A is incorrect because bridge grades have actually increased over time, from a C- in '88 to a C+ in '17. Answer C is incorrect because, while transit grades have gone down over time, they have not fallen as precipitously as aviation scores. Answer D is incorrect because school grades have improved slightly in recent years.

**56. H** Answer H is the best choice because schools were at one point given an F, which is the worst conceivable grade and also the only F on the report card, but have improved to a D+ in recent years. While these grades are still low, it does represent major improvement from the worst conceivable situation. Answer E is incorrect because bridges have improved just two thirds of a letter grade in 20 years, while schools have improved more than a full letter. Answer G is incorrect because transit scores have actually gone down over time.

**57. B** Answer B is the best choice because the cumulative GPAs do not reflect the averages of the grades above them (this can clearly be seen in 2005, where the GPA is a D in spite of two D+s and a C appearing in the table). Also, the presence of school in the table when it did not appear in the passage should signal to the reader that there are many different categories of infrastructure beyond the ones mentioned in the passage. Based on that information, the reader should be able to infer that there were other grades on the report card in addition to the four categories in the selection. The term "Selection" in the title of the table should also be a major indicator that it is just part of a larger whole. Answer A is incorrect because there is nothing in the passage or report card to suggest that the Society of Civil Engineers is "fake." Answer C is incorrect because we have no way of knowing the "harshness" of these grades (or those of any teacher) without actually seeing the evidence ourselves. Therefore, the reader can't possibly know the "harshness" of the grades for certain. Answer D completely incorrect because a quick look at the individual grades and GPAs reveals that there must be more factors taken into account than just the four being presented in the selection (again, 2005 is a prime example of this).

ARGOPREP
ARGOPREP.COM/SHSAT

**You can find detailed video explanations to each problem in the book by visiting: ArgoPrep.com**

**58. 8** You are given a composite function question where you first have to plug in the value of 8 to the function $f(x)$.

$f(8) = 8^2 + \sqrt[3]{8}$
$f(8) = 64 + 2$
$f(8) = 66$

$g(66) = \sqrt{66 - 2}$
$g(66) = \sqrt{64}$
$g(66) = \boxed{8}$

**59. 1,824**

You are given that the perimeter is equal to 172. The formula for finding the permitter of a rectangle is $2(l) \times 2(w) = P$. We are given both the length and width and plugging that into the formula gives us :

$2(3x - 1) + 2(3x + 9) = 172$.

Now simplify and solve for $x$.

$6x - 2 + 6x + 18 = 172$
$12x + 16 = 172$
$12x = 156$
$x = 13$

Plug the value of $x$ back into the expression for length and width to find the respective measurements.

Length: $3(13) - 1 = 38$
Width: $3(13) + 9 = 48$

The question asks you to find the area. Formula for the area of a rectangle is length $x$ width. The length is 38 and width is 48. $38 \times 48 = 1{,}824$.

**60. 0.5** This is a probability question. No matter how many times you flip a coin, you will always have a $\frac{1}{2}$ or 0.5 chance of getting Heads or Tails. Therefore, the answer is 0.5.

**61. 40** If we draw a diagram for this question, it is easy to see that a right triangle is formed and the pythagorean theorem must be used to find the length of how high up the building wall can be reached by the crane.

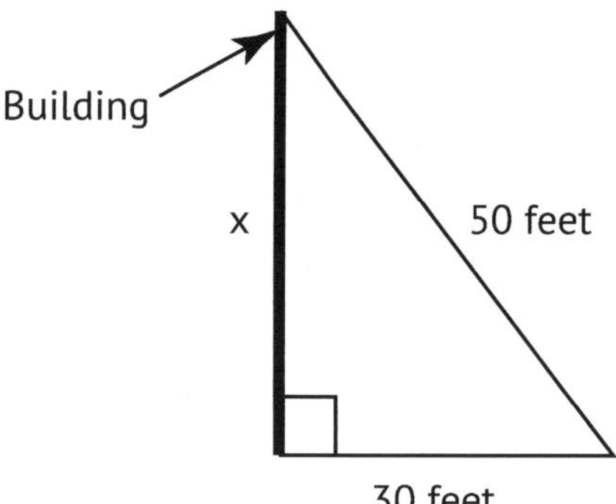


$x^2 + 30^2 = 50^2$
$x = 40$

You should know that 3, 4, 5 or any multiples of 3, 4, 5 in the same order is a Pythagorean triplet. Knowing this will save you time on the exam as calculations are not necessary.

**62. −4** Cross multiply $(x + 3)$ and 12 to get $12x + 36$.

You now have the following equation.
$12x + 36 = x - 8$
Solve for $x$
$x = -4$

**63.** **F** $\sqrt{25} + \sqrt{64} = 5 + 8 = 13$

**64.** **C** Simplifying this equation gives

$2r = 100$
$r = 50$

The answer is F.

**65.** **G** A square with a perimeter of 16 has a side length of a fourth of the perimeter. So the side length is 4. To find the area of that square, we must square the side length, giving us 16 again.

The answer is G.

**66.** **B** A number whose square is 81 is 9. 10% of 9 is 0.9 or answer B.

**67.** **H** The range is just the difference between the largest and smallest number. This is just 12 – 1 or 11. The answer is H.

**68.** **C** If P is the perimeter, and A is the area, we must find A in terms of P. We must divide P by 4 to get the side length of the square. Then we must square that value. This gives us $\frac{P^2}{16}$ or answer C.

**69.** **G** It takes Anayet 30 minutes to travel from his workplace to home. So it takes him 60 minutes to travel from his home to his workplace. In total, he spends 90 minutes traveling, and since the distance between his home to his workplace is 45 miles, the total distance for the round trip is 90 miles.

His average speed is 1 mi/ min. The answer is G.

**70.** **D** Dividing by $a$ gives us answer choice D.

$$\frac{(a^2 + a)}{a} = a + 1$$

**71.** **H** Sarah knows that the coin is a trick coin with only heads on both sides. So her expected probability of the coin landing on heads is 1. John's expected probability is 0.5. 1 is two times bigger than 0.5.

The answer is H.

**72.** **A** 0 is the number that when added to any number, doesn't change that number's value. Squaring 0 gives 0 still.

The answer is A.

**73.** **H** Be careful. The question asks for how many nonzero numbers are between 3 and 5. There are an infinite number of numbers between those two integers.

The answer is H.

**74. C** We know that the diameter of the circle must be 4. So, the side length of the square is also 4. We can use the Pythagorean Theorem to find the length of the diagonal of the square. This gives us $4\sqrt{2}$ or answer C.

**75. G** There are 6 integers between 0 and 5 inclusive and 4 integers between 1 and 6 inclusive. The absolute value of the difference between 6 and 4 is 2. The answer is G.

**76. B** If every three steps he takes, he rotates 30°, then if he took 18 steps, he rotated 30° 6 times. 6 times 30° is 180 degrees, which is a half of a full revolution. The answer is B.

**77. F** We must find 20% of 20 first. That is 4. Then we must take 20% of 4, which is 0.8. The answer is F.

**78. B** The sequence, 3, 5, 7 adds up to 15. The difference between 7 and 3 is 4. The answer is B.

**79. F** In 10 days, the goo decreased by 2 half lives. So each half life is 5 days. The answer is F.

**80. C** Here, we must realize that the numerator is a difference of perfect squares. That allows us to write,

$$\frac{(9^2 - 8^2)(9^2 + 8^2)}{9^2 + 8^2} = 9^2 - 8^2 = 81 - 64 = 17$$

The answer is C.

**81. F** Jackie puts a penny away every 2 minutes. Right after the first 2 minutes, 50% of the jug is filled. She puts 1 penny in the jar at that moment. Then she starts to fill 50% of the empty space left. Well, there is 50% of empty space left, so she starts to reach the filling of 75% of the jug. But before she fills 75% of the jug, the jug already has less than 30% of empty space left. So, she is just left with 1 penny at that instant.

The answer is F.

**82. D** We see that for every 4 triangles, we need 2 circles to balance it. In other words, we need 2 triangles for every circle. We also need 1 square for every 2 triangles. Therefore, there is a one to one ratio between the number of circles and squares. So we need 70 circles to balance 70 squares. The answer is D.

**83. F** $(\frac{2}{9})$ is the same as $.\overline{2}$. Solving for the missing number gives us. $\overline{3} = \frac{1}{3}$.

The answer is F.

**84. A** Factoring 232, gives us $2^3 \bullet 29$.

The answer is A.

**85. G** We can take note of the sequence that each symbol takes. The 6th symbol is also the 12th symbol and the 18th symbol and so on. The 438th symbol will be divisible by 6 as well. This means that the 6th symbol is also the 432nd symbol and therefore the 438th symbol as well.

The answer is G.

**86. C** Cross multiplying gives,

$32x = pt$ and solving for $t$ gives,

$t = \frac{32x}{p}$

The answer is C.

**87. G** $(\frac{52}{3})$ equates to $17.\overline{3}$ and the least integer greater than that is 18.

The answer is G.

**88. C** $5^5 + 5^5 + 5^5 + 5^5 + 5^5 = 5(5^5) = 5^{a+1}$
so then:
$a + 1 = 6$ and $a = 5$.

The answer is C.

**89. H** We know that, $(x^2 + y^2) = x^2 + 2xy + y^2$ and if this is to equal $x^2 + y^2$, then $2xy$ must be equal to 0. In other words, $xy = 0$.

The answer is H.

**90. A** Two circles can intersect at 2 points at maximum.

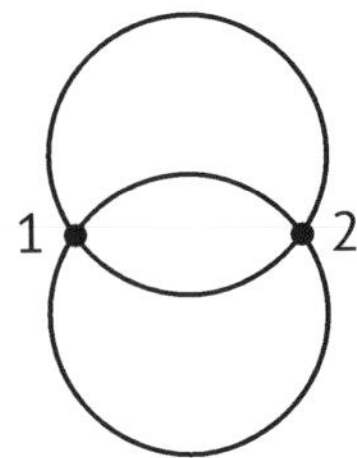


**91. G** The cumulative product of the set {1, 2, 3, 0} is the sequence, 1, 2, 6, 0. The mean of this sequence is the sum of the terms divided by the number of terms in the sequence. This equates to $(\frac{9}{4})$ or 2.25. The answer is G.

**92. B** The only nonpositive, nonnegative integer is 0. So the answer is 1.

The answer is B.

**93. E** A chord must touch the circle at two points. The only segment that does this is the diameter. The answer is E.

**94. C** $y(x) = 0$ at only 2 points, B and E, which are at the roots of the function.

The answer is C.

**95. F** Using the fact that there is 30° between every two consecutive ticks on the clock, we can see that at 2:00, 60 ° is formed between the hands.

The answer is F.

**96. D** The answer to this question depends on the number of marbles in the bag.

The answer is D.

**97. H** The expression can be rewritten as, $(36)(36) - 36 = 36(36 - 1) = 36(35)$ and since $a = 35$, then we have,

$(a + 1)(a) = a^2 + a$.

The answer is H.

**98. C** Equating the two perimeters for the octagon and circle respectively gives, $8a = 2\pi r$ and solving for $r$ gives,

$r = \frac{4a}{\pi}$

The answer is C.

**99. E** The greatest integer less than 1.5 is 1 and the least integer greater than 1 is 2. The answer is E.

**100. C** We know that, $\tau = 2\pi$ and the area of the semicircle is, $\frac{\pi r^2}{2}$.

Solving for $\pi$ and plugging in the area gives, $\frac{\tau r^2}{4}$.

The answer is C.

**101. H** If $F = -kx$, then either $k$ or $x$ must be negative since $F$ is greater than 0. We do not know which is negative, so we cannot determine a definite answer. The answer is H.

**102. C** We must square the side length to get the area.

$(7^a)^2 = 7^{2a}$

The answer is C.

**103. F** Set the two radii equal to each other and solve for $x$.

Plug the value of $x$ back into one of the expressions for the radius to solve for $r$. We have the expression $2x$. Plugging in the value of x gives us 12 • 2 = 24. The radius of the circle is 24.

The dotted section represents a fourth of the whole circumference which is $\frac{2\pi(24)}{4} = 12\pi$.

The answer is $12\pi$ or answer choice F.

**104. C** The value of $x$ must be a positive fraction, so the smallest value in the set would be the one that takes $x$ to the highest power. The answer is C.

**105. F** There are 360° that the hands must move to complete a full revolution and to be at the same time of 5:35. If every 15°, 5 minutes passes, then (24 • 5) minutes will have passed by the time it is 5:35 again. This is 2 hours.

The answer is F.

**106. B** This equation simplifies to,

$x^2 - 4 = ax^2 + bx - c$ and,

$a = 1$

$b = 0$

$c = -4$

so the sum of $a$, $b$ and $c$ is $-3$. The answer is B.

**107. G** This question requires to count the steps. It is only after 17 steps does Natalie reach the 7 step distance from point A.

The answer is G.

**108. B** We must pick a value of $n$ that makes the expression 0, since 0 is neither positive nor negative. This occurs when $n$ is the negative of $m$. The answer is B.

$C(m + -m) = 0$

**109. H** The third side cannot be uniquely determined since we do not know if these two sides are legs of the hypotenuse or if one of the sides is a hypotenuse. The answer is H.

**110. B** $2 + (\frac{1}{3}) = (\frac{7}{3})$ and multiplying the numerator and denominator of $(\frac{7}{3})$ by 2 gives $(\frac{14}{6})$. Equating this with $(\frac{14}{b})$ gives that $b = 6$. The answer is B.

**111. H** If $h$ doubles, then $V$ gets multiplied by a factor of 2. If $r$ triples, then $V$ gets multiplied by a factor of 9 since we are squaring $r$. We multiply 2 and 9 to get 18. The answer is H.

**112. D** The answer cannot be uniquely determined since we do not know if $x$ is negative or positive.

**113. E** Formula for percent decrease is:

$$\frac{\text{Original Number} - \text{New Number}}{\text{Original Number}} \times 100$$
$$= \text{Percent Decrease}$$

$$\frac{280{,}000 - 240{,}000}{280{,}000} \times 100 = 14.3\%$$

**114. B** To find the median, rearrange the numbers from lowest to greatest.

230000, 240000, 240000, 260000, 280000

The median value is 240,000 and by increasing it by 10% gives us 240,000 x 1.1 = 264,000. Therefore, the correct answer choice is B.

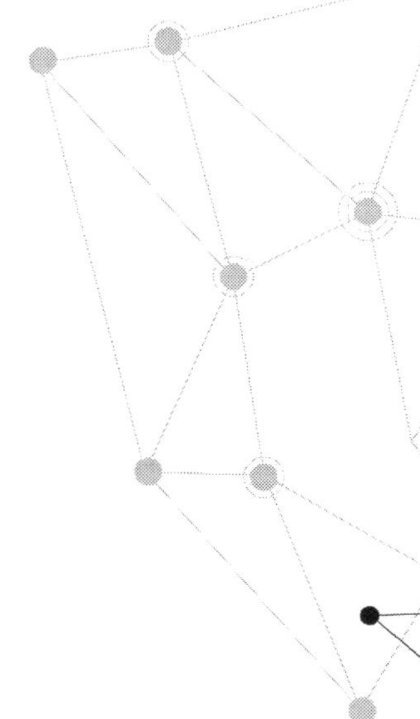

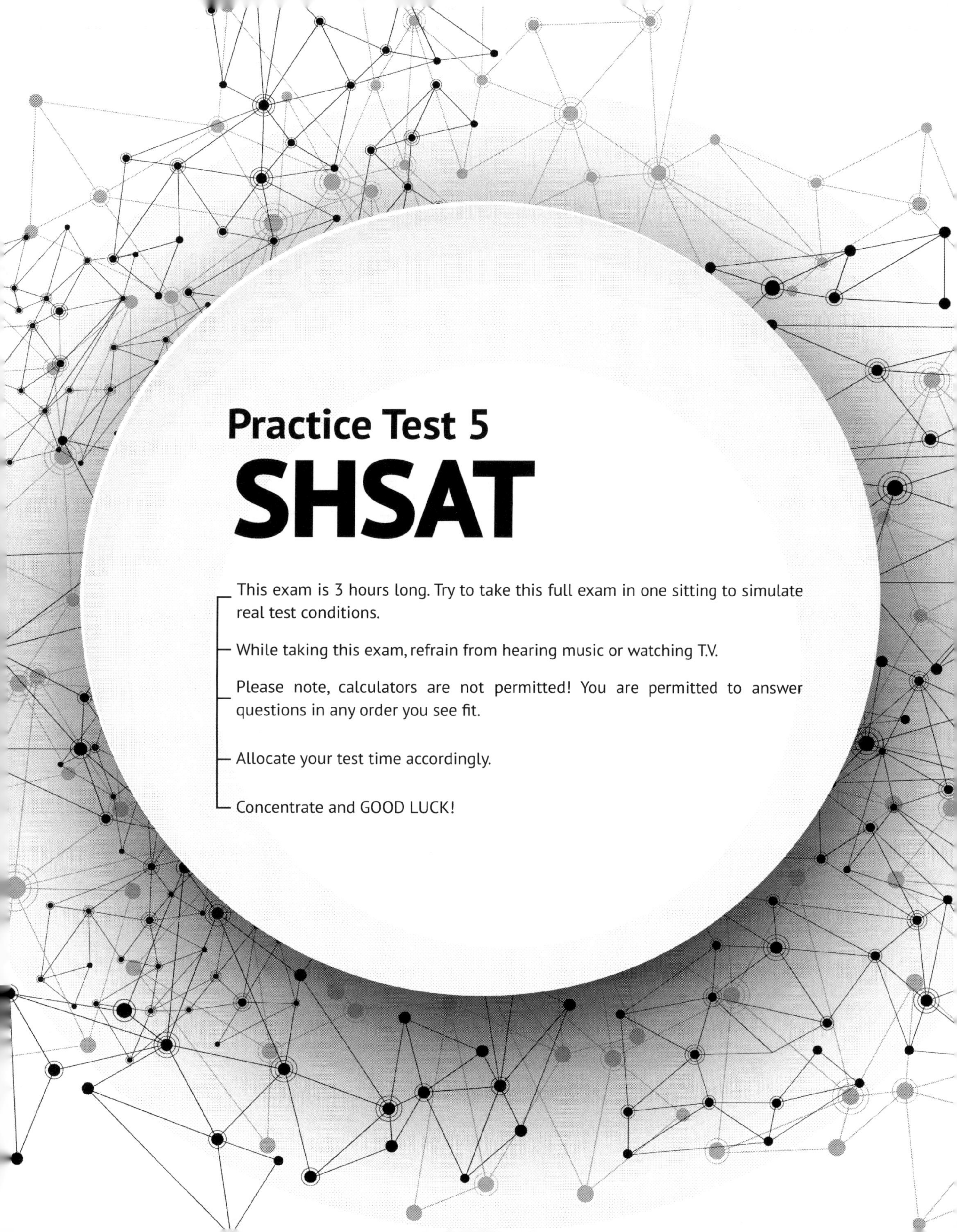

# Practice Test 5
# SHSAT

- This exam is 3 hours long. Try to take this full exam in one sitting to simulate real test conditions.
- While taking this exam, refrain from hearing music or watching T.V.
- Please note, calculators are not permitted! You are permitted to answer questions in any order you see fit.
- Allocate your test time accordingly.
- Concentrate and GOOD LUCK!

**You can find detailed video explanations to each problem in the book by visiting: ArgoPrep.com**

# SHSAT PRACTICE TEST 5

## ANSWER SHEET

### ENGLISH LANGUAGE ARTS

1. Ⓐ Ⓑ Ⓒ Ⓓ
2. Ⓔ Ⓕ Ⓖ Ⓗ
3. Ⓐ Ⓑ Ⓒ Ⓓ
4. Ⓔ Ⓕ Ⓖ Ⓗ
5. Ⓐ Ⓑ Ⓒ Ⓓ
6. Ⓔ Ⓕ Ⓖ Ⓗ
7. Ⓐ Ⓑ Ⓒ Ⓓ
8. Ⓔ Ⓕ Ⓖ Ⓗ
9. Ⓐ Ⓑ Ⓒ Ⓓ
10. Ⓔ Ⓕ Ⓖ Ⓗ
11. Ⓐ Ⓑ Ⓒ Ⓓ
12. Ⓔ Ⓕ Ⓖ Ⓗ
13. Ⓐ Ⓑ Ⓒ Ⓓ
14. Ⓔ Ⓕ Ⓖ Ⓗ
15. Ⓐ Ⓑ Ⓒ Ⓓ
16. Ⓔ Ⓕ Ⓖ Ⓗ
17. Ⓐ Ⓑ Ⓒ Ⓓ
18. Ⓔ Ⓕ Ⓖ Ⓗ
19. Ⓐ Ⓑ Ⓒ Ⓓ
20. Ⓔ Ⓕ Ⓖ Ⓗ
21. Ⓐ Ⓑ Ⓒ Ⓓ
22. Ⓔ Ⓕ Ⓖ Ⓗ
23. Ⓐ Ⓑ Ⓒ Ⓓ
24. Ⓔ Ⓕ Ⓖ Ⓗ
25. Ⓐ Ⓑ Ⓒ Ⓓ
26. Ⓔ Ⓕ Ⓖ Ⓗ
27. Ⓐ Ⓑ Ⓒ Ⓓ
28. Ⓔ Ⓕ Ⓖ Ⓗ
29. Ⓐ Ⓑ Ⓒ Ⓓ
30. Ⓔ Ⓕ Ⓖ Ⓗ
31. Ⓐ Ⓑ Ⓒ Ⓓ
32. Ⓔ Ⓕ Ⓖ Ⓗ
33. Ⓐ Ⓑ Ⓒ Ⓓ
34. Ⓔ Ⓕ Ⓖ Ⓗ
35. Ⓐ Ⓑ Ⓒ Ⓓ
36. Ⓔ Ⓕ Ⓖ Ⓗ
37. Ⓐ Ⓑ Ⓒ Ⓓ
38. Ⓔ Ⓕ Ⓖ Ⓗ
39. Ⓐ Ⓑ Ⓒ Ⓓ
40. Ⓔ Ⓕ Ⓖ Ⓗ
41. Ⓐ Ⓑ Ⓒ Ⓓ
42. Ⓔ Ⓕ Ⓖ Ⓗ
43. Ⓐ Ⓑ Ⓒ Ⓓ
44. Ⓔ Ⓕ Ⓖ Ⓗ
45. Ⓐ Ⓑ Ⓒ Ⓓ
46. Ⓔ Ⓕ Ⓖ Ⓗ
47. Ⓐ Ⓑ Ⓒ Ⓓ
48. Ⓔ Ⓕ Ⓖ Ⓗ
49. Ⓐ Ⓑ Ⓒ Ⓓ
50. Ⓔ Ⓕ Ⓖ Ⓗ
51. Ⓐ Ⓑ Ⓒ Ⓓ
52. Ⓔ Ⓕ Ⓖ Ⓗ
53. Ⓐ Ⓑ Ⓒ Ⓓ
54. Ⓔ Ⓕ Ⓖ Ⓗ
55. Ⓐ Ⓑ Ⓒ Ⓓ
56. Ⓔ Ⓕ Ⓖ Ⓗ
57. Ⓐ Ⓑ Ⓒ Ⓓ

### MATHEMATICS

63. Ⓔ Ⓕ Ⓖ Ⓗ
64. Ⓐ Ⓑ Ⓒ Ⓓ
65. Ⓔ Ⓕ Ⓖ Ⓗ
66 Ⓐ Ⓑ Ⓒ Ⓓ
67. Ⓔ Ⓕ Ⓖ Ⓗ
68. Ⓐ Ⓑ Ⓒ Ⓓ
69. Ⓔ Ⓕ Ⓖ Ⓗ
70. Ⓐ Ⓑ Ⓒ Ⓓ
71. Ⓔ Ⓕ Ⓖ Ⓗ
72. Ⓐ Ⓑ Ⓒ Ⓓ
73. Ⓔ Ⓕ Ⓖ Ⓗ
74 Ⓐ Ⓑ Ⓒ Ⓓ
75. Ⓔ Ⓕ Ⓖ Ⓗ
76. Ⓐ Ⓑ Ⓒ Ⓓ
77. Ⓔ Ⓕ Ⓖ Ⓗ
78. Ⓐ Ⓑ Ⓒ Ⓓ
79. Ⓔ Ⓕ Ⓖ Ⓗ
80. Ⓐ Ⓑ Ⓒ Ⓓ
81. Ⓔ Ⓕ Ⓖ Ⓗ
82. Ⓐ Ⓑ Ⓒ Ⓓ
83. Ⓔ Ⓕ Ⓖ Ⓗ
84 Ⓐ Ⓑ Ⓒ Ⓓ
85. Ⓔ Ⓕ Ⓖ Ⓗ
86. Ⓐ Ⓑ Ⓒ Ⓓ
87. Ⓔ Ⓕ Ⓖ Ⓗ
88. Ⓐ Ⓑ Ⓒ Ⓓ
89. Ⓔ Ⓕ Ⓖ Ⓗ
90. Ⓐ Ⓑ Ⓒ Ⓓ
91. Ⓔ Ⓕ Ⓖ Ⓗ
92. Ⓐ Ⓑ Ⓒ Ⓓ
93. Ⓔ Ⓕ Ⓖ Ⓗ
94. Ⓐ Ⓑ Ⓒ Ⓓ
95. Ⓔ Ⓕ Ⓖ Ⓗ
96. Ⓐ Ⓑ Ⓒ Ⓓ
97. Ⓔ Ⓕ Ⓖ Ⓗ
98. Ⓐ Ⓑ Ⓒ Ⓓ
99. Ⓔ Ⓕ Ⓖ Ⓗ
100. Ⓐ Ⓑ Ⓒ Ⓓ
101. Ⓔ Ⓕ Ⓖ Ⓗ
102. Ⓐ Ⓑ Ⓒ Ⓓ
103. Ⓔ Ⓕ Ⓖ Ⓗ
104. Ⓐ Ⓑ Ⓒ Ⓓ
105. Ⓔ Ⓕ Ⓖ Ⓗ
106. Ⓐ Ⓑ Ⓒ Ⓓ
107. Ⓔ Ⓕ Ⓖ Ⓗ
108. Ⓐ Ⓑ Ⓒ Ⓓ
109. Ⓔ Ⓕ Ⓖ Ⓗ
110. Ⓐ Ⓑ Ⓒ Ⓓ
111. Ⓔ Ⓕ Ⓖ Ⓗ
112. Ⓐ Ⓑ Ⓒ Ⓓ
113. Ⓔ Ⓕ Ⓖ Ⓗ
114. Ⓐ Ⓑ Ⓒ Ⓓ

### MATHEMATICS (GRID IN)

**58**

| | | | | |
|---|---|---|---|---|
| ⊖ | | | | |
| | ⊙ | ⊙ | ⊙ | ⊙ |
| | 0 | 0 | 0 | 0 |
| | 1 | 1 | 1 | 1 |
| | 2 | 2 | 2 | 2 |
| | 3 | 3 | 3 | 3 |
| | 4 | 4 | 4 | 4 |
| | 5 | 5 | 5 | 5 |
| | 6 | 6 | 6 | 6 |
| | 7 | 7 | 7 | 7 |
| | 8 | 8 | 8 | 8 |
| | 9 | 9 | 9 | 9 |

**59**

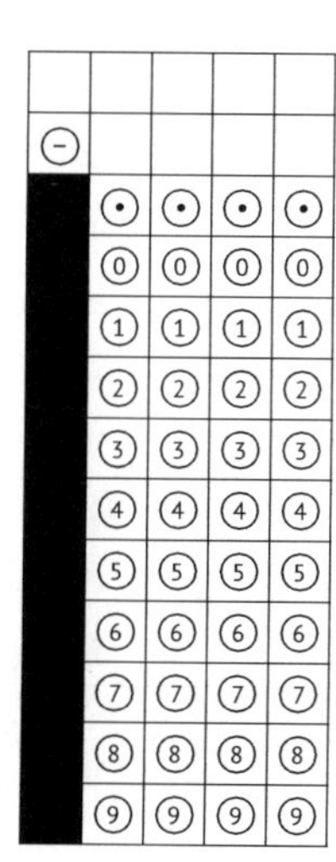

**60**

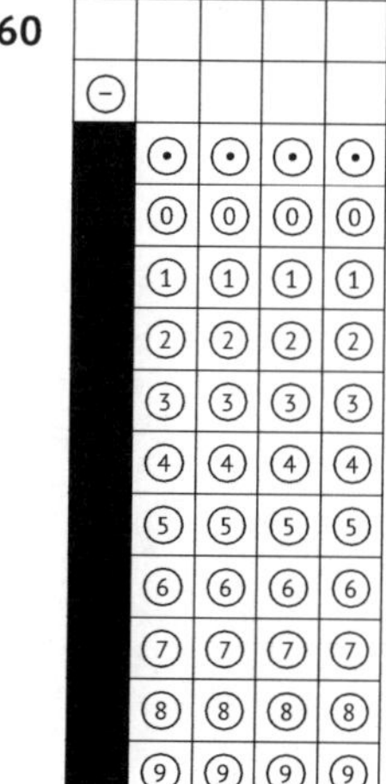

**61**

| | | | | |
|---|---|---|---|---|
| ⊖ | | | | |
| | ⊙ | ⊙ | ⊙ | ⊙ |
| | 0 | 0 | 0 | 0 |
| | 1 | 1 | 1 | 1 |
| | 2 | 2 | 2 | 2 |
| | 3 | 3 | 3 | 3 |
| | 4 | 4 | 4 | 4 |
| | 5 | 5 | 5 | 5 |
| | 6 | 6 | 6 | 6 |
| | 7 | 7 | 7 | 7 |
| | 8 | 8 | 8 | 8 |
| | 9 | 9 | 9 | 9 |

**62**

| | | | | |
|---|---|---|---|---|
| ⊖ | | | | |
| | ⊙ | ⊙ | ⊙ | ⊙ |
| | 0 | 0 | 0 | 0 |
| | 1 | 1 | 1 | 1 |
| | 2 | 2 | 2 | 2 |
| | 3 | 3 | 3 | 3 |
| | 4 | 4 | 4 | 4 |
| | 5 | 5 | 5 | 5 |
| | 6 | 6 | 6 | 6 |
| | 7 | 7 | 7 | 7 |
| | 8 | 8 | 8 | 8 |
| | 9 | 9 | 9 | 9 |

ARGOPREP
ARGOPREP.COM/SHSAT

**DIRECTIONS:** For questions 1 to 5, you will be asked to recognize and correct errors in sentences or short paragraphs.

**1.** Read this sentence.

> The water cycle has three main steps evaporation, condensation, and precipitation.

Which of the choices below is the best revision of the sentence?

**A.** The water cycle has three main steps: evaporation, condensation, and precipitation.
**B.** The water cycle has three main steps (evaporation, condensation, and precipitation).
**C.** The water cycle has three main steps, and those steps are evaporation, condensation, and precipitation.
**D.** The water cycle has three main steps; evaporation, condensation, and precipitation.

**2.** Read this paragraph.

> (1) The First Amendment famously promises that the government will not limit the people's freedom of speech. (2) It also guarantees that the government cannot establish an official religion or limit the practice of any religions that citizens might believe in. (3) The First Amendment goes on to establish citizens also have the rights to assemble to spread ideas and petition the government to make changes. (4) Finally, a free press is legally protected to help ensure that the other rights are safeguarded.

Which sentence could be added before Sentence 1 as a topic sentence?

**E.** The Bill of Rights contains the first ten amendments to the Constitution of the United States.
**F.** The First Amendment provides five basic freedoms for citizens.
**G.** The Founding Fathers believed it was important for people to be protected from government.
**H.** The First Amendment is the most important part of the Bill of Rights.

CONTINUE ON TO THE NEXT PAGE ➡

**3.** Read this paragraph.

(1) The Charles River in Boston, Massachusetts is a haven for rowers from all around the world. (2) On any given day, amateur paddlers and collegiate competitors rows side by side. (3) Each October since 1965, the Head of the Charles Regatta has attracted the top rowers from the United States and beyond to compete in a variety of races. (4) Competitors are grouped into a variety of classes based on age, experience level, and number of rowers. (5) More than 11,000 rowers participate in the Head of the Charles over its two-day span.

Which sentence should be revised to correct a subject-verb agreement error?

**A.** Sentence 2
**B.** Sentence 3
**C.** Sentence 4
**D.** Sentence 5

---

**4.** Read this paragraph.

(1) Hockey is surprisingly popular in the United States in spite of the fact that most people consider football and baseball to be far more "American." (2) Even in warm weather cities like San Jose and Los Angeles, hockey has won over many American fans. (3) Conversely, some Americans think of hockey as being a Canadian sport. (4) In areas like New England and Minnesota, recreational hockey leagues dominate basketball and softball in popularity.

How could Sentence 2 and Sentence 3 best be combined to clarify the relationship between ideas?

**E.** Even in warm weather cities like San Jose and Los Angeles, hockey has won over many American fans, but conversely, some Americans think of hockey as being a Canadian sport.
**F.** Even in warm weather cities like San Jose and Los Angeles, hockey has won over many American fans even though some still think of hockey as being a Canadian sport.
**G.** Even in warm weather cities like San Jose and Los Angeles, hockey has won over many American fans; some still think of hockey as being a Canadian sport.
**H.** Even in warm weather cities like San Jose and Los Angeles, hockey has won over many American fans, although some still think of hockey as being a Canadian sport.

---

**5.** Read this paragraph.

(1) Every Fourth of July, people across the nation celebrate the birth of the United States of America. (2) Familes around the country practice a variety of traditions including backyard barbecues, frolicking in public parks, and coming together at night for fireworks. (3) Americans never lost sight of what July Fourth is all about, though. (4) People still take time to recognize the wisdom of the Founding Fathers and the bravery of early patriots.

Which sentence should be revised to correct an inconsistent verb tense?

**A.** Sentence 1
**B.** Sentence 2
**C.** Sentence 3
**D.** Sentence 4

**CONTINUE ON TO THE NEXT PAGE ➡**

**DIRECTIONS:** Read the passage below to answer questions 6 to 11. The questions will focus on improving the writing quality of the passage to follow the conventions of standard written English.

---

### School Segregation

(1) Slavery in the United States officially ended with the Emancipation Proclamation of 1863. (2) Even though they were no longer slaves, black southerners were still discriminated against in many fundamental ways. (3) One example of this prejudiced treatment is the segregation of public schools throughout the South. (4) School segregation meant that black and white students had to go to separate schools. (5) The system lasted from about 1877 until 1954.

(6) In 1896, the Supreme Court ruled that racial segregation of schools was legal as long as the conditions were "separate but equal." (7) Conditions in black schools were consistently worse throughout the history of segregation. (8) The white public school system, on the other hand, was propped up with millions of dollars of additional taxpayer funding and had preferential access to the best teachers, materials, and facilities.

(9) Formal segregation was ruled illegal by the Supreme Court in 1954 in the famous decision *Brown vs. Board of Education of Topeka*. (10) The court explained in their majority decision that having separate educational facilities for each race was inherently unequal. (11) While *Brown vs. Board* ended government-sanctioned school segregation, the issue did not disappear instantly. (12) Schools throughout the South dragged their feet on integration for years, making it a drawn out, painful process for many southerners, black and white. (13) Today, education cannot be legally segregated, but schools in historically black neighborhoods are still some of the most underserved in the nation.

6. Which revision eliminates the use of passive voice in Sentence 2
   - **E.** Black southerners were discriminated against in many fundamental ways, even though they were no longer slaves.
   - **F.** Black southerners, no longer slaves, were discriminated against in many fundamental ways.
   - **G.** White southerners continued to discriminate against their black neighbors, even though they were no longer slaves.
   - **H.** Black people were discriminated against throughout the South, even though they were no longer slaves.

CONTINUE ON TO THE NEXT PAGE ➞

7. Which revision is necessary to correct Sentence 3?

   A. Change **this** to **these**
   B. Change **is** to **was**
   C. Change **throughout** to **in**
   D. Change **South** to **south**

---

8. What is the best way to combine Sentence 4 and Sentence 5 to clarify the relationship between ideas?

   E. School segregation, which lasted from about 1877 to 1954, meant that black and white students had to go to separate schools.
   F. From 1877 to 1954, school segregation existed,which meant that black and white students had to go to separate schools.
   G. White and black students had to go to separate schools from about 1877 to 1954, and that system was known as segregation.
   H. The system that lasted from about 1877 to 1954 was called school segregation, and that meant that white and black students had to go to separate schools.

---

9. Which transition should be added to the beginning of Sentence 7?

   A. Therefore
   B. Consequently
   C. For example
   D. However

10. Which sentence would best follow and support Sentence 7?

    E. Imagine how the students in segregated schools must have felt when they saw the huge differences between black and white schools.
    F. Black schools were faced with a shortage of qualified teachers, a lack of quality textbooks, and minimal government funding to maintain their facilities.
    G. This lack of institutional support made many people in black communities around the country feel neglected and rejected.
    H. Overall, this shabby treatment reduced African Americans' chances to better their lives.

---

11. Which sentence would best follow Sentence 8 to serve as a conclusion sentence for the second paragraph?

    A. Many people felt something had to be done to fix these conditions.
    B. Seventeen different states had formal school segregation programs.
    C. These disparities were clearly unequal, meaning that segregation was not only cruel but also illegal.
    D. Several organizations, including the United Nations, realized that this system was unjust.

CONTINUE ON TO THE NEXT PAGE ➡

ENGLISH LANGUAGE ARTS

Practice Test 5

**DIRECTIONS:** Read the passage below to answer questions 12 to 20. The questions will focus on improving the writing quality of the passage to follow the conventions of standard written English.

---

**Excerpt from "The Most Dangerous Game"**

By Richard Connell

"OFF THERE to the right--somewhere--is a large island," said Whitney." It's rather a mystery--"

"What island is it?" Rainsford asked.

"The old charts call it `Ship-Trap Island,'" Whitney replied." A suggestive name, isn't it? Sailors have a curious dread of the place. I don't know why. Some superstition--"

"Can't see it," remarked Rainsford, trying to peer through the dank tropical night that was palpable as it pressed its thick warm blackness in upon the yacht.

"You've good eyes," said Whitney, with a laugh," and I've seen you pick off a moose moving in the brown fall bush at four hundred yards, but even you can't see four miles or so through a moonless Caribbean night."

"Nor four yards," admitted Rainsford. "Ugh! It's like moist black velvet."

"It will be light enough in Rio," promised Whitney. "We should make it in a few days. I hope the jaguar guns have come from Purdey's. We should have some good hunting up the Amazon. Great sport, hunting."

"The best sport in the world," agreed Rainsford.

"For the hunter," amended Whitney. "Not for the jaguar."

"Don't talk rot, Whitney," said Rainsford. "You're a big-game hunter, not a philosopher. Who cares how a jaguar feels?"

"Perhaps the jaguar does," observed Whitney.

"Bah! They've no understanding."

"Even so, I rather think they understand one thing--fear. The fear of pain and the fear of death."

"Nonsense," laughed Rainsford. "This hot weather is making you soft, Whitney. Be a realist. The world is made up of two classes--the hunters and the huntees. Luckily, you and I are hunters. Do you think we've passed that island yet?"

"I can't tell in the dark. I hope so."

"Why?" asked Rainsford.

"The place has a reputation--a bad one."

"Cannibals?" suggested Rainsford.

"Hardly. Even cannibals wouldn't live in such a God-forsaken place. But it's gotten into sailor lore, somehow. Didn't you notice that the crew's nerves seemed a bit jumpy today?"

"They were a bit strange, now you mention it. Even Captain Nielsen--"

"Yes, even that tough-minded old Swede, who'd go up to the devil himself and ask him for a light. Those fishy blue eyes held a look I never saw there before. All I could get out of him was `This place has an evil name among seafaring men, sir.' Then he said to me, very gravely, `Don't you feel anything?'--as if the air about us was actually poisonous. Now, you mustn't laugh when I tell you this--I did feel something like a sudden chill."

CONTINUE ON TO THE NEXT PAGE ➡

**12.** Based on the passage, why are Rainsford and Whitney on a boat?

- **E.** They are explorers searching for the lost "Ship-Trap Island"
- **F.** They are traveling to their next destination on a hunting trip
- **G.** They are escaping from a pack of angry jaguars
- **H.** They are professional sailors

---

**13.** Which aspect of the setting plays a key role in establishing that Ship-Trap Island is very mysterious?

- **A.** The descriptions of the air
- **B.** The descriptions of the old sea charts
- **C.** The descriptions of the heat
- **D.** The image of the boat in the middle of the ocean

---

**14.** Why does Rainsford mention the distance of four yards?

- **E.** To illustrate how far away the island is supposed to be
- **F.** To illustrate the length of the boat
- **G.** To illustrate that it's impossible to see almost any distance
- **H.** To illustrate the distance from which he's comfortable shooting game

---

**15.** Which of these is the best definition for "rot" as it is used in the conversation between Rainsford and Whitney?

- **A.** Decomposition
- **B.** Disgusting ideas
- **C.** Nonsense
- **D.** Made by hand

**16.** Based on the passage, how do Whitney and Rainsford's personalities differ?

- **E.** Rainsford is more brash and aggressive, whereas Whitney is more cautious and empathetic.
- **F.** Whitney is more brash and aggressive, whereas Rainsford is more cautious and empathetic.
- **G.** Rainsford is more adventurous and brave, whereas Whitney is more meek and cowardly.
- **H.** Whitney is more adventurous and brave, whereas Rainsford is more meek and cowardly.

---

**17.** Based on the passage, what is Whitney's opinion of Captain Nielson?

- **A.** He is superstitious and cowardly
- **B.** He is suspicious and secretive
- **C.** He is self-important and overly serious
- **D.** He is brave and tough

---

**18.** Based on the passage, the word "Game" in the title most likely refers to:

- **E.** A card game that Whitney and Rainsford play to pass the time on the boat
- **F.** An animal being tracked or pursued by hunters
- **G.** A manipulation or ruse
- **H.** Willingness to try or do new things

**CONTINUE ON TO THE NEXT PAGE ➞**

**19.** Based on the text, approximately where does this scene take place?

**A.** Europe
**B.** South America
**C.** North America
**D.** Asia

---

**20.** Which of these is not a concern of Whitney's?

**E.** The fact that the sailors are superstitious about the island
**F.** The fact that Captain Nielson seems wary of the area they are in
**G.** The fact that hunting is terrifying for animals
**H.** The fact that there may be cannibals on the island

CONTINUE ON TO THE NEXT PAGE ➡

ARGOPREP
ARGOPREP.COM/SHSAT

# READING COMPREHENSION

Practice Test 5

**DIRECTIONS:** Analyze the passages below, and answer the commensurate questions. Only use information provided within the passage for your answers. There is only one answer for each question.

---

Long ago, when you were a little boy or a little girl – perhaps not so very long ago, either – were you never interrupted in your play by being called in to have your face washed, your hair combed, and your soiled apron exchanged for a clean one, preparatory to an introduction to Mrs. Smith, or Dr. Jones, or Aunt Judkins, your mother's early friend? And after being ushered into that august presence and made to face a battery of questions which were either above or below your capacity, and which you consequently despised as trash or resented as insult, did you not, as were gleefully vanishing, hear a soft sigh breathed out upon the air, "Dear child, he is seeing his happiest days?" In the concrete, it was Mrs. Smith or Dr. Jones speaking of you. But going back to general principles, it was Commonplacedom expressing its opinion of childhood.

There never was a greater piece of absurdity in the world. I thought so when I was a child, and now I know it; and I desire here to brand it as at once a platitude and a falsehood. How the idea gained currency, that childhood is the happiest period of life, I cannot conceive. How, once started, it kept afloat, is equally incomprehensible. I should have supposed that the experience of every sane person would have given the lie to it. I should have supposed that every soul, as it burst into flower, would have hurled off the imputation. I can only account for it by recurring to Lady Mary Wortley Montague's statistics, and concluding that the fools are three out of four in every person's acquaintance.

I, for one, lift up my voice emphatically against the assertion and do affirm that I think childhood is the most undesirable portion of human life, and I am thankful to be well out of it. I look upon it as no better than a mitigated form of slavery. There is not a child in the land that can call his soul, or his body, or his jacket his own. A little soft lump of clay, he comes into the world and is moulded into a vessel of honor or a vessel of dishonor long before he can put in a word about the matter. He has no voice as to his education or his training, what he shall eat, what he shall drink, or wherewithal he shall be clothed. He has to wait upon the wisdom, the whims, and often the wickedness of other people. Imagine, my six-foot friend, how you would feel to be obliged to wear your woollen mittens when you desire to bloom out in straw-colored kids, or to be buttoned into your black waistcoat when your taste leads you to select your white, or to be forced under your Kossuth hat when you had set your heart on your black beaver: yet this is what children are perpetually called on to undergo. Their wills are just as strong as ours, and their tastes are stronger, yet they have to bend the one and sacrifice the other; and they do it under pressure of necessity.

CONTINUE ON TO THE NEXT PAGE ➡

**21.** What is this passage mostly about?

- **A.** Why it is great to be a child.
- **B.** Why being told what to do is bad.
- **C.** To prove that people are fools.
- **D.** To illustrate that, contrary to popular belief, childhood is the worst time of life.

---

**22.** What does the author imply about the belief that childhood is the happiest time of one's life?

- **E.** It is a commonly held belief.
- **F.** It is a lie we tell ourselves.
- **G.** It is never true.
- **H.** It is always true.

---

**23.** What do we know about the author's childhood?

- **A.** She was never allowed to decide what she would wear.
- **B.** She was never allowed to leave the house when she wanted.
- **C.** She did not prefer it to her adult life.
- **D.** She was happier at the time of her childhood.

**24.** What is one reason listed as to why childhood is considered by the author to be the worst time in one's life?

- **E.** You need to focus too much on school.
- **F.** You do not get to play as much as when you are an adult.
- **G.** You do not get to boss people around as much as when you are an adult.
- **H.** Many important decisions are not in your control.

---

**25.** Why does the author ask the six-foot friend to imagine needing to wear mittens?

- **A.** To illustrate how distasteful mittens are.
- **B.** To illustrate that we take for granted our right to decide mundane actions.
- **C.** The illusion requires a cold habitat.
- **D.** The author believes her friend would look good in mittens.

---

**26.** What, if true, would most strongly weaken the author's main claim?

- **E.** Children are given some decision making.
- **F.** Adults are not entirely free to decide everything.
- **G.** Making decisions can be tiresome.
- **H.** People are happiest when others decide what is good for them.

**CONTINUE ON TO THE NEXT PAGE ➡**

If you asked a group of people which verb they would use to describe how their favorite foods are made, many people would say, "They're cooked!" However, a strong percentage of people would also say, "They're baked!" Although the two processes may seem very similar at first blush, cooking and baking are actually markedly different methods of creating food. Many people even say that cooking is an art, while baking is a science. Even in the culinary world, bakers and chefs are prepared separately and learn completely different techniques.

Since eating is a daily necessity, cooking's clear goal is to make food that is tasty and nutritious. In order to accomplish this, chefs can call on a variety of ingredients and flavor combinations to create a near infinite smorgasbord of delicious treats. By switching just a few local ingredients or incorporating a signature technique, chefs can reinvent a classic dish with a fresh, personal spin. Once chefs have a clear understanding of cooking fundamentals, they are free to experiment to create bold new flavor combinations and innovative techniques.

Bakers create breads, cakes, and other treats that rival the flavors of the world's finest chefs, but their road to creating delicious food is a more disciplined one. Baking involves creating dough, which must rise to be tasty and digestible. Getting that dough to rise involves facilitating specific chemical reactions that require a leavening agent, such as yeast or baking soda. For the dough to rise correctly, the ratio of ingredients must be in proper proportion, or the cake, bread, or other delicious baked good will not have an appealing taste, texture, or appearance.

Many great chefs are utterly terrified of baking. Since they have been trained to experiment and make adjustments on the fly, the idea of putting something in an oven and walking away for half an hour can be very intimidating for them. On the other hand, many bakers find cooking to be overwhelming because there is such a wide variety of ingredients that somebody must know how to use to become a great cook. Bakers love that they can create dozens of different delectable treats from a few basic ingredients like sugar, flour, salt, and water.

Baking and cooking are both crucial for mankind to survive and thrive. Creating food to feed the world is a key responsibility, which cooks and bakers around the world all work hard each day to accomplish. By creating food, they are also culinary caretakers of their ethnic, regional, and cultural heritage. Bakers and cooks both make the world a better place, but don't mistake them for each other!

**27.** Which of the following best tells what this passage is about?

**A.** Baking is better than cooking because it is more scientific.

**B.** Cooking is better than baking because it is more artistic.

**C.** Cooking and baking are very different processes, even though they seem quite similar.

**D.** Cooking and baking are both rewarding hobbies that many people enjoy.

**CONTINUE ON TO THE NEXT PAGE ➡**

**28.** Based on context clues, what is a "smorgasbord?"

- **E.** A regional specialty dish unique to a certain part of the world
- **F.** A restaurant that serves the most exotic food on earth
- **G.** A European cooking competition
- **H.** A wide array of hot and cold snacks.

---

**29.** Based on the passage, why might somebody believe that cooking is "an art?"

- **A.** Chefs have a great deal of freedom when they cook and can adjust to incorporate new ingredients and techniques as they work.
- **B.** When they cook, chefs create a plate of food that can rival the beauty of the works of famous painters.
- **C.** Food is a daily necessity, and without cooks, many people around the world would starve.
- **D.** Cooks have different individual styles and passions, whereas baking is the same all around the world.

---

**30.** Based on the passage, why might somebody believe baking is "a science?"

- **E.** Bakers make complex creations out of very simple, basic elements.
- **F.** Baking relies on creating specific reactions in proper proportion, so recipes and measurements must be precise.
- **G.** Baking involves using and heating a lot of glassware, as does laboratory science.
- **H.** Bakers have to worry about mastering the taste, texture, and appearance of their goods, which means they need a lot of complex knowledge.

---

**31.** Based on the passage, which of these processes would probably be hardest for a chef who wasn't familiar with baking?

- **A.** Frosting a cupcake
- **B.** Writing properly spaced and sized text on a cake
- **C.** Choosing herbs to season an herb bread
- **D.** Making cinnamon roll dough

---

**32.** How are cooks and bakers both "culinary caretakers of their ethnic, regional, and cultural heritage?"

- **E.** They create food that makes people happy and reminds them of home, family, and traditions.
- **F.** Cooks and bakers can get jobs at museums where they recreate food that people ate in different locations and eras.
- **G.** The most important part of a cook or baker's identity is their ethnic, regional, and cultural heritage.
- **H.** Cooks and bakers work together to feed the world, so they are unsung cultural heroes.

**CONTINUE ON TO THE NEXT PAGE ➞**

Golf is popular around the world with people of all ages, nationalities, and athletic backgrounds. Although uninitiated television viewers often assume golf is boring, millions of enthusiasts appreciate the rewarding thrill of a shot well played. People enjoy golf because it provides hundreds of individual opportunities for strategizing and success. While golf may have a reputation as an exclusive game reserved for elites, it's actually one of the most straightforward sports to play and understand.

The object of the game in golf is to get a small, white ball into a hole that's typically between 100 and 500 yards away. Players hit the ball with a long club, counting the number of hits, or "strokes," it takes them to get from the starting point to the hole. A "round" of golf is consists of playing either nine or 18 of these holes and then tallying strokes at the end. In competitive play, the player with the lowest score wins the game; however, many people also like to play golf individually and simply try to break their personal best score.

Each player is allowed to carry up to 14 different clubs to help them hit the ball different distances. Those clubs are broken into four basic groups: woods, irons, wedges, and putters. Woods have bulbous metal heads (although, as their name suggests, they were once made from wood) and hit the ball the farthest, although at the lowest trajectory, of all the clubs. The biggest and longest wood is called the driver, and it is typically used for the first shot of each hole. Irons are used for distances under 200 yards and are numbered in ascending order from one to nine, with higher numbers counterintuitively representing shorter potential distances. Wedges are used near the green (the target area around the hole) to help players get into position to finish the hole. Each player has one putter, which is the club used to actually knock the ball into the hole from short distance.

During a round of golf, players are constantly strategizing, making decisions, and attempting to put their plans into action. Before each stroke, players must approximate their distance to the hole, decide which club would best fit their needs, determine the angle at which they need to line up to hit the ball, and settle on how far down they will choke on their grip. Once they've made these considerations, a player must decide how full a swing to execute, since hitting the ball the maximum possible distance is not always the best decision. Of course, all this decision-making can be complicated when the mind is filled with competitive anxieties, frustration, or feelings of self-doubt. For this reason, golfers must focus, clear their head, and focus on playing in the moment.

Of course, there are also a variety of external factors that golfers must consider. Courses are loaded with small bodies of water, which players must keep their ball out of or suffer a penalty stroke added to their score for that hole. Sand traps, also known as bunkers, are pits of sand around the course that players must hit their ball out of without letting their club touch the ground. If a player's club touches the sand, they must add a penalty stroke to their score also. These physical obstacles only add to the challenge that is golf's mental game.

**CONTINUE ON TO THE NEXT PAGE ➡**

**33.** Which answer best describes the purpose of this passage?

- **A.** To show the reader why golf is better than other sports
- **B.** To convince the reader to try golf
- **C.** To provide the reader with a brief explanation of golf
- **D.** To tell the reader a story about golf

---

**34.** Based on the passage, why might "uninitiated television viewers often assume golf is boring?"

- **E.** Golf is primarily a game of internal strategizing and disciplined execution.
- **F.** The rules of golf are highly complex and difficult to explain to new fans.
- **G.** Golf requires too much athletic skill for most people to appreciate.
- **H.** Televised golf has commercial breaks, which slow down the action.

---

**35.** Based on the passage, which iron could potentially hit a golf ball the farthest?

- **A.** Seven
- **B.** Five
- **C.** Two
- **D.** Four

**36.** If E, F, G, and H played a competitive round of golf together, which score would win the game?

- **E.** 120
- **F.** 79
- **G.** 84
- **H.** 102

---

**37.** Based on the passage, which of these scenarios is the worst outcome in terms of score?

- **A.** Dennis hit his ball into the water once.
- **B.** Dennis hit his ball into two sand traps, but he kept his club from touching the ground as he got it out both times.
- **C.** Dennis hit his ball into the water once, and then into two sand traps, but he kept his club from touching the ground both times as he got out of the bunkers.
- **D.** Dennis hit his ball into two sand traps, and he allowed his club to touch the ground both times that he hit the ball out.

---

**38.** Based on the passage, which is the best explanation of why golf can be frustrating?

- **E.** All the equipment you need to play golf is very expensive.
- **F.** When you're having a bad day on the golf course, you often have nobody to blame but yourself.
- **G.** Golfers are highly competitive and often give each other a hard time about past failures and embarrassing moments.
- **H.** Playing golf involves highly complex math.

**CONTINUE ON TO THE NEXT PAGE →**

**Lines Written in Early Spring**
By William Wordsworth

I heard a thousand blended notes,
While in a grove I sat reclined,
In that sweet mood when pleasant thoughts
Bring sad thoughts to the mind. (4)
To her fair works did nature link
The human soul that through me ran;
And much it grieved my heart to think
What man has made of man. (8)
Through primrose tufts, in that sweet bower,
The periwinkle trailed its wreaths;
And 'tis my faith that every flower
Enjoys the air it breathes. (12)
The birds around me hopped and played:
Their thoughts I cannot measure,
But the least motion which they made,
It seemed a thrill of pleasure. (16)
The budding twigs spread out their fan,
To catch the breezy air;
And I must think, do all I can,
That there was pleasure there. (20)
If this belief from heaven be sent,
If such be Nature's holy plan,
Have I not reason to lament
What man has made of man? (24)

**39.** What device does Wordsworth use to draw attention to his main point in the poem?

- **A.** Metaphor
- **B.** Simile
- **C.** Repetition
- **D.** Personification

**40.** Which best describes the overall tone of the poem?

- **E.** Reflective
- **F.** Inflammatory
- **G.** Uplifting
- **H.** Descriptive

---

**41.** Which of these is the best definition for "fair" as it is used in Line 5?

- **A.** Balanced
- **B.** Consistent
- **C.** Pale or light in color
- **D.** Beautiful

---

**42.** What does the speaker suggest is the main difference between nature and mankind?

- **E.** Nature always exists in harmony; humans cannot tap into that energy because we are burdened with consciousness.
- **F.** Nature always seems happy to exist in the moment; humans have instead chosen a life of dissatisfaction and forgotten how to live in the preset.
- **G.** Nature is always active and filled with life; humans make themselves miserable with laziness.
- **H.** Everything in nature is beautiful; only humans can create hate and ugliness.

---

**43.** Which device does Wordsworth use extensively in Lines 9-20 when describing nature?

- **A.** Metaphor
- **B.** Simile
- **C.** Repetition
- **D.** Personification

**CONTINUE ON TO THE NEXT PAGE →**

**44.** What is "this belief" that the speaker is referencing in Line 21?

- **E.** The belief that nature is an all-powerful force
- **F.** The belief that nature is filled with joy
- **G.** The belief that humanity is ruining the planet
- **H.** The belief that twigs spread out to catch breezes

---

**45.** Which other word from the poem is the nearest synonym for "lament," as it is used in Line 23?

- **A.** Grieved (Line 7)
- **B.** Trailed (Line 10)
- **C.** Measure (Line 14)
- **D.** Thrill (Line 16)

---

**46.** To what does the speaker compare nature in Stanzas 2 and 6?

- **E.** Humanity
- **F.** A goddess
- **G.** Birds and flowers
- **H.** Lamentations

**47.** Which of these statements would the speaker of the poem be most likely to agree with?

- **A.** Most people need to spend more time communing with nature.
- **B.** Deforestation and the destruction of natural habitats are two of the biggest challenges facing humanity today.
- **C.** Most people allow the cares and challenges of daily life to prevent them from having fun.
- **D.** People should view plants and animals as equals, not as lesser beings.

**CONTINUE ON TO THE NEXT PAGE ➞**

**Basketball Statistics**

In the twenty-first century, nearly all sports fans are aware of the statistics and analytical data surrounding their games of choice. Over the last twenty years, the use of statistics to quantify player achievement, determine player quality, and inform player salaries and contracts has exploded. Basketball in particular has emerged as a game in which statistical analysis is key to understanding the impact that individual players have on the game.

Basketball has many different statistical categories, but let's stick to the very basics. The most fundamental stats are minutes (MIN) and points (PT). A professional basketball game is 48 minutes long, but due to the endurance the sport requires, very few players participate in more than 40 minutes of any given game. Points simply represent how many points that player scored for his or her team during that time in the game. At a glance, it might be easiest to think that the player with the most points was far and away the best player on the court, but there are many other ways to analyze what happened to the game and make a more informed conclusion.

When players are on offense, not all of them are looking to shoot the ball every time it's in their hands. Some players, especially point guards, prefer to make passes that set up other players for points. If a player makes a pass that sets his or her teammate up for a bucket, he or she is awarded an assist (AST). Players with a large number of assists are generally regarded as unselfish team players because they guide their team toward taking the best shot rather than the first shot they see. On the other hand, a player will not be awarded an assist unless his or her teammate makes their shot, so racking up a large number of assists is also indicative of being on a high-percentage shooting team.

Players can also contribute significantly to their teams by getting rebounds (REB). Rebounding is the act of recovering the ball after a missed field goal attempt. Getting rebounds can be beneficial in different ways, depending on the situation. When a player's team is on offense, getting a rebound means another opportunity to put up a shot. This is sometimes called a "second-chance" opportunity and often provides the offense the chance to get the better of the defense before they can react. When a player gets a rebound on defense, it means they have cut off their opponent's scoring chance and can move the ball down the court to take their turn on offense. Defensive rebounds help teams create dramatic swings in the score of the game, as it creates more offensive opportunities during times when the opposition is struggling worst.

There's no one statistic that quantifies how good a defensive player someone is, but blocks (BLK) and steals (STL) are two numbers that help explain the impact a player has on the defensive end. Blocks are blocked shots and represent the number of times a player used his or her hands to prevent an opponent's shot from reaching the hoop. Steals represent the numbers of times a player intercepted a pass or took the ball away from an opponent. Great defensive players also typically get a lot of rebounds, but it's also possible for a defensive player to become statistically underrated because offensive numbers like points and assists are much easier to notice than solid guarding ability, which is not simple to transform into a number.

**CONTINUE ON TO THE NEXT PAGE ➞**

| Partial Box Score Showing Statistics for Smithtown Rats Starters | | | | | | | | |
|---|---|---|---|---|---|---|---|---|
| Player Name | MIN | PTS | ORB | DRB | REB | AST | STL | BLK |
| Mason | 36 | 11 | 1 | 3 | 4 | 9 | 3 | 0 |
| Smith | 22 | 18 | 3 | 0 | 3 | 3 | 1 | 0 |
| Abdul | 34 | 29 | 2 | 5 | 7 | 1 | 1 | 0 |
| Lilly | 25 | 6 | 2 | 9 | 11 | 0 | 2 | 4 |
| Chen | 32 | 16 | 0 | 7 | 7 | 4 | 1 | 2 |

**48.** Which of these is the best definition for "quantify" as it is used in Paragraph 1?

**E.** To count
**F.** To assess the quality of
**G.** To measure using numbers
**H.** To describe

---

**49.** Based on the passage, why would statistical data potentially impact player salaries?

**A.** Better statistics indicate that a player is superior to others and therefore should be paid more.
**B.** Better statistics indicate that a player understands the game on a higher level than others and therefore should be paid more.
**C.** Better statistics indicate that a player is responding to the coaching style of his or her current teacher and therefore should be paid more.
**D.** Better statistics indicate that a player is a positive influence on the locker-room and therefore should be paid more.

**50.** Based on the passage, why is the player with the most points not always the best player on the court?

**E.** Because having the most points could potentially mean that player is a ball-hog and refuses to support his or her teammates
**F.** Because a player could impact the game just as significantly in other ways, such as setting up other players with assists or playing defense
**G.** Because the player with the most points could still be on the losing team
**H.** Because the player with the most points might have also made a dumb mistake that lost his or her team the game

---

**51.** Which other word in the passage is a synonym for "bucket" as it is used in Paragraph 3?

**A.** "Points" (Paragraph 2)
**B.** "Offense" (Paragraph 3)
**C.** "Passes" (Paragraph 3)
**D.** "Field goal" (Paragraph 4)

CONTINUE ON TO THE NEXT PAGE ➡

**52.** If a point guard passes the ball to his or her teammates the same number of times in two different games, how could he or she have 6 assists in one game and 11 assists in the other?

**E.** Assists are dependent on teammates making shots, so the point guard's teammates might have had a worse shooting night in the game where he or she got 6 assists.
**F.** The point guard might have turned the ball over more times in the game with 6 assists, and turnovers cancel out assists.
**G.** The point guard might have been playing against a better defensive team in the game with 6 assists, and those defensive players were able to block his or her assists.
**H.** Assists are dependent on minutes, so the point guard may have played fewer minutes in the game with 6 assists.

---

**53.** Based on the passage, why does the offense have an advantage over the defense in "second-chance" situations?

**A.** Because they cut off the other team's chance to score which creates an opportunity to shift the score more dramatically
**B.** Because defenders were focused on the previous play and trying to get the rebound, which means they might not be as aware or perfectly positioned as they were on the initial play
**C.** Because, in a second chance situation, players can pass to their teammates to earn an assist rather than shooting the ball themselves
**D.** Because, in a second chance situation, the defense is usually frustrated that they didn't get the rebound, which makes them more susceptible to being scored against

**54.** Why are good defensive players often statistically underrated?

**E.** There are no statistics that quantify defense, which makes offensive numbers much easier to appreciate.
**F.** Good defensive players typically get a lot of rebounds, which aren't appreciated as much as points.
**G.** Blocks and steals are not tied to player salaries and contracts the way points, rebounds, and assists are
**H.** Points and assists on offense are easy to quantify, but there are many skills involved in defense that don't translate into numbers well.

---

**55.** Based on the partial box score, which player on the Smithtown Rats is the most likely to be the point guard, and how can you tell?

**A.** Lilly is likely the point guard because he has the fewest points
**B.** Lilly is likely the point guard because he has the most rebounds
**C.** Mason is likely the point guard because he has the most assists
**D.** Mason is likely the point guard because he has the most steals.

---

**56.** Based on the partial box score, which player is likely the best or most important defender on the Smithtown Rats?

**E.** Lilly
**F.** Chen
**G.** Abdul
**H.** Smith

**CONTINUE ON TO THE NEXT PAGE ➡**

**57.** Which inference is critical to fully understanding the box score?

**A.** Concluding that the Smithtown Rats won the game

**B.** Concluding that the Smithtown Rats lost the game

**C.** Concluding that "ORB" and "DRB" stand for "offensive rebound" and "defensive rebound"

**D.** Concluding that "ORB" is more important than "DRB"

**CONTINUE ON TO THE NEXT PAGE ➞**

ARGOPREP
ARGOPREP.COM/SHSAT

## MATHEMATICS
INSTRUCTIONS

## 90 MINUTES • 57 QUESTIONS

Select the best answer from the choices given by carefully solving each problem. Bubble the letter of your answer on the answer sheet. Please refrain from making any stray marks on the answer sheet. If you need to erase an answer, please erase thoroughly.

**Important Notes:**

1. There are no formulas or definitions in the math section that will be provided.
2. Diagrams may or may not be drawn to scale. Do not make assumptions based on the diagram unless it is specifically stated in the diagram or question.
3. Diagrams are not in more than one plane, unless stated otherwise.
4. Graphs are drawn to scale, therefore, you can assume relationships according to the graph. If lines appear parallel, then you can assume the lines to be parallel. This is also true for right angles and so forth.
5. Simplify fractions completely.

***THIS EXAM IS MORE DIFFICULT**

# Practice Test 5*

**GRID IN PROBLEMS (Questions 58-62)**

*Directions: The following five questions are grid-in problems. On the answer sheet, please be sure to write your answer in the boxes at the top of the grid. Start on the left side of each grid.*

**58.** Given p @ t = $\frac{p}{4}(1 - t^2)$, calculate 7 @ 3.

**59.** Solve $-7(3n + 5) = -6n + 25$ for $n$.



CONTINUE ON TO THE NEXT PAGE →

**60.** Bob is making mini fondant cakes for the next bake sale. Each cake costs Bob \$1.80 to make. If he sells the cakes for \$3.00 each, how many will he have to sell to make a profit of exactly \$36.00?

**61.** A car travels for 3 hours at a speed of 55 miles per hour and then for the next 2 hours travels at a speed of 65 miles per hour. Find the average speed of the car for the entire journey.

**62.** If $x = -1$ and $y = 2$, what is the value of the expression $2x^3 - 3xy$?

CONTINUE ON TO THE NEXT PAGE ➡

**MULTIPLE CHOICE PROBLEMS (Questions 63-114)**

**63.** Find the next term in the series:
0, 1, 1, 2, 4, 7, 13, 24...

**E.** 28
**F.** 37
**G.** 44
**H.** 48

---

**64.** Which is true about *A* and *B*?

$A = \sqrt{65} - 9$
$B = \sqrt{50} - 8$

**A.** $A = B$
**B.** $A > B$
**C.** $A > 1$
**D.** $B > A$

---

**65.** Which is a solution of the following equation?

$$\frac{(x^2 + x - 6)}{(x - 2)} = 0$$

**E.** −2
**F.** −3
**G.** 0
**H.** 2

**66.** John is stacking boxes directly upon each other. He stacks at 1 box per minute initially and every minute after that, his stacking rate increases by 1 box per minute. If each box is 5 inches tall, in how many minutes will the stack be 30 inches tall.

**A.** 2 min
**B.** 3 min
**C.** 5 min
**D.** 6 min

---

**67.** A Dilob has a mass of 20.2 milligrams. What is the Dilob's mass in grams?

**E.** 0.0202 g
**F.** 0.202 g
**G.** 2.02 g
**H.** 20.2 g

---

**68.** Jesse goes to the store. He buys a magazine for \$8. Then he sells it for \$10 and buys it back again for \$11. He finally sells it for \$12. What was his profit?

**A.** −\$1
**B.** \$0
**C.** \$2
**D.** \$3

**CONTINUE ON TO THE NEXT PAGE ➡**

**69.** If $f(\gamma) = 2f(\delta)$ and $\gamma = 2\delta$, what is a possible function for $f$?

**E.** $x$
**F.** $x^2$
**G.** $2x^2$
**H.** $\sqrt{x}$

---

**70.** A substance's length doubles every hour. At 2PM it was 3 meters. What was the length at 11AM that same day?

**A.** 0.375 meters
**B.** 0.5 meters
**C.** 0.75 meters
**D.** 1 meter

---

**71.** Which is true of these three functions?

$f = x^{x^4}$
$g = (x^x)^4$
$h = x^{4^x}$

**E.** $f = g$
**F.** $h = g$
**G.** $f = g + h$
**H.** $f \neq g$

---

**72.** Linda scored a 66, 82, 81, and 92 on her English exams. What score must Linda obtain on the next english test to have an average of exactly 84?

**A.** 84
**B.** 87
**C.** 95
**D.** 99

---

**73.** If today is Saturday, what day of the week will it be in 365 days from now?

**E.** Tuesday
**F.** Thursday
**G.** Friday
**H.** Sunday

---

**74.** What is the remainder of **7,700,000,000,202** divided by **9?**

**A.** 0
**B.** 1
**C.** 2
**D.** 3

---

**75.**

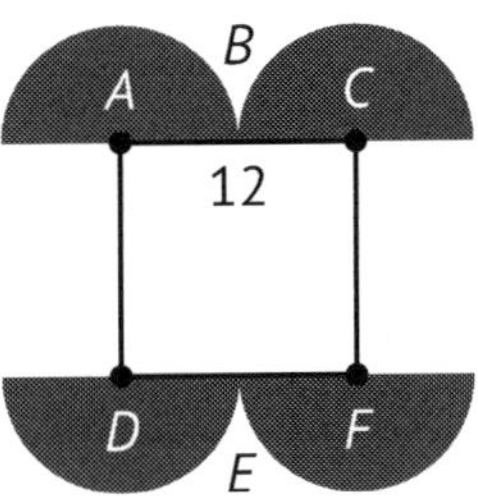


In the figure above $\overline{AB} = \overline{BC} = \overline{DE} = \overline{EF}$ and the side of the square is 12. Points $B$ and $E$ are the midpoints of the square. Find the area of the shaded region.

**E.** $12\pi$
**F.** $24\pi$
**G.** $36\pi$
**H.** $72\pi$

**CONTINUE ON TO THE NEXT PAGE ➞**

**76.** $8^{x+3} = 64^{3x}$, what is the value of $x$?

**A.** $\frac{1}{2}$

**B.** $\frac{3}{5}$

**C.** $\frac{5}{3}$

**D.** 2

---

**77.** If $A \blacktriangleright\blacktriangleleft B = AB(\frac{A}{B}) - 2^3$

then what is the value of $3 \blacktriangleright\blacktriangleleft 2$?

**E.** 1

**F.** $13\frac{3}{7}$

**G.** $14\frac{3}{7}$

**H.** $13\frac{7}{4}$

---

**78.** If the average of 11 numbers is 15, then what is the sum of these 11 numbers?

**A.** 26
**B.** 121
**C.** 165
**D.** 225

**79.** What is the average of
$(9b - 7) + (7 - 3b) - (-3 - 3b) + (6 + 3b)$

**E.** $3b + \frac{9}{4}$

**F.** $\frac{9}{4}b + 3$

**G.** $3b + 2$

**H.** $2b + 3$

---

**80.** $\frac{y^{-1} \bullet y^3 \bullet y^4 \bullet y^5 \bullet y^6}{y^6 \bullet y^5 \bullet y^4}$

**A.** $y^{-4}$
**B.** $y^{-2}$
**C.** 1
**D.** $y^2$

---

**81.** If the pattern continues, what will be the 50th symbol?

★ ♥ → ← ∗ ↑ ★ ♥ → ← ...

**E.** ←
**F.** ∗
**G.** ★
**H.** ♥

CONTINUE ON TO THE NEXT PAGE ➡

**82.** A trapezoid has base lengths in the ratio of 2:6. If the area of a trapezoid is 260 and the altitude is 5, then what is the length of the longer base?

**A.** 20
**B.** 26
**C.** 65
**D.** 78

---

**83.** $\frac{4}{9}$ is the square root of what number?

**E.** $\frac{1}{2}$

**F.** $\frac{2}{3}$

**G.** $\frac{8}{18}$

**H.** $\frac{16}{81}$

---

**84.** In the following system of equations,
$3x + 7y = 24$
$9x + 4y = 21$

What is $(x, y)$?

**A.** (1, 1)
**B.** (1, 3)
**C.** (3, 1)
**D.** (2, 4)

---

**85.** If [trapezoid: $a$ $b$ / $c$ $d$] means $\sqrt{abcd}$, then what is the value of [trapezoid: 1 12 / 3 4] ?

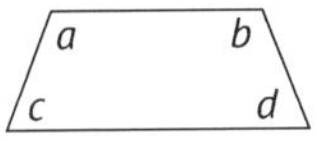

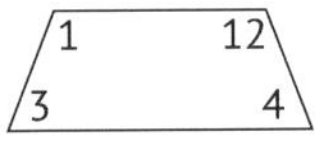

**E.** 3
**F.** $\sqrt{12}$
**G.** $\sqrt{24}$
**H.** 12

---

**86.** Which of the following is bigger, the first or the second? Assume $X$ does not equal $Y$.

First: $\frac{X}{X - Y}$ Second: $\frac{Y}{Y - X}$

**A.** They are equal
**B.** First
**C.** Second
**D.** Not enough information

**CONTINUE ON TO THE NEXT PAGE ➞**

**87.**

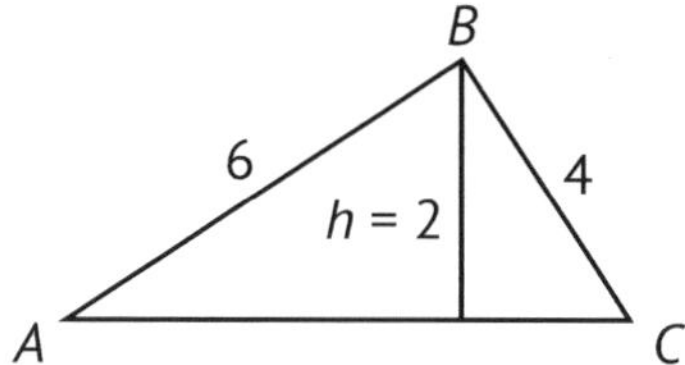


Figure not drawn to scale

In the figure above, triangle *ABC* has an area of 20 square inches, where the height is 2 inches. If a square has the same perimeter as the triangle above, then what is the area of the square?

**E.** 56 sq.in
**F.** 56.15 sq.in
**G.** 56.25 sq.in
**H.** 56.50 sq.in

---

**88.** The following table shows the class test average score in MsJones' Biology class over the years she has been teaching for. What is the median class test score for the years shown?

Average Test Score in Ms. Jones' Biology Class

| Year | 2007 | 2008 | 2009 | 2010 | 2011 | 2012 | 2013 | 2014 | 2015 |
|---|---|---|---|---|---|---|---|---|---|
| Avg. Test Score | 74 | 83 | 74 | 71 | 92 | 84 | 69 | 89 | 91 |

**A.** 74
**B.** 83
**C.** 84
**D.** 89

**89.** The wheels of a car have a diameter of 10 meters. If the speed of the car is 50 meters per hour, how many revolutions does one wheel make in **one hour?**

**E.** 5

**F.** $\frac{50}{\pi}$

**G.** 10

**H.** $\frac{5}{\pi}$

---

**90.** A circle is inscribed in a square. What is the probability that a penny, if thrown, will fall in the shaded region below?

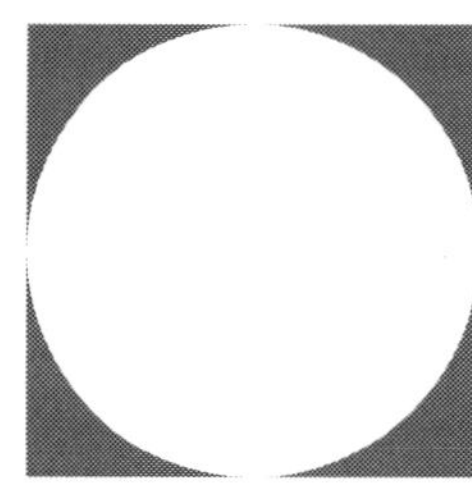

**A.** 1

**B.** $\pi - 2$

**C.** $1 - \frac{\pi}{4}$

**D.** $(\frac{\pi}{2})$

CONTINUE ON TO THE NEXT PAGE ➡

**91.** What is: $\frac{(10\%) \cdot (10\%)}{100\%}$?

**E.** 1%
**F.** 10%
**G.** .001
**H.** 1

---

**92.** The greatest integer function of *x*, gives the largest integer that is less than *x* and is represented by: $\lfloor x \rfloor$, what is $\lfloor 10\% \rfloor + 1$?

**A.** 1
**B.** 1.1
**C.** 11
**D.** 11%

---

**93.** Sara is stuck in a circular field. She knows that the area of the circular field is 100 square meters. She walks at a speed of 10 meters per minute. How long will it take her to walk from one end of the circular field to the other end assuming she must cross through the center.

**E.** $\sqrt{\frac{100}{\pi}}$
**F.** $2\sqrt{\frac{100}{\pi}}$
**G.** $10\sqrt{\frac{100}{\pi}}$
**H.** $0.2\sqrt{\frac{100}{\pi}}$

**94.** The Fibonacci Sequence involves taking two previous numbers and adding them together to get the next. If the first two Fibonacci numbers are 0 and 1, what is the mean of the first 5 Fibonnaci numbers?

**A.** $\frac{5}{6}$
**B.** $\frac{7}{6}$
**C.** $\frac{7}{5}$
**D.** 1

---

**95.** If
1 slack = $x$ vaks
9 vaks = 12 hips,

How many slacks are in 24 hips?

**E.** 2
**F.** $\frac{9}{x}$
**G.** $\frac{18}{x}$
**H.** $\frac{x}{9}$

---

**96.** What is the value of $\frac{11^2}{10^2}$?

**A.** 12.1
**B.** 121
**C.** .121
**D.** 1.21

CONTINUE ON TO THE NEXT PAGE ➡

**97.** If $(a\check{}b) = a + b - b^2$, then what is the value of this expression when $a = 5$ and $b = 2$?

**E.** 2
**F.** 3
**G.** 4
**H.** 5

---

**98.** How many nonpositive integers are **between** −3 and 5, inclusive?

**A.** 1
**B.** 3
**C.** 4
**D.** 6

---

**99.** A number is squared and added to its reciprocal. If that number is represented by $x$, what is the expression?

**E.** $x^2 + 1$

**F.** $x^2 + \frac{1}{x}$

**G.** $x^2 + \frac{1}{x^2}$

**H.** $\frac{x^4 + 1}{x^2}$

**100.** If I increase the size of a ball by 50% two times in a row, what is the percent increase assuming that the initial size of the ball was 20.

**A.** 25%
**B.** 50%
**C.** 75%
**D.** 125%

---

**101.**

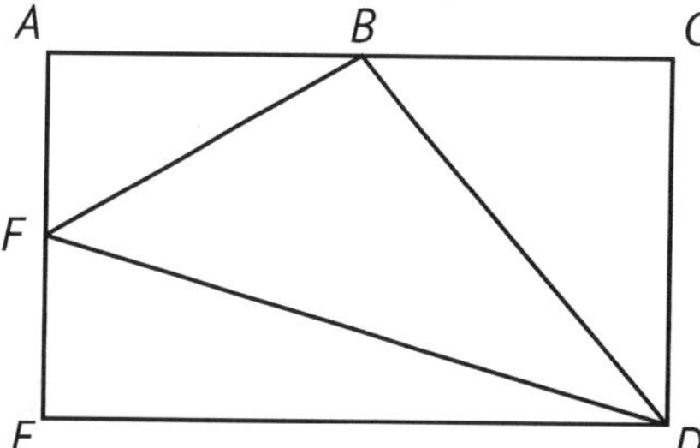


In the figure above, the rectangle *ACDE* has an area of 440 square meters. The points *B* and Fare the midpoints of the sides *AC* and *AE* respectively. What is the area of the triangle, *BCD?*

**E.** 56
**F.** 110
**G.** 200
**H.** 220

CONTINUE ON TO THE NEXT PAGE ➡

**102.** The least common multiple of two numbers, $x$ and $y$ can be represented by:

*LCM*($x$, $y$). The following is true for the concept of the least common multiple:

If we can find integers, $a$ and $b$ for both $x$ and $y$ respectively such that $ax = by = LCM(x, y)$, then $ax$ or $by$ is the least common multiple of $x$ and $y$.

What is the least common multiple of $\sqrt{2} \cdot \pi$?

**A.** $2\pi\sqrt{2}$
**B.** $2\pi$
**C.** $2\pi^2$
**D.** Does not exist

---

**103.** For how many values of $x$ is the function not equal to 1?

$$f(x) = \frac{x-3}{x-3}$$

**E.** 0
**F.** 1
**G.** 2
**H.** 3

---

**104.** If today is Monday, what day will it be in $49^2$ from now?

**A.** Tuesday
**B.** Wednesday
**C.** Thursday
**D.** Monday

**105.** If $f(x) = x^3$, then how many times greater is $f(4)$ than $f(2)$?

**E.** 2
**F.** 3
**G.** 4
**H.** 8

---

**106.** Convert $\frac{3}{40}$ to a decimal.

**A.** 0.0075
**B.** 0.075
**C.** 0.06
**D.** .75

---

**107.** How many prime numbers are between 4 and 16 inclusive?

**E.** 2
**F.** 3
**G.** 4
**H.** 5

---

**108.** How many perfect squares are between 9 and 25 exclusive?

**A.** 0
**B.** 1
**C.** 2
**D.** 3

**CONTINUE ON TO THE NEXT PAGE ➡**

**109.** An octagon, a triangle and a circle all have the same perimeter (circumference for the circle). Which is true of the areas of these shapes? ($O$ = area of octagon, $T$ = area of triangle, and $C$ = area of circle).

**E.** $O < C < T$
**F.** $O = T = C$
**G.** $C > T = C$
**H.** $C > O > T$

---

**110.** If $(\frac{x}{y}) = x^2$, then what is $(\frac{x}{y}) - (\frac{x}{y})^2$ ?

**A.** $x^2y$
**B.** $x^4$
**C.** $x^2(1 - x^2)$
**D.** $x^2(1 + x^2)$

---

**111.** In a scaled drawing, 1 millimeter represents 150 meters. How many square millimeters on the drawing represent 1 square meter?

**E.** $\frac{1}{150}$
**F.** $\frac{1}{22,500}$
**G.** $\frac{1150}{22,500}$
**H.** 22,500

**112.** A rectangle is drawn on a coordinate plane. If the coordinates of one corner of the rectangle is (0, −5) and the coordinates of the opposite corner is (7, 3), then what is the area of the rectangle?

**A.** −21
**B.** 21
**C.** 56
**D.** 105

---

**113.** Which one of the following is equivalent to the expression

$\frac{(xy)^3(z)^0}{x^3y^4}$, when $xyz \neq 0$?

**E.** $xyz$
**F.** $xz$
**G.** $\frac{1}{y}$
**H.** 1

---

**114.** How many distinct prime factors does 2,520 have?

**A.** 3
**B.** 4
**C.** 7
**D.** 48

**THIS IS THE END OF THE TEST. IF THERE IS TIME REMAINING, YOU MAY CHECK YOUR ANSWERS TO**

**CONTINUE ON TO THE NEXT PAGE ➡**

# SHSAT PRACTICE TEST 5
## ANSWER KEY

### PART 1 (ENGLISH LANGUAGE ARTS)

**Revising/Editing**

1. **A**
2. **F**
3. **A**
4. **H**
5. **C**
6. **G**
7. **B**
8. **E**
9. **D**
10. **F**
11. **C**

**Reading Comprehension**

12. **F**
13. **A**
14. **G**
15. **C**
16. **E**
17. **D**
18. **F**
19. **B**
20. **H**
21. **D**
22. **E**
23. **C**
24. **H**
25. **B**
26. **H**
27. **C**
28. **H**
29. **A**
30. **F**
31. **D**
32. **E**
33. **C**
34. **E**
35. **C**
36. **F**
37. **D**
38. **F**
39. **C**
40. **E**
41. **D**
42. **F**
43. **D**
44. **F**
45. **A**
46. **F**
47. **C**
48. **G**
49. **A**
50. **F**
51. **D**
52. **E**
53. **B**
54. **H**
55. **C**
56. **E**
57. **C**

### PART 2 (MATHEMATICS)

**Math**

58. **-14**
59. **-4**
60. **30**
61. **59**
62. **4**
63. **G**
64. **D**
65. **F**
66. **B**
67. **E**
68. **D**
69. **E**
70. **A**
71. **H**
72. **D**
73. **H**
74. **A**
75. **H**
76. **B**
77. **E**
78. **C**
79. **E**
80. **D**
81. **H**
82. **D**
83. **H**
84. **B**
85. **H**
86. **D**
87. **G**
88. **B**
89. **H**
90. **C**
91. **E**
92. **A**
93. **H**
94. **C**
95. **G**
96. **D**
97. **F**
98. **C**
99. **F**
100. **D**
101. **F**
102. **D**
103. **F**
104. **D**
105. **H**
106. **B**
107. **G**
108. **B**
109. **H**
110. **C**
111. **F**
112. **C**
113. **G**
114. **B**

You can find detailed video explanations to each problem in the book by visiting:
**ArgoPrep.com/SHSAT**

# Practice Test 5 (Answers and Explanations)

**1. A** Answer A is the best choice because a colon is the correct punctuation mark to introduce a list. Answer B is incorrect because, by placing the steps in parentheses, the author downplays the importance of that information, making it seem almost unnecessary when it is actually the main idea of the sentence. Answer choice C is incorrect because it adds the unnecessary, wordy phrase "...and those steps are..." Answer choice D is incorrect because it uses a semicolon to introduce the list, which is the job of the colon.

**2. F** Answer F would make the best topic sentence because it clearly states the overarching topic that Sentences 1 through 4 are all about. Answer E is a true statement of fact that is related to paragraph, but it is not specific enough to be the best topic sentence. Answer G is similarly a related fact, but not a clear statement of the main idea of Sentences 1 through 4. Answer H is not a strong topic sentence because it is a statement of opinion (as it could be reasonably disagreed with). Since the rest of the paragraph is clearly explanatory, rather than argumentative, it should have a topic sentence that is a clear statement of fact.

**3. A** Answer A is correct because Sentence 2 contains the subject-verb agreement error "...amateur paddlers and collegiate competitors rows side by side." Since "paddlers and... competitors" is a plural subject, the plural verb "row" is required. Answers B, C, and D are all incorrect because "Regatta has attracted," "Competitors are grouped," and "rowers participate" all make correct use of subject-verb agreement.

**4. H** Answer H combines the sentences in a way that clarifies the logical relationship between the two, making it the correct answer. By using the comma and the word "although," Answer H connects the two sentences in a grammatically correct way that shows the relationship between the two sentences better than the original passage. Answer E is incorrect because it simply combines the two sentences using the conjunction "and," doing little to enhance the complementary relationship of the two ideas. Answer F is incorrect because it uses the word "even" in a repetitive manner and fails to insert a comma before "even" to ease flow for the reader. Answer G is also incorrect because it simply combines the two sentences using a semicolon, which does not demonstrate the connection between the two ideas as well as the "although" in Answer H.

**5. C** This paragraph is consistently written in the present tense, so Answer C is correct because it contains the past tense phrase "Americans never lost sight..." The addition of the modifier "Americans have never lost sight..." would bring the sentence into the present tense to make it consistent with the rest of the paragraph. Answers A, B, and D are all incorrect because they contain only present tense verbs.

**6. G** Passive voice occurs when the subject of a sentence is having action done to them rather than being the actor of the verb. Sentence 2 contains the passive voice construction "black southerners were still discriminated against." Answer G is correct because it restructures the sentence to make "White southerners" the new subject of an active voice construction ("White southerners continued to discriminate..."). Answers E, F, and H are all incorrect because they all fail to identify and correct the passive voice construction "...were discriminated against..."

**7.** **B** The first two paragraphs of this passage are consistently written using past tense verbs, which is appropriate since historical information is the theme. Answer B is correct because it makes the tense of Sentence 3's verb consistent with the rest of the paragraph and clarifies the timeline of events for the reader. Answer A is incorrect because "these" is a plural pronoun, which would disagree in number with its object "treatment." Answer C is incorrect because "throughout" is a more specific, descriptive preposition than "in." By using "throughout," the author communicates that this was a wide-ranging, systematic problem rather than something that happened in a few places. Answer D is also incorrect because when speaking of the American South, particularly as it relates to issues of the Civil War and segregation, "the South" is treated as a proper noun and should therefore be capitalized.

**8.** **E** Answer E is the best combination of Sentences 4 and 5 because it combines all of their main ideas in a grammatically correct way while also significantly reducing wordiness. Answers F and H are both incorrect because, although they include the main ideas of both sentences, they are essentially jumbles of comma-separated clauses, which could easily confuse the reader. Answer G is also incorrect because it uses the unnecessarily wordy statement "...and that system was known as," which hurts the flow of the sentences and paragraph.

**9.** **D** Answer D is correct because the content of Sentence 7 (that black schools were subject to worse conditions) is directly contrary to the ideas laid out in Sentence 6 (that schools should be "separate but equal"). The transition "However" is used to indicate unexpected or contrary information, making it the perfect fit for Sentence 7. Answers A and B are both incorrect because "Therefore" and "Consequently" both suggest that the content of Sentence 7 is the logical conclusion of Sentence 6, which it is not. Answer C is also incorrect because the author is not presenting information in Sentence 6 that supports Sentence 7.

**10.** **F** Answer F is the best choice because it provides concrete examples that support the claim made in Sentence 7. By providing evidence, an author can strengthen their point and clarify ideas to the reader. Answer E is incorrect because it doesn't match the tone of the rest of the passage (as the author speaks directly to the reader). Answer G is provides a valuable detail that would fit in the overall passage, but it is not the best choice to provide direct support to Sentence 7 because it doesn't provide any examples or directly elaborate on the conditions laid out in Sentence 7. Answer H is also incorrect because, while it is a true statement that could have a place in this passage, it does not directly support Sentence 7.

**11.** **C** Answer C is the best conclusion sentence because it continues to develop the ideas that came before it (that conditions were clearly unequal in the different schools) while also calling back to the topic sentence (by referencing the "separate but equal" doctrine). Wrapping up ideas and reminding the reader of the paragraph's purpose are the two main roles of a conclusion sentence, so Answer C is an excellent choice. Answers A and D are both incorrect because they abruptly transition into talking about solutions rather than concisely summarizing the problem that had been laid out in the paragraph (as Answer C does). Answer B is also incorrect because, while it is an interesting and relevant fact, it does not serve any of the purposes of a conclusion (summarizing, transitioning, signposting for the reader, etc.).

**12. F** Answer F is the best choice because there are numerous references throughout the passage to the two characters being big game hunters as well as mentions that they are going to hunt upon arriving at their destination. Whitney clearly states, "We should have some good hunting up the Amazon." Answer E is incorrect because, while they are interested in the mysterious island, there is nothing in the text to suggest that they are professional explorers or on some mission to locate the island – it is simply a topic of conversation. Answer G is incorrect because there are no actual jaguars in the scene, and the jaguar is only mentioned as an example of an animal that is hunted and that they hope to hunt in the future. Answer H is incorrect because Whitney and Rainsford refer to the crew of the ship as "they," which clearly communicates that they are not formally members of the crew themselves.

**13. A** Answer A is the best choice because Connell frequently describes the air at key moments in the passage. In the passage's opening lines, the two characters discuss the denseness of the air and the way it affects their ability to see. At the end of the passage, Captain Nielson also suggests that the quality of the air suggests that something evil or mysterious is about to happen. Answer B is incorrect because the old sea charts are never described in any depth, only mentioned briefly. Answer C is incorrect because, while the heat is mentioned several times in the passage, it isn't directly associated with the mysterious qualities of the island the way that the dense, thick air is, making Answer A a better choice. Answer D is incorrect because the author never describes the shape, size, or qualities of the boat in any specific way in the passage.

**14. G** Answer G is the best choice as it represents a correct interpretation of Rainsford's point. Whitney suggests that even Rainsford's trained eye cannot see 4 miles in the dark and dense air of the Caribbean night. Rainsford agrees and reinforces that it's far harder to see than even Whitney is appreciating by effectively saying "I can't even see 4 yards tonight, let alone 4 miles!" Answer E is incorrect because the island is supposed to be much further off than four yards; Rainsford just uses four yards as an example of a short distance. Answer F is incorrect because the author never describes the length of the boat specifically. Answer H is incorrect because Rainsford is established as having a very good eye under regular conditions; he just can't see four yards in these incredibly challenging conditions, making Answer G the best choice.

**15. C** Answer C is the best choice because, in the context of the conversation, Rainsford is telling Whitney, "Don't be ridiculous!" when he says "Don't talk rot." His following remarks ("Bah!" and "Nonsense!") should have been major indicators to the reader. Answer A is incorrect because there is no description of anything physically rotting or decomposing in the passage. Answer B is incorrect because Rainsford thinks Whitney is being silly, not gross or disgusting. He isn't disgusted by Whitney's ideas, he just thinks they're stupid. Answer D is incorrect and probably represents the reader mis-associating "rot" with the homophone "wrought," which means "made by hand."

**16. E** Answer E is the best choice because Rainsford's lack of sympathy for hunted animals and dismissal of superstitions about the island show that he has little regard for the thoughts and feelings of others, whereas Whitney's appreciation of the perspectives of both the animals and the crew show him to be more of a thinker. Answer F is incorrect because it completely inverts the two characters' qualities as they are presented in the text. Answer G is incorrect because Whitney is never portrayed as cowardly – he is still an accomplished hunter after all – but rather as careful and thoughtful, making Answer E a better choice. Similarly, Answer H is incorrect because Rainsford is certainly never portrayed as meek or cowardly. On the other hand, he seems like someone who has a "take charge and take action" approach, making Answer E the best choice.

**17. D** Answer D is the best choice because Whitney describes Nielson as a "tough-minded old Swede" and suggests that anything that legitimately concerns the captain should be of major concern for he and Rainsford. Answer A is incorrect because Whitney describes respect for the captain's toughness and chalks up her words to caution rather than cowardice. Answer B is incorrect because Captain Nielson is presented as having told Whitney some important information, so there's nothing secretive about his character. Answer C is incorrect as well because Nielson's words clearly show respect for Captain Nielson, so he would not attribute negative qualities to him such as "self-importance." If anything, he suggests that the captain is cautious on behalf of the whole crew, which speaks to his toughness, bravery, and sense of responsibility, not his cowardice.

**18. F** Answer F is the best choice because it identifies the passage's frequent mentions of hunting and hunters as the source of the title. Answer E is incorrect because they are never mentioned as playing any game during the scene. If anything, they are simply described as standing on the deck of a ship, looking out into the darkness. Answer G is incorrect because there is no suggestion anywhere in the passage that anybody is being conned, manipulated, or intentionally misled. Answer H is incorrect because the concept of "being game" for something is relatively new, and the word was not used in that way when this text was written. The "Game" in the title clearly refers to game animals (animals that are hunted), since the characters have an extended conversation about the morality of hunting.

**19. B** Answer B is the best choice because the text provides several reference points to animals and geographical features that communicate the setting to be located near South America. The two travelers say they are headed to Rio (which is in Brazil) and that they hope to travel up the Amazon River, which is the largest River in South America, to hunt jaguars, which are indigenous to South America. Additionally, the text refers to the "Caribbean night," which suggests their boat is located near the Caribbean Sea, which is to the immediate north of the South American continent. Answer A is incorrect because the characters clearly describe weather, animals, and geographic reference points that are located in South America. The only European country specifically mentioned in

the passage is Sweden, and it is only mentioned as the origin point of Captain Nielson. Answer C is incorrect because all of the reference points in the passage are features of South America, not North America. There are no Jaguars in North America, and both the Amazon and Brazil are clearly located in South America. Answer D is similarly incorrect because there are no reference points to any geographic or cultural features of Asia or Asian countries in the passage.

**20. H** Answer H is the best choice because Whitney immediately dismisses the idea that cannibals live on the island, saying, "Even cannibals wouldn't live in such a God-forsaken place." All the other answer choices represent concerns Whitney expresses in the passage. Answer E is incorrect because Whitney mentions the "curious dread" the sailors have about the island at the very beginning of the passage and also mentions its "suggestive name" of Ship-Trap Island, displaying that he appreciates their concern. Answer F is incorrect because Whitney characterizes Nielson as a "tough old Swede" and admits that he did feel a chill in the air when Captain Nielson told him the place was evil. Answer G is incorrect because the argument between Whitney and Rainsford in the middle of the passage clearly displays that Whitney has some misgivings about stirring up "the fear of pain and the fear of death" in animals.

---

**Passage 2 ("Long ago, when you were a little boy..."):**

**21. D** Answer D is the best choice because, throughout the text, the author vehemently disagrees that childhood is the best part of life and resents the assertion by adults that it is. Lines 34-36 articulate this point clearly by saying, "I for one lift up my voice emphatically against the assertion, and do affirm that I think childhood is the most undesirable portion of human life." Paragraph 1 introduces the idea that adults overrate and over-sentimentalize childhood, Paragraph 2 explains that the author disagrees, and Paragraph 4 contains a fleshing out of the author's point featuring several examples as evidence. Answer A is incorrect because it represents the exact opposite of the author's point of view. Answer B is incorrect because being told what to do is only one of the many problems the author identifies with childhood. Answer C is also incorrect because, while the author would probably agree that adults who romanticize childhood are fools, the main argument of the passage is about the nature of childhood, not the foolishness of adults.

**22. E** Answer E is correct because, throughout the passage, the author addresses the idea that childhood is the happiest time in life as if it is a commonly held belief. By associating this idea with "Commonplacedom" (Line 17), the author establishes that he or she believes the romanticism of childhood is very commonplace. Answer F is incorrect because the author makes this point explicitly in Lines 19-58 rather than implying anything. Answers G and H are both incorrect because the author does not use absolutes like "always" or "never" in the passage, and never makes the claim that nobody has a happy childhood.

**23. C** Answer C is correct because in Lines 35-37, the author clearly states, "I think childhood is the most undesirable portion of human life, and I am thankful to be well out of it." These words clearly display that the author prefers her adult life to her childhood. Answer A is incorrect because, while the author identifies clothing as a realm in which children have minimal freedom (Lines 45-55), she never says outright that she was never allowed to pick her own clothes. Similarly, Answer B is incorrect because the author never explicitly states that she herself was not allowed to leave the house. Answer D cannot be correct because the author clearly states in Lines 35-37 that she prefers her adulthood over childhood.

**24. H** Answer H is the best choice because Lines 40-58 all provide examples of ways in which children are not in control of the major decisions surrounding their lives. Answer E cannot be correct because schools are never mentioned in the passage. Answer F is incorrect as well because the passage never makes any reference to adults having the freedom to play. Answer G cannot be correct because the passage suggests that children are powerless and adults are the ones who do the bossing around, while Answer G asserts the exact opposite.

**25. B** Answer B is the best choice because in Lines 48-55, the author describes to the "six-foot friend" that children often have choices made for them, even in situations that don't really matter, such as how to dress. The author asks the adult to "imagine... how you would feel, to be obliged to wear your woolen mittens when you desire to bloom out in straw-colored kids, or to be buttoned in your black waistcoat when your taste leads you to select your white... yet this is what children are perpetually called to undergo." Answer A is incorrect because the author does not make any judgement about the fashionableness of mittens in the passage. Answer C is incorrect because the author asserts throughout the passage that children everywhere are treated this way, and uses other examples besides just warm gloves (such as being forced to wear the black waistcoat over a white one). Answer D cannot be correct because the author is not suggesting their friend wear mittens; rather, she suggests "Imagine if you were forced to wear mittens."

**26. H** Answer H is the best choice because if people prefer not to make decisions, then being told what to do would actually make them very happy. Answer E is not the best answer because, the author would probably argue, that making "some" decisions is not enough. Answer F is not the best answer because, while true, the fact that adults don't have total freedom doesn't forgive putting overly stringent limits on the freedom of children. Answer G is not the best answer either because the fact that decision-making is hard does not mean that people would prefer to have all their decisions made for them.

**Passage 3 ("If you asked a group of people which verb they would use"):**

**27. C** Answer C is correct because it provides the best summary of the main ideas of the passage. The reader could easily infer this by reading the first (introduction) paragraph and the final sentence of the final (conclusion) paragraph. Answers A and B are incorrect because they both assume that the writer is arguing that one style is superior to the other, which is untrue. The passage compares the two, but it does not make judgments about their value. Answer D is also incorrect, although it is a true statement. While Answer D correctly identifies the subjects of the passage (cooking and baking), it fails to identify what the passage is saying about them (that they are surprisingly different).

**28. H** Answer H is correct because it is nearest to the dictionary definition of "smorgasbord," which is: "a buffet offering a variety of hot and cold meats, salads, hors d'oeuvres, etc," or, "a wide range of something; a variety." Readers could easily determine that Answer H is correct based on the words "variety," "combinations," and "infinite" appearing in the same sentence. Answers E through G are all incorrect. There is no textual basis for Answer G. Answers E and F suggest a partial, but incomplete, understanding of the sentence.

**29. A** The ability of chefs to adjust and make changes on the fly is emphasized in the second and fourth paragraphs, making Answer A correct. Like artists, chefs can tweak their food as it cooks - unlike bakers, who are constrained within their recipes and must patiently wait while their goods bake in the oven. Answer B is a reasonable conclusion, but not the best answer as supported by the passage. Answer C demonstrates that the reader is trying to connect the answer to the passage (as "Food is a daily necessity" closely mirrors the beginning of paragraph 2). However, Answer C is still incorrect because preventing people from starving is not considered one of the artistic aspects of food. The first half of Answer D ("Cooks have different individual styles and passions") is the beginning of a good answers, but the second half ("baking is the same all around the world") is an untrue and oversimplified statement. Although it accesses one of the passage's key ideas, Answer D is not the best answer.

**30. F** Paragraphs 3 and 4 emphasize the precise and repeatable nature of baking, making Answer F correct. Answer E is incorrect, but it does show the reader trying to connect the answer to the text, as the phrase "very simple, basic elements" mirrors the content of the final sentence of Paragraph 4. Answer G is incorrect and has no basis in the passage because glassware is never mentioned. Answer H is incorrect because needing to master the taste, texture, and appearance of food is not exclusive to bakers, and therefore, cannot be the reason why baking is more scientific than cooking.

**31. D** Answer D is the best answer because Paragraph 3 emphasizes that creating dough is one of the hardest (and most scientific) processes that bakers must master. Given what the reader has been told about chefs (that they enjoy flexibility and making adjustments), the regimented approach required to make dough is most likely to be difficult for a chef. Answers A and B are incorrect with no textual basis. Answer C is incorrect because, due to their need to master a variety of ingredients and flavors, chefs might actually be good at selecting herbs for a bread.

**32. E** Answer E is the best answer because it combines the idea of making food for the world (one of the main ideas of the final paragraph) with ideas that relate to culture (home, family, and tradition). Answer F is incorrect and most likely suggests the reader misinterprets the use of the word "caretaker." Answer G is not the best answer because it could be reasonably disagreed with, and many chefs and bakers might not agree that their ethnic, regional, and cultural heritage are the most important parts of their identities. Answer H is incorrect because, while it hits on the main idea of the last paragraph, it does not address the actual elements of culture (home, family, and traditions) in the way that Answer E does.

**Passage 4 ("Golf is popular around the world..."):**

**33. C** Answer C is the best answer because this passage provides a general explanation of the rules of golf, the procedure of playing, and the challenges most often faced by players. Answer A is incorrect because the author never directly addresses other sports and only talks about golf on its own merits. Answer B is incorrect because, while the passage clearly has a favorable view of golf, it does not actively attempt to persuade anybody in include any calls to action. Answer D is also incorrect because the passage does not contain any distinct narrative or story, as it is purely explanatory.

**34. E** Answer E is correct because the passage repeatedly emphasizes that golf is a game of mental strategizing and planning, which are internalized activities that can't be appreciated through a television. Answer F is incorrect because, as Paragraph 2 demonstrates, the fundamental rules of golf are fairly straightforward. Answer G is incorrect because the passage mentions twice that golf is accessible to people of all ages and body types, contradicting this assumption. Answer H, while somewhat factual, is not the best answer because, as the passage details, fast-paced "action" is not the most important or intriguing part of golf.

**35. C** Paragraph 3 explains that irons "are numbered in ascending order from one to nine, with higher numbers counter intuitively representing shorter potential distances." Using either knowledge of the term "counter intuitively" or by using context clues such as "shorter potential outcomes," readers can can determine that smaller numbered irons actually hit the ball farther, making Answer C correct. Answers A, B, and D are all incorrect because the two iron, the club represented by the lowest number, has the potential to hit the ball the longest distance.

**36. F** The final sentence of Paragraph 2 clearly establishes that "the player with the lowest score wins the game." Since 79 is the lowest of the available numbers, Answer F is correct. Answers E, G, and H are all incorrect because none of those numbers represent the lowest (winning) score.

**37. D** Based on Paragraph 5, hitting a ball into the water adds one stroke to a player's score, as does grounding a club in a sand trap. Answer D is the correct choice because it is the only scenario that portrays Dennis racking up two penalty strokes. Each time he grounds his club in the sand trap accounts for one additional stroke, giving him a score of +2. Answer A is incorrect because it shows Dennis incurring only one penalty stroke (for hitting the ball into the water). Answer B actually shows Dennis committing no penalty strokes because he avoided grounding his club in the sand trap. Answer C shows Dennis receiving only one penalty stroke (for hitting his ball into the water) because he did not ground his club either time he was in a sand trap.

**38. F** Answer F is correct because the passage repeatedly emphasizes the individualistic, internalized nature of golf. Answer F is closely aligned with the passage because it demonstrates the "dark side" of the main point of Paragraphs 3-5. Answer E is incorrect and has no textual basis because the passage never mentions cost or expense in any way and, if anything, works to dispel the stereotype that golf is a rich person's game in Paragraph 1. Similarly, Answer G has no textual basis because, if anything, the passage stresses golf as a casual game that is often played with no stakes at all. Answer H is incorrect because the scoring of the game is described and demonstrated as being simple in the passage itself.

**Passage 5 ("Lines Written in Early Spring"):**

**39.** **C** Answer C is the best choice because Wordsworth ends the poem by repeating "What man has made of man?" a line which appeared previously in Line 8. Clearly, this repetition at the end of the poem is intended to draw attention to the previous idea as the main point of the piece. The line effectively draws direct contrast between the harmony and happiness of nature and the drudgery of human life, which Wordsworth describes and suggest throughout the rest of the poem. Answers A, B, and C are all incorrect, although metaphor, simile, and personification are all used in the poem, because it is the repeated line that Wordsworth uses to tie things together at the end and remind the reader of the point he is making.

**40.** **E** Answer E is the best choice because Wordsworth establishes in Line 2 that the speaker is "reclined" in a "grove," which is a very relaxing environment that would promote imaginative thinking and reflection. His descriptions of the joy and beauty of nature (Lines 9-20) show that he is reflecting upon the world he sees around him, and his repeated line "What man has made of man" displays that he is extending his thinking from beyond what he sees around him and is contrasting it with the life of humans. All of this clearly shows reflective thinking. Answer F is incorrect because, although the speaker is making a point that many people may disagree with, he does not present it in an overly forceful or offensive "in your face" manner; on the contrary, he makes his point in a very peaceful, reflective manner, making Answer E the better choice. Answer G is incorrect because the speaker clearly has some reservations about human life and is not entirely positive on the outlook of humanity. He says he "laments" man's condition and wonders "What man has made of man?" both of which are far from uplifting. Answer H is incorrect because, while the poem is deeply descriptive, "descriptive" is not necessarily a tone (as it is not an attitude or flavor, so speak), and Answer E is still a better, more specific answer because it actually analyzes what effect the descriptions create.

**41.** **D** Answer D is the best choice because the rest of the poem describes the beauty and harmony of nature in great detail. "[H]er fair works" essentially means "Nature's beautiful qualities" in the context of the passage. Answer A is incorrect because the speaker is not describing nature as "fair" in the sense of legal equity but rather as beautiful. Answer B is similarly incorrect because the speaker is not discussing our modern concept of "fairness," but rather beauty. Answer C is incorrect as well because he is not describing something fair like "fair skin," but rather describing all of nature as "fair," meaning beautiful. Given the incredible detail in which Wordsworth describes the beauty and harmony of nature, Answer D is clearly the best choice.

**42. F** Answer F is the best choice because it reflects an understanding of both Wordsworth's point about nature and his point about the human condition. The happiness and carefree quality of nature is described in Lines 11-20. The speaker describes that "every flower / Enjoys the air it breathes" (Lines 11-12), describes the birds as playing (Line 13), and states that growing plants feel "pleasure" (Line 20). The dissatisfaction of man is revealed in Lines 21-24 when Wordsworth writes, "If this belief from heaven be sent / If such be Nature's holy plan, / Have I not reason to lament / What man has made of man?" In these lines, Wordsworth is directly contrasting the human condition to the carefree and happy ways of nature. Answer E is incorrect because Wordsworth clearly believes that humanity is or should be capable of living in happiness like nature. In Lines 5-7, Wordsworth clearly communicates that the spirit of nature is linked to the human soul, which demonstrates that he believes man has chosen his life of cares. Answer G is incorrect because Wordsworth doesn't cite laziness as one of humanity's problems at any point but rather seems to think man cares *too much* about things. Answer H is incorrect because Wordsworth never says that humanity is inherently destructive and terrible, rather he laments "What man has made of man," essentially saying he believes that humanity can do better. Answer F is the only choice that correctly reflects the viewpoints in the poem.

**43. D** Answer D is the best choice because, throughout Lines 9-20, Wordsworth treats the plants and animals within nature as characters, giving them human or human-like qualities. In Stanza 3, Wordsworth personifies the flowers by imagining that they enjoy fresh air. In Stanza 4, Wordsworth personifies the birds by describing them like happy children playing. In Stanza 5, Wordsworth personifies growing plants as taking pleasure in reaching up and outward with their twigs and branches. Answers A and B are both incorrect because Wordsworth is treating the features of nature as characters, not directly comparing them to anything else, as an author does with a metaphor or simile. Answer C is incorrect as well because, while Wordsworth does use the word "pleasure" in both Stanza 4 and Stanza 5, he uses personification as the main feature or device throughout the body of the poem, making Answer D a better, more complete choice.

**44. F** Answer F is the best choice because, in the opening line of the final stanza, Wordsworth is essentially pointing backwards and drawing attention to the worldview that he lays out in Lines 9-20. He is essentially saying "If my theory that nature is joyous and humanity has chosen to be miserable is true, then I feel bad for all of us" in the final stanza. Answer E is incorrect because "this belief" isn't just a belief in the power of nature; it's a belief in the happiness and harmony of nature, as described in the body of the poem. Answer G is incorrect because, in spite of his love of nature and frustration with humanity, Wordsworth never specifically mentions the environmental impact of humanity upon nature in the poem. Answer H is incorrect because it refers back simply to Lines 17-20 without taking in the "big picture" of the entire poem. "This belief" expressed in Line 21 is the belief that nature is a happy, harmonious place, as laid out in the body of the poem.

**45. A** Answer A is the best choice because "grieve" and "lament" both mean to express sadness. The repeated line "What man has made of man" (Lines 8 & 24) should have been a major indicator to the reader, as the words "grieved" and "lament" are both used immediately before the phrase, suggesting that both verbs reflect how the speaker feels about the condition of man. Answer B is incorrect because the speaker is describing the growth of a flower in Line 10, not anything connected to his frustration with the condition of mankind. Answer C is incorrect because "measure" is used in the poem to mean "to figure something out." When the speaker says he cannot "measure" the thoughts of the birds, he means that he can't tell what they're thinking. Answer D is incorrect because a "thrill" is a positive feeling and therefore in direct opposition to the way the speaker feels about humanity, as expressed in Lines 21-24.

**46.** **F** Answer F is the best choice because in both Stanzas 2 and 6, the speaker connects nature to concepts associated with the divine, such as creation and heaven. In Stanza 2, the speaker says, "her fair works did nature link / The human soul that through me ran" (Lines 5-6). The phrase "her fair works" establish nature as a female creator. Since creating the world is generally associated with gods or divinity, this description immediately establishes nature as a goddess. In fact, the description of how the human soul is connected to nature suggests that nature may be the goddess who created mankind originally. In Stanza 6, the speaker refers to "Nature" (Line 22) with a capitalized first letter, much like many people in western cultures capitalize "God." The speaker also describes nature as having a "holy plan" and sending ideas from "heaven," both of which support the idea that nature is presented as or compared to a goddess in the poem. Answer E is incorrect because the speaker contrasts nature and humanity, accentuating the differences rather than comparing them and accentuating the similarities in the poem. Answer G is incorrect because the speaker describes the birds and flowers in Stanzas 3-5, not the stanzas the question points toward. Answer H is incorrect because the speaker laments the condition of man, not the condition of nature in the poem. Nature is presented as a benevolent and beautiful goddess, making Answer F the best choice.

**47.** **C** Answer C is the best choice because, even though the speaker might agree with all four statements, Answer C is directly connected to Wordsworth's main point, as it is presented in Lines 5-8 and 21-24. Wordsworth laments "what man has made of man," meaning that he is frustrated that humanity has chosen the opposite path of nature, focusing on frustrations and challenges rather than being happy to exist. Answer A is incorrect because, even though the author would probably agree with it, there are no specific places in the passage where the speaker expresses the need for more people to observe nature; rather, he suggests people need to act more like the plants and animals in nature. Answer B is incorrect because the speaker of the poem does not make any mention of the impact humanity has on nature; he only focuses on the fact that he wishes humanity could be more like nature. Answer D is also incorrect because, while the author clearly respects plants and animals, he never specifically mentions ways in which humans are unfair to them. The speaker would probably agree with all these viewpoints, but only Answer C is squarely rooted in the text, making it the best choice.

**Passage 6 ("Basketball Statistics"):**

**48. G** Answer G is the best choice because, based on context, "quantifying" is using statistics to measure player achievement, quality, and reasonable salaries. The words "statistics" and "data" should have been major indicators to the reader. Answer E is not the best choice because Answer G provides a much more detailed, specific answer. "Counting" is just one way to use numbers in a simple, sequential order. "Quantifying" something using data might involve any number of steps or calculations, making it far more complex than counting. Answers F and H are both incorrect because they ignore the importance of numbers to "quantifying." Descriptions and assessments that do not included numbers are "qualitative" rather than "quantitative," making Answer G the best choice.

**49. A** Answer A is the best choice because, as Paragraph 1 explains, the entire goal of statistics is to quantify player achievement and determine player quality. Since someone's skill and ability at their job should ideally determine their salary in a meritocracy, that means that statistics are crucially important to determining how much players get paid. Answer A is incorrect because statistics do not reflect someone's knowledge in any way, only their performance. Answer C is incorrect because there is nothing in the passage in particular about coaching, and the answer therefore has no textual basis. Answer D is incorrect because there is nothing in the passage about locker-room culture, and being an exceptional player doesn't preclude someone from having a negative personality.

**50. F** Answer F is the best choice because Paragraphs 3-5 all describe ways that a player can impact the game in major ways without scoring points. The passage also consistently suggest that all the different contributions that players can make are equally valuable in different ways. Although Paragraph 2 states that points is one of the two most fundamental statistics, that is not presented to mean that it is one of the most important things of all; rather, it simply means it is one of the easiest and most basic that one needs to understand to watch the game. Answer E is incorrect because, while the passage emphasizes the importance of passing, there is nothing explicitly mentioned about the idea of being a "ball-hog." Answer G is incorrect because being on the losing team doesn't preclude somebody from being the best individual player in a given game; it just means their team lost. Answer H is similarly incorrect as well because making one mistake wouldn't preclude someone from being the best player; it simply means they made a bad mistake and still could've been the most impactful player otherwise.

**51. D** Answer D is the correct choice because "bucket" in Paragraph 3 and "field goal" in Paragraph 4 are both used to mean "made shot." A "field goal attempt" is presented in Paragraph 4 as a shot that misses, so the reader can infer that a "field goal" is a made shot. Answer A is incorrect because points are what you get by making shots; points and made shots are not exactly the same thing, especially since some shots in basketball are worth different numbers of points. Answer B is incorrect because a "bucket" isn't just offense – it's the product of a successfully

completed offensive possession, making Answer D a better choice. Answer C is successful as well because, while passes can set up "buckets," a pass and a shot are certainly established as two different actions in the passage.

**52. E** Answer E is the best choice because Paragraph 3 of the passage clearly states, "On the other hand, a player will not be awarded an assist unless his or her teammate makes their shot, so racking up a large number of assists is also indicative of being on a high-percentage shooting team." This means that a player's teammates must be making shots for that player to get assists. Answer F is incorrect because there is nothing in the passage about turnovers or any statistics cancelling each other out. Answer G is incorrect because, based on Paragraph 5, shots are what gets blocked, not assists. Answer H is incorrect because there is no connection at all between assists and minutes, and a reduction in minutes would not affect the situation presented in the original question whatsoever, since it clearly states the player passed "the same number of times."

**53. B** Answer B is the best choice because Paragraph 4 clearly states that a second-chance situation "often provides the offense the chance to get the better of the defense before they can react." Answer B clearly describes ways in which the defense might be struggling to react: they could be positioned poorly, or they might not be as aware of everything that's happening on the floor. Answer A is incorrect because it is describing a defensive rebound, not an offensive one. Answer C is incorrect because players can always pass to their teammates for assists, so that is not an exclusively feature of second-chance situations. Answer D is incorrect as well because, while it is potentially true in some scenarios, there is no predictable way to say when teams will become frustrated, which leaves Answer B as a better answer overall.

**54. H** Answer H is the best choice because it reflects the best understanding of the final sentence of Paragraph 5: "Great defensive players also typically get a lot of rebounds, but it's also possible for a defensive player to become statistically underrated because offensive numbers like points and assists are much easier to notice than solid guarding ability, which is not simple to transform into a number." The last part of the sentence is especially crucial, in which the text states that quantifying guarding in numerical statistics is incredibly difficult. Answer E is incorrect because it's untrue that no defensive statistics exist. Blocks and steals are presented specifically as two stats that give voice to defensive accomplishments. Answer F is incorrect because rebounds are presented in the text as easily quantified accomplishments, so there's no connection between getting a lot of rebounds and being underrated on defense. In fact, based on the text, a defensive player who got a lot of rebounds would be relatively unlikely to become underrated because he or she would have a skill that was relatively easy to appreciate statistically. Answer G is also incorrect because there is nothing in the passage about which stats are most relevant (or completely irrelevant) to contract negotiations and salaries.

**55. C** Answer C is the correct choice because it reflects the best understanding of Paragraph 3. Paragraph 3 establishes that assists are earned by passing to other players on the team and specifically says, "Some players, especially point guards, prefer to make passes that set up other players for points." This establishes that point guards are among the most likely players to pass, meaning Mason's 9 assists make him the most likely point guard. Answer A is incorrect because there is no correlation expressed anywhere in the passage between being a point guard and not scoring. The text says that point guards often prefer to pass, but that does not preclude them from scoring as well. Answer B is incorrect because there is no statistical correlation between rebounds and being a point guard. Only assists are specifically mentioned as the realm of point guards. Answer D is incorrect as well, even though it identifies Mason as the point guard, because it assumes steals are the indicator, which is not the case. Based on Paragraph 3, assists are the best predictor of point guard success, making Answer C the best choice.

**56. E** Answer E is the best choice because Lilly's team-leading block and defensive rebound totals suggest that he probably has a positive defensive impact. Although the passage establishes that defense is hard to quantify with statistics, Lilly's blocks, steals, and defensive rebounds are the best possible indicators of overall defensive performance. Answer F is incorrect because, while defensive rebounds and blocks indicate that Chen is probably a good defensive player, neither total is as high as Lilly's, making Answer E the best overall selection. Answer G is incorrect because even though Abdul has a good number of defensive rebounds, he does not have the block or steal numbers that put him in the same tier as Lilly or Chen. It is still possible Abdul is a great defensive player; however, if he is, he is one of the statistically underrated defenders that Paragraph 5 refers to. Answer H is also incorrect because Smith had no blocks and no defensive rebounds with just one steal, meaning his accomplishments on defense, if substantial, went unnoticed in terms of official statistics.

**57. C** Answer C is the best choice because the passage never specifically explains the acronyms "ORB" and "DRB." Paragraph 4 establishes that "REB" stands for rebound and explains the difference between an offensive and defensive rebound, but it never explicitly presents those letters to the reader until they appear in the box score. However, based on context (the fact that they appear right next to "REB" and that the total of "ORB + DRB" always equals the "REB" total should be major indicators), the reader should be able to figure out what the acronyms each stand for. Understanding this is fundamental to complete comprehension of the data table/box score. Answers A and B are both incorrect because the actual result of the game is inconsequential when it comes to understanding the individual statistical accomplishments of each player. The passage and box score examine statistics as reflections of individual player accomplishment, not indicators of team success in any way. Answer D is incorrect because, as Paragraph 4 explains, offensive and defensive rebounds are both beneficial and important, just in different ways.

**58. -14** Plug in your given values:

$= \frac{7}{4}(1 - 3^2)$

$= \frac{7}{4}(-8)$

$= -\frac{56}{4}$

$= -14$

**59. -4** $-7(3n + 5) = -6n + 25$
$-21n - 35 = -6n + 25$
$-15n = 60$
$n = -4$

**60. 30** If Bob sells the cake for $3.00 and it costs him $1.80 to make one, his profit for each cake sold is $1.20. The question asks how many cakes Bob needs to sell in order to make a profit of exactly $36.00. We can divide $36 by $1.2 to get 30. Bob will need to sell 30 cakes to make a profit of $36.00.

**61. 59** To solve this problem we need to know the average speed formula which is:

$$\text{Average Speed} = \frac{\text{Total Distance Covered}}{\text{Total Time}}$$

First calculate the total distance covered. For the first 3 hours the car traveled 55 miles per hour, so (55 • 3) = 165 miles. For the remaining 2 hours the car travels 65 miles per hour, so (65 • 2) = 130 miles. 165 miles + 130 miles = 295 miles. The total distance covered by the car is 295 miles. The total time taken is 5 hours. Divide 295 miles by 5 hours to get your average speed which is 59 miles per hour.

**62. 4** $2x^3 - 3xy$
$2(-1)^3 - 3(-1)(2)$
$(2 \cdot -1) - (-3 \cdot 2)$
$-2 + 6$
$= 4$

**63. G** After inspection, it can be seen that if you sum the first three terms, you get the next term. If you continue this pattern of adding the previous three terms to get the next, you can find the next term in the series to be,
7 + 13 + 24 = 44.

The answer is G.

**64. D** To make this problem easier, you can square all the numbers for A and B to get rid of the square root to help you see which value is greater.
$A = (\sqrt{65})^2 - 9^2$
$B = (\sqrt{50})^2 - 8^2$
$A = 65 - 81 = -16$
$B = 50 - 64 = -14$
As you can see the value of B is greater than A. Therefore, the correct answer is D.

**65. F** This equation can be factored as,

$$\frac{(x-2)(x+3)}{(x-2)} = (x+3) = 0,$$

so $x = -3$. The answer is F.

**66. B** During the first minute, he stacks one box. During the second minute, he stacks 2 more boxes on that 1 box he had originally. During the third minute, he stacks 3 more boxes on everything making the total 6 boxes, and since each box is 5 inches tall, that is 30 inches in total. It took 3 minutes to reach 30 inches.

The answer is B.

**67. E** We simply must divide by 1000 to convert from miligrams to grams. 0.0202g is the answer or answer choice E.

**68. D** If we assume negative values for costs and positive values for profit, we can write, –$8 + $10 – $11 + $12= +$3, so his profit is $3 or answer choice D.

**69. E** Substituting $\gamma = 2\delta$ into the function gives us, $f(2\delta) = 2f(\delta)$ which only happens for a non-constant linear function. The only non-constant linear function shown is, $x$, or answer choice E.

**70. A** 11AM is 3 hours before 2PM. If the length doubles every hour, then three hours before, it was $\frac{1}{2^3}$ the length at 2PM or $(\frac{3}{8}) = 0.375$ meters.

In other words, we have to cut the length in half three times.

The answer is A.

**71. H** None of these functions are equal to each other. The answer is H.

**72. D** Using the definition of averages and using $x$ as the score for the next test, we have:

$$\frac{66 + 82 + 81 + 92 + x}{5} = \frac{321 + x}{5} = 84,$$

which simplifies to $x = 420 - 321 = 99$, or answer choice D.

**73. H** Every 7 days from Saturday, it will be Saturday again. 7 can go into 365,52 times with a remainder of 1 day. So it will be 1 day after Saturday, which is Sunday.

The answer is H.

**74. A** A number is divisible by 9 if all of the digits of that number sum up to a number divisible by 9, which in this case, does. The answer is 0 or answer choice A.

**75. H** The length of $AB$ is 6, since $B$ is the midpoint of $AC$. The radius of each semicircle is then, 6 and there are 4 identical semicircles, which is equivalent to 2 circles. The area of 1 circle is $36\pi$, so the area of both circles is $72\pi$, or answer choice H.

**76. B** This equation can be simplified to, $8^{x+3} = (8^2)^{3x} = 8^{6x}$, so $x + 3 = 6x$, or $x = (\frac{3}{5})$. The answer B.

**77. E** The right hand side of the equation simplifies to $A^2 - 8$. So, we only need to worry about the value of A. The value of A is 3 and we can plug that in to our expression.

$3^2 - 8 = 1$. The answer is E.

**78. C** We simply have to multiply 11 by 15 to find the sum. The answer is 165 or answer choice C.

**79. E** Adding all of the terms and dividing by 4 gives,

$$\frac{12b + 9}{4} = 3b + \frac{9}{4}$$

The answer is E.

**80. D** This simplifies to, $\frac{y^{17}}{y^{15}} = y^2$.

The answer is D.

**81. H** Each symbol repeats every 6 symbols Later. For example, the first symbol appears at position 1, 7, 13 and so on. So, the second symbol will appear at 2, 8, 14, ..., 50. The answer is H.

**82. D** The area of a trapezoid with bases $a$ and band altitude, $h$, is:

$A = \frac{(a + b)h}{2}$ and we know what $h$ is and we know what $A$ is. Plugging those in and solving for $a + b$ gives us, $a + b = 104$. We also know the ratio of the base lengths if $(\frac{2}{6})$ which means, or $3a = b$. Plugging this into $a + b = 104$ and solving for $b$ gives us a value for $b$ of, $b = 78$ or answer choice D.

**83. H** The square root of $(\frac{16}{81})$ is $(\frac{4}{9})$.

The answer is H.

**84. B** Multiplying the first equation by −3 and adding it to the second equation gives, $-17y = -51$ or $y = 3$. If $y = 3$, then we can plug that value into the first equation and solve for $x$ to give us $x = 1$. The solution is (1, 3).

The answer is B.

**85. H** Multiplying all of the numbers in the trapezoid and taking the square root of that gives us, $\sqrt{144} = 12$

The answer is H.

**86. D** This answer depends on the signs of $X$ and $Y$ so the answer is D.

**87. G** If we call the unknown side, $AC$, $x$, we have that the perimeter of the triangle is, $P = 10 + x$ and the area is $(\frac{2}{2})x = 20$.

We can solve for $x$ to get $x = 20$, which means the perimeter of the triangle is, 30, which is also the perimeter of the square. All of the sides of a square are equal and the area is the side length squared. So, the area of the square is

$(\frac{30}{4})^2$ square inches = 56.25 square inches.

The answer is G.

**88. B** To solve this problem, we must align the scores in order from least to greatest (or greatest to least) and find the middle number. The middle number is 83, so the answer is B.

**89. H** In one hour, the car travels 50 meters and the circumference of the wheel is $2\pi r = 10\pi$, with a radius of 5 meters. Given this, we can find the number of revolutions that occur in one hour. This will be 50 meters divided by $10\pi$ which is $\frac{5}{\pi}$.

The answer is H.

**90. C** To find this probability, we must divide the area of the shaded region by the area of the square. Let's say that the radius of the circle is *r*. Then, the side length of the square is *2r*. The area of the square is then, $4r$. The area of the circle is $\pi r^2$ and the area of the shaded region is the difference between these two areas, $r^2(4 - \pi^2)$, and once we divide this by $4r^2$, we get:

$$\frac{r^2(4 - \pi^2)}{4r^2} = 1 - \frac{\pi}{4}$$

which is answer choice C.

**91. E** We know that 100% = 1, so we can simplify this to just 10% times 10%, which is 0.01 or 1%. The answer is E.

**92. A** 10% = 0.1. The greatest integer less than 0.1 is 0. 0 + 1 = 1.

The answer is A.

**93. H** We know that the area is 100 square meters, so we can find the diameter (2 times the radius, *r*) by equating, $\pi r^2 = 100$, which gives a diameter of, $2\sqrt{\frac{100}{\pi}}$ and dividing this by her speed gives us the time it takes for her to traverse the diameter which is, $0.2\sqrt{\frac{100}{\pi}}$. The answer is H.

**94. C** Using this formula of adding the previous 2 terms to get the next, we have for the first 5 terms,

0, 1, 1, 2, 3 which sums to 7.

The mean is $(\frac{7}{5})$ or answer choice C.

**95. G** If there are 9 vaks in 12 hips, then there are 18 vaks in 24 hips. There are $(\frac{18}{x})$ slacks in 24 hips or 18 vaks.

The answer is G.

**96. D** This simplifies to,

$(\frac{11}{10})^2 = (1.1)^2 = 1.21$,

or answer choice D.

**97. F** Plugging in the values for *a* and *b* into the equation gives us, $5 + 2 - 2^2 = 3$. The answer is F.

**98. C** The integers that are nonpositive within that range are, −3, −2, −1 and

0. There are 4 non positive integers. So the answer is C.

**99. F** A number squared is $x$. It's reciprocal is $(\frac{1}{x})$. The sum is,

$x^2 + \frac{1}{x}$. The answer is F.

**100. D** If the original size is 20, then it increases by 50%, the size will be 30. Then the size will be 45 if we increase it by 50% again. The percent increase from 20 to 45 is 125%.

The answer is D.

**101. F** Labeling the sides AB and BC as $x$, respectively and the sides, AF and FE as $y$, respectively, we can represent the area of the rectangle as, $4xy = 440$. This means that $xy = 110$. $x$ represents the base of triangle BCD, and y represents only half of the height. In order to represent the height, we need to multiply $y$ by 2, and we get $2xy$. Since we doubled $y$, 110 is also doubled so we have $2xy=220$. $2xy$ represents base times height and the formula for the area of the triangle is $A = \frac{1}{2}bh$. Since we know bh is 220, we have $A = \frac{1}{2}(220) = 110$. The area of triangle BCD is 110. The answer is F.

**102. D** Since $\sqrt{2}$ and $\pi$ are both irrational, there are no integers, a and b that can satisfy the definition of $LCM(x, y)$.

The answer is D.

**103. F** This function is undefined and not equal to 1 when the denominator is 0, which occurs when $x = 3$. The answer is 1, or answer choice F.

**104. D** Since $49^2$ is divisible by 7, the answer is still Monday. The answer choice is D.

**105. H** $f(4)$ can be written as $4^3$ or $2^6$.
$f(2)$ can be written as $2^3$.
The question becomes, how much greater is $2^6$ than $2^3$. The answer is $2^3$ greater, or 8 times greater. The answer is H.

**106. B** $(\frac{3}{40}) = 0.075$. The answer is B.

**107. G** There are four prime numbers between 4 and 16 inclusive. They are:
5, 7, 11, 13. The answer is G.

**108. B** The only perfect square between 9 and 25 exclusive is 16.

The answer is B.

**109. H** The more sides the figure has, the bigger the area, holding the perimeter constant. So, an octagon would have a bigger area than a triangle, and a circle would have the largest area. The answer is H.

**110. C** Plugging in what the formula tells us gives us,

$x^2 - x^4 = x^2(1 - x^2)$ or answer C.

**111. F** If 1 mm represents 150 m, then 1 sq. mm represents 22,500 sq. m. So then, 1 sq. m. is simply $(\frac{1}{22,500})$ sq. mm.

The answer is F.

**112. C** If we draw the two points that represent the corners of the rectangle, we see that the rectangle would look like this:

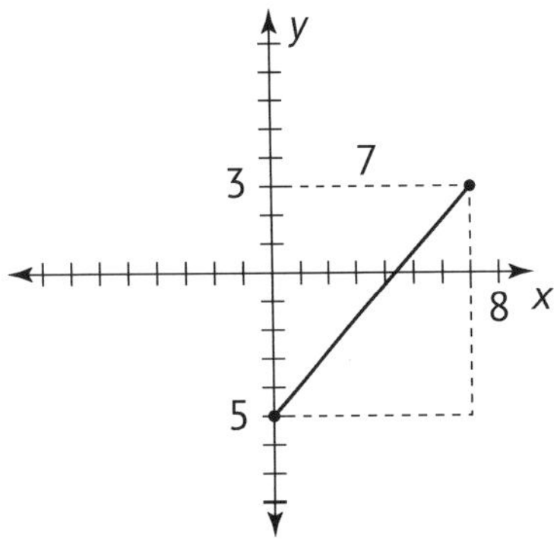


The area is 8 • 7 = 56. The answer is C.

**113. G** Simplify the following expression. $x^3$ cancels out and $z^0$ is simply one. $\frac{y^3}{y^4}$ results in $y^1$ and we are left with $\frac{1}{y}$.

**114. B** The prime factors of 2520 are 2•2•2•3•3•5•7. There are 4 distinct prime numbers making the answer 4 or answer choice B.

Made in the USA
Middletown, DE
03 October 2021

49563362R00212